INTERVENTIONS

Conor Cunningham

GENERAL EDITOR

It's not a question of whether one believes in God or not. Rather, it's a question of if, in the absence of God, we can have belief, any belief.

"If you live today," wrote Flannery O'Connor, "you breathe in nihilism." Whether "religious" or "secular," it is "the very gas you breathe." Both within and without the academy, there is an air common to both deconstruction and scientism — both might be described as species of *reductionism*. The dominance of these modes of knowledge in popular and professional discourse is quite incontestable, perhaps no more so where questions of theological import are often relegated to the margins of intellectual respectability. Yet it is precisely the proponents and defenders of religious belief in an age of nihilism that are often among those most — unwittingly or not — complicit in this very reduction. In these latter cases, one frequently spies an accommodationist impulse, whereby our concepts must be first submitted to a prior philosophical court of appeal in order for them to render any intellectual value. To cite one particularly salient example, debates over the origins, nature, and ends of human life are routinely partitioned off into categories of "evolutionism" and "creationism," often with little nuance. Where attempts to mediate these arguments are to be found, frequently the strategy is that of a kind of accommodation: How can we adapt our belief in creation to an already established evolutionary metaphysic, or, how can we have our evolutionary cake and eat it too? It is sadly the case that, despite the best intentions of such "intellectual ecumenism," the distinctive voice of theology is the first one to succumb to aphonia — either from impetuous overuse or from a deliberate silencing.

The books in this unique new series propose no such simple accommodation. They rather seek and perform tactical interventions in such debates in a manner that problematizes the accepted terms of such debates.

They propose something altogether more demanding: through a kind of refusal of the disciplinary isolation now standard in modern universities, a genuinely interdisciplinary series of mediations of crucial concepts and key figures in contemporary thought. These volumes will attempt to discuss these topics as they are articulated within their own field, including their historical emergence, and cultural significance, which will provide a way into seemingly abstract discussions. At the same time, they aim to analyze what consequences such thinking may have for theology, both positive and negative, and, in light of these new perspectives, to develop an effective response — one that will better situate students of theology and professional theologians alike within the most vital debates informing Western society, and so increase their understanding of, participation in, and contribution to these.

To a generation brought up on a diet of deconstruction, on the one hand, and scientism, on the other, Interventions offers an alternative that is *otherwise than nihilistic* — doing so by approaching well-worn questions and topics, as well as historical and contemporary figures, from an original and interdisciplinary angle, and so avoid having to steer a course between the aforementioned Scylla and Charybdis.

This series will also seek to navigate not just through these twin dangers, but also through the dangerous "and" that joins them. That is to say, it will attempt to be genuinely interdisciplinary in avoiding the conjunctive approach to such topics that takes as paradigmatic a relationship of "theology and phenomenology" or "religion and science." Instead, the volumes in this series will, in general, attempt to treat such discourses not as discrete disciplines unto themselves, but as moments within a distended theological performance. Above all, they will hopefully contribute to a renewed atmosphere shared by theologians and philosophers (not to mention those in other disciplines) — an air that is not nothing.

CENTRE OF THEOLOGY AND PHILOSOPHY

(www.theologyphilosophycentre.co.uk)

Every doctrine which does not reach the one thing necessary, every separated philosophy, will remain deceived by false appearances. It will be a doctrine, it will not be Philosophy.

Maurice Blondel, 1861–1949

This book series is the product of the work carried out at the Centre of Theology and Philosophy (COTP), at the University of Nottingham.

The COTP is a research-led institution organized at the interstices of theology and philosophy. It is founded on the conviction that these two disciplines cannot be adequately understood or further developed, save with reference to each other. This is true in historical terms, since we cannot comprehend our Western cultural legacy unless we acknowledge the interaction of the Hebraic and Hellenic traditions. It is also true conceptually, since reasoning is not fully separable from faith and hope, or conceptual reflection from revelatory disclosure. The reverse also holds, in either case.

The Centre is concerned with:

- the historical interaction between theology and philosophy.
- the current relation between the two disciplines.
- attempts to overcome the analytic/continental divide in philosophy.
- the question of the status of "metaphysics": Is the term used equivocally? Is it now at an end? Or have twentieth-century attempts to have a postmetaphysical philosophy themselves come to an end?
- the construction of a rich Catholic humanism.

I am very glad to be associated with the endeavours of this extremely important Centre that helps to further work of enormous importance. Among its concerns is the question whether modernity is more an interim than a completion — an interim between a pre-modernity in which the porosity between theology and philosophy was granted, perhaps taken for granted, and a postmodernity where their porosity must be unclogged and enacted anew. Through the work of leading theologians of international stature and philosophers whose writings bear on this porosity, the Centre offers an exciting forum to advance in diverse ways this challenging and entirely needful, and cutting-edge work.

Professor William Desmond, Leuven

A THEOLOGY
OF GRACE
IN SIX
CONTROVERSIES

Edward T. Oakes, S.J.

WILLIAM B. EERDMANS PUBLISHING COMPANY
GRAND RAPIDS, MICHIGAN

Imprimi potest: V. Rev. Douglas Marcouiller, S.J.
                     Provincial, Missouri Province of the Society of Jesus
                     September 1, 2013

Nihil obstat: Rev. Thomas G. Weinandy, O.F.M., Cap.
                     Censor deputatus
                     Capuchin College, Washington, D.C.
                     August 29, 2013

Imprimatur: Francis Cardinal George, O.M.I., Ph.D., S.T.D
                     Archbishop of Chicago
                     September 4, 2012

In accordance with Canon 824, permission to publish was granted by His Eminence, Francis Cardinal George, O.M.I., Archbishop of Chicago. The *Nihil obstat* and *Imprimatur* are official declarations that the book is free from doctrinal and moral error. No implication is contained therein that those who have granted the *Nihil obstat* and *Imprimatur* agree with the content, opinions, or statements expressed. No legal responsibility is assumed by the grant of this permission.

Published 2016 by
Wm. B. Eerdmans Publishing Co.
2140 Oak Industrial Drive N.E., Grand Rapids, Michigan 49505

Printed in the United States of America

22 21 20 19 18 17 16   7 6 5 4 3 2 1

Library of Congress Cataloging-in-Publication Data

Names: Oakes, Edward T., author.
Title: A theology of grace in six controversies / Edward T. Oakes, S.J.
Description: Grand Rapids, Michigan: Eerdmans Publishing Company, 2016. |
    Series: Interventions
Identifiers: LCCN 2015045476 | ISBN 9780802873200 (pbk: alk. paper)
Subjects: LCSH: Grace (Theology) | Salvation—Christianity. | Catholic Church—Doctrines.
Classification: LCC BT761.3 .O225 2016 | DDC 234—dc23
    LC record available at http://lccn.loc.gov/2015045476

www.eerdmans.com

Come you indoors, come home; your fading fire
Mend first and vital candle in close heart's vault.

Gerard Manley Hopkins, S.J.
"The Candle Indoors"

To the members of the
Academy of Catholic Theology

Contents

Foreword

Fr. Edward Oakes was one of the most sparkling and brilliant people I've ever known. I had the privilege of working with him for ten years at Mundelein Seminary—first as a faculty colleague and then as rector. He was one of those scholars who not only made you think about things in a new way but reminded you why you became a student of theology in the first place. After a conversation with Fr. Oakes, you were not just better informed; you felt more intellectually alive. He also had a passion for the notoriously "hard" questions in theology, those areas that most academics prefer to set aside or postpone: the relation between the divine mind and human mind in Jesus, evolution vs. creation, the possibility of universal salvation, and especially the play between nature and grace. The book you are about to read is a series of remarkably illuminating meditations on that uniquely complicated issue. I can testify firsthand that Fr. Oakes composed and polished these essays in the very last months of his life, just after he was diagnosed with terminal cancer. I will never forget a conversation I had with him during that final summer. After he explicated a dimension of the nature/grace problem with his customary boyish enthusiasm, he paused and then said, "I'm just so happy with my life right now!" I think it is safe to say that he wrote these reflections on grace at a strangely graced moment of his life.

Ludwig Wittgenstein—a philosopher with whom Fr. Oakes resonated—famously remarked that his own work represented an attempt to let the fly out of the fly bottle. I thought of Wittgenstein's image frequently as I read through these essays, for time and again, Oakes is showing us a way out of the classical (and frustrating) dilemmas surrounding the nature/grace dynamic. As we butt our heads over and again on the side of the bottle, honoring all that must legitimately be honored, he says, "Perhaps you could think of it this way."

I would like to highlight just a few of the scintillating resolutions that Fr. Oakes proposes. Within Roman Catholic circles, the nature/grace debate has often centered on competing texts within the oeuvre of Thomas Aquinas. There are certain passages in the *Summa theologiae* that unambiguously state that human nature has its own proper finality apart from the elevation of grace. But other passages in that same masterwork state, with equal clarity, that the singular end of the human being is the intimate friendship with God that can be accomplished only through grace. In the twentieth century, Reginald Garrigou-Lagrange and his disciples placed special stress on the former texts and Henri de Lubac and his followers emphasized the latter texts, giving rise thereby to a dispute that roiled Catholic theology mightily in the years prior to Vatican II. Fr. Oakes does not even try to resolve the matter of interpreting Thomas correctly, blithely admitting that there is a real and finally irresoluble tension in the master's writings.

What he does instead is show us an unexpected way out of the fly bottle, appealing to a relatively unknown Catholic thinker of the nineteenth century, Matthias Joseph Scheeben. Scheeben's distinction between grace and nature is every bit as sharp as Garrigou-Lagrange's, but he does not present the relationship between the two in an extrinsicist manner, imagining grace as a "penthouse atop a skyscraper." Rather, he changes the metaphor from architecture to matrimony and conceives nature as a kind of bride thoroughly transformed and marvelously elevated by her marriage to grace. And this serves, Oakes argues, to honor de Lubac's valid concerns about leaving nature as a self-contained reality bereft of any intrinsic relation to grace. A total resolution of the dilemma? No. A path forward, a way out of the fly bottle? Absolutely.

Fr. Oakes admits that Catholic doctrines concerning the Blessed Virgin Mary often prove insuperable stumbling blocks to rapprochement with Protestantism. The dogma of the Assumption has no biblical warrant, and the dogma of the Immaculate Conception seems to call into question the indispensability of Christ for salvation. But if we attend to this latter doctrine with greater concentration, we might, Oakes suggests, find a surprising point of contact with the classically Protestant teaching on the primacy of grace. For it would be difficult to imagine a more radical statement of justification by grace alone than the assertion that Mary, from the moment of her conception, which is to say, without any possible cooperation on her part, was saved through God's gracious love. And to make this connection even clearer, Oakes cites the formal statement of Pope Pius IX concerning the controversial doctrine: "We declare, pronounce, and define that the Most Blessed Virgin Mary, at the first instance of her conception, was preserved from all stain of original sin . . . in virtue of the merits of Jesus Christ." In other words, Mary was saved in the absolute sense not by her own merits but by Christ's, not through her works but through sheer grace. Could this most Catholic of teachings prove to be a bridge to the most distinctively Protestant of teachings?

I won't belabor things by summarizing each of Fr. Oakes's deeply creative resolutions. Suffice it to say that even the most skeptical of readers will find ample material in this book to intrigue, beguile, and invite further exploration. One of the passions of Oakes's life was his participation in the Evangelicals and Catholics Together project. The six interrelated essays on nature and grace represent, in my judgment, one of the most promising and intellectually satisfying ecumenical endeavors in fifty years. They also function as a capstone to a life dedicated to *fides quaerens intellectum*.

Most Rev. Robert Barron

Acknowledgments

I would first of all like to thank Francis Cardinal George, OMI, archbishop of Chicago and Chancellor of the University of St. Mary of the Lake/Mundelein Seminary, where I teach, for graciously providing the *Imprimatur* for the book; to Fr. Thomas G. Weinandy, OFM, Cap., for serving as his *Censor deputatus* and for providing the *Nihil obstat;* to Fr. Douglas Marcouiller, S.J., the provincial of the Missouri Province of the Society of Jesus for providing the *Imprimi potest*, and to his *Censor deputatus*, Fr. J. J. Mueller, S.J. Properly handled, ecclesiastical "censorship" should prove no more burdensome than sending manuscripts to referees; and in my case the censors were not only not burdensome at all but also quite helpful.

When I was about halfway through research on the fourth chapter I received a diagnosis of Stage-Four (meaning inoperable) pancreatic cancer that had also spread to the liver, which meant that almost half of the book had to be written during a series of chemotherapy sessions, which could be debilitating at times. Writing a book is often a solitary and sometimes lonely business; but in my illness I have learned how deeply collaborative any kind of writing can be. I am accordingly especially grateful to the Rector/President of Mundelein Seminary, Fr. Robert Barron, for his unstinting support during my ordeal, and to Fr. Thomas Baima, Vice-Rector for Academic Affairs and Academic Dean, and to Dr. Elizabeth Nagel, President of the Pontifical Faculty, for their willingness to "temper the wind to the shorn lamb" by allowing me a reduced schedule of classes, and to Dr. Matthew Levering, for taking over those lectures in my remaining schedule when my health so dictated.

To Dr. Levering I am also grateful for permission to use portions of my article "Scheeben the Reconciler," previously published in *Nova et Vetera*, which he edits, in the first chapter; and to Joseph Mangina, editor of

Pro Ecclesia, for permission to use my article "Predestination and Mary's Immaculate Conception" as the core of the sixth chapter. Lorraine Olley, Library Director, Anna Kielian, in charge of interlibrary loans, and Natalie Jordan in the periodical section all provided invaluable assistance and even allowed me to check out materials via "remote control" by their doing the check-out for me at the circulation desk and sending them to my *scriptorium* through the kind assistance of two work-study students, John Bosco Lutaaya and Joseph Tran, who were both a real boon to me, especially during the summer heat.

The medical personnel at the Kellogg Cancer Institute, where I am currently being treated, are too numerous to mention here by name; but they have all been unfailingly competent, caring, lucid in their explanations, and supportive in my goal of finishing this book. In this vast "cloud of witnesses," however, I would like to single out my oncologist, Richard de W. Marsh, MD, and his assistant Margaret Whalen, RN, for accompanying me every step of the way during this ordeal. I also wish to thank Mary Schufreider, RN, Jesuit Health Care Coordinator for the Chicago Province of the Society of Jesus, who was there from the beginning of my diagnosis and taught me how to give myself daily insulin injections and helped me negotiate my way to the many specialists I have been seeing.

But of all the people who have most come to my rescue during this ordeal, I must thank above all one of my doctoral students, Fr. Jeffrey Njus, of the diocese of Lansing, Michigan, who began doctoral studies at Mundelein just as I received my diagnosis. Because he had already completed his course work while previously working on a Licentiate, he has been free to serve as my "designated driver" to and from therapy sessions, as my resident "oncological dietician" (keeping me away from foods that might exacerbate the diabetes that has been an attendant byproduct of my malfunctioning pancreas), and above all as my eagle-eyed copyeditor of this manuscript. More than one person in my faculty residence has mentioned what a godsend Fr. Njus has proved to be; and right they are.

Finally, I wish to thank all the members of the Academy of Catholic Theology to whom this book is dedicated in gratitude for their electing me its President for the year 2013–2014. Because my cascading health problems only became acutely noticeable in late May, I was unable to attend the Academy's annual convention in the third week of May 2013 in Washington, DC (the first meeting of ACT I ever missed). Whether I will be able to attend the meeting in May 2014 of course lies in the hands of God and his holy providence. But whether present or absent, I wanted this book to serve as a sign of my esteem for this fine group of colleagues, from whom I have learned so much. At all events, whether I end up being able to attend or not, I take consolation from these words of St. Paul: "If we live, we live to the Lord; and if we die, we die to the Lord. So, whether we live or whether we die, we belong to the Lord" (Rom. 14:8).

EDWARD T. OAKES, S.J.
University of St. Mary of the Lake
Mundelein, Illinois

Introduction

Around the year AD 524 a Roman aristocrat by the name of Anicius Man-
lius Severinus Boethius (c. 480–c. 524) was arrested on a charge of high
treason by his overlord, the Ostrogothic king Theodoric. Needless to say,
while languishing in prison as he was awaiting execution, Boethius deeply
regretted having abandoned his earlier philosophical life for the sake of
political advancement in the cutthroat world of the Ostrogothic throne
room. But now, in the few months remaining before his execution, he had
a chance to return to the rarefied consolations that come from pondering
philosophical and theological questions, including those that will be the
subject of this book: what is God's providence? does predestination trump
human free will? how can the harshness and brutality of history be reconciled with the goodness of God? why are human affairs so turbulent when
seen against the backdrop of the serenity of heaven?

Quite lost in his efforts to answer these questions on his own, Boethius
soon found himself comforted by a celestial visitor, Lady Philosophy—who,
however, could only offer him this one "solace": her insistence that his
puny, finite mind will *never* be able to resolve his questions. For, after Boethius pleads with her to "reveal these mysteries and explain those things
that are clouded and hidden," he describes her answer this way:

> She hesitated a moment, then smiled and at last replied: "This is the
> great question, isn't it? It is a problem that can never be fully solved even
> by the most exhaustive discourse. For when one part of the conundrum
> is resolved, others pop up, like the heads of the Hydra. What is needed
> to restrain them is intellectual fire. Otherwise, we are in a morass of
> difficulties—the singleness of providence, the vicissitudes of fate, the
> haphazardness of events, God's plan, predestination, free will. All these

knotty questions come together and are intertwined.... [So] you must be patient for a bit while I construct the arguments and lay them out for you in proper sequence."[1]

Few topics in dogmatic theology can be more Hydra-headed, vexatious or indeed downright wearisome than the issue of grace, which does indeed require patience if one is to see the arguments laid out in their proper sequence. In the course of many centuries, distinctions have arisen that can only baffle the uninitiated: sanctifying grace, habitual grace, prevenient grace, actual grace, sacramental grace, condign grace, sufficient grace, irresistible grace, and on and on. What are all these distinctions *for*? It all seems so arbitrary, like those labels on paint samples in a hardware store: cobalt blue, Wedgewood blue, sky blue, navy blue, azure blue, baby blue, zephyr blue, Mediterranean blue, indigo blue, and on and on. Yes, the eye can distinguish the subtle differences in shades, even if the labels attached to them seem rather arbitrary; but can that really be said of grace?

But even a cursory glance at the history of theology shows that more rides on these seemingly arcane debates than first meets the eye. For the issue of grace both determines and is determined by a host of other issues that everyone admits are crucial to the Christian religion. What ultimately motivates all debates on grace is this central issue: *what are God's intentions for the world?* Take the example of the many religions of the world. Assuming that all events in history are enfolded somehow in God's providence, what does the immense variety of world religions mean? Are they all fundamentally manifestations of the human longing for God that can all be subsumed under one overarching category, so that each religion is more or less equally valid as a path to God under the popular rubric of "it's all the same God anyway"? Or do they all make fundamentally incompatible truth-claims that cannot be adjudicated inside history?

A moment's reflection will show that both options help to determine, and are determined by, one's views on the relationship of nature and grace. If all human beings are *naturally* religious (even when they are avowed secularists and atheists), and if all religions (and ideologies) give equal access to the transcendent, then this must imply that there is a more or

---

1. Boethius, *The Consolations of Philosophy*, trans. David R. Slavitt (Cambridge, MA: Harvard University Press, 2008), 130–31. One of the twelve labors of Hercules was to slay the nine-headed snake Hydra, a task made more challenging because two more heads of the snake sprouted up to replace the one severed, a dilemma that Hercules could only prevent when he seared the stumps with burning brands.

less seamless transition from (man's) nature to (God's) grace. But if one religion (Christianity, say) raises a truth claim over all the others that can be shown on its own grounds to be true over against the truth claims of all the other religions (and ideologies), then this too must imply that grace is somehow radically distinct from man's religious nature, without which grace man will wander in darkness until he encounters the true grace of the one true religion.

If the latter position is the option one takes, then the witness of the Bible raises even more difficult problems regarding a theology of grace. There we hear stories of God's choice of Abel over Cain, of Jacob over Esau, indeed of Israel over the other nations (the name "Israel," it should be remembered, is a patronymic for the nation as a whole drawn from the name given to Jacob after he wrestled with the angel of the Lord). But even the election of Israel is internally volatile: for within Israel itself a "Remnant" of tribes (Judah and Levi) survives the vicissitudes of history, while the so-called "lost tribes" are wiped out of history by the Assyrians. Not even election, it would seem, proves to be that gracious, at least in human terms. As Rabbi Abraham Heschel wisely notes:

> From the beginnings of Israelite religion the belief that God had chosen this particular people to carry out His mission has been both a cornerstone of Hebrew faith and a refuge in moments of distress. And yet, the prophets felt that to many of their contemporaries this cornerstone was a stumbling block; this refuge, an escape. They had to remind the people that chosenness must not be mistaken as divine favoritism or immunity from chastisement, but, on the contrary, that it meant being more seriously exposed to divine judgment and chastisement.[2]

Now whether theologians first decide to solve the problem of pluralism in religion and then develop a theology of grace to justify that position, or first work out a theology of grace and nature and then draw out the implications of that theology when taking up the question of pluralism, is itself an intriguing methodological question, one that need not detain

---

2. Abraham J. Heschel, *The Prophets* (New York: HarperCollins, 1962), Vol. I: 32. This point will be crucial in our treatment of the doctrine of divine election in the third chapter and the nature of religious experience in the fifth. The key to these chapters can be found in the prophet Amos: "Hear this word that the Lord has spoken against you, O people of Israel, against the whole family which I brought up out of the land of Egypt: You only have I known of all the families of the earth. Therefore I will punish you for all your iniquities" (Amos 3:1–2).

us here. For the real point is simply that the two issues are inextricably linked—and deeply relevant. What should strike the reader as immediately obvious is that one's position regarding pluralism in religion both determines and is determined by the position one adopts regarding the relationship of nature to grace. The closer the link between nature and grace, then the easier it will be to detect signs of grace in all the religions of the world without exception, including even those ideological "religions" like secularism and communism. Even atheism can be looked on as an episode of grace, given the right perspective.[3]

But if grace is regarded as more or less "extrinsic" to human nature, landing upon some people and not others, then we are forced to look for signs of God's presence in the world using a different norm than the ubiquity of religion as an anthropological constant. In other words, with an "extrinsic" view of grace, we are leaving open the possibility that God speaks to some and not others, chooses some and not others, saves some and not others. If that is the case, then we must admit a greater distinction between nature and grace than some theologies will allow.

In any event, the point about the debate on nature and grace is that, at least when conducted properly, decisions on these matters should not be determined by an individual's preference for how he would *like* God to act; rather, the decision should be made according to an analysis of what it actually means for a nature to have a nature, and for grace to be a grace. Nature and grace are concepts that operate within theology by certain inherent "laws" of conceptual clarity, which is why scholastic theology felt compelled to draw so many fine distinctions as it became increasingly clear how subtle is the relationship between nature, free will, grace, predestination, justification, and so forth.

In facing all these complex issues, this book will be governed by one central axiom: *controversies clarify.* Theologians are, by profession if not by nature or personality, a disputatious lot. But there is a reason for that,

3. A telling example of such a shift in perspective would be Vatican II's Pastoral Constitution on the Church in the Modern World: "Atheism results not rarely from a violent protest against the evil in this world, or from the absolute character with which certain human values are unduly invested, and which thereby already accords them the stature of God. . . . Yet believers themselves frequently bear some responsibility for this situation. . . . Hence believers have more than a little to do with the birth of atheism. . . . While rejecting atheism, root and branch, the Church sincerely professes that all men, believers and unbelievers alike, ought to work for the rightful betterment of this world in which all alike live" (*Gaudium et spes* § 19, 21).

especially when it comes to so elusive a topic as grace: for only by seeing what is at stake in the debate—which only emerges in the course of controversy—can one understand why the issue matters. Of course a book on controversies need not itself be controversial, any more than a book on heresies must be heretical. In fact, in the various controversies treated in this book, I have tried to reach some kind of resolution, using key theologians who, in my estimation, have gone furthest in resolving the respective controversies.

Thus in the nature/grace debate, I rely on the nineteenth-century German Catholic theologian Matthias Joseph Scheeben. In the debate over sin, justification, and merit, I rely on St. Thérèse of Lisieux (declared a Doctor of the Church by Pope John Paul II in 1997). In the debate over evolution and original sin I rely on two encyclicals by Pope Pius XII, *Divino Afflante Spiritu* and *Humani Generis,* and on Pope John Paul II's Letter on Evolution to the Pontifical Academy of Sciences of 1996. In the very knotty issue of free will and predestination I rely on Karl Barth's shifting of the terms of the debate to Christology and away from Augustine's focus on the fate of the individual soul. And in the course of relying on Barth I make use as well of Fr. Robert Barron's notion of God's "non-competitive transcendence" and of Fr. Brian Shanley's similar interpretation of St. Thomas. The fifth chapter, however, I have decided to leave unresolved, not just for reasons of my waning health, but also to give students a chance to work out a resolution on their own in classroom discussions. Finally, my approach to Mary's mediating role in the distribution of graces comes from my discussions on Mariology during recent meetings of Evangelicals and Catholics Together and represents my own solution.[4]

Given how the issue of grace ramifies into nearly every other area of theology, the topics chosen for each of the six chapters could be multiplied at will. Nonetheless, this book will cover only those issues normally treated

4. Those who read the book straight through from start to finish will notice that certain citations recur, particularly from the work of Joseph Ratzinger/Pope Benedict XVI but also from a few other authors, which I have done not for the sake of sounding repetitious but to facilitate teachers using select chapters in, say, a course on theological anthropology; and since, at least in my estimation, the citations are relevant at each juncture, I have decided to risk repetition for the sake of flexibility. Also, because so many students lack acquaintance with the overarching narrative of Christian theology (and indeed, often of Western civilization itself), I have added the birth- and death-dates of most major figures mentioned in this book, omitting only either the most obvious ones (Augustine, Aquinas) or those mentioned only in passing.

in a single semester in a course on the theology of grace in the typical seminary or university classroom. There will therefore be no independent treatment of, for example, a theology of the Holy Spirit, or of the efficacious instrumentality of the sacraments as conduits of grace, or of the kinds of moral behavior that do or do not result in a loss of the life of grace, as these topics are usually covered in courses of their own. But the fact that so many of these other areas of theology both determine and are determined by a theology of grace is one more indication of the relevance of grace for all areas of theology, even in its most arcane moments.

So let the controversies begin.

CHAPTER 1

Nature and Grace

*The creature is darkness insofar as it comes out of nothing. But in as
much as it has its origin from God, it participates in his image; and
this leads to likeness to him.*

St. Thomas Aquinas, *De veritate* q. 18, a. 2, ad 5

The words *nature* and *grace* have a wide range of meanings, both inside and
outside theology. One way to begin to understand that range would be to
start simply with etymology. *Nature* comes from the Latin *natura*, itself a
noun formed from the Latin deponent intransitive verb *nascor, nasci, natus
sum*, meaning "to be born" which gives to English, among a host of other
words, terms like *nativity, nation* (which originally meant the land where
one was born), and *innate*, meaning "inborn" or "inherent," which in turn
implies the concept of something *essential* to the make-up or constitution
of a particular entity. What is natural, then, can, in certain contexts, refer
to what is essential to something's identity.[1] Thus, expressions like "It's only

1. It is this last meaning that Thomas stresses the most: "We should note that the word
natura is derived from *nascendo* [being born]. Hence the nativity of living beings—that is, of
animals and plants—was first called *natura*, as though the word were *nascitura* [something
that is being born]. Then the term *natura* was extended to the *principle* of this nativity. And
because the principle of such nativity is *internal*, the name 'nature' was further employed
to designate the *interior principle of movement*. . . . And because natural motion, especially
in procreation and generation, has as its term the essence of a species, that essence of a
species—signified by its definition—is called *nature*." Thomas Aquinas, *Quaestio disputata de
unione Verbi incarnati*, art. 1; emphases added. This latter meaning has now won out as the
primary one: "By far the commonest native meaning of *natura* is something like sort, kind,
quality, or character. When you ask, in our modern idiom, what something 'is like,' you are

1

human nature" assert (or at least imply) that a particular "natural" behavior or trait is inherent to a human being. Correlatively, when a behavior is described as "unnatural," the implication is not that such behavior is *impossible* to perform (like pigs flying, which is certainly unnatural in the absolute sense) but *deplorable*.[2]

Grace, on the other hand, comes from the Latin noun *gratia*, a word with another wide range of semantic content; one Latin dictionary lists these meanings (as determined by the context where they occur): "agreeableness," "esteem," "favor" (in the sense of a service done outside of one's ordinary duties), "indulgence," and finally, in a very common idiom, "thanks" or "*grati*tude." As with *natura*, *gratia* too is a nominal form derived from a Latin deponent verb, here *grator, gratari, gratus sum*, meaning "to give thanks to" or "to con*gratu*late," from which the adjective *gratus* came to mean "pleasing." In all of these usages the semantic range stresses what is *not* essential, that is, what is *gratu*itous, to the entity in question but comes to it as something extra, unexpected, or not required for a nature to be a nature.[3]

---

asking for its *natura*. When you want to tell a man the *natura* of anything you describe the thing." C. S. Lewis, *Studies in Words* (Cambridge: At the University Press, 1960), 24.

2. Lewis: "Since *natural* can mean 'having due affection,' or *pius*, *unnatural* of course means the reverse. Thus old Hamlet's ghost says that, while all murder is 'most foul,' his own murder was 'strange and unnatural,' because it was fratricidal. Anything which has changed from its sort or kind (*nature*) may be described as *unnatural*, provided that the change is one the speaker deplores. Behavior is *unnatural* or 'affected,' not simply when it is held to be a departure from that which a man's *nature* would lead to of itself, but when it is a departure for the worse. When the timid man forces himself to be brave, or the choleric man to be just, he is not called *unnatural*. '*Unnatural* vices' are so called because the appetite has exchanged its characteristic and supposedly original bent . . . for one which most men think worse. (Perpetual continence, though equally a departure from [nature], would be, and is, called *unnatural* only by those who disapprove of it.)" Lewis, *Studies*, 43–44; all emphases in the original.

3. One relic of that range of meanings referring to the *not-required* survives in English in the term used by restaurants: "gratuity," meaning a tip offered to the waiter as something added on to the bill in gratitude for excellent service. Granted, as tips become more socially expected, not giving a tip can look conspicuous; and some restaurants even affix a (now quite misnamed) "gratuity" to the bill. But outside of that context, no one is legally obliged to pay a tip, provided of course one is willing to endure some ugly stares on leaving the restaurant, whereas not paying a bill can land one in Small Claims Court. The point is that restaurateurs have a right in law to *demand* payment of a bill; but a tip, precisely as a gratuity, is unowed, not required in law, and thus "graciously" given. There is also a pejorative connotation to the word *gratuitous*, as in a "gratuitous insult." But there too the root meaning of "undeserved" or "unearned" is preserved.

Thus we speak of someone's gracious manners, the graceful turn of a ballet dancer, a king's gracious pardon, or a gracious gesture like holding open a door for someone overloaded with packages. All of which has been usefully summarized by the French theologian Jean Daujat in this way:

> The word "grace" is a literal translation of the Latin *gratia*, equivalent to the Greek *charis* and derived from the Latin adjective *gratus*, meaning "pleasing." Thence is derived the sense of something granted to someone, as being pleasing to him without its being strictly his due, a gratuitous favor granted to an individual without its being an obligation, and finally a "pardon," a free remission of a penalty incurred. The word also has an important use in aesthetics, so that La Fontaine says it means "something still more than beauty," and another French writer remarks that the word suggests something that charms us because it expresses or symbolizes something supremely lovable and attractive, such as trust, tenderness, etc. Thus there is a sense in which grace stands for moral qualities. On a last analysis, love is the essence of grace. What we admire in a smile, in gracious manners, in beautiful speech is really the goodness which lies behind them.[4]

This passage begins to hint at the paradox of grace. For if love is the essence of grace, then something peculiar enters the picture here: we all *need* love, but love is not love if it has been coerced out of the supposed lover. We all have heard stories of children raised in wealthy homes whose parents give them every material blessing but deprive them of love, thereby warping them (Victorian fiction is filled with such stories). Yet, in a sense, love is not *due* anyone. What is the value of love if it is not freely given? Thus the paradox: we need love but cannot demand it. Love is love precisely because it is a gift freely—that is, gratuitously—given:

> The fundamental meaning of the word "grace" is bound up with love. What pleases us, what we find agreeable, is what we love; but from the first form of love, which is an attraction to the loved object, we pass on to a higher form of love which is a "giving" to the [one] being loved. The lover seeks what is pleasing to the beloved. Real love is always expressed by a giving and, above all, by a giving of one's self. *The gift that comes from*

---

4. Jean Daujat, *The Theology of Grace*, trans. by a nun of Stanbrook Abbey (New York: Hawthorn Books, 1959), 10–11.

love, all that is generosity prompted by love, such is the deepest meaning of the word "grace." From this comes the idea of all that is given without its being the due of the recipient: of all that is purely a gift, of which a pardon, or remission of a punishment, is only one particular and derived sense. So also we have the words "gratuitous," "gratuity," "gratuitously." What is gratuitous is pleasing because it is something given, and it is love that gives. The same meaning is to be found in the expression to be—or not—in someone's "good graces."[5]

Something analogous to that paradox—a requirement than can only be fulfilled by a free gift—can be seen at work in the centuries-long debate on nature and grace in Christian theology. On the one hand, God did not *have* to create the world, and so in that sense creation is "gratuitous."[6] On the other hand, once God creates, he has created *natures*, that is, creatures with their own inherent identity and specific goals, the fulfillment of which is required for them to maintain those natures.

Christian doctrine has consistently maintained what is technically known as God's *aseity*, his full self-sufficiency. God is not needy and so did not create the world out of any inherent desperation, the way a lonely child makes a toy and invents a personality to go along with it in order to create an imaginary friend to assuage the pain of isolation. Moreover, Scripture asserts that the act of creation is intimately bound up with Christ's own

5. Daujat, *Theology of Grace*, 11; emphasis added. This insight also of course has scriptural warrant: "Love is patient, love is kind. It does not envy, it does not boast, it is not proud. It is not rude, it is not self-seeking, it is not easily angered. It keeps no record of wrongs. Love does not delight in evil but rejoices with the truth. It bears all things, believes all things, hopes all things, endures all things" (1 Cor. 13:4–7).

6. On the last page of his book *The First Three Minutes*, Steven Weinberg famously said: "The more the universe seems comprehensible, the more it also seems pointless." As the theologian Larry Chapp points out, the concept of *pointless* semantically overlaps with that of *gratuitous*. Humans often do pointless things "gratuitously," that is, for no ulterior purpose but just for the sheer fun of it, such as children building sandcastles on the beach, or prehistoric societies etching geometric patterns in pottery. Whimsy is itself a kind of grace. Weinberg, in other words, is "close to the kingdom" but not quite there (yet). In Proverbs, a personified Wisdom speaks of her playful delight at God's creation: "When he marked out the foundations of the earth, I was beside him like a little child and was daily his delight, rejoicing before him always, rejoicing in his inhabited world and delighting in the sons of men" (Prov. 8:29c–31). On this passage see Hugo Rahner, *Man at Play* (New York: Herder and Herder, 1967), 20, who notes that the Septuagint translates the Hebrew word for *rejoicing* with the Greek word for *dancing* (*choreuzein*). For the idea that all culture is a form of gratuitous, "pointless" play, see Johan Huizinga, *Homo Ludens: A Study of the Play Element in Culture* (Boston: Beacon Press, 1950).

incarnation—a gratuitous act on God's part if ever there was one. For as St. Paul says: "All things were created through him [Christ] and for him" (Col. 1:16b). That word *for* especially indicates the ultimate purpose of creation: to be united with Christ when all of creation will dwell in God, "who put everything under Christ; [and] when he has done this, then the Son himself will be made subject to him who put everything under him, so that God may be all in all" (1 Cor. 15:27c–28). For Christian revelation, nothing is obviously more gratuitous than the incarnation; but creation itself, as Paul teaches, was created through and for Christ so that all natures will be suffused with the divine presence.

In this perspective, nature becomes not just an analogue, a symbol, or an indicator of grace, a mere *pointer* to grace, but a true exemplification and *instantiation* of grace: For the entire universe has been gratuitously created *in* Christ and is destined for union at the end with that same Christ through whom and for whom creation was aboriginally made, and separation from whom would thus seem to entail a violation of one's very created nature. In this way, God's aseity confirms the gracious character of creation, as Daujat rightly stresses:

> It remains to see why God created, seeing that he is perfectly self-suffic-ing in his infinite perfection to which nothing is wanting. He is in no way obliged to create, for creation adds nothing to him who needs nothing. God, who is infinite freedom, is absolutely free to create or not to create. Hence creation, which brings nothing to him, is on his part purely gratuitous, pure generosity, a pure gift to the creature of everything that it has within it. Being, good, perfection, and therefore creation is a pure act of love, purely the overflow or superabundance of love. God creates in order to give, because he is infinite generosity and love.[7]

Despite the obvious truth of this passage, and despite even more the christological hymns in Colossians, one line from which was cited above, the truth expressed by them must be paired with others that *contrast* grace over against nature. For insoluble problems arise when the grace of creation is seen as seamlessly segueing into the grace of redemption. Indeed, other passages from Scripture stress how completely unmerited and unexpected grace is when it encounters the unsuspecting sinner, who is by *nature* a child of wrath (the added italics stress this special gratuity):

7. Daujat, *Theology of Grace*, 46.

5

As for you, you were dead in your transgressions and sins, in which you used to live when you followed in the ways of this world and of the ruler of the kingdom of the air, the spirit who is now at work in those who are disobedient. All of us also lived among them at one time in the passions of our flesh, gratifying the cravings of flesh and senses, and we were *by nature* children of wrath, *like everyone else*. But God who is rich in mercy, out of his great love for us, made us alive in Christ even when we were dead in our transgressions—*it is by grace that you have been saved*—and raised us up with him and seated us with him in the heavenly places in Christ Jesus, so that in the ages to come he might show the *immeasurable* riches of his grace in kindness toward us in Christ Jesus. For by grace you have been saved through faith, and *this is not of your doing; it is the gift of God*—not the result of works, so that no one may boast. (Eph. 2:1–9)

To be sure, Paul adds in the very next verse a further balance, where he says: "For we are what he has *made* us, *created* in Christ Jesus for good works, which God prepared beforehand to be our way of life" (v. 10). So the paradox remains even from verse to verse in various biblical passages. Of course, Paul is speaking here (mostly) of the operations of grace after the event of sin, which utterly changes the calculus, as it were, of the nature/grace relation—so much so that the next chapter will be devoted to the contrast between sin and grace.

Still, even when the fact of sin is provisionally "bracketed" for purposes of conceptual analysis, Scripture does not always speak of created nature as merely a subspecies of grace sharing the same ontological identity with the grace of redemption. Nature *as such*, in other words, is seen as the contrasting reality to "pure" grace. Thus in Romans the Apostle will say (again, with italics given to stress the contrast): "For I am sure that neither death, nor life, nor angels, nor principalities, nor things present, nor things to come, nor powers, nor height, nor depth, nor anything else *in all creation*, will be able to separate us from the love of God in Christ Jesus our Lord" (Rom. 8:38–39). That this contrast holds true even for nature before the fall of Adam Paul makes clear here:

What is sown is perishable, what is raised is imperishable. It is sown in dishonor, it is raised in glory. It is sown in weakness, it is raised in power. It is *sown a physical body*, it is raised a spiritual body. Thus it is written, "The first Adam became a living being" [Gen. 2:7]; the last Adam became a life-giving spirit. *But it is not the spiritual which is first but the physical, and then the spiritual.* The first man was *from the earth, a man of dust*; the second man is from heaven. *As with the man of dust, so are those who are of the dust*; and as is the man of heaven, so are those who are of heaven. Just as we *have* borne the image of the man of dust, we *shall* also bear the image of the man of heaven. I tell you this, brethren: *flesh and blood cannot inherit the kingdom of God, nor does the perishable inherit the imperishable.* (1 Cor. 15:42–50)[8]

Traditionally, the two prongs of this paradox—nature considered in itself as a true subspecies of grace, and grace considered as radically disjunctive from nature—come with a terminology: those who stress the continuity between nature and grace are called "intrinsicists," while those who stress the disjunction between the two are known as "extrinsicists." However traditional these terms have become, they can be misleading. No alleged extrinsicist really thinks creation has no relationship to Christ, just as no one who has been attacked as an intrinsicist thinks God took no free initiative to save the human race after the event of sin, still less that God "owes" us salvation, no matter how much we might crave rescue from the human plight, and no matter how restless the human heart is without God.[9] All supposed extrinsicists agree with St. Augustine that no one is

---

8. As the great medieval Dominican Albertus Magnus pointed out, nothing is more "extrinsic" to nature than the resurrection: "The resurrection is in no way a natural process; the fact that it is a final goal does not make it natural. Of course, if by 'nature' one means that natural being that man is, it can be said that man exists for the sake of resurrection; but this 'for the sake of' refers to the final purpose of the creation of man, not of nature. The ground of creation is not, in fact, nature; hence the final goal of creation is not actually the final goal of nature." Albertus Magnus, *De Resurrectione*, tractate 1, q. 3; cited in Hans Urs von Balthasar, *Theo-Drama: Theological Dramatic Theory*, Vol. V: *The Last Act*, trans. Graham Harrison (San Francisco: Ignatius Press, 1998), 375.

9. The invention of these two terms, at least as they are used in the nature/grace debate, has often been attributed to the French Catholic philosopher Maurice Blondel (1861–1949), but in fact, whether or not he originated them, he used them to express two equally *unacceptable* extremes: "I shall make use of certain barbarous neologisms with a view to fixing attention and throwing into relief the exclusive character of each thesis.... [They] are opposite extremes, but of the same kind, based upon similar habits of mind, suffering from analogous philosophical lacunae, and aggravating one another by their conflict." Maurice Blondel, *History and Dogma*, trans. Alexander Dru and Illtyd Trethowan (Grand Rapids, MI: Eerdmans, 1964/1904), 225. According to Blondel, monarchist Catholics were able to ally themselves with the atheist Charles Maurras because their extrinsicism prevented them from seeing that Christians must act as a *leaven* transforming society from within. See Pe-

more intimately interior to the soul than God; and no alleged intrinsicist so stresses the total interiority of God to the soul as to become a gnostic, the kind of person who, in Emily Bronte's poem, could make this kind of prayer:

> And am I wrong to worship where
> Faith cannot doubt, nor hope despair,
> Since my own soul can grant my prayer?
> Speak, God of Visions, plead for me:
> And tell why I have chosen thee.

Nonetheless, shopworn and misleading though these terms can be when addressing and describing what various theologians have actually thought about this issue, the polarity represented by them can serve as useful markers for outlining the various legitimate options *within* these extremes. On the one hand, no one wants to make grace so irrelevant to the most fundamental longings of the human heart that God's offer of salvation can easily be shrugged off and which some happen to accept the way others take up a hobby like building model trains. On the other hand, grace cannot meet us as something *expected*, as something long overdue. Some authors explain their concerns using the analogy of Old Testament to New: throughout the Old Testament the prophets had promised a Messiah who would liberate the Jews from oppression; but this liberation, when it came, arrived in a way whose acceptance required an *overthrow* of those very expectations that the Bible had inculcated.

Another way of possibly resolving this issue would be to look at an expression drawn from ordinary language: "There but for the grace of God go I." This remark can of course be meant in the literal, religious sense but is often said merely to express relief at having made a narrow, unexpected and unforeseen escape. But that idiom also points out how nature's *varia-*

---

ter J. Bernardi, *Maurice Blondel, Social Catholicism, and Action française: The Clash over the Church's Role in Society during the Modernist Era* (Washington, DC: Catholic University of America Press, 2009), 167–73, 189–207. On the other side of the ledger, it should also be noted that Blondel vigorously denied that his attacks on "extrinsicism" meant he was an intrinsicist, which in his terms meant being a pragmatist or a Kantian: "He recognized the ontological implications of first principles, the objective value of knowledge in all its stages, the objective truth of concepts, and the living immanence of realities in them." Henri Bouillard, *Blondel and Christianity*, trans. James M. Somerville (Washington, DC: Corpus Books, 1969), 39, citing Maurice Blondel, "fidélité conservée par la croissance même de la tradition," *Revue Thomiste* 40 (1936): 611–25.

tions—in outcome, gradations, talents, and the like—can serve as an analogue to grace strictly defined. Even the most consistent extrinsicists admit that nature often serves as a parable of grace, despite their insistence that nature and grace must not be conflated. This parabolic indicator of grace in nature has been expressed with admirable clarity by the nineteenth-century theologian Daniele Palmieri:

1. Every act of conceding that something is "necessary" in nature belongs to an infinite hierarchy of *gradations*, of which each one can seem like a "grace" to other narrower [lower] gradations.
2. The *de facto* immense *wealth* of creation, for example, of the animals and plants ordered to man, has a specific "graced" character as such.
3. Much that corresponds to human nature in general is not meant for each individual, for example, bodily and mental integrity, prosperity, and so on, especially since certain natural laws exclude the possibility that each isolated individual can partake of all these goods. They are thus, for the individual, "grace" in a preeminent way.
4. God could have ordered the world in many other different ways: that he chose *this* total arrangement that furnishes so much beneficence to the individual as well as to the whole can certainly be characterized as a "grace."
5. Finally, the whole environment, necessarily ordered to an innate dynamic as such, is *de facto* and constantly contingent and so has a "gracious" character to it in all its details.[10]

Thus we can come to our first conclusion: no so-called extrinsicist thinks grace is so utterly disconnected from nature that it makes no dif-

10. D. Palmieri, *Tractatus de gratia divina actuali* (1885), 7–8; emphases added. Reductionists will obviously object especially to Palmieri's first point, that "higher" developments represent something genuinely *new*, unexpected and "unowed." But reductionism collapses as soon as one realizes the impossibility of writing a research article on, for example, "The Role of Atoms in Supply-Side Economics." The chemist and philosopher of science Michael Polanyi gets at something like the same point when he says: "[I]t is as meaningless to represent life in terms of physics and chemistry as it would be to interpret a grandfather clock or a Shakespeare sonnet in terms of physics and chemistry; and it is likewise meaningless to represent mind in terms of a machine or of a neural model. Lower levels do not lack a bearing on higher levels; *they define the conditions of their success and account for their failures, but they cannot account for their success, for they cannot even define it.*" Michael Polanyi, *Personal Knowledge: Toward a Post-Critical Philosophy* (Chicago: University of Chicago Press, 1962), 18, 382; Polanyi's italics.

ference to one's eternal fate how one relates to God's offer of grace; and no alleged intrinsicist has ever collapsed the distinction between God and the creature as to be, in effect, a pantheist or a gnostic. In that regard, all Christian theologians without exception agree with this fundamental anthropological starting point, so aptly and concisely expressed by Hans Urs von Balthasar (1905–88):

> Thus, though man is created in the image and likeness of God, he is formed from the dust of the earth. Though he is called to be the highest, the nearest to God, he is by origin the lowliest. What lies behind him— the dust of his origin—is a constant reminder that he must not confuse the archetype with the image; the fact that he is an image is a constant reminder that he must conform himself to the archetype on which he is patterned. In other words, *man's first state is to be at a twofold remove*— at a remove from God and from nothingness. Because he comes from nothing, he retains, however great his likeness to the archetype, an even greater and ineradicable unlikeness. Nor can he increase his likeness to God by becoming more and more unmindful of his origin in order thereby to be more like God. On the contrary, it is only in the measure of his striving to be in the image and likeness of God, even though always at a remove from God, that man fulfills the purpose for which he was created. He achieves the highest measure of this likeness when he has the humility neither to forget nor to deny for an instant his condition of not-being God, the nothingness of his origin.[11]

In other words, the very concept of grace *requires* that it be set against what is not-grace, that is, against nature. For grace is, ultimately, as we saw above, a relationship established in love; but no love can exist unless the lovers remain distinct from one another:

> Any effort to establish an identity of archetype with image would bring about man's immediate destruction. For it was only because he was at a remove from God that the grace that called him into being could also bestow upon him the grace of likeness. It is only because he is not-God, because he comes to meet God as the unalterably not-God, that he shares in the independence, unity, personality and freedom of his

---

11. Hans Urs von Balthasar, *The Christian State of Life*, trans. Sister Mary Frances Mc-Carthy (San Francisco: Ignatius Press, 1983), 67; Balthasar's italics.

Creator. If a mirror were to be so like what it mirrored that it had become identical with it, what was mirrored would cease to exist. If the two lovers were to attempt so to possess one another that the two were fused into one, then love—if such a thing were possible—would fall into nothingness. To understand any movement of love at all, the lover must proceed from the sure state of his own existence.[12]

So deeply is this reality of not-being-God inscribed in man's essence—that is, in his nature—that this dilemma has become part of Western literature's common coinage, for which this famous passage from Alexander Pope's *Essay on Man* (Epistle II.1) may serve as the most rhetorically effective example:

> Know then thyself, presume not God to scan;
> The proper study of mankind is man.
> Placed on this isthmus of a middle state,
> A being darkly wise and rudely great:
> With too much knowledge for the sceptic side,
> With too much weakness for the stoic's pride,
> He hangs between, in doubt to act or rest;
> In doubt to deem himself a god or beast;
> In doubt his mind or body to prefer;
> Born but to die, and reasoning but to err.
> Alike in ignorance, his reason such,
> Whether he thinks too little or too much:
> Chaos of thought and passion all confused;
> Still by himself abused or disabused;
> Created half to rise and half to fall;
> Great lord of all things, yet a prey to all;
> Sole judge of truth, in endless error hurled:
> The glory, jest, and riddle of the world![13]

12. Balthasar, *Christian State of Life*, 67–68. As Pope St. Leo the Great (c. 400–461) says so well: "As God does not change by his condescension, so man is not swallowed up by being exalted." Leo the Great, *Epistula 28: ad Flavianum*, 3–4 (*PL* 54, 763–67): "Sicut enim Deus non mutatur miseratione, ita homo non consumitur dignitate." I owe this reference to Fr. Richard Schenk, O.P., to whom thanks.

13. Pope's debt to Pascal has long been recognized, as here: "Man's greatness lies in his capacity to recognize his wretchedness. A tree does not recognize its wretchedness. So it is wretched to know one is wretched, but there is greatness in the knowledge of one's

These, then, are the confines of the debate from which theologians rarely stray—and when they do, incoherence quickly sets in. But even though nearly everyone admits that the God-creature distinction remains in force even in the most intimate union with God, the history of theology shows that different emphases become possible, from which then different schools of thought arise. So while no one confesses to being an admitted extrinsicist or intrinsicist (nor, correlatively, is the accusation ever justified when it is leveled by one side against the other), still it is possible to *veer* toward one extreme or the other. Thus, some theologians will stress the *continuity* between nature and grace by emphasizing the gratuity of creation coupled with the single will of God that the whole human race be saved; while others will stress the *discontinuity* between man's lost state and the quite unexpected divine initiative to save (at least part of) the human race.

While both sides of this debate operate within orthodox boundaries, as we have seen, the dispute between them is not minor; for a lot rides on it, above all God's ultimate intentions in creating and saving the world, as was already pointed out in the Introduction. The trouble is, Christians (including theologians) often take a position on those wider, more burning issues first and *then* cobble together a theology of the nature/grace relation to justify—or at least shore up—an already adopted position. Such a procedure is not, in and of itself, problematic. For there is nothing about the theology of grace that says it has to come first, either logically or chronologically; and in the history of theology one often notes a reciprocal interchange between, say, the issue of eschatology and that of grace, with one reinforcing the other and without any evident cause-effect priority of one over the other.

That said, since this book is a work not on eschatology, nor on the

---

wretchedness." Blaise Pascal, *Pensées*, trans. Honor Levi (Oxford: Oxford University Press, 1995), 36–37. For that reason, all the Christian saints recognize that no matter how intimate our union with God becomes through grace, the distance between God and the creature will never be abrogated: "Man is indeed called to love, but only in a manner that permits him to live to the full his condition as creature. He not only may, but must, strive for the highest degree of love; but this highest degree must be accompanied by the most complete realization of his true state as creature. In a word, love must have the inner form of dependence and submission; it must be identical with the glorification of the Eternal Archetype by means of reverential service" (Balthasar, *Christian State of Life*, 68). This duality is also reflected in two sayings of Jesus: "I no longer call you servants, but friends" (John 15:15); but: "So you too, when you have done all that is commanded of you, say: 'We are unworthy servants; we have only done what is our duty'" (Luke 17:10).

church's relation to the modern world, nor on the diversity of world religions in light of divine providence, but strictly on grace, the question to be addressed here is this one: is there some way of resolving the debate between continuity and discontinuity in the nature/grace relation when it is *taken in isolation* from other issues, so that it can then cast retrospective light on all these other topics?

Perhaps there is, although at first glance the ins and outs of this controversy might seem arcane, one of those debates that generate a lot of heat and dust among theologians but which will probably strike the non-expert as providing little light. If not pointless, the debate often strikes the outsider as at least remote from everyday concerns. But on closer analysis, this seemingly arcane controversy can in fact prove highly illuminating for other issues as well: and this can be seen above all in the question of whether man has, by virtue of his nature as a created being, a *natural* desire for God.

Now, given St. Augustine's famous line early in his *Confessions* that our heart is restless until it rests in God, it would seem that tradition holds in the affirmative, that is, that man does indeed have a natural desire for God. But in fact that answer, while perhaps superficially obvious, runs into difficulties. Perhaps for Augustine, the issue admitted of a simple answer, but not for Aquinas. Here, in simplified terms, is how the Augustinian tradition sees it, according to William O'Connor:

> St. Augustine knew as well as Aristotle that man's will tends by a necessity of its nature towards happiness, the notion of which is imprinted on our minds. He also knew that true happiness or beatitude is found only in God. It is but a step to identify the happiness we are seeking by a necessity of our nature with God, and there does not seem to be any reason to doubt that St. Augustine made this step. Since God is in fact the soul's beatitude, it is all one with him to say that the soul is borne by its nature towards happiness and to say that it is borne by its nature toward God.[14]

This insight was so obvious to Augustine that the alternative seems never to have entered his mind; and in fact he explicitly says in the *Soliloquies* that every being capable of loving is loving God whether he is aware of

---

14. William R. O'Connor, *The Natural Desire for God*, The Aquinas Lecture, 1948 (Milwaukee: Marquette University Press, 1948), 18–19.

it or not.[15] Partly, this is an outcome of his Platonic epistemology, whereby man comes to the knowledge of the truth, *any* truth, only because of a prior divine illumination enlightening his soul, a view also shared by St. Bonaventure.[16] Now obviously, if God must be so directly involved in the attainment of truth, even natural truths, then man must have a natural desire for God correlative to his natural desire for the truth, as O'Connor explains:

> St. Augustine placed, or rather discovered, in the soul of every man, prior to grace *and prior even to conscious reflection*, a natural desire for God as our beatitude. . . . [S]o long as the divine illumination of truth was retained in the Augustinian tradition, a natural desire for God followed upon it as a necessary consequence. We see this in the teaching of St. Bonaventure, a pure Augustinian, for whom the soul has an innate knowledge of the existence of God as its supreme good, since it is made in His image and likeness. This gives rise to a natural desire for God as our beatitude: "The soul naturally tends toward the one in whose image it has been made, in order that in Him it may be beatified."[17]

Aquinas, however (and notoriously for his time), denied this special divine illumination and with Aristotle held that natural truths were accessible to the human mind through entirely natural faculties.[18] Given Plato's

15. "O God, thou who art loved, wittingly or unwittingly, by everything that is capable of loving. . . ." Augustine, *Soliloquies* I, 2.

16. "Shall we say, as St. Thomas Aquinas was to answer, that since God has made man a rational animal, the natural light of reason must be able naturally to perform its proper function, which is to know things as they are, and thereby to know truth? Or shall we say with St. Augustine, that truth being necessary, unchangeable, and eternal, it cannot be the work of a contingent, mutable, and impermanent human mind interpreting unnecessary, changeful and fleeting things? Even in our minds truth is a sharing of some of the highest attributes of God; consequently, even in our minds, truth is an immediate effect of the light of God." Etienne Gilson, *The Unity of Philosophical Experience* (San Francisco: Ignatius Press, 1999; originally published in 1937), 43–44. See as well: Etienne Gilson, *Pourquoi saint Thomas a critiqué saint Augustin* (Paris: J. Vrin, 1981): "Le thomisme serait donc né . . . d'une décision philosophique pure. Opter contra la doctrine de Platon, pour celle d'Aristote, c'était s'obliger à reconstruire la philosophie chrétienne sur d'autres bases que celles de saint Augustin" (126).

17. O'Connor, *Natural Desire for God*, 24–25; emphasis added. The internal quotation is from Bonaventure's *De mysterio Trinitatis* I, 1, 10.

18. See *ST* I, q. 84, a. 5 and I, q. 88, a. 3. Admittedly, in these two passages Thomas seems to be trying to harmonize his position with Augustine's, not disagree with it; but that is the usual habit among medieval theologians, as one scholar rightly notes: "Thomas probably

great prestige among most medieval theologians of that time, and given as well the correlative suspicion with which Aristotle was regarded in the thirteenth century, not to mention the overpowering weight of Augustine's authority in theological debate (not least in matters of grace), and given the wholesale adoption of the theory of divine illumination by Bonaventure, Thomas Aquinas certainly caused a stir, not least because his epistemology made God much more *obscure* and the path to God correlatively that much more arduous.[19]

It is often forgotten how nugatory are the results of Thomas's Five Ways—which lead, to be sure, to "what all men call God"; but still, although we can be sure of God's "factual" existence, we still can know nothing of God's essence: "Created things are not sufficient to represent the Creator," says Thomas. "Hence we cannot possibly arrive at perfect knowledge of the Creator from creatures; in addition, because of the weakness of our intellect, we cannot even know all that created things manifest of God."[20] And, as O'Connor explains, the effect of that position on the question of man's natural desire for God is direct and immediate, and indeed revolutionary:

> Is it not true that God is our beatitude? Has it not been revealed that the vision of God is the end of man? That is the whole point. It is a *revealed* truth that the vision of God is the only historical end man has ever had, so that the purely natural man with a purely natural end has never existed. Does this mean that the human will by its very nature

did not yet recognize the immense doctrinal distance between the historical Augustine and his own epistemology. Yet Aquinas was hardly the first scholastic to interpret the Latin Father somewhat loosely." Bernhard Blankenhorn, O.P., "Aquinas as Interpreter of Augustinian Illumination in Light of Albertus Magnus," *Nova et Vetera*, English Edition, Vol. 10, No. 3 (Summer 2012): 689–713; here 699.

19. For Thomas, this arduous journey to God establishes the creaturely basis for the theological virtue of hope, as he says here: "Now hope implies desire accompanied by the rousing of one's spirit [*animi*] as tending to something arduous [*quasi in quoddam arduum tendens*]" (*De veritate* q. 28, a. 4). The renowned Thomist moral theologian Servais Pinckaers explains this passage as follows: "Hope has for its object *bonum arduum*, an arduous good that is difficult to attain. The object of hope is one from which we are separated by a great distance, a distance which makes us simultaneously afraid that we will not be able to achieve it, while at the same time spurring us on with the effort required to achieve it." Servais Pinckaers, O.P., "The Natural Desire to See God," *Nova et Vetera*, English edition, Vol. 8, No. 3 (Summer 2010): 627–46, here 643.

20. Thomas Aquinas, *De veritate* q. 5, a. 2, ad 11; and: "Although uncreated truth exceeds all created truth, yet there is nothing to prevent created truth from being better known to us. Things that are less known in themselves are known better by us" (ibid., q. 10, a. 12, ad 6).

has an innate, necessary tendency towards God, or the vision of God, as our beatitude? Does it mean that the intellect is tending by its nature as intellect, prior to all actual knowledge, towards this vision as the only object that can finally put an end to its unlimited craving for truth? In other words, has every intellectual creature a natural desire for the beatific vision? When the question is worded in this fashion St. Thomas' answer is, I believe, a straightforward no.[21]

What accounts for this strange turn of events? How could Thomas deny what seemed so obvious to Augustine, who said that, since we were aboriginally created for union with God, we must accordingly bear within our natures a trace of that divine intention? How could God's purposes not be inscribed in our very desires? As we saw above, part of the reason for this shift made by Thomas stems from his denial of divine illumination in the human soul giving access to natural truths. This denial makes God inherently obscure. But Thomas also has another argument: free will. If matters were as Augustine held, then man would gravitate toward God of necessity, the way a hungry teenager gravitates toward the school cafeteria line at lunchtime. But such is obviously not the case: men are constantly rebelling against God. As Pascal asked so pointedly: "If man is not made for God, why is he only happy with God? If man is made for God, why is he so hostile to God?"[22] *Ergo*, man is not created with a natural desire for God, and this despite all previous tradition, as O'Connor explains:

> St. Augustine taught that even in this life the mind sees or makes an identification of God with man's beatitude, so that the will cannot help being drawn towards Him by natural necessity. For St. Thomas we do not see in this life an identification of God with the good in general or with happiness. For this reason the human will is not drawn by natural necessity towards God or the vision of God as the object that consti-tutes our beatitude. *The knowledge of God we have in this life is indirect, mediate, abstract, obscure.* It does not present God to us as He really is. If an object appeared to us as good from every point of view, the will would of necessity tend towards it and seek its rest in it. This will be the case in the next life when we shall see God as He is, but we do not see Him now. We know from revelation that He is our true beatitude

21. O'Connor, *Natural Desire for God*, 26–27; emphasis added.
22. Pascal, *Pensées*, 8.

and ultimate end and we should freely adhere to Him, *even though we cannot do so by natural necessity.* The mere fact that we are capable of turning away from God as our ultimate end proves that we have not a determined tendency towards Him as our beatitude as we have towards happiness in general.[23]

As is well known (at least among those theologians invested in this debate), the twentieth-century Jesuit theologian Henri de Lubac (1896–1991) took the exact opposite position. In an oft-cited passage, he made this claim:

It is said that a universe might have existed in which man, though without necessarily excluding any other desire, would have his rational ambitions limited to some lower, purely human, beatitude. Certainly I do not deny it. But having said that, one is obliged to admit—indeed one is automatically affirming—that in our world as it is this is not the case.... In me, a real and personal human being, in my concrete nature—that nature I have in common with all real men, to judge by what my faith teaches me, and regardless of what is or is not revealed to me either by reflective analysis or by reasoning—the "desire to see God" cannot be permanently frustrated without an essential suffering. To deny this is to undermine my entire Credo. For is not this, in effect, the definition of the "pain of the damned"? And consequently—at least in appearance—a good and just God could hardly frustrate me, unless I, through my own fault, turn away from him by choice.[24]

But where does that freedom come from, and what does it say about man's natural desire for God? De Lubac does not say. For as we saw above, O'Connor takes Thomas's side (or what he takes to be the doctrine of the Common Doctor in this matter) precisely to avoid the implications of necessity entailed in the Augustinian view. And sure enough, no sooner has de Lubac seemed to concede a freedom on the part of a human person to reject his deepest desire, he lapses back into calling this natural desire entirely constitutive of the human person:

23. O'Connor, *Natural Desire for God*, 29–30; emphases added. As the author points out: "It is important ... to see that to desire to know an object is not the same as desiring an object already known" (ibid., 35), a distinction that was lost on Augustine but is crucial for resolving this knotty issue.

24. Henri de Lubac, *The Mystery of the Supernatural*, translated by Rosemary Sheed, Introduction by David L. Schindler (New York: Crossroad, 1998), 54, emphasis added.

The infinite importance of the desire implanted in me by my Creator is what constitutes the infinite importance of the drama of human existence.... For this desire is not some "accident" in me. It does not result from some peculiarity, possibly alterable, of my individual being, or from some historical contingency whose effects are more or less transitory.... It is in me as a result of my belonging to humanity as it is, that humanity which is, as we say, "called." *For God's call is constitutive.* My finality, which is expressed by this desire, is inscribed upon my very being as it has been put into this universe by God. And, by God's will, I now have no other genuine end, no end really assigned to my nature or presented for my free acceptance under any guise, except that of "seeing God."[25]

Notice here how de Lubac is arguing backward from eschatology to his assertion that man has an innate, natural desire for God; for the pains of hell are due precisely to the eternal frustration of that desire. Of course, the hypothesis of a limbo for infants who die before baptism would claim the opposite; for here would be a post-mortem realm where natural desires could be fulfilled without an eternal frustration.[26] But that hypothesis has largely been abandoned, not least because the Second Vatican Council seems to have undercut it with its assertion of a *single* end for man: "For, since Christ died for all men, and *since the ultimate vocation of man is in fact one, and that divine*, we ought to believe that the Holy Spirit, in a manner known only to God, offers to every man the possibility of being associated with this paschal mystery."[27]

That text, more than any other from that epochal council, explains

25. de Lubac, *Mystery of the Supernatural*, 54–55.

26. The invocation of the idea of limbo reserved for unbaptized infants (who in this limbo supposedly never notice their deprivation of their supernatural destiny) in order to support the hypothesis of a pure nature, however, soon runs into its own contradictions. Not only does it have to face Col. 1:16 and John 1:1–4 (which assert that all creation came *through* Christ and/or the Word), but it must also face its own insistence that *natura pura* does not actually obtain in the world as it was actually created by God. As Reginald Garrigou-Lagrange rightly points out: "All theologians agree that this state of pure nature never existed." Reginald Garrigou-Lagrange, *Grace: Commentary on the* Summa theologica *of St. Thomas, IaIIae, q. 109–14*, trans. Dominican Nuns of Corpus Christi Monastery (St. Louis: B. Herder, 1952), 23. Thus, if a *limbus infantium* does exist, then so does a pure nature untouched by Christ; but this latter is denied by all parties, as it would deny the trinitarian/christological foundation of creation.

27. *Gaudium et Spes* §22; cited from *The Documents of Vatican II*, ed. Walter M. Abbott, S.J. (New York: America House Press, 1966), 221–22; emphasis added.

why de Lubac's reassertion of Augustine's view won out during roughly the first forty years after the council. Very few dissenting voices could be heard in that time against de Lubac's programmatic statement in *Surnaturel* that the "spirit just *is* desire for God."[28] Given the way the debate was framed in those postconciliar years, such a consensus can hardly come as a surprise, as seen in this memoir by someone who lived through and was trained in that time:

> Declaring "pure nature" not to belong to the subject matter of theology was also the remedy against what Maurice Blondel labeled an "extrinsicist" view of grace, or what we as students referred to as "Suárez's cream cake." It is the well-known picture of nature and grace as two tiers, one on top of the other, without an intrinsic connection between the two. Human nature is complete in itself, and it might well do without grace, that is, without a personal relation to God. Without the cream of grace, it would be a little dry and less tasty, but the cake of nature is not really affected by the cream topping. However, from a religious, and hence also from a theological perspective, such a view was completely unacceptable. It alienated grace and faith from our personal, concrete, everyday life and from the larger reality of society and the world by promoting a flight into a distinct spiritual realm. It domesticated and isolated theology, confining it to the little, sheltered niche of the supernatural, fully disconnected from the humanities and sciences.[29]

Given recent criticisms leveled against de Lubac, it takes some imagination to see why his argument proved so convincing. Bernard Mulcahy (as it happens, a strong critic of de Lubac's thesis) summarizes de Lubac's argument with admirable and sympathetic objectivity here:

> Against the notion of pure nature, first, it may be objected that pure nature is not, and has never been, the state of any real human being.... Second, one may object that the notion of pure nature is alien to the

28. Henri de Lubac, *Surnaturel: Etudes historiques*, nouvelle édition, preparée et préfacée par Michel Sales, S.J. (Paris: Desclée de Brouwer, 1991), 483: "Paradoxe de l'esprit humain: créé, fini, il n'est pas seulement doublé d'une nature; il est lui-même nature. Avant d'être esprit pensant, il est nature spirituelle. ... L'esprit est donc désir de Dieu."

29. Harm Goris, "Steering Clear of Charybdis: Some Directions for Avoiding 'Grace Extrinsicism' in Aquinas," *Nova et Vetera*, English edition, Vol. 5, No. 1 (Winter 2007): 67–79; here 69.

Christian tradition. . . . In fidelity to tradition, the argument goes, we ought to imitate the early doctors and ignore the idea of pure nature. . . . Third, it has been objected that the idea of pure nature is dualistic. . . . [leaving theology] unable to think of grace except as a sort of alien invader, a foreign organism which seizes our nature and forces us to be its host. In addition, to treat nature and grace as only extrinsically related is to imply that grace leaves our natural, everyday human life untouched, reserving its effects for a separate "religious" part of our humanity. . . . Fourth, and finally, it is said that the idea of pure nature is to blame for certain ills of the modern Church and world. The critics of *natura pura* . . . hold that this scholastic concept has contributed to the marginalization of Christianity in the Western world. Alone or in combination with other principles, the idea of pure nature is made to carry the blame for atheistic humanism, capitalism, secularism, and an array of other phenomena which the critics of pure nature find objectionable.[30]

But recently, new voices have insisted they be heard, claiming that de Lubac went too far. Part of their case is historical. For one of the most controversial aspects of de Lubac's claim was that Thomas *agreed with de Lubac* and that therefore most of the later commentators misunderstood Thomas from the ground up on this issue. While it is of course theoretically possible that the commentators understood Thomas better than he understood himself, and that therefore the commentary tradition represents a legitimate development of the thought of the Common Doctor,[31] most of those who object to de Lubac claim the historical Thomas is on their side.

30. Bernard Mulcahy, O.P., *Aquinas's Notion of Pure Nature and the Christian Integralism of Henri de Lubac: Not Everything Is Grace*, American University Studies, Series VII: Theology and Religion, Vol. 314 (New York: Peter Lang, 2011), 4–5. One might also mention, at a popular level, the famous last line of Georges Bernanos's novel *A Diary of a Country Priest*, where the expiring priest said on his deathbed that grace is everywhere, a novelistic echo of the Little Flower's line "everything is grace": "Si vous me trouviez morte un matin, n'ayez pas de peine: c'est que Papa le bon Dieu serait venu tout simplement me chercher. Sans doute, c'est une grande grâce de recevoir les Sacrements; mais quand le bon Dieu ne le permet pas, c'est bien quand même, tout est grâce." Thérèse de L'Enfant de la Sainte Face, *Oeuvres Complètes* (Paris: Cerf, 1988), 1009.

31. This seems to be Garrigou-Lagrange's position: "one cannot follow St. Thomas by falling into a material literalism." P. R. Garrigou-Lagrange, "La possibilité de la grâce est-elle rigoureusement démonstrable?" *Revue thomiste* no. 94 (Mars-Avril 1936), 214, footnote 20: "il ne faut pas, pour suivre saint Thomas, tomber dans un littéralisme matériel."

So who is right, O'Connor or de Lubac? In retrospect, it has now become clear that there are texts in the Thomist corpus that could be used by either side, a point now becoming increasingly evident in the course of this drawn-out battle. As Steven Long rightly points out:

> It helps to put to rest the exegetic difficulty. It is without doubt true that there is a problem in the very texts of Aquinas, and a problem which seemingly does not allow much room for maneuver with respect to its solution: because the doctrinal points which constitute the elements of the problem—one is almost tempted to say "constitute the contradiction"—are starkly and clearly stated in St. Thomas's texts. Yet the realization that there are indeed *two* sets of texts, one of which was not merely an interposed corruption, itself marks a decisive advance toward correct interpretation of Thomas's teaching. . . . The second set of texts hedges about, and delimits, the possible signification of the first set, and vice versa. That is, on the supposition that we do not wish to suppose St. Thomas's texts to exhibit raw incoherence, then we need to read these texts in relation one to another.[32]

Part of the problem stems from the fact that Thomas never addressed, at least explicitly, the specific question that motivated the twentieth-century controversy, when the terms of the debate shifted from *desire* to *exigency*, a much stronger term suggesting an essential requirement for a nature to function as a nature (like the exigency for food in animals), which God would accordingly be "obliged" to fulfill, which would violate the root meaning of grace. We have already cited Paul's defense of the gratuity of grace here: "As for you, you were dead in your transgressions and sins. . . . But because of his great love for us, God, who is rich in mercy, made us alive with Christ even when we were dead in transgressions—it is by grace that you were saved" (Eph. 2:1, 4–5).

But that passage does not really address the question that has been

---

32. Steven A. Long, *Natura Pura: On the Recovery of Nature in the Doctrine of Grace* (New York: Fordham University Press, 2010), 13, 15; emphasis in the original. Despite his own anti-de Lubac position, O'Connor agrees that Thomas cannot be easily reconciled with himself: "St. Thomas, apparently, flatly denies what he has so vigorously affirmed concerning the existence of a natural desire. Since this is the case, it is difficult to appeal to any text whether for or against a natural desire for God, for one set of texts can always be offset by another." William R. O'Connor, *The Eternal Quest: The Teaching of St. Thomas Aquinas on the Natural Desire for God* (New York: Longmans, Green and Co., 1947), 12.

animating so much of the contemporary debate. For, once grace has been given, further questions arise: Are we allowed to feel more than just the appropriate *gratitude* for having received this gift that we could never have merited or deserved? That is, does the unmerited gift of grace cast a retrospective light on our past life of sin so that we are also permitted to feel *relief* that we have been rescued from a plight that we had long recognized prior to receiving grace? Is grace, then, like a trace mineral (zinc, for instance) whose absence from one's diet led to a kind of vague physiological malaise whose discontents (caused by factors not yet suspected) were never fully appreciated in their outermost extremity until the homeostasis of good health returned with a healthier, more balanced diet, but had nonetheless led to a felt listlessness that went on for years? In other words, does grace heal the soul's prior malaise in a way that makes grace seem, at least retrospectively, *like the answer to a spiritual exigency*, defined here as a crying need that had all along caused man to ache for grace ever since his expulsion from the Garden of Eden—a longing, moreover, that he had been *noticing* all along?

The usual answer in modern theology, starting with the condemnations of Michael Baius (1513–89) and Cornelius Jansenius (1585–1638)—both of whom had answered "Yes" to those questions—has been that man cannot have been given an inherent, innate exigency for grace, under the Aristotelian rubric that natural desires cannot be in vain.[33] Applying that

---

33. "We call a shoe pointless when it cannot be worn. But God and nature create nothing that is useless." Aristotle, *On the Heavens* Book I, ch. 4 (271a30). The context here is actually not human artifacts like shoes but, as the title of the treatise indicates, Aristotle's discussion of the necessarily circular orbits of celestial bodies. The application of this principle, which properly belongs in Aristotle's long superseded astronomy, to theological discussions of nature and grace is ironic indeed. At all events, and only adding to the irony, both Baius and Jansenius accepted that premise too, which is why they held that original sin had so devastated human nature and not just merely deprived our first parents of the (supposedly extraneous) grace of original justice: because grace and nature belong together, they reasoned, loss of grace necessarily entails the ruin of nature. Although they came to diametrically different conclusions about the way grace operates in postlapsarian man, they both wanted to stress the devastating effects of original sin on human nature, for which Aristotle's axiom proved useful. Condemnation of these views obviously required that orthodox theologians make a firmer—or at least less ambiguous—distinction between nature and grace, which then proved an important catalyst for the Thomist commentators. But because the commentators *also* accepted Aristotle's principle that nature does nothing in vain, they were perforce compelled to posit natural ends in man that were independent of his ultimate felicity in heaven. The theses of Baius and Jansenius will be discussed in more detail in the third chapter, on original sin. For purposes of this chapter, all that need be said

Stagirite axiom,[34] theologians argued as follows: if God had implanted an exigency for grace as part of our very nature, he would accordingly "owe" us grace, which would of course destroy its gratuity, making it no longer truly grace but something we could, *horribile dictu*, "count on." Hence, by an ineluctable logic, man has no innate, natural desire for God.

While this denial of a natural spiritual exigency is plausible—even inevitable in the wake of Baius and Jansenius—a problem lurks if that answer becomes too one-sided. For Scripture reveals that *all* of creation (and not just the human spirit) does indeed "groan" for its fulfillment in Christ:

> We know that the whole creation has been groaning as in the pains of childbirth right up to the present time. Not only so, but we ourselves, who have the firstfruits of the Spirit, groan inwardly as we wait eagerly for our adoption as sons, the redemption of our bodies. For in this hope we were saved. But hope that is seen is no longer hope at all. Who hopes for what he already has? But if we hope for what we do not yet have, we wait for it patiently. (Rom. 8:22–25)

What makes this passage so fascinating is the way Paul easily ascribes a natural longing to all creation (which can hardly be said to have "sinned"); yet he goes on to assert a further longing for *something not our due*. Crucially, as he points out, human longing is one for *adoption*. Now adoption refers to a legal status to which obviously a person has no claim: even a bedraggled, desperately hungry, rag-clad waif cannot go to a court of law and demand to be taken in by any family of his arbitrary choosing. Certain rights accrue naturally to natural-born children; adoption, however, is a freely bestowed legal status by which the one being adopted is (as we say) "graciously" allowed to belong legally to a particular family. My hapless parents were stuck with me and my dreadful infantile caterwauling upon

---

here is that the condemnation of their heresies forced a more precise distinction to be made, even in our prelapsarian first parents, between nature and grace.

34. The Stagirite invokes the same principle to biology too, of course: "Again, some members of the class of fishes are neither male nor female, as we see in eels and a kind of mullet found in stagnant waters. But whenever the sexes are separate, the female cannot generate perfectly by herself alone, for then the male would exist in vain, and nature makes nothing in vain." Aristotle, *On the Generation of Animals* Book II, ch. 5 (741b2). The operation of this principle in the nature/grace debate makes it difficult to account for Paul's insistence that "creation was subjected to futility, *not by its own choice*, but by the will of the one who subjected it" (Rom. 8:20).

my entrance into the world; but I have no claim to the estate of Bill Gates. (The novels of Charles Dickens, especially *David Copperfield* and *Great Expectations*, often hinge on this universally recognized reality.)[35]

Although, as said above, Thomas did not directly address this particular question as phrased this way, his extraordinarily subtle discussion of the nature/grace relation did have an enormous influence in later debate—*and for both sides*. On the first side of the ledger, we have St. Thomas's argument that to know God is the end of every intelligent substance:

> Since all creatures, even those devoid of understanding, are ordered to God as to an ultimate end, all achieve this end to the extent that they participate somewhat in His likeness. Intellectual creatures attain it in a more special way, that is, through their proper operation of understanding Him. Hence, this must be the end of the intellectual creature, to understand God. (*Summa contra Gentiles* III, 25.1)

From this consideration, Thomas directly concludes in this same chapter that man's desire for God is entirely natural: "There is naturally present in all men the desire to know the causes of whatever things are observed.... Therefore, man naturally desires, as his ultimate end, to know the first cause. But the first cause of all things is God. Therefore, the ultimate end of man is to know God" (*Summa contra Gentiles* III, 25.11). Furthermore, for Thomas, following Aristotle here, no natural desire may be in vain (*ST* I, q. 75, a. 6; *Compendium theologiae* 104). Finally, there is this stark, quasi-Augustinian statement:

> Final and perfect happiness can consist in nothing else than the vision of the divine essence.... If therefore the human intellect, knowing the essence of some created effect, knows no more of God than that he is, the perfection of that intellect does not yet reach simply the First Cause, but there remains in it the *natural* desire to seek the cause. Wherefore it is not perfectly happy. Consequently, for perfect happiness the intellect needs to reach the very essence of the First Cause. And then it will have its perfection through union with God as with that object in which *alone* man's happiness consists. (*ST* I-II, q. 3, a. 8; emphasis added)

35. The preceding four paragraphs are adapted from my article "Scheeben the Reconciler: Resolving the Nature/Grace Debate," *Nova et Vetera*, English edition, Vol. 11, No. 2 (Spring 2013): 435–53.

In some passages, Thomas even compares man's natural desire for God with biological instincts, as Howard Kainz rightly points out.[36] According to Kainz, Thomas means this term to be taken quite literally: the faith-instinct is univocally parallel to the instincts for self-preservation, sexual congress and hunger for knowledge, differing only in the object of the instinct's exigent craving. Although in this passage Thomas uses the milder term "inclination," he does so in the context of speaking of those drives that later biologists will call "instincts," especially that of self-preservation:

> In man there is first of all an inclination [*inclinatio*] to good in accordance with the nature he has in common with all substances—inasmuch as every substance seeks the preservation of its own being, according to its nature; and by reason of this inclination, whatever is a means of preserving human life and of warding off its obstacles belongs to the natural law. Secondly, there is in man an inclination to things that pertain to him more specifically, according to that nature which he has in common with the other animals; and in virtue of this inclination those things are said to belong to the natural law which nature has taught to all animals, such as sexual intercourse, education of offspring and so forth. Thirdly, there is in man an inclination to good according to the nature of his reason, which nature is proper to him; thus man has a natural inclination to know the truth about God. (*ST* I-II, q. 94, a. 2)

Although *inclinatio* is the word of choice here, Thomas uses the stronger word "instinct" in other passages to explain not biological drives but, fascinatingly, *the universality of natural religion.* Religion is an anthropological constant, says the Common Doctor, because man has an instinctive drive to worship God: "under the state of the law of nature, man was moved, by inward instinct alone [*solo interiori instinctu*] and without any outward law, to worship God; [furthermore] the sensible things to be employed in the worship of God were also determined by inward instinct [*ita etiam ex interiori instinctu*]" (*ST* III, q. 60, a. 5, ad 3). Elsewhere Thomas says: "man feels that he is obligated [*obligatum*] by some sort of natural instinct [*quodam naturali instinctu*] to pay reverence to God in his own way, from whom comes the beginning of man's being and of all good" (*ScG* III, c. 119).[37]

---

36. Howard P. Kainz, *The Existence of God and the Faith-Instinct* (Cranbury, NJ: Susquehanna University Press, 2010).

37. The prehistoric paintings in the caves of Lascaux in the Dordogne region of south-

So, relying on these passages, does Thomas hold, as de Lubac claimed, that each human being has an innate natural desire for God, an exigency for the beatific vision? There is, after all, no biological drive without a corresponding exigency, no instinct without an object to crave (including the drive to know, as per the scholastic axiom: *intellectus caret omnibus illis quas natus est intelligere*: "the intellect craves all those things it is born to know"). Given Thomas's terminology here, the obvious answer seems to be Yes: if we have a natural instinct to revere the God of our origins, then we must desire union with God by that same natural instinct.

But that affirmative answer can only prove convincing if we also air-brush away another set of texts that argue the contrary. For elsewhere Thomas could not be clearer that man has a *twofold* end, one inherent in his nature as a created, embodied intellect, and the other, an added, supernatural one bestowed on him gratuitously, one given to him in order to lead him to desire supernatural union with God. This position is especially clear in a passage that seems directly to contradict the passage cited immediately above (not to mention the teaching of Vatican II in *Gaudium et Spes* §22, also cited above):

> Man is perfected by virtue, [which enables him to perform] those actions whereby he is directed to happiness. . . . Now man's beatitude or happiness is twofold [*Est autem duplex hominis beatitudo sive felicitas*]. . . . One is proportional to human nature, a happiness, that is, which man can obtain by means of his natural principles. The other is a happiness surpassing man's nature, and which man can obtain by the power of God alone, by a kind of participation of the Godhead. . . . And because such happiness surpasses the capacity of human nature, man's natural principles, which enable him to act well according to his capacity, do not suffice to direct man to this same [supernatural] happiness. Hence it is necessary for man to receive from God some additional principles, whereby he may be directed to supernatural happiness, even as he is directed to his connatural end by means of his natural principles, albeit not without divine assistance. (*ST* I/II, q. 62, a. 1)[38]

---

western France (made roughly 17,000 years ago) and the even earlier ones at Chauvet in the Ardèche Département of southern France (dated 30,000 years ago) are notoriously difficult to interpret—since, when they were painted, literacy had not been invented; and without texts to go on, there is no way to interpret why they were made. One suspects, though, based on these passages, that Thomas would hold that the paintings were made for religious reasons.

38. Although Thomas does not mention the bishop of Hippo directly here, something

In an earlier work, Thomas makes virtually the same point but in even starker terms: "The final good of man is twofold. One is in proportion to human nature, the other is a good that exceeds this proportion, since the forces of nature are not sufficient to obtain it, *or even to think about it or desire it* [*nec ad cogitandum vel desiderandum*]. This is eternal life, which is promised to man solely by divine generosity" (*De veritate* q. 14, a. 2; emphasis added).[39]

Among historians of theology, an almost universal consensus holds that the vast majority of Thomist commentators stress—and develop—this side of Thomas's teachings on the natural desire to see God, the side that insists on the twofold ends of man, as Lawrence Feingold has shown in massive detail in a highly regarded study.[40] Out of that development came the introduction of two technical terms that have themselves become heated topics of debate: *elicited desire* (as opposed to natural), and *obediential potency.* The first refers to a desire to know God as First Cause born out of philosophical wonder; the second to God's ability to create a new nature as the basis for the gift of supernatural grace strictly defined.

As to the first term, *elicited desire*, Feingold admits that "texts of St. Thomas concerning the natural desire to see God do not directly address or explicitly determine the question of whether the natural desire in question is elicited or innate, which explains the divergence of views which have existed and which still exist in this matter."[41] But the distinction was made because it seemed to solve the problem of God creating a nature with an

---

like Augustine's view gets expressed in the third objection, to which Thomas offers this reply: "The reason and will are naturally directed to God, inasmuch as He is the beginning and end of nature, but [only] in proportion to nature. But the reason and will, according to their nature, are not sufficiently directed to Him in so far as He is the object of supernatural happiness" (ibid., ad 3). The break with Augustine is now complete.

39. A point repeated here: "Now everlasting life is a good exceeding the proportion of created nature, since it exceeds its knowledge and desire" (*ST* I/II, q. 114, a. 2). Also here: "Man merits not by desiring a happiness which he naturally seeks, but by desiring something special, *which he does not seek naturally* [*quod non naturaliter appetit*], such as the vision of God, in which nonetheless as a matter of fact [*secundum rei veritatem*] his happiness does consist" (*De veritate* q. 22, a. 7; emphasis added).

40. Lawrence Feingold, *The Natural Desire to See God according to St. Thomas Aquinas and His Interpreters*, second edition (Naples, FL: Sapientia Press, 2010). In the majority he includes Denis the Carthusian (1402–71), the Dominicans Thomas de Vio (1469–1534; better known as Cardinal Cajetan), Bartolomé de Medina (1527–1580), Domingo Báñez (1528–1604), and the Jesuit Francisco Suárez (1548–1604). In the minority are the Dominican Domingo de Soto of Salamanca (1494–1560) and the Jesuit Francisco de Toledo (1532–1596).

41. Feingold, *Natural Desire*, xxxiii.

innate desire that he would then "have" to fulfill. Moreover, elicited desire can account for why so many are not moved to worship God, who alone can fulfill all our desires, of whatever species, as Feingold explains here:

> The object, *once considered*, naturally attracts the will and thus specifies its act to be one of desire or love and not indifference. This means that objects of natural willing are not always being willed in act, but only when the object is considered. This distinction is important with regard to the natural desire to see God. In order for this to be a natural desire, it is not necessary for rational creatures to always actually desire it, but only when the mystery of God is considered. It may be that a thought-less or worldly person, or an atheist, never considers this, and therefore never actually desires it.[42]

Corresponding to the distinction between natural and elicited desires is the correlative distinction between natural and obediential potency. Once again, the distinction was made to avoid tying nature too closely to grace, which would entail what the scholastics called a *debitum naturae*, meaning a nature to which God "owed" grace. A purely "natural" potency means a potential that its nature is bound to actualize, whereas an "obe-diential" refers to a potency that is fulfilled *only when a new nature takes the place of the old one*, as when John the Baptist said that "God can raise up out of these stones children of Abraham" (Matt. 3:9). But for de Lubac of course, that is just the problem: now actual nature has become so divorced from a supposedly *miraculous* nature that secular man can shrug off the announcement of the good news of salvation as irrelevant to his concerns.

However, that was not quite the point that the Thomist commenta-tors were making. St. Paul does, after all, speak of us becoming a new *cre-ation*: "Therefore, if anyone is in Christ, he is a new creation; the old has gone, the new has come" (2 Cor. 5:17). Now clearly Paul is not referring here to pagan stones having been transformed *first* into different *kinds* of souls now capable of hearing the gospel, upon which sits atop the grace

---

42. Feingold, *Natural Desire*, 21; emphasis added. The advantage of this distinction is that it gives anthropological grounding to Pascal's insight that we keep from attending to our relation to God by what he calls *divertissements* (distractions): "The only thing that consoles us for our miseries is distraction, yet that is the greatest of our wretchedness. Because that is what mainly prevents us from thinking about ourselves and leads us imperceptibly to dam-nation. Without it we should be bored, and boredom would force us to search for a firmer way out, but distraction entertains us and leads imperceptibly to death." Pascal, *Pensées*, 10.

of redemption. And so a further distinction was made between a "generic" obediential potency based on God's *potentia absoluta* to do anything not inherently self-contradictory (like his ability to create children of Abraham out of stones), and a "specific" obediential potency, based on God's *potentia ordinata*, by which he operates using the natural materials he has already created. Thus, humans, as a spiritual and intellectual species, do have a capacity for the beatific vision; it's just that *human nature cannot actualize this potential on its own: for not only must the potential be given as a grace (but here as part of the grace of creation), so too, and preeminently, must the actualization*; and that is what is meant by "obediential" potency.

Now as anyone with even a passing acquaintance with scholastic philosophy and theology knows, scholastic thinkers are fond of distinctions, overly so to their critics. (Renaissance writers like Erasmus and Petrarch were particularly scathing in that regard.) But generally speaking, these distinctions arise because they serve a purpose, they *function*; specifically they bring to light previously unsuspected contradictions and resolve them through a more nuanced treatment of terms. Such, I believe, is the case here. Of course, not every distinction actually serves its purpose; and if de Lubac is right, the utility of terms like "elicited desire" and "obediential potency" has long met (and passed) its sell-by date. But others, like Steven Long, disagree and claim that, absent this distinction, only confusion will result:

> Inasmuch as creatures can be said to be in potency to that which only the divine power can bring forth in them, it nonetheless remains true that God can bring about certain effects only in certain natures. For example: only a knowing and loving creature can, through the active agency of God, be brought to graced knowledge and love of God. If God can raise up sons of Abraham from the very rocks, this can only be by rendering them no longer to be rocks. By contrast, the life of grace *through the active agency of God* perfects human persons, *uplifting* human nature without destroying or mutating it.[43]

Here perhaps is the most crucial issue in this debate: how much agency should be attributed to God and how much to the human person? (This issue, as it happens, dominates the entire theology of grace, as the rest of

43. Steven A. Long, "Obediential Potency, Human Knowledge, and the Natural Desire for God," *International Philosophical Quarterly* 37 (March 1997): 45–63, here 45; emphases added.

the chapters of this book will show.) For de Lubac, since man as spirit just *is* the desire for God, the human person will always be actively seeking God, whether he realizes it or not, and whether or not the individual puts God at the center of his life. But Long denies this, precisely to preserve the gratuity of grace:

> A rock cannot know and love God without ceasing to be a rock—it cannot even be "helped" to know and love because it lacks any such faculties that might be so helped. By contrast, while a human person cannot know and love God in direct vision and embrace him without supernatural aid, with such aid the human person may partake in intrinsically supernatural divine friendship: and this is the specific notion of obediential potency as applied to the relation of grace to nature. *It is a wholly passive potency* that yet presupposes as its subject some determinate nature that is such that when aided by the active agency of God it may achieve a certain specific range of actuation. It is because of man's essentially spiritual nature that he has an obediential potency to the spiritual life.[44]

Because this issue of agency touches so directly on the question of predestination and free will, a full discussion of agency, divine and human, will have to be postponed until the chapter specifically devoted to that topic. (It obviously also affects the whole question of "merit," treated in the next chapter.) Suffice it to say here that the distinctions between natural and elicited desires and between natural and obediential potency, arcane though they might seem at first glance, carry vast implications for other issues, which is perhaps another way of saying that these distinctions perform a function and cannot be dismissed as mere scholastic hairsplitting.

Whatever be the outcome of that debate, there can, however, be no doubt that these terms cannot be found in so many words in Thomas, as Feingold himself concedes, as we saw above, although many of his texts do lead to a legitimate development of his thinking by his commentators, as we also saw above. Still, the point bears stressing: Thomas does not treat the matter of God's debt to nature (*debitum naturae*), nor does he distinguish natural from elicited desire, or speak of obediential potency, in the

---

44. Steven A. Long, "On the Loss, and Recovery, of Nature as a Theonomic Principle," *Nova et Vetera*, English edition, Vol. 5, No. 1 (Winter 2007): 133–83, here 165–66; emphasis added.

same way modern commentators do. Thomas certainly does not react in horror to the idea that God might "owe" us anything, as we see here:

> In the divine operations debt may be regarded in two ways, as due either to God, or to creatures, and in either way God pays what is due. *It is due to God that there should be fulfilled in creatures what his will and wisdom require*, and what manifests his goodness. In this respect God's justice regards what befits him, inasmuch as he renders to himself what is due to himself. It is also due to a created thing that it should possess what is ordered to it. . . . Thus God also exercises justice when he gives to each thing what is *due* to it by its *nature* and *condition*. (*ST* I, q. 21, a. 1, ad 3; emphases added).[45]

What is fascinating about this passage is that it can be used by either side, for Thomas never addresses the question at hand: does this nature have a burning exigency for God, which puts God under the "obligation" (but only to himself!) to sate that exigency; or is that nature such that God can add a higher desire, a higher nature, a higher calling?[46] Thomas

45. Thomas is here answering the third objection, which runs: "The act of justice is to pay what is due. But God is no man's debtor"—which is precisely the objection raised against de Lubac!

46. Although he does not address them directly, Denys Turner seems to join Long and Feingold here: "For ours is like the condition of the person who is self-deceived: not only is he self-ignorant, but he has somehow managed to hide from himself how it is that he is himself the cause of that ignorance and that he has a reason for remaining in it undisturbed. Therefore, for Thomas it takes grace to know that we are in need of grace. . . . Grace, therefore, does not exactly answer to our desire, as if we knew what our desire is. Grace answers to desires that only it can arouse in us, showing us what it is that we really want: grace is *pure gift*, the gift we could not have known that we wanted until we were given it. . . . And prayer answers to the very desire that prayer itself discovers; prayer uncovers the hidden desire precisely *by* answering it." Denys Turner, *Thomas Aquinas: A Portrait* (New Haven, CT: Yale University Press, 2013), 171–72. Here, however, Turner, in this last line, might be overarguing his case; since petitionary prayer often springs from purely natural needs: "Give us this day our daily bread." First hunger, then prayer. One way of squaring this circle comes from the recently published "Prayer Journal" of the American novelist Flannery O'Connor, a notebook she kept while at the Iowa Writers' Workshop in 1946–47: "My dear God, Supplication. This is the only one of the four [types of prayer] I am competent in. It takes no supernatural grace to ask for what one wants and I have asked You bountifully, oh Lord. I believe it is right to ask You too and to ask our Mother to ask You, but I don't want to overemphasize this angle of my prayers. Help me to ask you, oh Lord, for what is good for me to have, for what I can have and do Your service by having." Flannery O'Connor, "Journals: My Dear God: A young writer's prayers," *The New Yorker* (September 16, 2013): 26–30, here 28.

never addressed that question directly, as we can see from the fact that he bequeathed to his disciples two seemingly contrary sets of texts that are left to his later interpreters to harmonize.[47]

Reconciling these two sets of apparently opposing positions has of course not been an easy task, the difficulty of doing which no doubt accounts in large measure for the protracted length and irresolvability of this debate over the centuries. But that is a burden for historical theologians to work out, since their method by definition is to deal strictly with the Thomist texts as they stand. Of more immediate concern in this chapter is the more strictly systematic, conceptual or dogmatic question: can developments in more recent centuries be brought to bear to reconcile these two positions, especially in the light of Vatican II?

For the debate does seem rather to have reached a stalemate.[48] Yet all

47. One problem with de Lubac's interpretation was his flagrant selectivity in citing the Thomist corpus, a blindspot that recent scholarship has been quick to expose, and this despite his undoubted achievements conceded by all. Mulcahy gives the best overall assessment here: "The general aim of Henri de Lubac's life's work was, by his own account, to make the treasures of the Catholic past known and appreciated in the modern world. . . . To a marvelous extent, de Lubac was successful [in] this purpose. He called the Church to acknowledge its Jewish origins, and to a new respect for the Jewish people. His *Corpus Mysticum* furthered liturgical renewal and infused ecclesiology with a fresh sense of the ancient doctrine that the Eucharist constitutes the Church. Through his scholarly research, he helped spark interest in patristic and medieval exegesis, contributed to the rehabilitation of Origen, and initiated the production of *Sources chrétiennes*, one of the century's greatest patrological resources. His books on all these topics have been widely read and widely translated, influencing educated Catholics and at least two popes; his *Catholicisme* recently received the extraordinary accolade of being singled out in a papal encyclical, Benedict XVI's *Spe salvi*, for reminding the Church of the communal nature of salvation. To these achievements must be added his witness of tireless fidelity and self-sacrifice, including his personal bravery in opposing anti-Semitism during the German occupation of France during World War II. Despite all this, it must be admitted that de Lubac's scholarship was often flawed. This is not surprising when we consider that he did not have the benefit of any instruction beyond his ordination studies, and that his scholarship tended to be more broad than deep. . . . Unfortunately, he was frequently impatient with specialists and more rigorous scholars who opposed his interpretations. In his haste to communicate his discoveries, he sometimes gave very partial readings of textual evidence. We find him, on a number of occasions, using quotations which seem to prove his arguments but which, in their original contexts, do not support him. It might be conceded that de Lubac, on such occasions, intends his quotations for merely rhetorical effect; but, still, quoting authorities out of context does tend to give a false impression." Mulcahy, *Aquinas's Notion of Pure Nature*, 147–48.

48. Politics, both socioeconomic and ecclesiastical, plays its part here too in keeping the debate stretched out, with Milbank the socialist arrayed against the neo-Thomists Fein-

along, a solution has been at hand, one offered already in the nineteenth century. It will be the thesis in the rest of what follows that the theology of the German Matthias Joseph Scheeben (1835–1888) has given us a viable solution to this problem.[49] Although he was highly regarded in the first half of the twentieth century, changes in the postconciliar outlook quickly led to widespread neglect of his writings.[50] But, as will become evident in what follows below, the time has come for him to be restored to his rightful place in the contemporary debate, for his theology of the nature/grace relation does in fact offer not just a way out of the dilemma outlined above but also the path to real reconciliation of positions seemingly opposed.

One reason the influence of a neglected theologian can return is because later generations come to realize that this unfairly ignored theologian has already solved a controverted problem *even before the controversy arose*. Such, I maintain, is the case with Scheeben on the issue now before us. For what he has managed to do, at least in my estimation, is to concede all the distinctions necessary for keeping grace gratuitous and for delineating nature as a correlative reality independent of grace; but he made all those distinctions for the purpose of showing how nature and grace exist and live in an intimate union, made more intimate precisely *because* they are distinct realities (thereby addressing de Lubac's concern that grace not get so cordoned off from the reality of nature that it becomes irrelevant).[51]

---

gold and Hütter. If war has been called the conduct of diplomacy by other means, according to some interpreters, the nature/grace debate is the politics of the culture wars pursued in theology's seminar room. See Sean Larsen, "The Politics of Desire: Two Readings of Henri de Lubac on Nature and Grace," *Modern Theology*, Vol. 29, No. 3 (July 2013): 279–310.

49. I owe this insight to Andrew Swafford, STD, who first pointed out Scheeben's relevance to me in this debate. The paragraphs below closely track (but with revisions) what I said in "Scheeben the Reconciler," cited above.

50. No less a luminary than John Courtney Murray wrote his dissertation in 1938 on Scheeben, later republished as: John Courtney Murray, S.J., *Matthias Joseph Scheeben's Doctrine on Supernatural Faith* (New York: Edwin Mellen, 1987). See also John Courtney Murray, S.J., "The Root of Faith: The Doctrine of M. J. Scheeben," *Theological Studies*, Vol. 9 (1948): 20–46.

51. Fascinatingly, Scheeben is admired by theologians usually taken by most observers to be radically opposed in their outlook, such as Balthasar and Garrigou-Lagrange: "The sympathetic citation of his work by twentieth-century theologians as different as Hans Urs von Balthasar, a child of the so-called 'new theology' of the 1940s and 1950s, and Reginald Garrigou-Lagrange, champion, in the years immediately preceding the Second Vatican Council, of 'strict observance' Thomism, attests to his mediating role." Aidan Nichols, O.P., *Romance and System: The Theological Synthesis of Matthias Joseph Scheeben* (Denver: Augustine Institute Press, 2010), 19.

Scheeben scholars have long noticed his insistence that grace must be defined over against nature, which cannot be done unless nature is granted its own self-subsistent reality independent of grace. For example, Aidan Nichols boldly puts it this way:

> Right from his earliest work, *Natur und Gnade* of 1861, Scheeben has insisted on an extremely sharp distinction between nature and supernature, nature and grace. Indeed, were one [to go] looking for texts to illustrate what early twentieth-century critics of neo-Scholasticism called "extrinsicism" and mid-twentieth-century theologians of the *nouvelle théologie* movement [named] "a two-storey model" of the nature/grace relationship, one could do a lot worse than quarry some texts from Scheeben's writings.[52]

What is more, Scheeben clearly held to a theory of man's two-fold end, an idea that de Lubac found especially repugnant but which Scheeben seems to have taken for granted, based on the irrefragably obvious anthropological data in front of him (and us) of stunted human ambitions terminating in death. In his words: "Rational creatures, with the nature they have, cannot improve indefinitely. Their progress lasts just so long as the development of their natural faculties will last. But since their natural faculties are finite, the development of rational creatures must also have a determined and *limited* end."[53]

Similarly, Scheeben anticipates the teaching of Pope Pius XII in his 1950 encyclical *Humani Generis* when he frankly asserts the possibility that God could have given man—had he so chosen—a purely natural end: "In addition to the supernatural order of human development established, revealed, and inaugurated by Christ, man has a natural order, based on his

52. Nichols, *Romance and System*, 288. Cyril Vollert, Scheeben's Jesuit translator, agrees: "His most notable contribution to Neo-Scholasticism is his service in bringing the supernatural, in its full purity and beauty, back to the center of theological thought." Cyril Vollert, S.J., "Introduction," Matthias Joseph Scheeben, *Nature and Grace*, trans. Cyril Vollert, S.J. (St. Louis: B. Herder Book Co., 1954), xiii.

53. Matthias Joseph Scheeben, *The Glories of Divine Grace*, trans. by a monk of St. Meinrad's Abbey (New York: Benziger, 1886), 46; emphasis added. Further: "The Church necessarily supposes that there is a natural goal and end; for it teaches that the end now appointed for nature, consisting as it does in the beatific vision of God, is absolutely supernatural, and is to be communicated to us by a special grace. And yet there must be a necessary [natural] end for nature." Scheeben, *Nature and Grace*, 93.

nature. This would be the permanent order destined for man if God had not decreed something better.... This means that a purely natural state would be possible, that is, a state without any genuine supernatural elements."[54]

So important for Scheeben is this rigid distinction between nature and grace that he finds it not just in the Thomist commentary-tradition (where all agree it is to be found, at least in the vast majority of authors), and not just in Thomas himself (contrary to de Lubac's views); but he also traces the distinction back to the early fathers of the church (which de Lubac presumably would have found preposterous). These fathers, he claims, "insisted that grace does not merge with nature and that it even possesses a certain autonomy."[55] To add to the anti-de-Lubac side of the ledger, adding insult to injury, as it were, other passages imply that Scheeben would have been quite flabbergasted by de Lubac's claim that the pure-nature thesis *led* to secularism. For him quite the opposite is true:

> My cherished aim is to bring out the supernatural character of the Christian economy of salvation in its full sublimity, beauty, and riches. The main task of our time, it seems to me, consists in propounding and emphasizing the supernatural quality of Christianity, for the benefit of both science and life. Theoretical as well as practical naturalism and rationalism, which seek to throttle and destroy all that is specifically Christian, must be resolutely and energetically repudiated.[56]

In other words, without a resolute distinction between nature and grace, apologetics becomes impossible, which was also a principle of neo-Thomist attacks on de Lubac.

Astute observers will notice, however, a decided shift in accent that has taken place here from the standard neo-Thomist approach to apolo-

54. Scheeben, *Nature and Grace*, 86–87.

55. Scheeben, *Nature and Grace*, xix: "The Greek Fathers . . . considered grace in its supernatural and divine excellence, as a perfection that surpassed even what was true in the created world of nature. They saw grace in its relations with the mysteries of the Trinity, the Incarnation, and the Eucharist. Against rationalistic Nestorianism they pointed out that grace, like the Incarnation, has a supernatural, mysterious connection with the Godhead; against the Manichaeans, Gnostics, and Eutychians they brought to light the difference and opposition between nature and grace. . . . With remarkable penetration and incisiveness these Fathers, notably Cyril of Alexandria, triumphantly combated the naturalist and rationalist tendency that marked Nestorius and that had earlier appeared among the Arians. They remain the best allies in our conflict with modern rationalism" (ibid., xviii-xix).

56. Scheeben, *Nature and Grace*, xvii.

getics. As Gerald McCool points out, standard manual apologetics, based on Thomas's treatment of the so-called *praeambula fidei* (truths of natural theology that could be proved by reason alone), started with purely *rational* arguments (for the existence of God and the like) and only then proceeded to those truths that could be known solely by faith. According to these Roman Thomists: "By preserving that distinction [between faith and reason], scholastic philosophy could mount strong philosophical arguments for the credibility of revelation without compromising the transcendence of Christianity's revealed mysteries."[57] But then—at least in McCool's analysis—that style of apologetics had completely lost its ability to address the operative assumptions of the "cultured despisers" of Christianity living in the nineteenth century:

> Late nineteenth-century idealists considered the historical "facts of Christian revelation" proclaimed by its authentic witnesses as matters of no significance to them. Since man's interior life of consciousness required no knowledge of such external facts either for its intellectual or for its moral development, historical Revelation could be simply dismissed out of hand. Even if Christ had lived, and [even] if the alleged witnesses of Revelation had told the truth, these were just external facts of history. They were no different from thousands of other singular facts which ancient historians could verify. Brute, singular facts like these were completely "extraneous" to the vital needs of a consciousness whose immanent development must be directed by its own universal laws. On principle then, extrinsic historical facts, like the life of Christ or the preaching of St. Paul, could not be matters of concern either to the philosopher or to the philosophically enlightened intellectual. He had no need to know them. In fact, since they were useless distractions which might impede the progress of his inner life, he would be well advised to ignore them. The current Catholic apologetics had been devised to answer the arguments of eighteenth-century Enlightenment philosophers who were willing to debate the claims of Christian Revelation. But late nineteenth-century idealists had no intention of debating with Christian apologists. As a matter of principle, apologists were to be denied a hearing.[58]

57. Gerald A. McCool, *The Neo-Thomists* (Milwaukee: Marquette University Press, 1994), 34.
58. McCool, *The Neo-Thomists*, 47. Blondel, for one, took this objection seriously and in fact it forms the basis for his criticism of "extrinsicism," as his premier Anglophone biographer points out: "All it [extrinsicism] looks for from facts are signs for the senses and proofs for common sense. . . . It only extracts some abstract ideology from [history] that it then

For all these reasons—so effectively described by McCool—Scheeben realized that apologetics could only be, in the last analysis, simply *good theology*, that is, a theology that displayed the strictly supernatural character of Christianity *from the outset*. Such a move of course did not mean for Scheeben any concession to liberalism, which the Modernists took as their starting point in order to make the Christian message plausible to their skeptical contemporaries. Quite the contrary, Scheeben was intensely anti-liberal.[59] But his stress on the supernatural as the key locus for apologetics does come close to de Lubac's concern that the church's supernaturally validated message must be seen to address the *real* concerns of the age. Both Scheeben and de Lubac agree that apologetics will be chasing after a mirage if it vainly tries to address putatively self-sufficient secularists based on arguments drawn from their own self-justifying and closed-off rationalism.[60]

But where Scheeben shows his greatest divergence from the manual school is in his next step: his insistence that nature and grace must be kept conceptually distinct in order to make their "nuptial" union more effective:

---

presents as the object of faith, as if that were all there is to the true Christian faith. . . . Such a rudimentary way of reasoning, which is supposed to make us take the first step from facts to dogmas, convinces no one, least of all those who place their faith in reason. . . . It leaves all the key relations extrinsic to each other: the relation of the sign to the thing signified, the relation of facts to the dogmatics superimposed on them. . . . It separates facts and dogmas in such a way that they can only remain at odds with one another, whence the defensive and ultimately defeatist attitude it takes in the face of modern historical studies." Oliva Blanchette, *Maurice Blondel: A Philosophical Life* (Grand Rapids, MI: Eerdmans, 2010), 195.

59. John Courtney Murray even goes so far as to speak of Scheeben's "hatred" of liberalism: "One might perhaps best characterize these [early] years by calling them the period in which the one great theological hate of Scheeben's life was kindled to flaming intensity—his hate of rationalistic and naturalistic religious Liberalism. It may seem strange to speak of hate in connection with a man of Scheeben's quiet temper; however, the passion does show itself in the texts in which he attacks this particular error." John Courtney Murray, S.J., "The Root of Faith," 24. Nichols expresses the same point, albeit without Murray's psychologizing attribution of "hate" to Scheeben: "Ultramontane Scheeben certainly was. . . . However, Scheeben's articles in defense of [Vatican I] were essentially occasional pieces, unrepresentative of the general tenor of his theological work." Aidan Nichols, O.P., "Homage to Scheeben," in *Scribe of the Kingdom: Essays on Theology and Culture*, Volume I (London: Sheed & Ward, 1994): 205–13, here 205–6.

60. Pinckaers would seem to agree: "We do not find any trace in St. Thomas of the common modern presupposition according to which the intervention of faith and grace disrupts necessarily, as a foreign element, the activity of reason, liberty, and human nature" (Pinckaers, "Natural Desire," 638).

"When grace is transformed into the light of glory, the union will become an indissoluble spiritual marriage, a *matrimonium spirituale ratum et consummatum*. The freedom of nature at the side of grace will cease, because it will be thoroughly pervaded by grace and taken up into grace."[61]

Ludwig Wittgenstein famously said that we are bewitched by language. Metaphors, images, analogues are our fate. Under that rubric, Scheeben's change of imagery has a way of blocking the worst implications of the notorious two-tier model of the nature/grace relationship, with a "supernature" sitting atop nature, like a penthouse atop a skyscraper. As Nichols explains:

> Scheeben's *principal* organizing metaphor for the nature/grace relation is very different. It is drawn not from architecture but from marriage. It is nuptiality. Yes, he makes a sharp ontological distinction between nature and grace. But he treats nature and grace as intimately conjoined in a matrimonial bond, co-inhabiting, according to the divine covenant, in a connubial relationship, inter-penetrating in life and love. Scheeben is not only a theologian of the difference between the natural and the supernatural, he is *the* theologian of their *connubium* as well.[62]

Of course a mere change of imagery won't accomplish much without an argument demonstrating *why* nature and grace belong together in married bliss. For that we must turn to what is perhaps Scheeben's most radical move: his grounding of the nature/grace relation in the bond between the human and divine natures of Christ in the hypostatic union. Scheeben points out that Christ's human nature is (of course) a part of creation, but not his divine nature—which is, well, divine. While this sounds obvious (and is), its implications are vast. For one thing it means that God's power to create and sustain the universe in being is not the same as his power to become incarnate (which distinction is the ground for the distinction between grace and nature, even though God created graciously); and since the whole point of the incarnation is to restore man to friendship with God, this means that the union between man and God effected by grace requires far more than "topping off" nature with a superadded gift:

> In the ordinary created thing, God is present only as its maker and conserver. Without His presence in this way, things could not exist. But in

61. Scheeben, *Nature and Grace*, 337.
62. Nichols, *Romance and System*, 289; all italics in the original text.

the soul having grace He is present as sanctifier, giving Himself to the creature and sharing with him the holiness of His own being. *This recalls the way in which God the Father is in His only-begotten Son. . . .* Thus, as the presence of the Father in His Son is different from His presence in creatures, *similarly* the presence of the Holy Ghost in the souls of the just is different from His ordinary manner of dwelling in creatures.[63]

That Scheeben means the word "similarly" as no mere rhetorical flourish or as a kind of vague resemblance becomes apparent when he goes on to establish what the grounding of the nature/grace relationship in the incarnation actually entails: now we should no longer speak of mere adoption but of something *between* "adoptive" and "natural" sonship, something that, in his words, "closely interlaces the adoptive sonship with natural sonship."[64] Elsewhere, he radicalizes the Johannine concept that believers are "born of God" (John 1:13c) in this way:

Every child that is born receives its nature from its father. Therefore, the Second Person of the Holy Trinity is called Son and the First is called Father, because the Latter [that is, the Father] has shared His own Divine Nature of being with the Former [the Son]. . . . When through grace we receive a sharing of the Divine *Nature* and of the divine life, it is then true *in a strict sense* [*im eigentlichen Sinne*] that we are born of God.[65]

Especially in his later book *The Mysteries of Christianity* Scheeben hammers away at this point: just as the hypostatic union means the *substantial* union of God and man in Christ ("hypo-static" being the Greek-rooted equivalent to the Latin-rooted word "sub-stantial"), so too the union of God with the Christian is "similarly" *substantial*. Indeed, *as* substantial, this union means that grace can no longer be conceived as coming to man from without:

Thus the incarnation of the Son of God is the real basis for the adoption of the human race, and likewise conducts that adoption to a consummation that is unique in its sublimity. . . . This fatherhood is not merely

63. Scheeben, *The Glories of Divine Grace*, 74; emphases added.
64. Matthias Joseph Scheeben, *The Mysteries of Christianity* (St. Louis: B. Herder Book Co., 1946), 385.
65. Scheeben, *The Glories of Divine Grace*, 100; emphases added.

imitated in God's relationship to man, out of sheer grace, but *is joined to man substantially.* . . . The incarnation raises the human race to the bosom of the eternal Father, that it may receive the grace of sonship with all of its implied dignities *and rights* by a real contact with the source, rather than by a purely gratuitous influx from without.[66]

"Rights-talk" of course entails talk of obligations: If I have a right to free speech, the government has an obligation to respect that right and cannot throw me into jail for publishing a broadsheet. If I have a right to the free exercise of religion, you have an obligation not to interfere with that right. If I decide to worship Amon-Re or decide to go off on a tree-hugging tour of Crete in order to offer myself up to chthonic feminist deities, you're just going to have to grit your teeth and put up with my folly. If I have a right to privacy, you have an obligation not to tap my phone or record my phone conversations without my knowledge or permission.[67]

Given that indissoluble connection between rights and obligations, one would think that Scheeben would shy away from speaking of any claim we have on God, or any "right" we have over God, that approach being the surest way to undermine—indeed deny—the gratuity of grace. Of course, he would grant that nothing in the sin of Adam and Eve ever obligated God to save them and their progeny by sending his Son, which he did solely out of love (John 3:16). But once the incarnation took place, Scheeben frankly speaks of God's "obligations." Notice how he uses the modal verb *must* applied to God here:

If, then, the human race . . . becomes the body of Christ, and its members become the members of God's Son, if the divine person of the Son of God bears them in Himself as His own, then, with due proportion,

66. Scheeben, *Mysteries*, 384–85; emphases added.

67. I am deliberately phrasing the correlation between rights and obligations in the way criticized by Mary Ann Glendon's *Rights Talk: The Impoverishment of Political Discourse* (New York: The Free Press, 1991), who scores this formulation for the way it expels the intermediate terms of virtue and responsibility: "The American rights dialect is distinguished not only by what we say and how we say it, but also by what we leave unsaid . . . [the] habitual silences concerning responsibilities" (76). The binary logic of rights vs. obligations also neglects any standard for adjudicating rights in conflict (like the right to a free press vs. the right to a fair trial). But this very situation highlights the oddity of Scheeben's way of speaking of human rights *vis-à-vis* God and of God's (therefore correlative) "obligations" toward humans. But he does so—as will become clear in the next few paragraphs—because of the way he radicalizes the kind of "adoption" we receive from God.

must not the divine gift of the Son of God flow over to men, since they are His members? *Must* not God the Father extend to these members the same love as that which He bears for His natural Son, *must* He not embrace them in His Son *with one and the same love,* inasmuch as they belong to Him?[68]

As Scheeben continues to reflect on this analogy throughout *The Mysteries of Christianity,* the language he uses grows more radical until his formulations become very nearly eye-popping:

Because of Christ this sonship is no longer a mere adoptive sonship, since we receive it not as strangers but as kinfolk [*als Verwandte*], as members of the only-begotten Son, and *can lay claim to it as a right* [*und sie als ein Recht beanspruchen können*]. The grace of sonship in us has something of the *natural* sonship of Christ Himself, from which it is derived. *Because we are not mere adoptive children,* because we are members of the *natural* Son, we truly enter into the personal relationship in which the Son of God stands to His Father. *In literal truth, and not by simple analogy or resemblance,* we call the Father of the Word *our* Father, and in actual fact He is such not by purely analogous relationship, but by the very *same* relationship which makes Him the Father of Christ.[69]

In this way Scheeben seems to have answered, by anticipation, the objections raised in the twentieth century.[70] Yes, even when all these points

68. Scheeben, *Mysteries*, 377–78; emphases added. Here one is reminded of a line from de Lubac: "There can be no question of anything being due to the creature. But, one may perhaps say, it remains true none the less that once such a desire exists in the creature, it becomes the sign not merely of a possible gift from God, but of a certain gift." Henri de Lubac, *Mystery of the Supernatural,* 207.

69. Scheeben, *Mysteries*, 383; emphases added. Nor are these views to be found only in *Mysteries.* In other writings, he shows himself equally comfortable with talk of "rights": "As children of God, we have a far more intimate relation with God than adopted children have to their father.... We are his heirs and we have a right to this inheritance. This right is based on our birth." Scheeben, *The Glories of Divine Grace,* 100–101.

70. Geniuses are like that: they *anticipate.* I am reminded here of what Harold Bloom said of Shakespeare: "[This is] Shakespeare's most idiosyncratic strength: he is always ahead of you, conceptually and imagistically, whoever and whenever you are. He renders you anachronistic because he *contains* you; you cannot subsume him. You cannot illuminate him with a new doctrine, be it Marxism or Freudianism or Demanian linguistic skepticism. Instead,

are conceded, much is lost when the concepts of nature and grace are too quickly collapsed into each other. Yes, the existence of natural law itself testifies to ends purely natural (ethics being fundamentally a teleological discipline). Yes, the case of Aristotle's *Nicomachean Ethics* proves that a purely human "thriving" (*eudaimonia*) is an entirely appropriate standard for adjudicating purely intra-human ethical issues. Yes, Thomas (in one set of texts) insists that man has a twofold end, one natural and the other supernatural, one set forth in natural law and the other in divine revelation. But as early as his book *Nature and Grace* we find Scheeben insisting that for a Christian natural law has already been subsumed into the divine "law" of discipleship, of sonship, so that for a Christian there really is no such thing as an independent natural law:

> Who can fail to perceive . . . that the doctrine of supernature, which is an elevation of human nature above its own level, clarifies and specifies the transcendence of Christian morality over all philosophical, rational, and rationalistic morality. . . . *Philosophical ethics, in the sense of a system set up in opposition and defiance against theological morality, is unquestionably not a true and genuine morality.* For in the present order purely natural relationships do not exist alone and apart, and therefore cannot be made to prevail in isolated self-sufficiency.[71]

Even more ringingly, in the Epilogue to this early book and just a few pages before its end, Scheeben calls for an end to a Christian ethics conceived as a heteronomous imposition of alienating rules. In Christian discipleship morality is *lifted up* to something greater and higher—not in the Hegelian sense of *aufgehoben* (suspended, rendered invalid), but in the sense of being raised up to make us what we have always been destined to be:

---

he will illuminate the doctrine, not by prefiguration but by postfiguration, as it were: all of Freud that matters most is there in Shakespeare already, with a persuasive critique of Freud besides. The Freudian map of the mind is Shakespeare's; Freud seems only to have prosified it. Or, to vary my point, a Shakespearean reading of Freud illuminates and overwhelms the text of Freud; a Freudian reading of Shakespeare reduces Shakespeare, or would if we could bear a reduction that crosses the line into absurdities of loss. *Coriolanus* is a far more powerful reading of Marx's *Eighteenth Brumaire of Louis Napoleon* than any Marxist reading of *Coriolanus* could hope to be." Harold Bloom, *The Western Canon: The Books and School of the Ages* (New York: Riverhead, 1994), 24.

71. Scheeben, *Nature and Grace*, 275; emphasis added.

How poverty-stricken and mean Christian morality appears when it is regarded merely as the morality of man (that is, the ethics based on man's natural moral dignity as found in his reason and free will) rather than as the morality of the sons of God! . . . To grasp the truth that we really are Christ's brothers, we must go into the question of our conformity with Him in His divine no less than in His human nature. And grace may not be regarded merely as a corroborating factor in moral life; it must be apprehended and presented as the new foundation of that life, pertaining to a higher order. Then we shall develop a true moral theology, as distinct from a moral philosophy. Then we shall be able to preach from the pulpit a morality that shares in the excellence of dogmatic theology, a morality rooted in faith, grace, and the mysteries of Christianity.[72]

In other words, and in conclusion, the knotty and still unresolved debate over the nature/grace relationship *can* be resolved, but only by grounding that secondary problem in the prior and greater mystery of the incarnation. After all, the incarnation is that mystery that Thomas himself called the one that "among the divine works most especially exceeds reason; for nothing can be thought of which is more marvelous than this divine accomplishment, that the true God, the Son of God, should become true man" (*Summa contra Gentiles* IV, 27.1). And one of the most astonishing parts of that marvel is that Jesus, the very incarnate Son of God, could say to us, *jam non dico servos . . . vos autem dixi amicos*: "I no longer call you servants, but friends" (John 15:15).

All that now remains as the task for the rest of this chapter will be to present the results of the preceding analysis (that is, to summarize what can now be reliably said of the nature/grace relation) and then to describe why this seemingly arcane issue *matters*, for indeed it does matter, often in surprising ways.

As to results, I think it can now be said that both sides in this debate are right, in their own limited way. Although, as we have seen, the terms "extrinsicist" and "intrinsicist" do not denote the true position of any of the authors treated here, there are differences of approach that can perhaps be better denominated by these terms (which are admittedly my neolo-

---

72. Scheeben, *Nature and Grace*, 343. In other words, Scheeben is trying to get away from Augustine's notion of grace as mere *auxilium* (aid for living the moral life) and more on the notion favored by the Eastern Fathers of grace as the agent of our *apotheosis*, divinization.

gisms): *continuitists* and *discontinuitists*. The first group, best represented by de Lubac and one side of Thomas (who did, after all, say that grace builds on nature), insists on a continuity between nature and grace, lest the life of grace come to seem quite irrelevant to human concerns. The second, best represented by most of the Baroque commentators on Thomas and revived recently by Steven Long and Lawrence Feingold, and represented also by certain utterly clear texts from Thomas himself, insist on the discontinuity between nature and grace, lest grace be seen merely as a way for humans to realize their full potential (that is, *their* full potential, rather than finding the specific Christian mission God intends for every baptized Christian, which often leads to martyrdom and in all cases leads to a life of self-denial and taking up one's cross).[73]

Both concerns are legitimate, and both positions find (limited) validation in Thomas himself. But the positions are not strictly contradictory, even if Thomas never seemed to have realized the tension, at least in terms of contemporary debate. But, if Scheeben is right, the two can only be reconciled if the imagery of the debate moves away from architecture and becomes nestled in the imagery of love and marriage.

Recall what was said at the outset of this chapter: the word *grace* is, ultimately, a matter of love; but not love in the romantic sense, a protection against the cold winds of existence, the kind of love the poet Matthew Arnold spoke of in "Dover Beach." No, this is a love that *demands*, that *goes beyond* nature and its capacities, that makes no exceptions and brooks no opposition. As Balthasar says so well:

> Thus the principle is affirmed that the calling to love is an absolute one, admitting of no exception, and so ineluctable that failure to observe it is tantamount to total corruption. Let there be no doubt. We are here to love—to love God and to love our neighbor. Whoever will unravel the meaning of existence must accept this fundamental principle from

---

73. As Paul says: "All who want to live piously in Christ Jesus will suffer persecution" (2 Tim. 3:12), which Balthasar glosses this way (adding along the way more Pauline support for the position of the discontinuitists: "To be baptized, then, means totally to renounce a life lived according to one's own wishes, for 'it is no longer I that live, but Christ lives in me' (Gal. 2:20). Because 'Christ did not please himself, we . . . ought not to please ourselves' (Rom. 15:3, 1)." Balthasar, *Christian State of Life*, 339. See also: "God is careful to make plainly visible not only the general unworthiness, but also the natural ineptitude of the one called. He chooses whom he will; if the one he has chosen accepts this mission, he becomes, as it were, a new creation called by the Lord out of nothingness" (ibid., 398).

whose center light is shed on all the dark recesses of our loves. For this love to which we are called is not a circumscribed or limited love, not a love defined, as it were, by the measure of our human weakness. It does not allow us to submit just one part of our lives to its demands and leave the rest free for other pursuits; it does not allow us to dedicate just one period of our lives to it and the rest, if we will, to our own interests. The command to love is universal and unequivocal. It makes no allowances. It encompasses and makes demands upon everything in our nature: "with thy whole heart, with all thy soul, and with all thy mind."[74]

In finding legitimacy in both sides of the debate, I am not trying to be namby-pamby, wishy-washy, or any of the other terms that afflict theological peacemakers. Rather, my point to stress here is that the two positions come out of deep pastoral concerns; for what theologians on both sides recognize, as said above, is that this debate matters. Take, for example, Feingold's worry that, if grace is seen as too continuous with nature, people will take their salvation as their due: "[O]ne of the great pastoral problems of our time is that so many people, Catholics and non-Catholics alike, take Heaven for granted as something somehow due simply to natural goodness. This view debases Heaven by naturalizing it."[75] We have all been to funerals and wakes, I suspect, where a kind of dreamy Americanized eschatology is at work, where the deceased is eulogized as already in heaven, often in the most vulgarized terms. Thus, uncle Wilbur, an avid golfer, will be hymned as now enjoying swinging his nine iron in that great Country Club in the sky.[76]

This same breezy attitude also affects the attitude of many ordinary Catholics as they approach the sacraments. Paul's admonition to approach them "worthily" seems largely to have fallen into desuetude. But the warn-

74. Balthasar, *Christian State of Life*, 27.

75. Feingold, *Natural Desire*, 443. Also here: "The pastoral and spiritual solution to our crisis cannot lie in weakening the distinction between nature and grace, or [in] diminishing the coherence of the natural order, but only in rightly understanding how the Christian promise opens the horizon to what we already naturally desire in a dim and inefficacious way. Thus glory perfectly fulfills what nature would wish but dare not hope" (ibid., xxxvi).

76. When the aged senator from West Virginia, ninety-two-year-old Robert Byrd (known as the King of Pork for all the federal largesse he poured into his state), died in the summer of 2010, the Catholic (!) bishop of Charleston (the capital of West Virginia) chirruped that the Senator was surely now in heaven. One wonders if the burdened taxpayers from other states agreed, whose children will be saddled for generations to come with paying off the federal debt that was used to fund all that Appalachian bacon.

ing is clear: "Therefore, whoever eats the bread and drinks the cup of the Lord in an unworthy manner will be guilty of sinning against the body and blood of the Lord. . . . If we judged ourselves, we would not come under judgment. When we are judged by the Lord, we are being disciplined, so that we will not be condemned with the world" (1 Cor. 11:27, 31–32). Sounding almost like an extrinsicist, Paul further asks his congregation: "Did the word of God originate with you?" (1 Cor. 14:36).

This same worry actually, was de Lubac's concern, although it often goes unrecognized in the secondary literature (on both sides: those attacking and those supporting him). For soon after Vatican II de Lubac began attacking any lazy identification of nature and grace, especially in a lecture he delivered at Saint Louis University in 1968:

> Does not such an "openness" [or *aggiornamento*] become a forgetfulness of salvation and of the gospel, a tending toward secularism, a loosening of faith and morals? Finally, this "openness" becomes for others a loss of identity, in a word, the betrayal of our obligation toward the world. Because the Council, following the desire of John XXIII, did not wish either to define new dogmas or to pronounce anathemas, many conclude that the church no longer has the right to judge anything or anyone; they recommend a "pluralism" which is not the pluralism of the theological schools but that of entirely different beliefs from those of the normative faith. . . . The word "renewal" can cover a multitude of abuses![77]

Of course de Lubac never abandoned his view that a heavy stress on pure nature, independent of grace and sufficient to itself, had long since become jejune. Nor, one suspects, would he have been entirely happy with an excessive stress on human passivity when the human person meets grace, a position perhaps due to his membership in the Society of Jesus, a religious order whose members tend to stress, over against other schools (Thomist above all), the active freedom of the human will *vis-à-vis* God's offer of grace. That, however, is a topic for a later chapter. But before getting to that quite complex issue, we must first address how creation—very much including created human nature—has been affected by sin and how God "justifies" (puts right) that now marred creation.

---

77. Henri de Lubac, "The Church in Crisis," *Theology Digest*, Vol. 17, No. 4 (Winter 1969): 312–25; here 319; henceforth cited as de Lubac, "Church in Crisis." A revised version of this address was published in *Nouvelle Revue Théologique* vol. 91 (1969): 580–96.

CHAPTER 2

Sin and Justification

I say more: the just man justices,
  Keeps grace: that keeps all his goings graces;
Acts in God's eye what in God's eye he is—
  Christ.

Gerard Manley Hopkins, "As Kingfishers Catch Fire"

The topic of sin and justification resembles the issue of nature and grace in at least this respect: while both debates can get very arcane, they also both have a lot riding on the outcome of their respective debates. But in the case of nature and grace, the pastoral relevance of that debate had to be drawn out and made explicit. Most non-theologians, after all, spend little or no time worrying about the issue (even if, as we saw in the Introduction, most lay Christians carry around in their souls an implicit theology of grace, whether they realize it or not).

With the case of justification, however, at least *that* problem does not arise. Whatever else one can say about the Christian doctrine of justification, it certainly is of burning and immediate pastoral relevance. For the issue of justification—unlike most other issues pertaining to the theology of grace—eventually became church-dividing. At least here, no one has to spend any effort in establishing the pastoral, indeed ecumenical, relevance of what some Protestants call the *articulus stantis et cadentis ecclesiae*— that article of faith upon whose correct interpretation the very unity of the church depends. Of course, even in those churches and denominations that make "justification by faith alone" their founding principle (the Lutheran Church of the Missouri Synod, for example), ordinary pew-sitters might be quite unfamiliar with the intricacies of the doctrine and care little about them, might doze off at the first mention of the word *justification*, might not be able to define the difference between forensic and imparted justification if their lives depended on it; but the fact that this doctrine did once become church-dividing testifies to its inherent importance.[1]

In keeping with the aims of this book, little or no effort will be made here to contribute to the fields of scriptural exegesis or historical theology *per se*. Particularly in the case of Martin Luther, there is a heated debate among Luther scholars (themselves primarily Lutheran) about how his theology of justification is to be understood. They claim that the real Luther differs considerably from the one embedded in the Lutheran doctrinal confessions. But that dispute pales in comparison with the debate about what St. Paul means by justification (again, for the most part, this controversy is taking place among Protestant scholars). Basing themselves, they claim, on scientific rather than confessional principles of exegesis, they hold that Paul's view of justification bears little or no resemblance to Luther's. Obviously, a chapter such as this one cannot fail to take note of both debates, for any reappraisal of either Luther or Paul (or by some scholars, both) will obviously be of the highest significance for dogmatic theology. But *notice taken* is not the same as a *contribution made*. This chapter, in other words, will rely on scriptural exegesis and historical theology, not contribute to them.

Instead, and as much as possible, this chapter will stress what is entailed in the Christian *concept* of justification, with various positions—Catholic and Protestant—set out as fairly as possible, *sine ira et studio*, so that readers can at least understand what the debate is all about and why it led to a deep and abiding division in Western Christendom. As with the first chapter, we will begin with secular uses of the words *sin* and *justification*.

Nowadays, the word *sin* carries mostly a religious connotation, but it

---

1. In fact, one does not even need to be a regular churchgoer to live under the massive, albeit unacknowledged, impact of Reformation doctrine, as Brad Gregory rightly sees: "The place of the Reformation in European history seems clear. It falls between the Middle Ages and modernity as something long gone, over and done with. It seems distant from the political realities and global capitalism of the early twenty-first century, far removed from present-day moral debates and social problems. This book argues otherwise. What transpired five centuries ago continues today profoundly to influence the lives of everyone not only in Europe and North America but all around the world, whether or not they are Christians or indeed religious believers of any kind." Brad S. Gregory, *The Unintended Reformation: How a Religious Revolution Secularized Society* (Cambridge, MA: Harvard University Press, 2012), 1.

too has its roots in secular settings. For in the New Testament, the Greek word translated into English as *sin* is *hamartia*, which originally meant (in weaponry) "missing the mark" and then quickly came to mean more generically any error or wandering from some preset goal, as Josef Pieper explains here:

> We should recall at this point that both the Latin and the Greek terms for sin (*peccatum, hamartia*: used by the New Testament to characterize exactly what we mean by "sin") originally had another, non-ethical meaning. Perhaps it is neither surprising nor remarkable that, in the hundred times Homer uses the verb *hamartanein* to describe a simple action, he is referring to the fact that a warrior hurling his spear has failed to hit his target. But also in Aristotle, the noun *hamartia* and the verb *hamartanein* are clearly used, on average, much more often to indicate some non-ethical meaning of "missing the mark," such as the diagnostic lapses of a physician, grammatical errors of syntax, slips of the pen, and the like, even though in the *Nicomachean Ethics* the same word usually refers to moral failings.[2]

Further—because it implies in its generic meaning something that has gone awry and must, as the expression goes, be "put right"—*sin* is a correlative word, meaning a word that automatically implies its opposite: if something has strayed from a goal, then the word *straying* makes no sense unless we already know what that goal should be or should have been. The same of course holds true for *injustice* too, a word that makes no sense without a prior notion of what justice entails, which is why Aristotle says that justice and injustice are correlative terms: that is, injustice (like sin) is that which cries out to be set aright.[3]

As the analysis of this chapter proceeds, it will become ever clearer how many distinctions must be made when discussing justification (forensic, meritorious, imputed, imparted, spiritual, transformative, and so forth), not least because those adjectives became the catalyst for a divided Western Christendom. But with sin at least, the matter is relatively

2. Josef Pieper, *The Concept of Sin*, trans. Edward T. Oakes, S.J. (South Bend, IN: St. Augustine's Press, 2001), 16–17.

3. "Now often one contrary state is recognized from its contrary; . . . if good condition is known, bad condition also becomes known." Aristotle, *Nicomachean Ethics* V 1 (1128b18–20). In his commentary on this passage, Thomas hits upon a pithy summary: "The many forms of injustice make the many forms of justice quite clear." Thomas Aquinas, *In Eth.* V 1, no. 893.

straightforward, at least when we take sin in its widest, generic meaning (a meaning, as we saw, that it shares with injustice): as denoting that reality that has gone wildly awry, a sense that also directly entails the notion that it must be set right. As Pieper says in his monograph *Justice:*

> Among all the things that preoccupy us today, there seem to be few that are not connected with justice in a very intimate fashion. A survey of current problems reveals this clearly. . . . There are problems of "human rights," of a "just war" and war crimes, of responsibility in the face of unjust commands, the right of opposition against unlawful authority; capital punishment, dueling, political strikes, equality of rights for women. . . . And each one has an immediate connection with the notion of justice. Over and above that, however, anyone who judges the realities encountered in everyday life by the standard of "justice" will clearly see that evil and suffering in our world have many names, but primarily that of "injustice."[4]

In contrast to the word *injustice*, however, the word *sin* now carries, as we saw, an almost exclusively religious connotation, usually referring more to something gone awry between human beings and God, whereas injustice implies something more "horizontal," usually connoting more intra-human than human-divine relations. But for the believer, the special religious connotation of the word *sin* only adds to the dilemma. Injustice is of course intolerable, as anyone who suffers under unjust regimes knows (the reality of injustice largely dominates contemporary politics and is the motivation for all manner of policies and proposals to set things right); but that intolerability only intensifies for the believer when sin is factored into the picture. The discrepancy between not merely an unjust but a *sinful* world and an all-holy God can drive some Christians to thoughts of suicide. For example, St. Ignatius Loyola recounts this episode in his autobiography:

> He found no cure for his scruples. Many months had now passed since they had begun to torment him. Once when he was very upset by them, he began to pray with such fervor that he shouted out loud to God, saying "Help me, Lord, for I find no remedy among men nor in any creature. Yet if I thought I could find it, no labor would be too great for me. Even

---

4. Josef Pieper, *Justice*, trans. Lawrence E. Lynch (New York: Pantheon, 1955), 9.

though I should have to follow a little dog so he could help me, I would do it." While he had these thoughts, the temptation often came over him with great force to throw himself into a large hole in his room next to the place where he was praying.[5]

Although he never spoke specifically in terms of suicide, Martin Luther too recounts how his sinfulness made him despair of ever being able to relate to a just God. Speaking of his life as an Augustinian monk, he says:

> At such times God seems terribly angry, and with him the whole creation. At such a time there is no flight, no comfort, within or without, but all things accuse. At such a time as that the Psalmist mourns, "I am cut off from thy sight" [Psalm 31:22]. . . . In this moment, strange to say, the soul cannot believe that it can ever be redeemed. . . . All that remains is the stark-naked desire for help and a terrible groaning, but it does not know where to turn for help.[6]

Perhaps the most rhetorically effective account of this feeling of despair trying to reconcile an all-good God with the reality of sin comes from Cardinal Newman's autobiography:

> Starting then with the being of a God, . . . I look out of myself into the world of men, and there I see a sight which fills me with unspeakable distress. The world seems simply to give the lie to that great truth, of which my whole being is so full; and the effect upon me is, in consequence, as a matter of necessity, as confusing as if it denied that I am in existence myself. If I looked into a mirror, and did not see my face, I should have the sort of feeling which actually comes upon me, when I look into this living busy world, and *see no reflection of its Creator.*[7]

Note how this dismay can equally well describe the dismay of the atheist, and indeed his dismay often forms the very grounds for his disbelief: For the atheist, the image of God as omniscient, omnipotent, and all-good

---

5. From *The Autobiography of St. Ignatius Loyola*, trans. Joseph O'Callaghan (New York: Harper & Row, 1974), 35. Throughout, Ignatius speaks of himself in the third person.

6. Martin Luther, "Explanation of the Ninety-Five Theses," in *Luther's Works*, ed. Jaroslav Pelikan (Philadelphia: Fortress Press, 1967), Vol. 31, 129; *WA*, 1:579.

7. John Henry Cardinal Newman, *Apologia pro vita sua*, A Norton Critical Edition, edited by David J. DeLaura (New York: W. W. Norton & Co., 1968/1864), 186; emphasis added.

is simply too disjunctive with the world as presently constituted to be endured.[8] Newman certainly gets *that*:

> Were it not for this voice, speaking so clearly in my conscience and my heart, I should be an atheist, or a pantheist, or a polytheist when I looked into the world. I am speaking for myself only; and I am far from denying the real force of the arguments in proof of a God, drawn from the general facts of human society and the course of history, but these do not warm me or enlighten me; they do not take away the winter of my desolation, or make the buds unfold and the leaves grow within me, and my moral being rejoice. The sight of the world is nothing else than the prophet's scroll, full of "lamentation and woe."[9]

Indeed, *the more intensely the devout believer believes, the more intense will be his pain at having to live in the world,* whose mad ways seem to demand to be put back to rights, which of course only God can do. So, either God has taken such an initiative out of sheer graciousness, or the world invites God's utter rejection of what he has created:

> To consider the world in its length and breadth, its various history, the many races of man, their starts, their fortunes, their mutual alienation, their conflicts; and then their ways, habits, governments, forms of worship; their enterprises, their aimless courses, their random achievements and acquirements, the impotent conclusion of long-standing facts, the tokens so faint and broken of a superintending design, the blind evolution of what turn out to be great powers or truths, the progress of things, as if from unreasoning elements, not towards final causes, the greatness and littleness of man, his far-reaching aims, his short duration, the curtain hung over his futurity, the disappointments of life, the defeat of good, the success of evil, physical pain, mental anguish, the prevalence and intensity of sin, the pervading idolatries, the corruptions, the dreary hopeless irreligion, that condition of the whole race, so fearfully yet exactly described in the Apostle's words, "having

8. Oddly, the atheist does not usually then content himself with taking the world as it is: his protest against God, *being primarily a moral one,* is often the very basis for his ameliorative commitments. So for both believer and unbeliever, the world is, in Hamlet's words, "out of joint," the recognition of which led the prince to curse the fate that forced him to set it right.

9. Newman, *Apologia,* 186.

no hope and without God in the world,"—all this is a vision to dizzy and appall and inflicts upon the mind the sense of a profound mystery, which is absolutely beyond human solution. What shall be said to this heart-piercing, reasoning-bewildering fact? I can only answer, that either there is no Creator, or this living society of men is in a true sense discarded from His presence.[10]

Discarded from God's presence: that is the fundamental problem of justification: how has God put things right between himself and the world, given the reality of God's *justified* wrath? If God has not in fact discarded the world (as he well could have done), how does he now relate his gracious saving gestures to his justice, that is, without violating his all-holy nature? Needless to say, if that setting-the-world-aright is to happen, it must be God's work alone: "For it is by grace that you have been saved, through faith—and this not from yourselves, it is the gift of God" (Eph. 2:8). Assuming—as of course Newman does for other reasons—that God exists,[11] the world as God intended it is utterly out of whack, madly discrepant from his aboriginal intentions. The secularist might see only injustice, but the believer will see both, injustice and sin, and then ask how revelation describes God's initiative to set things right again.

But at this point an oddity of terminology arises. It comes as no surprise that Paul would speak above in terms of *grace*, for that word captures so well the idea that our salvation entirely depends on God, which we have no right to expect or any claim to raise. Yet Paul does not speak here

---

10. Newman, *Apologia*, 186–87; the internal quotation is from Paul (Eph. 2:12).

11. After an adolescent flirtation with atheism, Newman read a book by a Calvinist divine that convinced him he belonged to the elect, a theology he later abandoned but which left its mark on him, preventing him from lapsing back into atheism based on empirical arguments pointing to the state of the world: "When I was fourteen, I read [Thomas] Paine's Tracts against the Old Testament, and found pleasure in thinking of the objections which were contained in them. Also, I read some of Hume's Essays. . . . Also, I recollect copying out some French verses, perhaps Voltaire's, in denial of the immortality of the soul, and saying to myself something like 'How dreadful, but how plausible!' When I was fifteen (in the autumn of 1816), a great change of thought took place in me. I fell under the influences of a definite Creed, and received into my intellect impressions of a dogma which, through God's mercy, have never been effaced or obscured. . . . [My early Calvinism confirmed] me in my distrust of the reality of material phenomena [and] made me rest in the thought of two and two only absolute and luminously self-evident beings, myself and my Creator" (ibid., 15–16). We will notice later how Newman eventually abandoned this "Calvinist solipsism," and precisely by coming to a different view of justification.

solely of grace but also of *justification*. The trouble is, that word comes from *justice*, which conjures up a whole range of meanings relating to rights, claims, and obligations. At least on the surface, *grace* and *justice* seem antithetical, for one denotes an unexpected and unowed gift, whereas the other denotes obligation, of giving to each other what is due. Thus Pieper: "Wherefore all just order in the world is based on this, that man give man what is his due. On the other hand, everything unjust implies that what belongs to a man is withheld or taken away from him—and, once more, not by misfortune, failure of crops, fire or earthquake, but by man."[12]

Further, justice not only implies giving to each human being his due, but it also relies on the notion of *equality*, a word that might sound all-too-modern but which in fact has ancient pedigree, as we see from Thomas's definition of justice: "It is proper to justice as compared with other virtues to direct man in his relations with others, as it denotes a kind of equality, *as its very name implies*" (*ST* II/II, q. 58, a. 1; emphasis added);[13] but obviously there can be no notion of equality between Creator and creature, let alone between an all-holy God and the sinful human. Indeed, even quite apart from sin, Thomas says the very notion of linking justice to creation is incoherent: "[I]n the creation of things God did not work of necessity as though he brought things into being as a debt of justice" (*ScG* II, 28.1).[14]

Finally, if one must give another what is his due (it's *due* him, after all), this right/obligation can only be ensured by law, making law-abiding behavior another implication of justice. There is, in other words, no right (on my part) without a correlative obligation (on your part), and *vice versa*, an obligation that can only be enforced by law. Under that rubric, to disobey the law is to commit an injustice.[15]

Yet all three implicates entailed in the concept of justice *directly* con-

---

12. Pieper, *Justice*, 10. This definition is quite common; for example, Augustine: "Justice is the virtue which assigns to everyone his due." *City of God* XIX, ch. 21, trans. Henry Bettenson (New York: Viking Penguin, 1984), 882.

13. Following Aristotle: "The just, then, is the lawful and the equal, the unjust the unlawful and the unequal." *Nicomachean Ethics* V 1 (1129b1).

14. Pieper's more periphrastic translation runs: "Therefore, creation itself is not an act of justice; creation is not anyone's due." Pieper, *Justice*, 14.

15. The Aristotelian Mortimer Adler summarizes all three points in the definition here: "Justice consists in treating equals equally. . . . Justice [also] consists in rendering to each individual what he is due, giving to each person what belongs to him. . . . [Finally] we say that a person is just if he obeys the law of the community in which he lives. The just person is the law-abiding citizen." Mortimer Adler, *How to Think about the Great Ideas* (Chicago: Open Court, 2000), 265–66.

tradict the fundamental meaning of grace, as Paul makes clear in each instance: as to the first definition of justice, he denies that man is *due* anything from God here: "Now to one who works, his wages are not reckoned as a gift but as his due. Contrariwise, to one who does not work but trusts him who justifies the ungodly, his faith is reckoned as righteousness" (Rom. 4:4–5); second, Paul denies *equality*, not only between God and the human race as such, but also in God's treatment of individual humans, as here: "As it is written, 'Jacob have I loved but Esau hated.' . . . [And God] says to Moses, 'I will have mercy on whom I have mercy' " (Rom. 9:13, 15); and finally he denies that being *law-abiding* will in any way avail before God: "For all who rely on works of the law are under a curse" (Gal. 3:10).[16]

Yet, despite all this, Paul uses the word *justification* time and again for describing how God reestablished a right relationship between himself and the human race; and the question is why: Why, if justice implies obligation across the board, does Paul use a court-based term that presupposes equality, obligation, and law, when, in effect, he is really talking about God's gracious dealings with the human race, who is bound by no equality, obligation, or law? Such is the problem of justification in Christian theology.[17]

Even to begin to answer that question, however, brings up a knotty

---

16. Yet Paul can also say: "For it is not those who hear the law who are righteous in God's sight, but it is those who obey the law who will be declared righteous" (Rom. 2:13). It is especially in dealing with Paul's disconcerting variations in his statements about the law that commentators down through the ages confess bafflement. For example, Augustine says: "The verse, 'I do not understand my own actions' [Rom. 7:15] seems . . . to contradict Paul's earlier verse, 'Sin . . . wrought death in me through what is good' [7:13]." *Augustine on Romans: Propositions from the Epistle to the Romans [and] Unfinished Commentary on the Epistle to the Romans*, trans. Paula Fredriksen Landes (Chico, CA: Scholars Press, 1982), 17. Surveying modern Pauline scholarship, one commentator concludes: "It is symptomatic that the followers of the apostle have hardly ever been able to agree on what he really wanted to say. . . . It is in fact striking that more than one interpreter can state that Paul's theology of the law is just a lot of nonsense, unless of course you opt for his particular interpretation (different from most). We thus face a curious dilemma. On one hand, the clarity, profundity and cogency of Paul's theological thinking is universally praised. On the other hand, it does not seem possible to reach any unanimity whatsoever as to what his message really was." Heikki Räisänen, *Paul and the Law* (Philadelphia: Fortress Press, 1986), 3-4. While exegetes are still hotly debating how Paul understands the law, justification, and obedience, we will see later in this chapter how dogmatics might be able to offer a possible path to reconciliation.

17. Thus, Barth's deft formulation of the problem: "[H]ow can it be that peace is concluded between a holy God and sinful man—by *grace*, but in a way that is completely *right*?" Karl Barth, *Church Dogmatics*, IV/1: *The Doctrine of Reconciliation*, trans. G. W. Bromiley (Edinburgh: T. & T. Clark, 1956), 520; emphases added.

problem of translation. Unfortunately, Paul's Greek terminology does not map exactly with English usage, so that sometimes Paul will use a word that will require a certain English word on one occasion, and a different English word on another, and vice versa. For example (to go from English to Greek), the word *justice* can be translated into either the Greek *dikē* or *dikaiosunē*, although the latter is usually translated back into English as *righteousness*, which carries a different, usually more subjective connotation, something like *uprightness*.[18] Or (to go from Greek to English, and this most fatefully) *dikaiosunē* will be translated not only as *righteousness* but also as *justification* (justification: a *making*-just), which refers exclusively to *God's* action in restoring a right relation to the human race, even though the Greek *dikaiosunē* is a legal term referring to a *defendant's* exculpatory arguments in a court of law. The connotation of *making*-just, on the other hand, is better conveyed in Greek by its word *dikaiōsis*, which is, however, usually translated not as "justification" but as "acquittal."

Going from Greek to English gets even more complicated because sometimes the only words available for translating Paul's Greek come from the Teutonic roots of English and sometimes from Norman French; and sometimes English preserved both forms to mean basically the same thing (think of *freedom* and *liberty* here).[19] Although this situation seems complicated

18. Matters get even more complicated because recently in conversational English *righteousness* is often used to mean *self*-righteousness. The result is that when the Bible speaks of, especially, the "righteousness of God," contemporary listeners/readers pick up an implication of moral rigidity and unbending judgmentalism in the deity—ironically, just the image Luther had of God before his breakthrough discovery of justification by faith alone. For that reason, E. J. Goodspeed and Joseph Fitzmyer prefer to translate the term not as *righteousness* but as *uprightness*, as Fitzmyer explains here: "*dikaiosunē theou* ... is often translated as 'the righteousness of God,' which sometimes sounds like his self-righteousness. The Vulgate translated this Greek phrase as *justitia Dei*, which often appears in older Catholic versions (or in romance-language translations) as 'the justice of God.' This translation, however, was often misunderstood as God's 'vindictive or punitive justice,' as Luther the monk once understood it. Because of such problems, I follow E. J. Goodspeed's translation 'the uprightness of God, ... [denoting] the divine quality whereby God acquits his people, manifesting toward them his precious power in a just judgment.'" Joseph Fitzmyer, "Romans," in *The New Jerome Biblical Commentary*, ed. Raymond E. Brown, S.S., Joseph Fitzmyer, S.J., and Roland E. Murphy, O.Carm. (Englewood Cliffs, NJ: Prentice Hall, 1990), 830–68, here 834.

19. "Modern English has two parents, Norman French and Anglo-Saxon. In most cases this gives the English-speaker a richness of vocabulary which few other languages equal. We distinguish the Anglo-Saxon 'swine' (tended by Anglo-Saxon peasants in the field) from the French 'pork' (eaten by the conquering Normans at table). Anglo-Saxon was a Germanic language, and to this day Germans eat *Schweinfleisch*, 'swine flesh,' which strikes the En-

(and is), the noted Pauline scholar E. P. Sanders, whom we have just cited in the immediately preceding footnote, explains the matter clearly here:

> In the case of key words in Paul's vocabulary, however, we have a difficulty, since some forms drove others out, rather than remaining as duplicates. The best translation of Paul's word *dikaiosunē* is the Anglo-Saxon "righteousness," not the French "justification," since "justification" often carries the nuance of defensiveness or of a legal excuse, and we shall see that this was not Paul's meaning. Paul's cognate verb, *dikaioun*, however, no longer has an Anglo-Saxon equivalent. The verb *rihtwisian* [literally, to "rightwise"] was lost long ago, and we have only the French "justify." Similarly, [the French-derived] "faith" best translates Paul's *pistis*, since [the Anglo-derived] "belief" often connotes "opinion," which is far from what Paul meant. But English has no verb which corresponds to "faith," and so for Paul's verb *pisteuein* English translators have to use "believe." In this case the Anglo-Saxon verb has driven out the French.[20]

The following table (adapted from Sanders) will show which Greek terms have two English words available (drawn from Anglo-Saxon and Norman French) and which words have driven out their equivalents (marked by an *x*) through accidents of linguistic development:

	Greek	Anglo-Saxon	Norman French
Noun	*dikaiosunē*	righteousness	justification
Adjective	*dikaios*	righteous	just
Verb	*dikaioun*	x	to justify
Noun	*pistis*	belief	faith
Adjective	*pistos*	believing	faithful
Verb	*pisteuein*	to believe	x

To add to the complications, there is the immensely consequential question of how to interpret Paul's genitive case, especially in his term

---

glish-speaker as crude and unpalatable. In the dual vocabulary which its two parents afford English, words derived from Anglo-Saxon often have a common or earthy meaning (like 'swine'), while those derived from French are more polite or sophisticated. This reflects the fact that the Normans won the battle of Hastings and became the English nobility. The dual parentage usually allows us to make fine distinctions and nuances." E. P. Sanders, *Paul: A Very Short Introduction* (Oxford: Oxford University Press, 2001), 53.

20. Sanders, *Paul*, 53–54.

dikaiosunē theou ("the righteousness of God"). Generally speaking, Greek allows four different kinds of genitives: possession, subject of the action named in the noun, origin, and object of that same action.[21] It might baffle the reader unacquainted with this debate to learn this, but in a sense the Reformation began as a dispute over the genitive *of God* in Paul's term, usually translated as "the righteousness of God."[22] If the term is meant as a *possessive* genitive, then it is referring to a perfection that God possesses by being God, like God's infinity or goodness; or if it is a *subjective* genitive, then it refers to God's activity of saving by making humans "upright" before him. Both of these genitives largely overlap, inasmuch as they refer to God's *own* righteousness.[23]

But if *tou theou* is a genitive of *origin*, then Paul would be speaking of a righteousness (or justice) that proceeds from God to the potential believer (either by God merely *declaring* sinners acquitted even though they are actually guilty, or by genuinely *imparting* that righteousness in the soul of

21. I am ignoring here idiomatic uses of the genitive, like the Greek "genitive absolute," which roughly serves the same function as the Latin "ablative absolute." Greek in fact has no ablative case, which in Latin usually served to denote motion *from* or *origin*, a function absorbed by Greek to the genitive, which also denoted possession (as does the Latin genitive). In other words, the Greek genitive encompasses more concepts than the Latin genitive.

22. This dispute over the genitive as the crux of the issue between Catholics and Protestants emerges most clearly in the exchange of letters between Jacopo Cardinal Sadoleto (1477–1547) and John Calvin (1509–64). In the first letter, dated March 18, 1539, the Cardinal says: "[W]e obtain the blessing of complete and perpetual salvation by faith *alone* in God and in Jesus Christ. When I say by faith alone, I do not mean, as those inventors of novelties do, a mere credulity and confidence in God, by which, to the seclusion of charity and the other duties of a Christian mind, I am persuaded that in the cross and blood of Christ all my faults are unknown; *this indeed is necessary* and forms the *first* access which we have to God." Calvin could hardly object to *that* formulation, since similar statements could readily be found in the writings of the Reformers. But still, there is a problem, which he points out here: "Assuredly, we deny that in justifying a man they [works] are worth a single straw. . . . But what notion, you ask, does the very term *righteousness* suggest to us if respect is not paid to good works? I answer, if you would attend to the true meaning of the term *justifying* in Scripture, you would have no difficulty. For it does not refer to man's own righteousness, but to the mercy of God, which contrary to the sinner's deserts, accepts a righteousness for him by not imputing his unrighteousness." John Calvin & Jacopo Sadoleto, *A Reformation Debate: Sadoleto's Letter to the Genevans and Calvin's Reply*, trans. John C. Olin (New York: Fordham University Press, 2000), 29, 61; emphases added.

23. Here is an instance where English again proves its oddity: *righteousness* in this context means a property appertaining to God, whereas *justification* refers to his activity; but both words can translate, in the proper context, *dikaiosunē theou*.

the believer);[24] finally, if it is an *objective* genitive, then this righteousness is understood as a quality that *counts* before God or (to use a verb common in these discussions) "avails" with God, either because the human in question is "truly" just, or because it comes to him as a special gift from God, which must be recognized as such.[25] Again, these latter two usages overlap, inasmuch as they refer to God's transitive activity in *making* just.

A further complication must be mentioned before this chapter begins its properly dogmatic analysis, and that would be the movement that has now earned the moniker the New Perspective on Paul, which rejects the usual *psychological* interpretation of justification to a more *functional* reading of that key Pauline teaching. The psychological interpretation claims that Paul chose to speak of justification by faith and not by works in order to assuage a conscience plagued by the individual's (specifically Paul's own) inability to fulfill the requirements of the law, especially the Law of Moses but also including the ethical law. Going back at least as far as Augustine and made famous (and church-dividing) by Luther, this reading gains its plausibility from this passage in Romans describing what has become officially known as the Servility of the Will:

> We know that the law is spiritual; but I am carnal, sold under sin. I do not understand my own actions. For I do not do what I want, but I do the very thing I hate. Now if I do what I do not want, I agree that the law is good. So then it is no longer I that do it; but sin which dwells within me. For I know that nothing good dwells within me, that is, in my flesh. I can will what is right, but I cannot do it. For I do not do the good I want, but the evil I do not want is what I do. Now if I do what I do not want, it is no longer I that do it, but sin which dwells within me. So I find it to be

24. This distinction is the gravamen of the division between Luther's view (or what is generally taken to be his view) and that of the Council of Trent, as we will see below. The first is called *imputed* or *forensic* justification or righteousness, to stress the "legal" or "court-based" ("forensic") acquittal; the second is usually called *imparted* or *infused* and implies more than mere acquittal, something that genuinely affects the soul.

25. I have drawn this terminology and the schema behind it from N. T. Wright, *What Paul Really Said* (Grand Rapids, MI: Eerdmans, 1997), 101. At least as regards the difference between subjective and objective genitives, English has a way of resolving that difficulty unavailable in Greek. Take the expression "the love of God": that could refer either to the love God has for the world or to the love humans ought to feel for God. But when the possessive form "God's love" is used, the ambiguity is resolved. For in English idiom "God's love" means only the love that God expresses. Greek, however, has no other way to express the genitive than by such expressions as *tou theou.*

a law that when I want to do right, evil lies close at hand. For I delight in the law of God, in my inmost self, but I see in my members another law at war with the law of my mind and making me captive to the law of sin which dwells in my members. Wretched man that I am! Who will deliver me from this body of death? Thanks be to God through Jesus Christ our Lord! So then, I of myself serve the law of God with my mind, but with my flesh I serve the law of sin. (Romans 7:14–25)

Given the way readers of this passage down through the ages have seen their own experience of struggling against temptation reflected here, and given Augustine's own struggles with sexual passion and Luther's despair at being unable to live out his monastic rule to the letter, nothing seems more obvious than that Paul must be speaking of himself here too. Undoubtedly, he is making a universal point throughout this passage about the human condition in general; but the fact that he used the first-person singular pronoun *I* throughout must surely mean that he was also speaking of *his own inner psychological torment*. After all, like all humans, Paul was a man of flesh and blood, and he explicitly says, "with *my* flesh I serve the law of sin" (v. 25).

But according to Krister Stendahl (1921–2008)—who was, it bears mentioning, a Lutheran bishop of Sweden as well as, before that, a professor of New Testament at Harvard Divinity School—that interpretation cannot be right. For in those passages where Paul is undoubtedly speaking strictly about himself and without reference to the universal human condition, he betrays no inner turmoil of conscience. Quite the opposite in fact: "If any other man thinks he has reason for confidence in the flesh, I have more: circumcised on the eighth day, of the people of Israel, of the tribe of Benjamin, a Hebrew born of Hebrews; as to the law a Pharisee, as to zeal a persecutor of the church; *as to righteousness under the law blameless*" (Phil. 3:4–6; emphasis added).[26] For Stendahl, if this passage is taken seriously, it must mean not only that Luther was wrong, but so too was the entire western tradition of interpreting Paul, from Augustine on:

Especially in Protestant Christianity—which, however at this point has its roots in Augustine and in the piety of the Middles Ages—the Pauline awareness of sin has been interpreted in the light of Luther's

26. He makes the same claim here: "I advanced in Judaism beyond many of my own age among my people" (Gal. 1:14).

struggle with his conscience. But it is exactly at this point that we can discern the most drastic difference between Luther and Paul, between the sixteenth and the first century, and, perhaps, between Eastern and Western Christianity. A fresh look at the Pauline writings themselves shows that Paul was equipped with what in our eyes must be called a rather "robust" conscience. In Phil. 3 Paul speaks most fully about his life before his Christian calling, and there is no indication that he had had any difficulty in fulfilling the Law. On the contrary, he can say that he had been "flawless" as to the righteousness required by the Law (v. 6). His encounter with Jesus Christ . . . has not changed this fact. It was not to him a restoration of a plagued conscience; when he says that he now forgets what is behind him (v. 13), he does not think about the *shortcomings* in his obedience to the Law, but about his glorious *achievements* as a righteous Jew, achievements which he nevertheless now has learned to consider as "refuse" in the light of his faith in Jesus as the Messiah.[27]

To call this article revolutionary would be an understatement; for, among other implications, it showed that all previous interpretations of Paul's doctrine of justification, not just Luther's but also *all* interpretations in the West, both Catholic and Protestant, from Augustine on, were wrong from the ground up. Not for nothing, after all, did Augustine, and not some previous Jewish, pagan, or Christian author, write the first autobiography, a genre unknown before him; for it was he, says Stendahl, who invented the introspective conscience in the West. But his problem was not Paul's.[28]

27. Krister Stendahl, "The Apostle Paul and the Introspective Conscience of the West," in *The Writings of St. Paul*, A Norton Critical Edition, ed. Wayne A. Meeks (New York: W. W. Norton, 1972), 422–34, here 423; emphases added; originally published in *Harvard Theological Review* 56 (1963): 199–215.

28. For an example of a New Perspectivist who follows Stendahl directly here, see Sanders: "Luther saw the world and the Christian life quite differently. He was impressed by the fact that, though a Christian, he felt himself to be a 'sinner'; he suffered from guilt. Paul, however, did not have a guilty conscience. Before his conversion to being an apostle of Christ, he had been . . . 'blameless' (Phil. 3:6). As an apostle he could not think of anything which would count against himself at the final judgment, though he left open the possibility that God might find some fault (1 Cor. 4:4). Luther, plagued by guilt, read Paul's passages on 'righteousness by faith' as meaning that God reckoned a Christian to be righteous even though he or she was a sinner. Luther understood 'righteousness' to be judicial, a declaration of innocence, but also fictional, ascribed to Christians 'by mere imputation,' since God was merciful. . . . Luther sought and found relief from guilt. But Luther's problems were not Paul's, and we misunderstand him if we see him through Luther's eyes." Sanders, *Paul*, 57–58.

So if Augustine, Luther, and a host of Paul's readers, both Catholic and Protestant, were wrong, what *did* Paul mean by justification by faith? Given the centrality of that doctrine in Protestant theology, it has always seemed at least a bit embarrassing that Paul does not mention his teaching on that theme in every one of his epistles.[29] In fact, where he does bring it up, it is in letters dealing either with the place of Israel in God's providential drama of salvation after the advent of Christ or with the relation between contemporary Judaism and the new Christian dispensation (or, at times, relations between Jewish and Gentile Christians); and that is the clue.

The key here is not *how* Paul converted (that was after encountering Christ on the road to Damascus) but *when*. The first Christians in Jerusalem were of course all Jews and *continued to think of themselves as Jews*: they worshipped in the Temple (Luke 24:53); they continued to keep the Mosaic dietary laws (Gal. 2:12), and they admitted Gentiles into their community only if they were first circumcised (Acts 11:2; 15:1; Gal. 5:11) or only under some extraordinary revelation (Acts 10). But among those Jewish Christians in Jerusalem were some who were born not in Palestine but

---

29. Needless to say, because so much rides on this issue (not least the perceived doctrinal basis of the Reformation), many traditional Protestants insist that the New Perspectivists have got it all wrong. Although it would take this chapter too far afield to delve into this dispute at length, it can at least be noted here that the main opponents of the New Perspective are Seyoon Kim, *Paul and the New Perspective: Second Thoughts on the Origin of Paul's Gospel* (Grand Rapids, MI: Eerdmans, 2002), and John Piper, *The Future of Justification: A Response to N. T. Wright* (Wheaton, IL: Crossway Books, 2007). Piper ironically argues from *tradition* (along, of course, as he thinks, from Scripture): "If Wright is correct here, then the entire history of the discussion of justification for the last fifteen hundred years—Catholic, Protestant, and Orthodox—has been misguided. . . . This is a remarkable claim to make about church history. But Wright is ready to play the man" (60). But if the psychological interpretation of Paul is wrong, and if it comes from Augustine (first) and then was handed on without challenge until Stendahl called it into question, then arguments from tradition collapse. It is indeed ironic that Piper would so readily abandon his own *sola scriptura* principle. One more point: if Piper's last sentence sounds *ad hominem*, his target can hit back with an even greater ferocity: "Like America looking for a new scapegoat after the collapse of the Cold War and seizing on the Islamic world as the obvious target, many conservative writers, having discovered themselves in possession of the Pauline field after the liberals tired of it, have looked around for new enemies. Here is something called the New Perspective; it seems to be denying some of the things we have normally taught; very well, let us demonize it, lump its proponents together, and nuke them from a great height." N. T. Wright, "New Perspectives on Paul," *Justification in Perspective: Historical Developments and Contemporary Challenges*, ed. Bruce L. McCormack (Grand Rapids, MI: Baker House, 2006): 243–64, here 247. Presumably, readers of this passage can catch Wright out doing a bit of his own "lumping," and not just against his critics. But nobody ever said theology was a game of beanbag.

in the Diaspora and who accordingly usually spoke Greek as their native language, not Aramaic and/or Hebrew. When "ethnic" tension between the two groups arose, the crisis was resolved by, as it were, a "power-sharing agreement" (Acts 6:1–6) according to which seven Greek-speaking deacons were set aside for the task of meeting the needs of their fellow "Hellenes," all of whom had Greek names and one of whom (Nicholas) was a convert from paganism to Judaism before he converted to Christianity (v. 5).

There must have been something about these deacons' preaching, or at least Stephen's, that asserted or implied a disjunction between Judaism and the Christian gospel.[30] For *they* (Acts 6:8–14) and *not* the Hebrew-speaking Christians (Acts 5:33–42) were persecuted by the Jews of Jerusalem. Crucially, it was *that* gospel, the one preached by Stephen, that Paul was persecuting (Acts 8:1). Thus, at the moment of his conversion, Paul's logic seems to have been the following: Torah, the Law of Moses, is incompatible with the Christian gospel; hence the latter must be persecuted, since Torah is God's premier gift to his Chosen People. *Ergo*, the gospel must be a false gospel. But when he met Christ on the way to persecute the Greek-speaking Christians in Damascus, Paul saw that the gospel *is* true; but in that realization he was still operating under his previous logic: so now the Torah had lost its point.[31]

Following this analysis, the New Perspectivists claim that Paul always speaks of justification by faith in terms of this dilemma: what *now*, after the coming of Christ, is the role for the Mosaic Law? And the answer to that question is that the Law, in retrospect, was merely propaedeutic and that what the Jews *thought* it had been intended to accomplish had now devolved to faith in Christ, who alone justifies:

> Now before faith came, we were confined under the law, kept under restraint until faith should be revealed. So that the law was our custodian until Christ came, that we might be justified by faith. But now that faith has come, we are no longer under a custodian; for in Christ Jesus you are all sons of God, through faith. For as many of you as were baptized into Christ have put on Christ. There is neither Jew nor Greek, there

30. "Opposition arose, however, from members of the Synagogue of the Freedmen (as it was called)—Jews of Cyrene and Alexandria as well as the provinces of Cilicia and Asia.... They secretly persuaded some men to say, 'We have heard Stephen speak words of blasphemy against Moses and against God'" (Acts 6:9, 11).

31. Following here the analysis of Martin Hengel, *Between Jesus and Paul: Studies in the Earliest History of Christianity*, trans. John Bowden (London: SCM Press, 1983), 1–29.

is neither slave nor free, there is neither male nor female; for you are all one in Christ Jesus. And if you are Christ's, then you are Abraham's offspring, heirs according to promise. (Gal. 3:23–29)

In other words, Paul's doctrine of justification by faith serves this one great single purpose: to ensure Gentile inclusion in the people of God; it is, in other words, a *functional* doctrine, meant to serve wider purposes. The emphasis in Romans (the other letter besides Galatians where justification figures so prominently) is slightly different, partly due to its different setting.[32] But the basic functionality of the doctrine remains, with a new twist: not only did justification by faith establish the rightful place of Gentiles among the people of God, but it also guaranteed the essential *equality* of Jew and Gentile (a key correlate in the concept of justice, as we saw). True, he mentions that point once in Galatians (3:28, cited above), but in Romans the theme throbs like a steady drumbeat, which almost sounds numbing when arranged in a catena:

The gospel . . . is the power of God for salvation of every one who has faith, to the Jew first and also to the Greek. (1:16)

There will be tribulation and distress for every human being who does evil, the Jew first and also the Greek, but glory and honor and peace for every one who does good, the Jew first and also the Greek. For God shows no partiality. (2:9–11)

Are Jews any better off? No, not at all; for I have already charged that all people, both Jews and Greeks, are under the power of sin. (3:9)

For there is no distinction . . . (3:22)

Or is God the God of Jews only? Is he not the God of Gentiles too? (3:29)

32. "Paul was not under direct attack when he wrote Romans, and the letter is much less polemical than is Galatians. He had also listened to criticism of his position and had thought some more about the issues. The church at Rome was not of his founding, and this too affected the tone of the letter. He could berate the Galatians and threaten them, or appeal to their initial response to him and play on past sympathy and warmth. . . . These persuasive devices were not appropriate when writing to a church that was not his own, but others were. He was not too proud to use compliments when urging the Romans to hear him out." Sanders, *Paul,* 76.

[God makes known] the riches of his glory . . . [for] us whom he has called, not only from out of the Jews but also from the Gentiles (9:23–24)

For there is no distinction between Jew and Greek, the same Lord is Lord of all and bestows his riches upon all who call upon him. (10:12)

For God has consigned all people to disobedience that he may have mercy on all. (11:32)

Another theme that was only lightly touched on in Galatians but which was treated more prominently in Romans also came from the various objections his doctrine elicited, especially this one: if the law had lost its role in regulating behavior and was to be replaced by faith, not works, *what happens to ethics?* The implied criticism in the question clearly stung, because Paul seems flummoxed in trying to answer it: "Are we to continue in sin that grace may abound? By no means!" (6:1–2) Later in chapter 6 he makes clear he is still bothered: "Are we to sin because we are not under law, but under grace?" and can only respond in the same baffled way: "By no means!" (6:15) This dilemma accounts for the more positive assessment of the law in Romans than in Galatians: "And why not do evil that good may come, as some people slanderously charge us with saying?" (3:8) to which he replies: "Do we then overthrow the law by this faith? By no means! On the contrary, we uphold the law" (3:31). As Sanders says, "this has no counterpart in Galatians."[33]

Even more fascinating is another variation on the doctrine: when he takes up this problem of ethical behavior in more detail—as he clearly must, given the all-too-peremptory way he had been dealing with the issue so far—he no longer speaks of justification by faith but uses other terms, as Sanders notes here:

As the argument about the equal status of Jew and Gentile in the people of God rolls on, it is combined with Paul's concern about ethics and the law. In Romans 6, . . . he wishes to refute the idea that Christians, being free from the law, sin so that grace may abound (6:1–2), and he tries to explain how, without the law, ethics are maintained. He argues that Christians, being "in the Spirit," are able to put to death evil deeds and to fulfill what the law requires (8:1–14).[34]

33. Sanders, *Paul,* 78.
34. Sanders, *Paul,* 79–80.

From this shift in terminology we learn two things: first, that justification cannot be either the centerpiece or the linchpin of Paul's theology, precisely because it fails to address on its own terms the ethical dilemmas it raises; and second, therefore, that justification by faith cannot be *merely* forensic or imputed. True, Paul does say: "Now to the one who works, his wages are not reckoned as a gift but as his due. But to the one who does not work but instead trusts him who justifies the ungodly, his faith is *reckoned* as righteousness" (Rom. 4:4–5). This passage, perhaps more than any other in Romans, has been cited to claim that Paul holds to a theory of imputed or declared justification, along with the rest of Romans 4, which uses the verb *reckon* (*logizomai*) eleven times. But as Sanders points out:

> This [passage in Rom. 4] does not mean, however, that Paul thinks of righteousness as being fictitiously imputed to those who have faith, while they remain sinners in fact. In sharing Christ's death Christians have died to the old order. They no longer live in sin (6:2), but are "slaves" of righteousness, who have become obedient to God (6:15–18). Paul picked up "reckon" from Genesis [15:6] and then he repeated it, with no thought of a fictional, "merely imputed" righteousness.[35]

But if Paul is not speaking here of an imputed righteousness (or at least not merely so), then how does he understand it, and why is it so hard to get agreement among exegetes as to Paul's actual meaning? Given the current

---

35. Sanders, *Paul,* 79. One commentator argues that Paul's image of Christian manumission from the slavery of sin to the "slavery" of righteousness resolves Paul's dilemma in finding a place for works (and ethics) in his theology: "Christians are free in a number of respects, not least from the trammels of sin. But our freedom is with a view to our service.... Notice, for example, the striking juxtaposition in Gal. 5:13 of the ideas of freedom and slavery: 'You are called to be free, but ... through love be slaves to one another.'" David J. Williams, *Paul's Metaphors: Their Context and Character* (Peabody, MA: Hendrickson, 1999), 116. Perhaps because of the American Civil War and the long struggle of African-Americans to free themselves from the reverberating aftereffects of bondage, we flinch at Paul here; but as he himself concedes, it's only a metaphor, but still a useful one: "I am speaking in human terms, because of your natural limitations. For just as you once yielded your members to impurity and to greater and greater iniquity, so now yield your members to righteousness for sanctification. When you were slaves of sin, you were free in regard to righteousness. But then what return did you get from the things of which you are now ashamed? The end of those things is death. But now that you have been set free from sin and have become slaves of God, the return you get is sanctification and its end, eternal life" (Rom. 6:19–22). Note that Paul also speaks of manumission even in letters where justification is not mentioned (1 Cor. 6:20; 7:23).

irresolved state of the question among Pauline scholars, it seems best to move out of Pauline exegesis and enter the dogmatic question directly, especially in the light of the church-divisions caused by the different answers to this question. Newman put the issue most forcefully in his *Lectures on Justification*. His formulation is certainly tendentious (he had no patience with forensic justification); but the point here to stress is the radicality of the alternatives:

> Man did not become guilty except by becoming sinful; he does not become innocent except by becoming holy. God cannot, from His very nature, look with pleasure and favour upon an unholy creature, or justify or count righteous one who is not righteous. Cleanness of heart and spirit, obedience by word and deed, this alone in us can be acceptable to God; that is, this alone can constitute our justification.[36]

The classic Protestant position rejects Newman here because of the impossibility of achieving this so-called "cleanness of heart and spirit," of being obedient "in word and deed"—the very attempt to achieve which was the source of Luther's despair in his days as a monk. Perhaps the pithiest statement explaining the Protestant insistence on imputed, not imparted justification comes from Paul Tillich, who said that the principle of forensic justification can be reduced to this formulation—*justification means accepting that you are accepted even though you are unacceptable*:

> Do not try to do anything now; perhaps later you will do much. Do not seek for anything; do not perform anything; do not intend anything. Simply accept the fact that you are accepted. . . . After such an experience we may not be better than before, and we may not believe more than before. But everything is transformed. In that moment, grace conquers sin, and reconciliation bridges the gulf of estrangement. And nothing is demanded of this experience, no religious or moral or intellectual presupposition, nothing but *acceptance*.[37]

Leaving aside the historical question of whether either extreme (forensic or transformative) is fair to Luther's actual thought, these two po-

36. John Henry Cardinal Newman, *Lectures on the Doctrine of Justification* (London: Longmans, Green, and Co., 1900), 32.

37. Paul Tillich, *The Shaking of the Foundations* (New York: Charles Scribner's Sons, 1948), 162; Tillich's emphasis.

sitions, when taken abstractly as possible interpretations of the Pauline doctrine of justification, are clearly unbridgeable. The problem is that the dispute cannot be solved merely by exegesis, for all interpreters approach a text with prior commitments, whether they be ideological, philosophical, or theological.[38] (Augustine was a neo-Platonist, Thomas an Aristotelian, and Luther was trained in the nominalist tradition of William of Ockham; and one would have to lapse into total naïveté to think these philosophical commitments had no influence on their scriptural commentaries.)

Furthermore, a position in favor of imputed vs. imparted justification *ramifies*, determining a host of other positions, which of course, once they become church-dividing, further harden the initial positions taken, making a reexamination of the original issue all that more difficult. Above all, the two views on justification carry immense implications for how human *agency* is to be interpreted.[39] No wonder, then, that Luther so vociferously objected to Erasmus's defense of free will, for it undermined his own doctrine of justification directly, as Daphne Hampson explains:

> To Catholic ears, the Lutheran position has often sounded deterministic. It belongs to human dignity, to the dignity of the creation which God has made, that God does not simply overwhelm us or control us. The human must be allowed to perform a free act in relation to God. Hence the Tridentine talk of "freely co-operating" with God's grace. . . . For Catholicism, God respects our freedom. For Luther this would not make sense. To speak of a freedom in relationship to God is, for him, not to understand that God is God. We must rather allow God to deliver us into freedom. For Catholicism we have a "base" on which to stand (creation) also in relationship to God. For Luther we are falling apart;

---

38. Hans-Georg Gadamer's *Truth and Method*, trans. Joel Weinsheimer and Donald G. Marshall (New York: Crossroad, 1991), has largely convinced the world of that reality (see "The Reality of Authority and Tradition," 277–85). As Paul Ricoeur pointed out: "It was surely as a kind of provocation that Gadamer undertook his plea in favor of prejudice," which for the Enlightenment was just "what one must get rid of in order 'to dare to think.' . . . The rehabilitation of prejudice [however] does not signify submission to every tradition, but only the impossibility of removing oneself from the condition [of] historical transmission." Paul Ricoeur, *Hermeneutics: Writings and Lectures*, Volume 2, trans. David Pellauer (Cambridge: Polity, 2013), 73, 76.

39. In a sense, nearly every issue in the theology of grace touches on this question of free will: justification, original sin (the freedom of Adam and Eve before and after the fall), predestination, and even Mary's Immaculate Conception, all of which will be treated in the rest of this book.

we must first base ourselves in God through faith before we can begin to speak of human freedom.[40]

Described in this way, the two views of justification seem irreconcilable; but that is the point: when described as two extremes, they *are* irreconcilable. But a resolution becomes possible when each side is taken on its own terms and then is led through to a new resolution based on the internal contradictions lurking in each position, what Immanuel Kant called an "antinomy."[41] Take, for example, the internal contradiction inside the merely declaratory view of forensic justification, by which God declares acquitted the guilty defendant: what does that say *about God*? As Newman shrewdly noted, there is a problem here:

> Surely it is a strange paradox to say that a thing is not because He says it is; that the solemn averment of the Living and True God is inconsistent with the fact averred; [that] His accepting our obedience is a bar to His making it acceptable, and that the glory of His pronouncing us righteous lies in His leaving us unrighteous. Sure it is a paradox to maintain

---

40. Daphne Hampson, *Christian Contradictions: The Structure of Lutheran and Catholic Thought* (Cambridge: Cambridge University Press, 2001), 44. Of course that objection to Luther's view of freedom does not mean Catholics have always been fair to the Wittenberg reformer: "Again, it is far from the case that Luther thinks that the human lacks free will in the sense that a determinist might hold. As he well says, the kingdom of heaven was not made for geese! Luther's point is that I cannot perform a single act which should justify me with God" (ibid., 100). But even when that point is conceded, the fundamental difference remains: "Faith in the Lutheran sense of trust is not something which we possess in ourselves; it is not, in Catholic terminology, an 'infused virtue.' We are justified by trusting extrinsically in another (and not in ourselves). Faith is not a work; it is a response to a promise. . . . [I]n speaking of 'justification by faith,' Lutherans are not referring to a virtue infused by God which thenceforth becomes an intrinsic property of the human. They are referring to that act whereby I trust in another and not in myself. In other words they are proclaiming the Christian to live by an 'extrinsic' righteousness and not on account of anything about the way that he or she is" (ibid., 49, 98–99).

41. Technically speaking, an antinomy is a subset of paradox, which, *sensu stricto*, means a sentence that is self-contradictory on the surface but that speaks to a deeper truth ("Too swift arrives as tardy as too slow"). An antinomy, on the other hand, is a sentence that does not contradict itself on the surface but whose implications lead to the opposite conclusion, as when Zeno took the sentence "The world is finite" and then pointed out that one could then proceed to that finite boundary and throw a spear over the delimiting line, thereby extending the finitude of the world to infinity. (Thus, again strictly speaking, Zeno's so-called "paradoxes" are really antinomies.)

that the only safeguard of the doctrine of our being accepted freely and without price, is that of our hearts being left odious and offensive to God. How does it diminish the freedom of the gift that He does more? How does it exalt His grace, to say that He lets remain in the "filthy rags" of nature those whose obedience His omnipotence surely might make well-pleasing to Him, did He so will? We, indeed, can claim nothing; and if it be proved that Scripture promises no more, then it is presumptuous to seek it; but it is very certain that Scripture, again and again, speaks of our hearts and bodies, our thoughts, words, and works, as righteous; so it is not for want of Scripture warrant that we shrink from believing this gracious truth, but we are determined that the word righteous, in such passages, shall not really mean righteous; we put a second sense upon the word, we explain away the sacred text, and deny a sacred doctrine, all because we have a notion that we are exalting the fullness and richness of God's mercy by circumscribing it.[42]

What Newman in effect is saying here is that the whole debate, at least on the forensic side, is operating with a strange view of God's power to effect change in the Christian soul. Nay, he does more than imply it: in the next paragraph he says it outright:

Alas! it is an opinion too widely spread, too pertinaciously held, to need formal statement, that if God be supposed to impart any intrinsic acceptableness to our services, this must diminish our debt to Him; that the more He does for us, the less we must necessarily feel indebted to Him; and, though He give us all other graces, He cannot give humility with them. Far be from us notions as contrary to Scripture as they are disparaging to God's love; no, let us believe the comfortable truth, that the justifying grace of God effects what it declares.[43]

What Newman is getting at here, in his attacks on (mere) forensic justification, is a strange presupposition held by the proponents of (exclusive) imputed justification: that God's word must be ineffective *in re* (in fact) in order to be effective *in spe* (as promise). This dichotomy he denies outright: "He may bless, He may curse, according to His mercy or our deserts;

---

42. Newman, *Justification*, 78–79. Recall what was said above how Paul was forced to move away from forensic terminology when discussing ethics and obedience.

43. Newman, *Justification*, 79.

but if He blesses, surely it is by making holy; if He counts [as] righteous, it is by making righteous; if He justifies, it is by renewing; if He reconciles us to Himself, it is not by annihilating the Law, but by creating in us new wills and new powers for the observance of it."[44] By phrasing it in this way, Newman is then led to his most notorious conclusion:

> He [Luther] found Christians in bondage to their works and obser-vances; he released them by his doctrine of faith; and he left them in bondage to their feelings. . . . For outward signs of grace he substituted inward; for reverence towards the Church contemplation of self. And thus, whereas he himself held the proper efficacy of the Sacraments, he has led others to disbelieve it; whereas he preached against reliance on self, he introduced it in a more subtle shape; whereas he professed to make the written word all in all, he sacrificed it in its length and breadth to the doctrine which he had wrested from a few texts.[45]

It is the almost unanimous verdict of scholars that Newman was unfair to Luther here. As Thomas Sheridan rightly points out: "Newman did not read German and few of Luther's German works had been translated into English."[46] In the course of the lectures (thirteen in all), Newman even seems to give implicit acknowledgment to this charge of unfairness to the historical Luther, since he regularly cites in favor of his views the positions adopted by later noted Lutheran theologians, especially Philip Melanch-thon, in the heat of debate with Catholics.[47] For Newman's real target was

---

44. Newman, *Justification*, 34.

45. Newman, *Justification*, 340.

46. Thomas Sheridan, S.J., *Newman on Justification: A Theological Biography* (Staten Island, NY: Alba House, 1967), 240. Newman seems to have simply assumed (along with the Evangelicals of his day) that a forensic view of justification precluded the idea of an efficacious baptism, especially infant baptism. But this was not Luther's own view: see Jon-athan D. Trigg, *Baptism in the Theology of Martin Luther* (Leiden: Brill, 2001), who insists that for Luther there was no contradiction, but who also concedes Newman's difficulty: "*Prima facie* the baptismal doctrine is more plausibly cast as the negation of the great reformation doctrines than as their essential underpinnings" (3).

47. As Henry Chadwick shrewdly sees: "Newman's footnotes mainly refer to firmly Protestant authors, especially when he can find in them (as was not difficult) proposi-tions that cohered with his main contention, namely *that those who stand for imputed righteousness and those who stand for imparted righteousness are ultimately talking about one and the same thing.*" Henry Chadwick, "*The Lectures on Justification*," in *Newman after a Hundred Years*, ed. Ian Ker and Alan G. Hill (Oxford: Clarendon Press, 1990), 287–308, here

those Evangelicals, inside and outside the Church of England; and since he himself had adhered to the Evangelical wing of the Church of England, his lectures were, in a sense, an argument with his past self.[48] Newman's problem with his erstwhile Evangelical co-religionists was that they had conceded no ontological validity to the sacrament of baptism and placed everything on the act of faith, a view against which both Luther and Calvin vigorously fought, as Sheridan notes:

> Many of them [the Evangelicals] had, in fact, as Newman shows else-where, gone beyond not only the English but also the continental Reformers in their Protestantism and had become so hypnotized by certain slogans and pat phrases that they rejected many ideas and prac-tices of which Luther and Calvin themselves were staunch defenders. Whether or not it was justly said of Luther himself—and Newman seems to have questioned this later on—Newman's statement concerning him was perfectly applicable to many of the Evangelicals of his day.[49]

291; emphasis added. But such could not be said of the Evangelicals: "Newman distanced himself from the then widely held view among Evangelicals (a view which Philip Melanch-thon expressly disowned in his *Apology for the Augsburg Confession*) that to speak of justi-fication 'by faith alone' necessarily excludes any means of communicating grace through the dominical sacraments or apostolic ministers" (ibid., 295). The "money quote" from Melanchthon can be found here: "Excludimus autem opinionem meriti, non excludimus verbum aut sacramenta, ut calumniator adversarii." ("[By 'faith alone'] we exclude merit, not the word or sacraments, as our opponents slanderously claim.") Philip Melanchthon, *Apologia Confessionis Augustanae* (1531), ch. 4, sec. 7.

48. Chadwick again: "As is commonly the case with Newman's writings, the prose is never so brilliant or the argument so acute as when he is stating the position of those with whom he makes no secret of disagreeing. For Newman's *Justification* is a highly polemical work, and its main argument is directed against the beliefs which he himself had held as an Evangelical." Chadwick, "The *Lectures*," 289.

49. Sheridan, *Newman on Justification*, 240–41. The so-called Finnish interpretation of Luther has also undermined the historical accuracy of Newman's portrait of the Reformer of Wittenberg. According to this interpretation, once Luther's theology of justification is seen not as an independent *articulus stantis et cadentis ecclesiae* but as a part of his Chris-tology, everything changes: "According to Luther, Christ (in both his person and his work) is present in faith and is through this presence identical with the righteousness of faith. Thus, the notion that Christ is present in the Christian occupies a much more central place in the theology of Luther than in the Lutheranism subsequent to him. The idea of a divine life in Christ who is really present in faith lies at the very center of the theology of the Reformer." Tuomo Mannermaa, "Why is Luther So Fascinating? Modern Finnish Luther Research," in *Union with Christ: The New Finnish Interpretation of Luther*, ed. Carl E. Braaten and Rob-ert W. Jenson (Grand Rapids, MI: Eerdmans, 1998), 1–20, here 2. For a complete statement

But setting these essentially historical questions aside, let us return to the inner logic of the (purely) forensic interpretation. For the whole value of the forensic view, at least according to its proponents, is that it allegedly avoids the temptation to pride. For if there *is* a role for "works," that is, for a free response for which we are "response-able" and for which we can accordingly claim "credit" or "merit," then once again man is put in the role of demanding something of God that is his due. The way for the side advocating an imparted or transformative view of justification to address this question and allay the concerns of the forensicists would be, first, to *agree* with the objection and *admit* that justification excludes the idea of pride, of "earning" salvation, of merit understood as a claim on God. In other words, we must take the opposite (generally Catholic) position as *itself* an antinomy. That is, precisely by claiming an inner, transformative role to justification, one discovers that the justified sinner has no claim on God. Balthasar, as it happens, followed this strategy when he addressed the similar concerns of Karl Barth; he did this, above all, by considering the reality of temptation in the life of the justified Christian:

> Temptation mercilessly reveals the yawning chasm between Is and Ought, between what is and what should be. We see the depths of this fissure from an insight into God's justice and judgment. However harsh this view, it is a true one, even though it but hides the transfiguring vision of grace and transforming love. When we undergo temptation, we are exposed not only to a yawning and persistent abyss and to our incapacity to measure up. Worse, we feel how hopelessly distorted are our good works. Every single feature of human life is lost before God if grace is lacking—a grace that the sinner cannot count on and to which he has no right whatever. No one who has really found himself trapped

of his views, see: Tuomo Mannermaa, *Christ Present in Faith: Luther's View of Justification* (Minneapolis: Fortress Press, 2005). Although it would far transcend the competence of the author of this chapter to adjudicate the matter, Mannermaa does adduce a large number of Luther's texts to support his position, of which this one can serve for all the others: "We have said often enough that through faith we must be born God's children and gods, lords and kings, just as Christ is born in eternity a true God of the Father. And we must once again break out through love to help our neighbor with good deeds, just as Christ became man to help us all." Luther, *WA* 17 II, 74, 20–75, 11 (cited by Mannermaa at 14). But, without attempting to adjudicate the matter here, one can at least point out the irony that, if the Finnish interpretation is correct, then the notion that the unity of the church depends on subscribing to "justification by faith alone" as the later Lutheran confessions understood that term is once again undermined, and precisely by . . . Luther!

in the coils of temptation has ever been able to save even one of his works from the fire of divine judgment. No one in such a situation would ever even dream of laying claim to any reward.[50]

In other words, it is only *within* a life which takes seriously the necessity to *be* just in fact that one realizes how far one is from that "fact." Only *by* attempting to exercise one's free will does one come to understand what is meant by the servility of the will. Only by accepting the "indicative voice" of our declared justification do we come to see how hard it is to obey the "imperative voice" of the Christian command to love. Only the infusion of justifying grace tells us how much we continue to depend on God's forensic decree that we are innocent even though we know we are guilty:

> In temptation, we come to appreciate how much of a dead-end sin really is. The sinner might do what he will, choose according to his wishes; he might say Yes, say No, saying nothing at all. No matter. Whatever he does will be a contortion if grace (which he cannot count on!) does not come to transform *everything* in him from the very roots. And even though it has been given especially to the saints to stare most intently at this naked truth, something of this insight lies within every Christian conscience. Anyone who truly loves God will taste of this chastisement. It is just that the saints are given to see without veils what the rest of us would just as soon not care to know.[51]

One of those saints was Paul: "My conscience is clear, but that does not make me innocent. It is the Lord who judges me" (1 Cor. 4:4). Basing itself on this text, the Council of Trent solemnly declared in its "Decree on Justification":

> Moreover, it must not be asserted that those who are truly justified should unhesitatingly determine within themselves that they are justified and that no one is absolved from his sins and justified unless he believes with certainty that he is absolved and justified and that absolution and justification are brought about by this faith alone, as if whoever lacks this faith were doubting God's promises and the efficacy of

50. Hans Urs von Balthasar, *The Theology of Karl Barth: Exposition and Interpretation*, trans. Edward T. Oakes, S.J. (San Francisco: Ignatius Press, 1992), 375–76.

51. Balthasar, *Barth*, 376; Balthasar's italics.

Christ's death and Resurrection. For just as no man should doubt God's mercy, Christ's merit, and the power and efficacy of the sacraments, so also, whoever considers himself, his personal weakness, and his lack of disposition may fear and tremble about his own grace, since no one can know with a certitude of faith that cannot be subject to error that he has obtained God's grace. (DH 1534)[52]

Those evangelical churches that subscribe to the principle "Once saved, always saved" have reacted and continue to react to this statement with horror; for it seems to undercut the very consolation that the doctrine of justification by faith alone means to offer the tormented conscience. But for Trent, the irony here is that such an alleged certainty leads to the very pride in one's status before God that Luther had found so oppressive: "Even though it is necessary to believe that sins are not forgiven and never have been forgiven except gratuitously by the divine mercy on account of Christ, nevertheless, it must not be said that sins are forgiven or have been forgiven to anyone who *boasts* of the confidence and certainty that his sins are forgiven and who rests on that alone" (DH 1533; emphasis added). But this statement most emphatically does *not* imply a justification by works or merits, on which Trent could not be clearer: "We are said to be justified gratuitously because nothing that precedes justification, neither faith nor works, merits the grace of justification; for 'if it is by grace, it is no longer on the basis of works; otherwise grace would no longer be grace' [Rom. 11:6]" (DH 1532).

Using traditional Aristotelian language of the four causes, Trent gives sole priority to God's gratuitous will in justifying the sinner (here the council takes the four causes in this order: final, efficient, instrumental, and formal):

The causes of this justification are the following: the final cause is the glory of God and of Christ and life everlasting. The efficient cause is the merciful God who gratuitously washes and sanctifies.... The meritorious cause is the most beloved only begotten Son of God, our Lord Jesus Christ, who, "while we were enemies" [Rom. 5:10], "out of the great love with which he loved us" [Eph. 2:4], merited for us justification by

52. Heinrich Denzinger, *Enchiridion Symbolorum definitionum et declarationum de rebus fidei et morum,* ed. Peter Hünermann (Freiburg im Breisgau: Herder, 2001). Abbreviated henceforth as DH.

his most holy Passion on the wood of the Cross and made satisfaction for us to God the Father. The instrumental cause is the sacrament of baptism, which is the "sacrament of faith," without which faith no one has ever been justified. Finally, the *single* formal cause is "the justice of God, not that by which he himself is just, but that by which he makes us just," namely the justice that we have as a *gift* from him and by which we are spiritually renewed. Thus, not only are we considered just, but we are truly called just and we are just [1 John 3:1], each one receiving within himself his own justice, according to the measure that "the Holy Spirit apportions to each one individually as he wills" [1 Cor. 12:11] and according to each one's personal disposition and cooperation. (DH 1529; emphases added)

As history was to prove, these formal dogmatic decrees from Trent made the gulf separating Catholic and Protestant understandings of justification unbridgeable, even if some Protestants were more nuanced in their approach to this issue than others, and despite the fact that throughout this decree Trent puts the emphasis—indeed, the exclusive emphasis—on God's gratuitous initiative.[53] But the last sentence of that decree proved

53. It was Trent's stress on God's gratuity in justifying the sinner that prompted Hans Küng to assert that Trent and Karl Barth were in essential agreement: "[O]n the whole there is fundamental agreement between the theology of Barth and that of the Catholic Church." Hans Küng, *Justification: The Doctrine of Karl Barth and a Catholic Reflection*, trans. Thomas Collins, Edmund E. Tolk, and David Granskou (New York: Thomas Nelson & Sons, 1964), 282. The news rather unnerved Barth, who later said that Küng's book contained "razor-sharp arguments for the thesis that there is no essential difference between Reformation doctrine on the central point of justification as now interpreted and presented by me and the doctrine of the Roman church, properly understood. So far the book has not been repudiated by Catholic officialdom over there [in Rome]; on the contrary, it has been openly praised by several prominent figures. What is one to say to that? Has the millennium dawned, or is it just waiting round the next corner? How one would like to believe it!" Karl Barth, *How I Changed My Mind*, ed. John D. Godsey (Richmond, VA: John Knox Press, 1969), 59–70. Barth later wrote a letter to Küng which became the Foreword to a later edition of the book, in which Barth made this remarkable statement: "If what you have presented in Part II of this book is actually the teaching of the Roman Catholic Church, then I must certainly admit that my view of justification agrees with the Roman Catholic view.... If the things you cite from Scripture, from older and more recent Roman Catholic theology, from Denzinger and hence from the Tridentine text, do actually represent the teaching of your Church and are establishable as such, ... then, having twice gone to the Church of Santa Maria Maggiore in Trent to commune with the *genius loci*, I may very well have to hasten there a third time to make a contrite confession—'Fathers, I have sinned' " (in Küng, *Justification*, xx).

the sticking point. Although Luther avoided talk of Aristotle's four causes, he could have nothing to object to in this passage until the last sentence, especially the lines "each one receiving within himself *his own* justice," and "according to each one's personal disposition and *cooperation*."

Cooperation: around that word will center the major dispute between most Protestants and all Catholics. Although a discussion of the role of free will and grace will have to be postponed until the chapter specifically devoted to that complex topic, its relevance here comes from the fact that Trent's admission of true cooperation by the individual human then opens the way for the council to speak of *merit* in ways that made the gulf between Protestants and Catholics permanent. For inherent in the concept of merit is giving someone his due based on what he has earned or deserved.[54] But Paul retorts: "What do you have that you did not first receive?" (1 Cor. 4:7b). To which the only answer can be that of the *Catechism of the Catholic Church*: "With regard to God, there is no strict right to any merit on the part of man. Between God and us there is an immeasurable inequality, for we have received everything from him, our Creator" (*CCC* §2007).

Trent of course agrees, as we saw above (DH 1532). Indeed, on this point all parties are agreed, as they all claimed Augustine as their touchstone.[55] But Protestants generally, and Lutherans especially, excluded *on that basis* any talk of merit. For, despite the genuine value of the recent Finnish scholarship on Luther, there are important passages in the Wittenberg theologian's writings against which Trent seems clearly to have in mind, such as this crucial one:

54. Thus the *Catechism of the Catholic Church*: "The term 'merit' refers in general to the *recompense owed* by a community or a society for the action of one of its members, experienced either as beneficial or harmful, deserving reward or punishment. Merit is relative to the virtue of justice, in conformity with the principle of equality which governs it" (*CCC* §2006).

55. In fact, many of the fathers at Trent insisted that it would be dangerous to make Luther the explicit target of its decrees: "Not all Catholic theologians, especially members of the Augustinian Order, were convinced 'the Lutherans' were altogether wrong in their teaching on both Original Sin and justification, and at Trent the Augustinians' prior general, Girolamo Seripando, was among them. A few others believed that in this instance the differences were more a matter of words than substance. Most felt that the most urgent matter was the accusation that the church taught and subscribed to Pelagianism, the you-can-save-yourself-if-you-just-try-hard-enough version of Christianity." John W. O'Malley, *Trent: What Happened at the Council* (Cambridge, MA: Harvard University Press, 2013), 104; and the English Reginald Cardinal Pole agreed with Seripando: at one session he told the assembled bishops they should avoid saying "Luther said it. Therefore it is false" (ibid., 108).

The saints are always intrinsically sinners and correlatively always extrinsically justified. But the hypocrites say they are intrinsically just and accordingly always extrinsic sinners. But I say we are intrinsically [sinners], that is, [sin is] in us in this manner: in our eyes, in our self-assessment; but we are extrinsically [just], that is, before God and in *his* estimation. Therefore, we are extrinsically just when we are just not from ourselves or from our works, but we are just solely from God's estimation.[56]

Here Trent demurred. Relying again on key Pauline texts such as his admonition to the Corinthians that they should be "abounding in the work of the Lord, knowing that in the Lord your labor is not in vain" (1 Cor. 15:58); to the Colossians that in whatever "you do, you should work at it with all your heart," since, says Paul, "you know that you will receive an inheritance from the Lord as a reward" (Col. 3:23-24); and from the Letter to the Hebrews that "God is not so unjust as to overlook your work and the love which you showed for his sake" (Heb. 6:10), Trent issued the following relevant anathemas:

Canon 1. If anyone says that, without divine grace through Jesus Christ, man can be justified before God by his own works, whether they be done by his own natural powers or through the teaching of the law, let him be anathema. (DH 1551)

Canon 4. If anyone says that the free will of man, moved and awakened by God, in no way cooperates by an assent to God's awakening call,

56. Because of the importance of this passage, it seems best to cite it in its original Latin (following Luther's peculiar orthography): "Sancti Intrinsece sunt peccatores semper, ideo extrinsece Iustificantur semper. Hypocrite autem intrinsece sunt Iusti semper, ideo extrinsece sunt peccatores semper. Intrinsece dico, i.e., quomodo in nobis, in nostris oculis, in nostra estimatione sumus, Extrinsece autem, quomodo apud Deum et in reputatione eius sumus. Igitur extrinsece sumus Iusti, quando non ex nobis nec ex operibus, Sed ex sola Dei reputatione Iusti sumus." Luther, *WA* 56, 268.27–269.2; cited in Alister E. McGrath, *Justitia Dei: A History of the Christian Doctrine of Justification*, second edition (Cambridge: Cambridge University Press, 1998), 199; my translation, emphases added. Ironically, Luther is using here the very terminology Maurice Blondel was later to use to describe the position of the anti-Modernist *Thomists* of his day! The link between the two camps is the concern to preserve the gratuity of grace: in Luther's case the gratuity of the grace of justification *vis-à-vis* the *sinner;* in the manual Thomist case, the concern was to preserve the gratuity of grace in relation to *nature*, pure or otherwise.

through which he disposes and prepares himself to obtain the grace of justification; and that man cannot refuse his assent if he wishes, but that like a lifeless object he does nothing at all and is merely passive, let him be anathema. (DH 1554)

Canon 9. If anyone says that the sinner is justified by faith alone in the sense that nothing else is required by way of cooperation in order to obtain the grace of justification and that it is not at all necessary that he should be prepared and disposed by the movement of his will, let him be anathema. (DH 1559)

Canon 12. If anyone says that justifying faith is nothing else than confidence in the divine mercy that remits on account of Christ or that it is this confidence alone that justifies us, let him be anathema. (DH 1562)[57]

Canon 24. If anyone says that the justice received is not preserved and even increased before God through good works, but that such works are merely the fruits and the signs of the justification obtained and not also the cause of its increase, let him be anathema. (DH 1574)

Leaving aside the knotty question of which Protestant theologians fell under these anathemas, what is clearly at work in them is a presupposition regarding a legitimate and genuine human agency, one operating even after the fall of Adam. Although (as said above) that issue will have to be taken up in the chapter on original sin and the succeeding one on free will, this point at least is clear: once a kind of graced free will is granted to postlapsarian humans, Catholic teaching coheres, expressed most clearly (and recently) here:

57. Canon 12 was for Karl Barth the crux of the issue: "If there is any corresponding faithfulness of sinful man to the faithful God, it consists only in this confidence. As [the sinner] gives God this confidence, he finds himself justified, but not otherwise. That was what the Reformers maintained." Karl Barth, CD, IV/1, 626. But I think Barth is misinterpreting Trent here, whose focus was on that kind of confidence that led to pride and false boasting, as can be seen in the next canon: "Canon 13. If anyone says that, to attain the remission of sins, everyone must believe with certainty and without hesitation based on his own weakness and lack of disposition that his sins are forgiven, let him be anathema" (DH 1563). The confidence Trent is objecting to here, in other words, is one born out of total passivity, even a refusal to acknowledge *any* act of personal assent of faith to justification, which would indeed be an odd position for Protestants to adopt, since they believe in justification by *faith* alone. The "act of faith" is, after all, an act.

The merit of man before God in the Christian life arises from the fact that *God has freely chosen to associate man with the work of his grace.* The fatherly action of God is first on his own initiative, and then follows man's free acting through his collaboration, so that the merit of good works is to be attributed in the first place to the grace of God, then to the faithful. Man's merit, moreover, itself is due to God, for his good actions proceed in Christ, from the predispositions and assistance given by the Holy Spirit. (*CCC* §2008; italics in the original)

Based on this distinction, the *Catechism* can even speak in terms of "rights," a language we first found in the works of Matthias Scheeben in the first chapter:

Filial adoption, in making us partakers by grace in the divine nature, can bestow *true merit* on us as a result of God's gratuitous justice. This is our right by grace, the full right of love, making us "co-heirs" with Christ and worthy of obtaining "the promised inheritance of eternal life." The merits of our good works are gifts of divine goodness. "Grace has gone before us; now we are given what is due. . . . Our merits are God's gifts." . . . [For] *the charity of Christ is the source in us of all our merits* before God. (*CCC* §2009, 2011; italics in the original)[58]

The crux of the issue comes perhaps to its best expression in the *Joint Declaration on the Doctrine of Justification* officially issued by the Lutheran World Federation and the Roman Catholic Church (under the auspices of the Pontifical Council for Promoting Church Unity and approved by Pope John Paul II on October 31, 1999). For here we have two bodies, separated by their respective confessions, seeking to bridge the gap. Here is their conclusion:

When Catholics say that persons "cooperate" in preparing for and accepting justification by consenting to God's justifying action, they see such personal consent as itself an effect of grace, not as an action arising

---

58. The first internal quote is from Trent (DH 1546), the second from Augustine's *Sermon 298,* where the bishop of Hippo is commenting on this verse: "Henceforth there is laid up for me a crown of justice, which the Lord, the just judge, will award on that Day" (2 Tim. 4:8): "He will award it, after all, for [Paul's] merits, which is why we can say he is the just judge. But even here, do not start swaggering, because your merits are his gifts." St. Augustine, *Sermons* III/8 (273–305A), *The Works of Saint Augustine: A Translation for the 21st Century,* trans. Edmund Hill, O.P. (Hyde Park: NY: New City Press, 1994), 227.

from innate human abilities. According to Lutheran teaching, human beings are incapable of cooperating in their salvation because as sinners they actively oppose God and his saving action. Lutherans do not deny that a person can reject the workings of grace. When they emphasize that a person can only receive (mere passive) justification, they mean thereby to exclude any possibility of contributing to one's own justification, but do not deny that believers are fully involved personally in their faith, which is effected by God's word.[59]

Because this issue of cooperation will have to be postponed for later chapters, perhaps the ongoing conflict between imputed vs. imparted justification can be resolved at this early juncture, not by trying to reconcile the meaning of human freedom before and after justification (where Catholics and Protestants truly seem to differ), but by looking at a presupposition that both sides share, one that also goes back to Augustine and which held sway until the twentieth century and which has recently become ripe for overthrow: the *individualism* that simply assumes without further ado that justification pertains only to the one making the act of faith.[60]

This individualistic interpretation of justification in fact is intimately connected to the psychological interpretation of Paul's teaching on this

59. Lutheran World Federation and the Roman Catholic Church, *Joint Declaration on the Doctrine of Justification* (Grand Rapids, MI: Eerdmans, 2000), nos. 20, 21. The question has now become whether the division enunciated here is merely terminological or involves something more substantive. At least according to the Lutherans who signed on to this statement, differences on this point are only terminological: "In the doctrine of 'justification by faith alone,' a distinction but not a separation is made between justification itself and the renewal of one's way of life that *necessarily* follows from justification *and without which faith does not exist*" (ibid., no. 26). Correlatively, the Catholics make this point about good works: "According to Catholic understanding, good works, made possible by the grace and working of the Holy Spirit, contribute to growth in grace.... When Catholics affirm the 'meritorious' character of good works, they wish to say that, *according to biblical witness*, a reward in heaven is promised to these works. Their intention is to emphasize the responsibility of persons for their actions, not to contest the character of those works as gifts, or far less to deny that justification *always* remains the unmerited gift of grace" (ibid., no. 38; all emphases added)

60. Another argument for a revisitation and reconsideration of prior formulas is one best left to the Lutheran side, but is no less valid for that: "We have to bear in mind that there is also a justification by works based on the 'possession' of the doctrine of justification; this happens when justification is replaced by justification through possessing the right dogmatic formula." Edward Schlink, "The Ecumenical Character and Claim of the Augsburg Confession," in *The Augsburg Confession in Ecumenical Perspective*, ed. Harding Meyer, Lutheran World Federation Report 6/7 (Stuttgart: Kreuz Verlag, 1980), 21.

topic. This presupposition too was never directly addressed, let alone questioned, because from Augustine on it was assumed that Paul was speaking of himself in Romans 7 when he said that "I" cannot do the good that "I" want to do. When Augustine notoriously said that infants who died before receiving baptism go to hell, he was operating out of that same presupposition: that salvation pertains to individuals only, which turned baptism into a kind of celestial life-insurance policy *for the individual alone.*[61]

As we saw, the great appeal of a forensic view of justification is that it prevents boasting. According to its advocates, by refusing to admit merit in the economy of salvation, imputed justification keeps believers focused on God's unmerited mercies and not on their own paltry efforts to measure up to those mercies. But as soon as the individual notices that *he* has faith but his neighbor does not, a kind of "there but for the grace of God go I" attitude is bound to creep in, leading to a kind of hoarding of one's saved status. In other words, individualism makes the temptation to self-righteousness all but inevitable. But as (then Cardinal) Joseph Ratzinger pointed out, such an attitude of regarding salvation as applying solely to the individual is simply not Christian:

> We cannot start to set limits on God's behalf; *the very heart of the faith has been lost to anyone who supposes that it is only worthwhile, if it is, so to say, made worthwhile by the damnation of others.* Such a way of thinking, which finds the punishment of other people necessary, springs from not having inwardly accepted the faith; from loving only oneself and not God the Creator, to whom his creatures belong. That way of thinking would be like the attitude of those people who could not bear the workers who came last being paid a denarius like the rest; like the attitude of people who feel properly rewarded only if others have received less. This would be the attitude of the son who stayed at home, who could not bear the reconciling kindness of his father. It would be a hardening of our hearts, in which it would become clear that we were only looking

---

61. The first major assault in the twentieth century on the citadel of individualism was Henri de Lubac's *Catholicism: Christ and the Common Destiny of Man,* Foreword by Joseph Cardinal Ratzinger, trans. Lancelot C. Sheppard and Sr. Elizabeth Englund, O.C.D. (San Francisco: Ignatius Press, 1988), one line from which ("By revealing the Father and being revealed by him, Christ completes the revelation of man to himself" [339]) was adopted by Vatican II's Pastoral Constitution on the Modern World ("The truth is that only in the mystery of the incarnate Word does the mystery of man take on light" [*Gaudium et Spes* §22]). This book also received the high honor of being quoted directly in Benedict XVI's 2007 encyclical *Spe Salvi.*

out for ourselves and not looking for God; in which it would be clear that we did not love our faith, but merely bore it like a burden. . . . It is a basic element of the biblical message that the Lord died for all—being jealous of salvation is not Christian.[62]

After his election to the papacy in 2005 Pope Benedict made this perspective part of the official teaching of the Catholic Church, where he pointed out that Christian hope never deserves the name *Christian* hope unless it is hope for the salvation of others:

> Our lives are involved with one another; through innumerable interactions they are linked together. No one lives alone. No one sins alone. No one is saved alone. The lives of others continually spill over into mine: in what I think, say, do and achieve. And conversely, my life spills over into that of others: for better and for worse. So my prayer for another is not something extraneous to that person, something external, not even after death. . . . It is never too late to touch the heart of another, nor is it ever in vain. In this way we further clarify an important element of the Christian concept of hope. Our hope is always essentially also hope for others; only thus is it truly hope for me too. As Christians we should never limit ourselves to asking: how can I save myself? We should also ask: what can I do in order that others may be saved and that for them too the star of hope may rise? Then will I have done my utmost for my own personal salvation as well. (*Spe salvi* §48)

Paul admonished the Corinthians to recall the fact that unmerited grace *means* just that: unmerited, which itself precludes any hoarding: "What do you have that has not first been given to you? If then you received it, why do you boast as if it were not a gift?" (1 Cor. 4:7). In other words, if a Christian feels justified and thereby righteous as a pure gift, *why not imitate God and give it away?* This, after all, was Paul's attitude with the Jews: "For I could wish that I myself were accursed and cut off from Christ for the sake of my brethren, my kinsmen by race" (Rom. 9:3).[63] From these two verses Balthasar draws this conclusion:

---

62. Joseph Cardinal Ratzinger, *God Is Near Us: The Eucharist, the Heart of Life*, trans. Henry Taylor (San Francisco: Ignatius Press, 2003), 35–36; emphasis added.

63. This was also the attitude adopted by the Little Flower, as recounted in her remarkable autobiography: "One night, not knowing how to tell Jesus that I loved Him and how much I desired that He be everywhere loved and glorified, I was thinking with sorrow that

Here we confront the mystery of man's solidarity in sin. Every personal sin is also a community sin: both in the sense of impairing the community but also being caused, to some extent, by the community's sin. Far from circumscribing sin, it makes it weightier, putting new burdens of responsibility on the sinner. And since the effects of evil committed and good deeds left undone increase and multiply relentlessly, our debt is not paid off when our personal guilt is forgiven.[64]

But that way of putting things only gets at the reverse side of the justification, the photographic negative, as it were, of the light of God's grace. For in the last analysis, the gulf separating the imputed vs. the imparted views of justification can be positively resolved only in *Christology*. True, all humans are bound in the solidarity of sin: "For all have sinned and fallen short of the glory of God" (Rom. 3:23). But we are also bound in solidarity with Christ: "So, just as one trespass led to the condemnation of all, one act of righteousness leads to acquittal and life for all" (Rom. 5:18). In other words, Christ could not have redeemed the world if *he* had distinguished his sinlessness from the sin of the world, otherwise redemption would never had taken place: "For our sake God made him who knew no sin to be sin so that in him we might become the righteousness of God" (2 Cor. 5:21), from which principle Balthasar draws this conclusion:

[T]he just man, to the extent that he shares an active portion in the holiness of the Redeemer, also receives a more active portion in the task of bearing a guilt not his own, thereby sharing in the very work of redemption. This finally reaches the point where he can no longer distinguish whether he is suffering for his own sins or for that of others. For Christ himself, when he was hanging on the Cross, no longer wished to make this distinction either. He endured God's malediction against sin, suffering vicariously for us all. And, because of Christ, the sinner who wants to share in these sufferings can no longer make this distinction either. The true follower of Christ joins Christ in that darkness that is all the more bitter because he knows that he can never suffer alongside of Christ. No,

He could never receive in hell a single act of love. So I told God that to please Him I would willingly consent to find myself plunged into hell, so that He might be eternally loved in that place of blasphemy." Thérèse de Lisieux, *The Story of a Soul*, trans. Robert J. Edmonson (Brewster, MA: Paraclete Press, 2006), 122. Her relevance for a Catholic-Lutheran *rapprochement* will be taken up at the end of this chapter.

64. Balthasar, *Barth*, 375.

this suffering highlights how deeply bound he is in solidarity with all his fellow sinners, who are jointly responsible for the Cross of Christ.[65]

As Chiara Lubich (the founder of the Focolare Movement) once said in a lecture on those attachments that hinder us from following the path of Christ: since everything is a gift from God, since all that we "possess" is really but a "loan" lent to us in fiduciary trust, what we must do is give it all back to God. If God really wants us to keep a particular gift, then it will come back to us. But if not, as she so memorably said, *throw it away.*

N. T. Wright gets at this same point by using the analogy of geocentrism vs. heliocentrism in astronomy. The New Perspectivists, he claims, interpret Paul in the Copernican manner, whereas his critics are stuck in a Ptolemaic worldview: "The theological equivalent of supposing that the sun goes round the earth is the belief that the whole of Christian truth *is all about me and my salvation.* ... Again and again the writers, from a variety of backgrounds, have assumed, taken it for granted, that the central question of all is 'What must I do to be saved?' or (Luther's way of putting it), 'How can I find a gracious God?' or 'How can I enter a right relationship with God?'"[66] But that cannot be right; or at least it cannot be the whole truth. For Wright, God's purposes go far beyond individual salvation:

> God is rescuing us from the shipwreck of the world, not so that we can sit back and put our feet up in his company, but so that we can be part of his plan to remake the world. *We* are in orbit around *God and his purposes*, not the other way around. If the Reformation tradition had treated the Gospels as equally important to the Epistles, this mistake might never have happened. But it has, and we must deal with it. The earth, and we with it, go round the sun of God and his cosmic purposes.[67]

65. Balthasar, *Barth*, 375.

66. N. T. Wright, *Justification: God's Plan and Paul's Vision* (Downers Grove, IL: IVP Academic, 2009), 23.

67. Wright, *Justification*, 24; Wright's italics. Readers might be reminded here of one of Wittgenstein's journal entries: "The spring which flows gently and limpidly in the Gospels seems to have *froth* on it in Paul's Epistles. Or that is how it seems to *me*. Perhaps it is just my own impurity which reads turbidness into them; for why shouldn't this impurity be able to pollute what is limpid? But to me it's as though I saw human passion here, something like pride or anger, which is not in tune with the humility of the Gospels. It's as though he *is* insisting here on his own person, *and doing so moreover as a religious gesture*, something which is foreign to the Gospel. I want to ask—and may this be no blasphemy—'What might Christ have said to Paul?' But a fair rejoinder to that would be: What business is that of

Barth too introduces a similar universalist point of view; but his is more grounded in Christology than in cosmology, although of course the two viewpoints are hardly antithetical. For Barth saw that Christ's atonement on the cross was the real source of justification. So, far from serving as a free-standing doctrine in Protestant dogmatics, justification must be grounded in the person and work of Christ. Although he did not adduce the same arguments as Stendahl, Sanders, and Wright, Barth does sound rather like a New Perspectivist *avant la lettre* here in this startling passage:

> The strength of Reformation theology is the directness with which it tried to place itself under Scripture. . . . But this very strength was perhaps its weakness—a too hasty identification of the biblical situation with its own, and therefore as a result of its own impetuous understanding of the present a failure to see many of the nuances [of the past], . . . or, conversely, because of its impetuous exposition of the texts, a lack of many of the necessary nuances and differentiations in its judgment of the present. . . . Certainly in Galatians (not to speak of other parts of Paul's writings and of Scripture generally) there were and are many more things to be discovered than what Luther discovered then. Certainly there was and is much more to be said of the Roman Church and Roman theology both then and since than what the Reformers said then. . . . We do not need to consider ourselves bound . . . by their attitude.[68]

The real problem Barth had with "pure" Reformed theology on this issue stems from his opinion that it was phrased too much in exclusively negative terms, lest the justified sinner "possess" anything that might avail before God. He never denied the value of God's "no" to boasting, but he recognized that something was lost if justification was not also expressed in positive terms, that is, as touching on the work of Christ. So he says: "But we must now go deeper. We have described faith as the humility which involves necessarily the exclusion of works. In so doing we have obviously described it in its negative form."[69] But if that is *all* that can be said, then not only is something lost, but something is also

---

yours? Attend to making *yourself* more honorable! In your present state you are quite incapable of understanding what may be the truth here." Ludwig Wittgenstein, *Culture and Value*, trans. Peter Winch (Chicago: University of Chicago Press, 1980), 30.

68. Barth, *CD* IV/1, 622–23. A few pages later Barth says of the Reformers: "They did not have the unequivocal backing of Paul for all their statements" (626).

69. Barth, *CD* IV/1, 628.

utterly distorted in preaching: "One thing is certain, that as an abstract admission of human weakness and nothingness such statements cannot have any meaning as a self-confession of the faith. . . . That we are good for nothing is true, but it is not so relevant that the confession of this truth has independent significance."[70]

What *does* have "independent significance" for Barth is Christ. In Christ Barth can now speak of the positive side of justification, a positivity that, among its other virtues, gets the debate off the fate of the individual believer and on to God's intentions for the world at large, as we see in this lyrical passage:

> [T]he self-demonstration of the justified man to which faith clings is the crucified and risen Jesus Christ who lives as the author and recipient and revealer of the justification of all men. It is in him that the judgment of God is fulfilled and the pardon of God pronounced on all men. . . . It happened that in the humble obedience of the Son he took our place, he took to himself our sins and death in order to make an end of them in his death, and that in so doing he did the right. *He* became the new and righteous man. It also happened that in his resurrection from the dead he was confirmed and recognized and revealed by God the Father as [the new and righteous man] for us and all men. . . . There is not one for whose sin and death he did not die, whose sin and death he did not remove and obliterate on the cross. . . . There is not one to whom this was not addressed as his justification in his resurrection from the dead. . . . There is not one who is justified in any other way than in him—because it is in him and only in him that an end, a bonfire, is made of man's sin and death, because it is in him and only in him that man's sin and death are the old thing which has passed away, because it is in him and only in him that the right has been done which is demanded of man. . . . There is not one whose peace with God has not been made. . . . There is not one of whom it is demanded that he should make and maintain this peace for himself, or who is permitted to act as though he himself were the author of it, having to make it himself and to maintain it in his own strength. There is not one for whom he has not done everything in his death and received everything in his resurrection from the dead. Not one. That is what faith believes.[71]

70. Barth, *CD* IV/1, 628.

71. Barth, *CD* IV/1, 629-30; emphasis added. For biblical support of this lyricism, see

Note the fascinating fact that these reconsiderations of the traditional Protestant understanding of justification by faith have come, for the most part, from Protestant scholars, prompting at least two Evangelicals to wonder out loud whether the Reformation is over.[72] But also as was noted above, Catholic theologians too have been doing their own reassessment, prompted in part, of course, by developments in twentieth-century Protestant theology, starting with Barth but also including the New Perspectivists. Such Catholic attention is no doubt inevitable, given the immense ecumenical implications of Protestant reconsideration; but that portion of Catholic reassessment can obviously be only reactive, a response to Protestants working on the dilemmas of their own tradition.

Perhaps of greater value is the influence that a certain Catholic has exerted on this debate who approached this issue anew without any thought for its ecumenical implications and, indeed, without any knowledge of Protestant theology at all. I am referring to St. Thérèse of Lisieux (1873–97), a pious Carmelite nun who had been raised in the hothouse atmosphere of late-nineteenth-century bourgeois French Catholicism and who became, after her death of tuberculosis at the age of 24, not only the most popular Catholic saint of the twentieth century but also was named a Doctor of the Church by Pope John Paul II in 1997. Her relevance to this debate can be especially seen in the "Act of Oblation to Merciful Love," which she wrote two years before her death, part of which says, in a prayer to God:

> After earth's exile, I hope to go and enjoy You in my homeland (*patrie*), but I do not want to lay up merits for heaven. I want to work for Your love alone with the one purpose of pleasing You, consoling your Sacred Heart, and saving souls who will love you eternally. In the evening of this life, I shall appear before You with empty hands, for I do not ask You, Lord, to count my works. All our justice is stained in Your eyes. I wish, then, to be clothed in Your own justice and to receive from Your love the eternal possession of yourself. I want no other Throne, no other Crown, but You, my Beloved![73]

---

inter alia: "Jesus Christ, the Just One, . . . is the atoning sacrifice for our sins, and not for ours only but also for the sins of the whole world" (1 John 2:1c–2).

72. See Mark A. Noll and Carolyn Nystrom, *Is the Reformation Over? An Evangelical Assessment of Contemporary Roman Catholicism* (Grand Rapids, MI: Baker Academic, 2005). See too *The Catholicity of the Reformation*, ed. Carl E. Braaten and Robert W. Jenson (Grand Rapids, MI: Eerdmans, 1996).

73. Thérèse de Lisieux, "Offrande à l'Amour miséricordieux," in *Story of a Soul: The Auto-*

This theme of either renouncing works or claiming she never had them to begin with crops up again and again in her writings, especially in remarks she made toward the end of her life, collected in a book known as the *Novissima Verba* and translated into English as *Last Conversations*, such as here: "I cannot rely upon anything, not on one single work of mine, for security." And here: "I am very happy to go to heaven very soon, but when I think of these words of God: 'My reward is with me, to render to each one according to his works' [Rev. 22:12], I tell myself that He will be very much embarrassed in my case. I haven't any works! He will not be able to reward me 'according to my works.' Well, then, He will reward me according to *His* works."[74] Basing himself on these and similar texts, Balthasar comes to this conclusion:

> Luther, brought face to face with Scripture, came to conclusions that might be considered remotely parallel to those of Thérèse: the personal certainty of salvation, the stress upon trusting *fiducia* as opposed to ascetic practices and other good works, the clear-cut preference for New Testament mercy as against Old Testament justice. And, in this sense, and once all due reservations have been made, the "little way" can be regarded as the Catholic answer to the demands and questions raised by Luther.[75]

---

biography of St. Thérèse de Lisieux, trans. John Clarke, O.C.D. (Washington, DC: Institute of Carmelite Studies, 1976), 277; original italics removed. Fittingly, this quotation closes the section on merit in the *Catechism of the Catholic Church* (#2011). One author claims that the *Catechism* uses these words "to express the church's understanding of the role of human effort and the role of God's grace in our sanctification." Joseph F. Schmidt, *Everything Is Grace: The Life and Way of St. Therese of Lisieux* (Jamesville, MD: The Word Among Us Press, 2007), 43. I thank Fr. Ed White for drawing my attention to this work.

74. The first quotation comes from the so-called Yellow Notebook, consisting of remarks made by the saint to her superior while in the convent infirmary trying to recover from tuberculosis, in Thérèse de Lisieux, *Last Conversations*, trans. John Clarke, O.C.D. (Washington, DC: Institute of Carmelite Studies, 1977), 137, dated August 6, 1897; the second from ibid., 43, dated May 15, 1897.

75. Hans Urs von Balthasar, *Two Sisters in the Spirit: Thérèse of Lisieux & Elizabeth of the Trinity*, trans. Donald Nichols and Anne Elizabeth Englund (San Francisco: Ignatius Press, 1992), 95–96; see also 243. The Irish theologian Thomas Norris comes to a similar conclusion: "Thérèse's theological audacity is reason to hope that the remaining difficulties on the road to unity between Lutherans and Catholics are far from insurmountable." Thomas Norris, "Bringing Martin Luther and Thérèse of Lisieux into Conversation," in *Inter-Church Relations: Developments and Perspectives, A Tribute to Bishop Anthony Farquhar*, ed. Brendan Leahy (Dublin: Veritas, 2008), 154–63, here 161. Another voice who joins in celebrating this "Lutheran

This remarkable *rapprochement* from both sides does not of course mean we have arrived at the eschaton of Protestant-Catholic reunion—far from it. There is first of all the question of the various denominations' *confessions*, official statements of belief stemming from the sixteenth and seventeenth centuries, which were deliberately formulated to mark off confessional differences.[76] Obviously, for those who insist that these confessions continue to bind *in the same way when they were first formulated*, genuine reunion—including recognition of each denomination's structures of authority and the sharing of the Lord's Supper together—is, to that extent, excluded.[77]

Carmelite" is Conrad de Meester, *With Empty Hands: The Message of St. Thérèse of Lisieux*, trans. Mary Seymour (Washington, DC: Institute of Carmelite Studies, 2002). Another scholar agrees: "This intimacy, a kind of Christ-in-me such as that of which St. Paul writes, . . . was that [to which] Thérèse gave primacy. This is Lutheran territory." Thomas R. Nevin, *Thérèse of Lisieux: God's Gentle Warrior* (Oxford: Oxford University Press, 2006), 296. This collective assessment takes on added resonance if the Finnish interpretation of Luther is correct.

76. The terminological distinction between ancient "creed" and denominational "confession" does not necessarily imply lack of binding power within each denomination, as Jaroslav Pelikan points out here: "When descendants of the Protestant Reformation use the word 'creed,' this is the designation for one or another of 'the three creeds, Nicene Creed, Athanasius's Creed, and that which is commonly called the Apostles' Creed.' . . . But when Lutherans, Anglicans, or Presbyterians use the word 'confession,' or even 'the confessions,' that usually means the particular confession or confessions of their own church or branch of Protestantism. . . . Specifically in the case of Lutherans, Anglicans, and Presbyterians, 'confession' refers to *The Augsburg Confession* of 1530 (and the entire *Book of Concord* of 1580) for Lutherans, or to *The Thirty-Nine Articles of the Church of England* of 1571 for Anglicans, . . . or to *The Westminster Confession of Faith* of 1647 for Presbyterians. All three of these 'confessions' are products of the Reformation era." Jaroslav Pelikan, *Credo: Historical and Theological Guide to Creeds and Confessions of Faith in the Christian Tradition* (New Haven, CT: Yale University Press, 2003), 457–58. These various confessions were of course more binding on the laity when the principle of *cuius regio, eius religio* held sway; but with the breakdown of the confessional state they usually operated only to bind seminaries and prospective clergy. More to our point, the confessions (at least the Lutheran ones) do not speak univocally on the matter of imputed vs. imparted justification. In particular there is a noticeable tension between the *Apology for the Augsburg Confession* and the *Book of Concord*: "With these statements about justification as making righteous and as regeneration, justification . . . is no longer taught merely as a reality in the judgment of God, but as a change of man, as a change of man also in man's judgment. As faith 'renews and changes the heart' [*Apology* IV, 125], so justification is also regeneration, that is, renewal and transformation of the sinner." Edmund Schlink, *Theology of the Lutheran Confessions*, trans. Paul F. Koehneke and Herbert J. A. Bouman (Philadelphia: Muhlenberg Press, 1961), 106–7.

77. Michael Horton is particularly insistent on this point: "Since Reformed views are defined by our confessions, especially on such a crucial doctrine, positioning departures

It does not fall within the compass of this chapter to present any ecumenical proposals that could move Protestant-Catholic dialogue along, or to examine the specific teachings on justification in the various confessions, except perhaps to note that history moves on and that, in this sublunary world of ours, change is the rule of life and Heraclitus rules as king. Only history can say whether trends *internally* generated in Protestant and Catholic theology, which have broken down more hardened views of the past, will prove crucial to the cause of church unity.[78] But at least this is clear from the preceding analysis of the *concept* of justification: it cannot serve as a stand-alone doctrine but entails, upon closer analysis, a set of dynamic antinomies, the pursuit of which leads both to greater clarity and (so the fervent Christian prays) to greater understanding of the position of each side. Which, even if it does not lead directly to full, visible church unity, can only be for the benefit of all the churches.

[from them] as progress might convey the impression that defenders of the confessional view are merely repristinating a tradition rather than confessing a faith that is as exegetically defensible today as it was in the sixteenth century." Michael Horton, "Traditional Reformed View," in *Justification: Five Views*, ed. James K. Beilby and Paul Rhodes Eddy (Downers Grove, IL: IVP Academic, 2011), 83.

78. The Dominican theologian Richard Schenk takes a rather jaundiced view of the situation, primarily because of all the issues skirted by the Joint Statement and as also reflected by the Open Letter penned by numerous Lutheran theologians in Germany who also lamented all the issues left unaddressed by the Joint Statement. These would include the different understanding of identical terms like *simul justus et peccator* and concupiscence, the question of merit, the abiding passivity of the justified sinner, the role of good works. See Richard Schenk, O.P., "The Unsettled German Discussions of Justification: Abiding Differences and Ecumenical Blessings," *Dialogue: A Journal of Theology*, Vol. 44, No. 2 (Summer 2005): 152–63.

CHAPTER 3

Evolution and Original Sin

Our life is a false nature—'tis not in
  The harmony of things,—this hard decree,
This ineradicable taint of sin,
  This boundless upas, this all-blasting tree,
  Whose root is earth, whose leaves and branches be
The skies which rain their plagues on men like dew—
  Disease, death, bondage, all the woes we see—
And worse, the woes we see not, which throb through
The immedicable soul, with heart-aches ever new.

Lord Byron, "Childe Harold's Pilgrimage"

Strictly speaking, the topic of evolution (a doctrine taught in biology) does not belong in a discussion of original sin (a theological doctrine).[1] But the days are long gone when a theologian can build a *cordon sanitaire* around the first three chapters of Genesis or around the fifth chapter of Romans and treat them on their own terms only, without regard for the deliverances of evolutionary biology.

In what follows, I shall be taking these two operative principles for granted and will not argue for them on their own terms (they are, in other words, formally similar to the axioms of Euclidean geometry: *assumed, not proven*): 1) evolution (defined here as "descent with modification") is true; and 2) a "literal" interpretation of a biblical text does *not* refer to the way fundamentalists and journalists use the term, but means an interpreta-

---

1. Especially when speaking of evolution, I am of course using the word *doctrine* here only in its generic meaning, to refer to a required teaching in a particular discipline.

tion *governed by the intent of the biblical authors*, as defined by scientific exegesis of biblical texts.

I define evolution as "descent with modification" because that is the one aspect of evolution that has been massively confirmed by empirical data, primarily genetics (with a modest assist from the fossil record): it refers to the fact that all life currently occupying this planet descended from a single cell roughly three and half billion years ago whose progeny showed slight modifications, leading to increased complexity in life forms, a thesis nicely summarized here:

> Whatever prompted life to begin, it happened just once. That is the most extraordinary fact in biology, perhaps the most extraordinary fact we know. Everything that has ever lived, plant or animal, dates its beginnings from the same primordial twitch. At some point in an unimaginably distant past some little bag of chemicals fidgeted to life. It absorbed some nutrients, gently pulsed, had a brief existence. This much may have happened before, perhaps many times. But this ancestral packet did something additional and extraordinary: it cleaved itself and produced an heir. A tiny bundle of genetic material passed from one living thing to another, and has never stopped moving since. It was the moment of creation for us all. Biologists sometimes call it the Big Birth.[2]

No doubt some people, and not just fundamentalists, regard this scenario as very nearly preposterous.[3] But surely the *fact* that a single cell can eventually

---

2. Bill Bryson, *A Short History of Nearly Everything* (New York: Broadway Books, 2003), 293–94. As Bryson notes, whether single self-reproducing cells formed multiple times but failed to leave behind successful progeny cannot be known (there obviously being no fossil record available for such simple, boneless life forms). But the fact *that* all life now living on our teeming planet did come from a single cell billions of years ago can be established in a number of ways, such as this one: "We are all the result of a single genetic trick handed down from generation to generation [for] nearly four billion years, to such an extent that you can take a fragment of human genetic instruction, patch it into a faulty yeast cell, and the yeast cell will put it to work as if it were its own. In a very real sense, it is its own" (ibid., 294). I ignore here the question of divine agency in the formation of this first self-reproducing life-form, as being irrelevant to the question of original sin. For an account of these wider issues (which pertain more to philosophical or natural theology than to strictly theological topics like original sin), and one moreover that eschews the rigmarole of intelligent-design theory (indeed the author is a convinced Darwinian), see: Robert J. Asher, *Evolution and Belief: Confessions of a Religious Paleontologist* (Cambridge: Cambridge University Press, 2012).

3. It is not so much the idea of descent with modification that is so puzzling as it is

develop into a complex lifeform cannot be so absurd as to be inherently impossible. For everyone now reading this sentence began *his or her own life* as a single cell. The famous geneticist J. B. S. Haldane (1892–1964) drolly put it this way, in an anecdote recounted by Richard Dawkins (b. 1941):

> The irascible genius J. B. S. Haldane, who did so much else besides being one of the three leading architects of neo-Darwinism, was once challenged by a lady after a public lecture. It's a word-of-mouth anecdote . . . but this is approximately how the exchange went:
>
> > *Evolution sceptic:* Professor Haldane, even given the billions of years that you say were available for evolution, I simply cannot believe it is possible to go from a single cell to a complicated human body, with its trillions of cells organized into bones and muscles and nerves, a heart that pumps without ceasing for decades, miles and miles of blood vessels and kidney tubules, and a brain capable of thinking and talking and feeling.
> >
> > *JBSH:* But madam, you did it yourself. And it only took nine months.[4]

---

the extraordinarily early date for the first appearance of life that baffles, since that seems to exclude the idea of randomness in the formation of the first self-replicating molecule: "But the present date [for the start of life on earth] of 3.85 billion years is stunningly early. Earth's surface didn't become *solid* until about 3.9 billion years ago" (Bryson, *Short History*, 293). Darwin himself wisely left to one side the question of the origin of life in his book *On the Origin of Species*, especially after experiments had shown that life does not spontaneously arise (as had been previously thought) from the rot of dead animal corpses. But while Darwin was right to eschew that particular problem as being irrelevant to his purposes, the enigma still remains and awaits an answer: how *did* life first arise and why so early? To which one agnostic with no interest in providing a religious answer says this: "In such a case, some scientists might choose to turn to religion for an answer. Others, however, myself included, would attempt to sort out the surviving less probable scientific explanations in the hope of selecting one that was still more likely than the remainder. We are far from that state now." Robert Shapiro, *Origins: A Skeptic's Guide to the Creation of Life on Earth* (New York: Simon & Schuster/Bantam Books, 1987), 130. The dogmatic theologian can of course take all this in stride; for as Thomas teaches: "Some things are contingent by nature. Divine providence does not impose necessity on things to the exclusion of contingency. . . . Whatever divine providence decrees shall happen inevitably and through necessity, happens inevitably and through necessity. Whatever it intends to happen contingently, happens contingently." Thomas Aquinas, *ST* I, q. 22, a. 4, *sed contra* and *respondeo*. In other words, evolution, very much including the evolution of man, can be as much of a fluke as some claim. But that fluke does not escape the providence of God.

4. Richard Dawkins, *The Greatest Show on Earth: The Evidence for Evolution* (New York:

Evolution of course also entails certain other facts about the world that will also be assumed in this chapter without further argument for them. Indeed many of these facts were discoveries made not only before but also after the publication of Charles Darwin's *On the Origin of Species* in 1859, but were in any case indispensable for its formulation, specifically: 1) the age of the earth (since evolution requires a vast swath of time in which to operate), now estimated to be roughly 4.5 billion years old; 2) the ability of breeders of pigeons and dogs to cull undesired traits by preventing reproduction of offspring with those traits and allowing only those specimens to reproduce that have the desired traits (a process known as "artificial selection"); and of course 3) the fossil record, which, broadly speaking, shows a trend from simplicity to complexity with each succeeding geologic age. All of these too are indisputable facts and will be assumed without further arguments for them in what follows.

But other facts, as well, must be assumed. Because of the immense heuristic power of Darwin's explanation for evolution, his theory launched scientists into wholly new and previously unimagined areas of research, beginning of course with genetics but also including recent developments in geology, specifically the discovery of plate tectonics, with its notion of a fluid earth.[5] These later developments, too, were crucial to establishing Darwinism on a new footing, a new footing it sorely needed; for in fact

---

Free Press, 2009), 211. This reality, which no one can deny, has obvious relevance to the debate on abortion; but neither Haldane nor Dawkins seems to have been aware of the ethical implications of their assertions. But still the fact remains: nothing we know at the present is more complicated than the human brain, yet we all began life as a single cell: "The bottom line is that life is amazing and gratifying, perhaps even miraculous, but hardly impossible—as we repeatedly attest with our own modest existences" (Bryson, *Short History*, 291).

5. The notion of plate tectonics took most of the twentieth century to gain acceptance. First proposed in 1908 by an amateur American geologist, Frank Bursley Taylor, and picked up by a German meteorologist, Alfred Wegener, in 1912, the theory was widely rejected until geologists first accepted the idea of a molten core at the center of the earth and oceanographers noticed vast mountain formations at the bottom of the seas when transoceanic cables were laid, so that by 1964 most geologists were convinced of the theory: "A symposium of many of the most important figures in the field was convened in London under the auspices of the Royal Society in 1964, and suddenly, it seemed, everyone was a convert. The Earth, the meeting agreed, was a mosaic of interconnected segments whose various stately jostlings account for much of the planet's surface behavior" (Bryson, *Short History*, 180). This history is worth noting because of the way it reinforced the findings and theories of evolutionary biology: "Animal fossils repeatedly turned up on opposite sides of oceans that were clearly too wide to swim. How . . . did marsupials travel from South America to Australia? How did identical snails turn up in Scandinavia and New England?" (ibid., 174).

Darwinism had fallen into a remarkable decline around 1900. But with the addition of these later discoveries, genetics especially, the initial heuristic power of early Darwinism became the basis for what is now called the neo-Darwinian synthesis.[6]

Presumably, these were the findings (and they are massive) that Pope John Paul II had in mind when he said, in a famous message to the Pontifical Academy of Sciences in 1996, that evolution can no longer be regarded as merely hypothetical but stands on well-established factual grounds: "It is indeed remarkable that this theory [of evolution] has been progressively accepted by researchers following a series of discoveries in various fields of knowledge. The convergence, neither sought nor fabricated, of the results of work that was conducted independently is in itself a significant argument in favor of this theory."[7]

So this is the first axiom of this chapter: that evolution is true, that all life currently alive on this planet ultimately derived from a single, self-replicating cell around 3.5 to 3.8 billion years ago. The second axiom asserts that the first three chapters of Genesis and the fifth chapter of Romans

6. "From the high point of the 1870s and 1880s, when 'Darwinism' had become virtually synonymous with evolution itself, the selection theory had slipped in popularity to such an extent that by 1900 its opponents were convinced it would never recover. Evolution itself remained unquestioned, but an increasing number of biologists preferred mechanisms other than selection to explain *how* it occurred." Peter J. Bowler, *Evolution: The History of an Idea*, revised edition (Berkeley, CA: University of California Press, 1989), 246. Darwinism's great challenge at the turn of the century was the problem of "blending," which was only resolved with the discovery of Mendelian genetics: "A Scottish engineer, Fleeming Jenkin, considered the problem and noted an important flaw in Darwin's argument. Darwin believed that any beneficial trait that arose in one generation would be passed on to subsequent generations, thus strengthening the species. Jenkin pointed out that a favorable trait in one parent wouldn't become dominant in succeeding generations, but in fact would be diluted through blending. If you pour whiskey into a tumbler of water, you don't make the whiskey stronger; you make it weaker. . . . In the same way, any favorable trait introduced by one parent would be successively watered down by subsequent matings until it ceased to be apparent at all. Thus Darwin's theory was not a recipe for change, but for constancy. Lucky flukes might arise from time to time, but they would soon vanish under the general impulse to bring everything back to a stable mediocrity. If natural selection were to work, some alternative, unconsidered mechanism was required. Unknown to Darwin and everyone else, eight hundred miles away in a tranquil corner of Middle Europe a retiring monk name Gregor Mendel was coming up with the solution." Bryson, *Short History*, 390–91.

7. Pope John Paul II, "Message to the Pontifical Academy of Sciences on Evolution," delivered on October 22, 1996, published in *Origins*, Vol. 26, No. 22 (November 14, 1996): 349–52, here, 351.

must be interpreted "literally," but only as that term is understood by the Catholic magisterium (in other words, *not* as that term is understood by either fundamentalists or journalists); and by magisterium in this context I am referring specifically to this important passage in Pope Pius XII's encyclical *Divino Afflante Spiritu*, promulgated on the feast of St. Jerome, September 30, 1943:

35. What is the literal sense of a passage is not always as obvious in the speeches and writings of the ancient authors of the East, as it is in the works of our own time. For what they wished to express is not to be determined by the rules of grammar and philology alone, nor solely by the context; the interpreter must, as it were, go back wholly in spirit to those remote centuries of the East and with the aid of history, archaeology, ethnology, and other sciences, *accurately determine what modes of writing*, so to speak, the authors of that ancient period would be likely to use, and in fact *did use*.

36. For the ancient peoples of the East, in order to express their ideas, did not always employ those forms or kinds of speech which we use today; but rather those used by the men of their times and countries. What those exactly were the commentator cannot determine as it were in advance, but only after a careful examination of the ancient literature of the East. The investigation, carried out, on this point, during the past forty or fifty years with greater care and diligence than ever before, has more clearly shown *what forms of expression were used in those far off times, whether in poetic description* or in the formulation of laws and rules of life or *in recording the facts and events of history*. The same inquiry has also shown the special preeminence of the people of Israel among all the other ancient nations of the East in their mode of compiling history, both by reason of its antiquity and by reasons of the faithful record of the events; qualities which may well be attributed to the gift of divine inspiration and to *the peculiar religious purpose of biblical history*.

37. Nevertheless no one, who has a correct idea of biblical inspiration, will be surprised to find, even in the Sacred Writers, as in other ancient authors, certain fixed ways of expounding and narrating, certain definite idioms, *especially of a kind peculiar to the Semitic tongues, so-called approximations, and certain hyperbolical modes of expression, nay, at times, even paradoxical, which even help to impress the ideas more deeply on the*

mind. For of the modes of expression which, among ancient peoples, and especially those of the East, human language used to express its thought, none is excluded from the Sacred Books, provided the way of speaking adopted in no wise contradicts the holiness and truth of God, as, with his customary wisdom, the Angelic Doctor already observed in these words: "In Scripture divine things are presented to us in the manner which is in common use amongst men." For as the substantial Word of God became like to men in all things, "except sin," so the words of God, expressed in human language, are made like to human speech in every respect, except error. In this consists that "condescension" of the God of providence, which St. John Chrysostom extolled with the highest praise and repeatedly declared to be found in the Sacred Books.

38. Hence the Catholic commentator, in order to comply with the present needs of biblical studies, in explaining the Sacred Scripture and in demonstrating and proving its immunity from all error, should also make a prudent use of this means, *determine*, that is, *to what extent the manner of expression or the literary mode adopted by the sacred writer may lead to a correct and genuine interpretation*; and let him be convinced that this part of his office cannot be neglected without serious detriment to Catholic exegesis. Not infrequently—to mention only one instance—when some persons reproachfully charge the Sacred Writers with some historical error or inaccuracy in the recording of facts, on closer examination it turns out to be nothing else than those customary modes of expression and narration peculiar to the ancients, which used to be employed in the mutual dealings of social life and which in fact were sanctioned by common usage.[8]

Drawing especially on the italicized lines, the following conclusions can be drawn: First, what modern readers might think of as the literal reading of a particular passage based on a superficial reading might not at all correspond to what the ancient author might have meant to convey; rather readers must first travel back in time, as it were, and attempt to get inside the worldview of the ancient writers (no. 35). Second, the question of *genre* (what Pius calls "forms of expression") is crucial; for it makes all the difference in the world if the ancient author is using *poetic expression*

8. Pope Pius XII, *Promotion of Biblical Studies: Divino Afflante Spiritu*, trans. National Catholic Welfare Conference (Boston: Daughters of St. Paul, 1943); all emphases added.

in recounting past events, especially given the ancient author's overriding purpose in displaying what the pope calls "the peculiar religious purpose of biblical history" (no. 36).[9] Third, the sacred writers were more concerned to achieve certain rhetorical effects than to narrate history in the manner of modern documentary historians, or even of Thucydides (no. 37). Finally, Catholic exegetes must seek to glean the intention of the authors by their *literary modes of expression* in order to come to an accurate interpretation (no. 38).[10]

The application of these principles can be seen by taking the example of the creation account in Genesis 1, where the order of the six days of creation goes as follows:

First day: creation of light
Second day: creation of the heavens and water
Third day: creation of land and vegetation
Fourth day: creation of the bodies of light (sun, moon, stars)

9. An offbeat example from modern times will explain the importance of genre. On October 30, 1938, Orson Welles adapted H. G. Wells's novel *War of the Worlds* as a radio play. The first two-thirds of the one-hour broadcast took the form of simulated news bulletins about an imminent invasion of Martians, which some listeners took to be a newscast about a real event; and they were especially prone to be duped if they had missed the "framing device" of the opening announcement saying the subsequent hour would be a radio play. As it happens, the broadcast took place without commercial breaks, as would also happen with breaking news. In other words, for those who did not know the genre, the verisimilitude of the broadcast prompted the credulous to believe an alien invasion was in progress. A biblical parallel would be the book of Jonah: assuming, as most biblical scholars now do, that this book is a kind of fictional saga, it constitutes a category mistake to wonder how a real man could survive in the belly of a whale for three days.

10. One of Thomas Aquinas's great innovations was to insist that if a biblical author used metaphorical language or other literary tropes, that belonged to the literal meaning. Previously, most patristic writers took it for granted that if, for example, the Psalmist says "the rivers clap their hands," that must belong to the spiritual sense of the text, since rivers don't "literally" have hands to clap. But Thomas moved the meaning of literal away from the sentence to the author's intention, a shift that would later bear fruit in *Divino Afflante Spiritu*: "Thomas's moving of metaphor into the literal sense was a distant harbinger of the inclusion of various literary and narrative structures within the literal sense, which allows for a more spiritual sense to be found not beyond but within the literal sense itself. For example, John's story of the cure of the man born blind is surely, at the symbolic level, which is *part of the intention of the text*, a catechesis on baptism. And the fourth evangelist surely is capable of encoding more than one meaning in the literal sense of the text." George T. Montague, *Understanding the Bible: A Basic Introduction to Biblical Interpretation* (New York: Paulist Press, 1997), 64; italics in the original.

Fifth day: creation of the creatures of heaven and the waters (birds, fish)

Sixth day: creation of land life (animals), including male and female humans

The oddity here, at least from the viewpoint of modern cosmogenesis, is that the creation of (presumably phototropic) plants (the third day) comes *before* the creation of the sun (the fourth day), an obvious impossibility from an evolutionary point of view of whatever stripe. But of course Genesis 1 is not *about* scientific cosmogenesis. Rather, a hymnic parallelism is established for purposes of worship. Hence the rolling cadences that initiate the story of each day:

God said	*Let there be . . .*
And it was so	*God saw that it was good*
And evening came and morning	*on day (X)*

Within those framing words, a further parallel is set up: the first three days God creates the *setting* and in the final three days God *populates* those settings with particular bodies according to this schema:

First day: light	Fourth day: *bodies* of light
Second day: heavens and waters	Fifth day: *creatures* of sky and water
Third day: land and plants	Sixth day: *land animals*, including man[11]

This example highlights the problems inherent in trying to find some point of contact between Genesis and modern scientific views. But these two narratives only become incompatible when the attempt is made to make them compatible. That is, only a felt need to harmonize leads to a perceived conflict, when in fact Genesis 1 is not in any way *about* the evolution

---

11. Tables drawn from Lawrence Boadt, *Reading the Old Testament: An Introduction* (New York: Paulist Press, 1984), 114. Another author notices another symmetry: on the third and sixth day, there is a twofold work (third day: land *and* vegetation; sixth day: animals *and* the first human pair), which also helps separate the first three days from the final three: "For every three days, a fourfold work; with the result that both the third and the sixth day have two works." Bertram Hessler, *The Bible in the Light of Modern Science*, trans. Sylvester Saller (Chicago: Franciscan Herald Press, 1960), 32. The very rolling cadences of Genesis 1 make clear that the text is doxological, and therefore probably liturgical; indeed perhaps it was sung or chanted in a Babylonian proto-synagogue during the Exile.

of the cosmos—which stands to reason, since the author(s) of Genesis could have had no way of anticipating the deliverances of our modern natural sciences. In saying this, I am not advocating a two-truth theory—far from it, in fact. We obviously live in one world, and so all texts of whatever provenance must bear some connection with the real world. But it does no good to try to fit ancient texts into modern molds, when the authors themselves wrote without any knowledge of modern science.[12] Rather, as Pius teaches, the direction must go in reverse: *we* must struggle to get into *their* minds.[13]

But once that task is completed (which is best left to exegetes trained in the skills required for this task and whose conclusions can be found in the many commentaries on the Bible), what then? Once we understand the doxological basis of Genesis 1, how does that insight get fitted into what we already know from modern cosmology? Here, I think, Pope John Paul II has once again pointed the way in a letter he sent to the head of the Vatican Observatory:

If the cosmologies of the ancient Near Eastern world could be purified and assimilated into the first chapters of Genesis, might not contem-

12. Hessler agrees: "Since the fundamental questions to be addressed here [in Genesis] are those of the religious man and not of one investigating the field of natural science, there can be no contradiction between the biblical report of the creation and the certain findings of natural science. Questions pertaining to natural science cannot be addressed to the Bible. It is also wrong to try to harmonize the Bible and natural science through artificial concordance theories. The statements of the two are on different levels" (Hessler, ibid., 42–43). A Calvinist biblical scholar agrees: "Christians today misread Genesis when they try to engage it, even minimally, in the scientific arena." Peter Enns, *The Evolution of Adam: What the Bible Does and Doesn't Say about Human Origins* (Grand Rapids, MI: Brazos Press, 2012), 43. This view is so close to unanimous among Old Testament scholars that a citation from the standard introductory textbook will suffice for the rest: "Anyone who is looking for a scientific account of the origin of the world can find plenty of discrepancies in the Priestly story. To the scientific mind it is odd to hear that the earth was created before the sun, or that light was created before the heavenly lights—the sun, moon, and stars. It is fruitless to try to harmonize this account with modern science by saying, for instance, that the six creative days correspond to geological periods, or that the creation of living things followed a pattern of evolution. The cosmology, or picture of the universe, presupposed in the story was inherited from Israel's cultural environment." Bernard W. Anderson, *Understanding the Old Testament*, third edition (Englewood Cliffs, NJ: Prentice Hall, 1974), 426.

13. Again, Enns agrees: "If we begin with assumptions about what inspiration 'must mean,' we are creating a false dilemma and will wind up needing to make tortuous arguments to line up Paul and other biblical writers with modes of thinking that would never have occurred to them" (ibid., 94–95).

porary cosmology have something to offer to our reflections upon creation? Does an evolutionary perspective bring any light to bear upon theological anthropology, the meaning of the human person as the *imago Dei*, the problem of Christology—and even upon the development of doctrine itself? What, if any, are the eschatological implications of contemporary cosmology, especially in light of the vast future of our universe? Can theological method fruitfully appropriate insights from scientific methodology and the philosophy of science? *Science can purify religion from error and superstition*; religion can purify science from idolatry and false absolutes. Each can draw the other into a wider world, a world in which both can flourish.[14]

These sentences are more revolutionary than they might at first seem. For the pope here is saying that just as Genesis purified Babylonian cosmology by inserting it into a monotheistic framework, *so too* can science do the same for the doctrine of creation.[15] Indeed the pope explicitly avows that an evolutionary perspective can contribute to the development of doctrine itself, for science, he says, "can purify religion from error and superstition."

Which now brings us to the topic of original sin in an evolutionary framework. The problem is similar to the attempt to make sense of the assertion that the earth ("the land") was created before the sun in Genesis 1: obviously, that can in no way be harmonized with what is now known of the evolution of our solar system, since the sun antedated the first self-replicating cell on earth by roughly a billion years. Similarly, the entire schema of evolutionary biology does not really "map out" with Genesis 2–3 at any point—above all, because Genesis 2 assumes (although it does not say it explicitly, in so many words) that Adam and Eve were without

14. "Letter of His Holiness Pope John Paul II to the Rev. George V. Coyne, S.J., Director of the Vatican Observatory," dated June 1, 1988, in *Physics, Philosophy and Theology: A Quest for Common Understanding*, ed. Robert J. Russell, William R. Stoeger, S.J., and George V. Coyne, S.J. (Vatican City: Libreria Editrice Vaticana, 1988), M11, M13; emphasis added.

15. Virtually all commentators agree on the pope's first point: that the Priestly authors of Genesis 1 took previous Babylonian material and reworked it: "While the Priestly authors obviously knew the Babylonian story, or one similar, and used its outline, they did not accept its theology . . . [affirming rather] the basic insights of Israel's faith: 1) that there is one God, without sexual gender, alone from the start, 2) who created from his goodness and wise plan a world of order, 3) in which matter is good and not the result of whim or magic, 4) but God's *word* decrees what is to be and establishes limits" (Boadt, *Reading*, 117).

parents, a hypothesis impossible to countenance in contemporary biology.[16] David Fergusson captures all these difficulties in this concise passage:

> In the standard expression of the doctrine in the work of Augustine, Aquinas and Calvin, it was assumed that the fall was a historical event involving the first human couple. After Darwin, however, scientific opinion seemed overwhelmingly to discount the possibility of a spatiotemporal fall. It could no longer be assumed that the human race had descended from a single couple created in a state of moral and physical integrity. Humans had descended from earlier hominids over a period of millions of years. Moreover, those conditions that produced suffering, conflict, and death had determined planetary life-forms long before the appearance of human beings and their deeds of transgression. The pervasiveness of evil and death could not be attributed to an initial fall from a state of perfection. In interpreting Genesis 3, therefore, commentators tended to view the ancient text as containing parabolic material that exercised an important descriptive function but not one of historical or scientific explanation. Just as Genesis 1 did not furnish us with details for scientific cosmology but with a characterization of the world as dependent upon God, so *mutatis mutandis* Genesis 3 attested the universality of sin and the alienation of human beings from God. It is description, not explanation.[17]

One possible way out of this dilemma—as well as serving as a possible point of contact with Genesis 1–3—is the doctrine of *monogenism*, meaning

16. The difficulties of Genesis 2 are only compounded by its different chronology from the previous chapter's timing in regard to the creation of plants. In Genesis 1, as we saw, the creation of plants preceded that of the sun by one day, and so three days before Adam's creation. In Genesis 2, however, the creation of plants *follows* Adam's: "In the day that the Lord God made the earth and the heavens, *when no plant of the field was yet in the earth* and no herb of the field had yet sprung up, . . . *then* the Lord God formed man of dust from the ground, and breathed into his nostrils the breath of life; and man became a living being. And the Lord God planted a garden in Eden, in the east; and there he put the man whom he had formed. And *then* out of the ground the Lord God made to grow every tree that is pleasant to the sight, and good for food" (Gen. 2:4b–5a, 7–9a). If the Priestly editor saw no reason to harmonize the first creation account in Gen. 1 with the second in Gen. 2, then we should take that same lesson to heart when dealing with evolution and original sin: each topic is not *about* what concerns the other.

17. David Fergusson, "Interpreting the Story of Creation: A Case Study in the Dialogue between Theology and Science," in *Genesis and Christian Theology*, ed. Nathan McDonald, Mark W. Elliott, Grant Macaskill (Grand Rapids, MI: Eerdmans, 2012), 155–174, here 168.

the doctrine that all human beings alive on the planet today descended biologically from a single pair of first parents, as defined by Pope Pius XII in his 1950 encyclical *Humani Generis* in these terms:

35. It remains for Us now to speak about those questions which, although they pertain to the positive sciences, are nevertheless more or less connected with the truths of the Christian faith. In fact, not a few insistently demand that the Catholic religion take these sciences into account as much as possible. *This certainly would be praiseworthy in the case of clearly proved facts*; but caution must be used when there is rather question of hypotheses having *some* sort of scientific foundation, in which the doctrine contained in Sacred Scripture or in Tradition is involved. If such conjectural opinions are directly or indirectly opposed to the doctrine revealed by God, then the demand that they be recognized can in no way be admitted.

36. For these reasons, the Teaching Authority of the Church does not forbid that, in conformity with the present state of human sciences and sacred theology, research and discussions, on the part of men experienced in both fields, take place with regard to the doctrine of evolution, in as far as it inquires into the origin of the human *body* as coming from pre-existent and living matter—for the Catholic faith obliges us to hold that souls are immediately created by God. However, this must be done in such a way that the reasons for both opinions, that is, those favorable and those unfavorable to evolution, be weighed and judged with the necessary seriousness, moderation and measure, and provided that all are prepared to submit to the judgment of the Church, to whom Christ has given the mission of interpreting authentically the Sacred Scriptures and of defending the dogmas of faith. Some, however, rashly transgress this liberty of discussion, when they act as if the origin of the human body from pre-existing and living matter were already completely certain and proved by the facts which have been discovered *up to now* and by reasoning on those facts, as if there were nothing in the sources of divine revelation which demands the greatest moderation and caution in this question.

37. When, however, there is question of another conjectural opinion, namely polygenism, the children of the Church by no means enjoy such liberty. For the faithful cannot embrace that opinion which maintains

either that after Adam there existed on this earth true men who did not take their origin through natural generation from him as from the first parent of all, or that Adam represents a certain number of first parents. Now it is in no way apparent how such an opinion can be reconciled with that which the sources of revealed truth and the documents of the Teaching Authority of the Church propose with regard to original sin, which proceeds from a sin actually committed by an individual Adam and which through generation is passed on to all and is in everyone as his own.[18]

The question here is how much this teaching has been modified, if only implicitly, in John Paul II's Letter on Evolution cited above. For especially, as regards no. 36, the question of evolution is no longer recognized by the later pope to be as hypothetical in 1996 as it was for the former pope in 1950. So any hope that the problem can be solved by denying one prong of the dilemma now seems foreclosed. Then there is the question of how monogenism is to be *defined*: is it a biological doctrine (as no. 36 implies) or a purely theological one (as no. 37 implies)? Actually, Pius XII never uses the word *monogenism* anywhere in the encyclical, but simply condemns *polygenism*, which he defines as holding either that there existed humans on earth who did not owe their existence to Adam, or that "Adam" stands for a plural number of first parents. But still, from condemning its opposite, the pope's meaning is clear: Catholics must hold that somewhere along the evolutionary line, all human beings owe their existence to one primordial pair.

Although monogenism might seem like a purely biological doctrine, to be discussed and adjudicated by biologists as they determine the sequence of descent with modification (to the extent that the evidence allows for a decision), and thus falling outside of the competence of the Catholic magisterium to decide the issue, nonetheless the fact of monogenism, in a certain sense, can be readily established using a little armchair biology. Each person currently existing on the planet came into being because of a single act of sexual intercourse by his or her two parents; thus, if the two parents had never met, that person would never have come into being. So monogenism applies to each of us through our parents. But each of those parents had parents of their own, making four grandparents to each person now alive. But of course if *either* of those sets of grandparents had

18. Pope Pius XII, *Humani Generis*, promulgated August 12, 1950 (Boston: Daughters of St. Paul, 1950), 14–15; emphases added.

never met, then either the person's mother or father would never have existed, nor would the person currently alive either. The same applies to the eight great-grandparents, the sixteen great-great-grandparents, and so on.

Thus, as each person traces his or her genealogy up the line of direct ancestors, what is being established is the *essential connection* of each direct ancestor having mated and given birth to an equally essential progenitor. No doubt these facts are behind the vast popularity of genealogical websites and the eager search for ancestors among so many moderns today: genealogical research helps to establish the radical *contingency* of human existence. True enough, but there is an oddity in the mathematics of these searches: as the number of our direct ancestors increases exponentially (one set of parents, two sets of grandparents, four of great-grandparents, eight of great-great-grandparents, and so on), the population of the earth declines the further back in history one goes. The only way to reconcile this conundrum is by what is known as "slot-duplication," which means that one human can occupy two "slots" of direct ancestors in the past along the family tree, as when first cousins marry:

> Only seven generations back, for instance, at roughly the time of the American Revolution, one already has *in theory* a hundred and twenty-eight ancestors on a hundred and twenty-eight separate lines. In fact the number is almost always smaller because of cousin intermarriage; when people who are already related marry, they occupy a second slot on the pedigree of their descendants, [which is called] duplication.[19]

Thus, as the number of *putative* ancestors grows exponentially, the actual *slots* can be filled with just one particular mating pair; and of course if those individuals had never mated, then the family tree would collapse down several lines, a phenomenon called "pedigree collapse." Eventually, analysis will lead to *all* putative slots being filled by one pair:

> Most geneticists are in agreement that . . . no human can be less closely related to any other human than approximately the fiftieth cousin, and

19. Alex Shoumatoff, *The Mountain of Names: A History of the Human Family* (New York: Simon & Schuster/Kodansha International, 1985), 78–79. The author draws this implication from pedigree analysis, obviously of direct relevance to the question of monogenism: "In other words, everybody belongs to one enormous pyramid of descendants that fans down from the first humans. . . . The kinship group to which we *all* belong . . . extends indefinitely in every direction" (ibid., 244–45).

most of us are a lot closer. . . . [T]he family tree of all of us, of whatever origin or trait, must meet and merge into one genetic tree of all humanity by the time they have spread into our ancestors for about fifty generations. The "family of man" which has been posited by many religions and philosophies—it was a central concept of the Enlightenment—actually exists.[20]

But does this *biological* establishment of monogenism really intersect in any helpful way with what Pius XII was teaching in *Humani Generis*? For, theologically considered, there are quite a number of issues left unaddressed by this armchair demonstration of biological monogenism. For one thing, evolution (in the strict sense, meaning descent with modification) insists that this putative first indispensable pair from whom all current humans descended, must themselves have had parents, making them too indispensable, and so on back into the mists of time. So where is the "real" Adam to be located along a whole series of indispensable ancestors?[21]

Second, if this indispensable pair must have as few contemporaries as

20. Shoumatoff, *Mountain of Names*, 244. If politics makes for strange bedfellows, genealogy makes them even stranger: "By charting the overlap in the pedigrees of recent American political figures, the genealogist William Addams Reitwiesner has discovered that . . . [President Jimmy] Carter and former President Nixon are sixth cousins (both descended from a New Jersey Quaker named Richard Morris, who lived before the American Revolution), . . . that the California senator Alan Cranston has in his constellation of known kin, through common descent from a man named Robert Bullard, who lived in Watertown, Massachusetts, in the early sixteen-hundreds: Queen Geraldine of Albania, Emily Dickinson, George Plimpton, the Dow Chemical family, Julie Harris, and Margaret Mead" (ibid., 245).

21. A further complication from slot-duplication is that this presumed essential monogenetic pair would share its indispensability with most of its contemporaries because of pedigree-collapse. Moreover (and weirdly), that array of indispensable pairs would have lived in the fairly recent past, as a recent article in *Nature* has shown: "If a common ancestor of all living humans is defined as an individual who is a genealogical ancestor for all present-day people, the most recent common ancestor (MRCA) for a randomly mating population would have lived in the very recent past. . . . [O]ur results suggest that the most recent common ancestor for the world's current population lived in the relatively recent past—perhaps within the last few thousand years. . . . [O]ur findings suggest a remarkable proposition: no matter the languages we speak or the color of our skin, we share ancestors who planted rice on the banks of the Yangtze, who first domesticated horses on the steppes of the Ukraine, who hunted giant sloths in the forests of North and South America, and who labored to build the Great Pyramid of Khufu." Douglas L. T. Rohde, Steve Olson, and Joseph T. Chang, "Modeling the recent common ancestry of humans," *Nature*, Vol. 431 (30 September 2004): 562–66, here, 562, 565.

possible, it would had to have originated in Africa, since genetics has now proved that all humans outside of Africa descended from early members of *Homo sapiens* who first made the trek out of Africa from something like 90,000 to 70,000 years ago and then went on to people the rest of the globe. Of course, by that time one must assume that most of the African continent must have already been well populated, pushing back further in time the placement of the (most recent) indispensable first parents with a minimum of contemporary members of the species.[22]

Third, with one *possible* exception, the doctrine of monogenism cannot be found in the Bible (the exception is Romans 5:12–19, whose exegesis will be taken up later in this chapter). It certainly cannot be found in Genesis, because after Cain has slain his brother Abel, God grants him the famous "mark of Cain," not as a curse, but to protect him from attacks *by other tribes* (Gen. 4:8–16). In fact, racists in the nineteenth century took the presence of these other "races" outside the Garden of Eden as proof of their own "divine" Adamic lineage in contrast to the more "bestial" genealogy of the "lower" races.[23] Ironically, this makes Pius's doctrine of monogenism

22. The revolution in genetics in the last half of the twentieth century has led to the discovery of what Steve Jones calls, in a deft phrase, "molecular surnames." Using the male Y chromosome, our ancestry can be traced back to central Africa around 100,000 years ago; the female mitochondrial line can be traced back another hundred thousand years before that. But the most recent indispensable couple can be traced back much earlier than that: "In a population of around a thousand people, everyone is likely to share the same ancestor about ten generations—some three hundred years—ago. The figure goes up at a regular rate for larger groups, which means that almost all native Britons can trace descent from a single anonymous individual on these islands who lived in about the thirteenth century. On the global scale, universal common ancestry emerges no more than a hundred generations ago." Steve Jones, *The Serpent's Promise: The Bible Retold as Science* (Toronto: Doubleday Canada, 2013), 55. Of course that pair would have had *its* own indispensable pair (the couple's respective parents), fanning out to grandparents and all the way back, showing once more how monogenism and polygenism (in the strict biological sense) mutually entail each other. As an aside, Jones, while generally reliable on the science, errs when he says in the opening sentence of the book that "Genesis was the world's first biology textbook." No it was not. The author(s) of Genesis had no interest in biology or in the evolution of the solar system. On this see the intelligent review of this book by the Thomist Timothy McDermott, "Genesis vs. Genetics," *Times Literary Supplement* (August 19, 2013): 21, who scores the book for providing "a perfectly good account of scientific (usually genetic) facts ... placed in parallel with a failed attempt at the same thing in the Bible." An application of Pius XII's definition of "literal" could have prevented this error.

23. In this they found unlikely allies among some Darwinians: "The subtitle of the *Origin* also made a convenient motto for racists: 'The Preservation of Favoured *Races* in the Struggle for Life.' Darwin of course took 'races' to mean varieties or species; but it was no violation

a quintessentially *progressive* doctrine! But does it do the *theological* work he wants it to do?

To begin to answer that question, we run into the same problem we encountered when trying to fit Genesis 1, with its praise of God for creating plants on the third day and the sun on the fourth day, into contemporary cosmology: there is no real intersection because neither worldview is concerned with what motivates the other view. Similarly with biological and theological monogenism: if they have to intersect, then Adam's sin would have to have taken place in Africa maybe 300,000 years ago, and by a couple that themselves had parents, who presumably were not that much different from their immediate ancestors. None of this of course is implied in Genesis, whose narrated events seem to be taking place in some vague location in Mesopotamia, where a serpent can talk, and where God takes regular afternoon strolls through his garden, clear signs of the folkloric background to the story. In fact, Pius XII concedes this very point in *Humani Generis*. After reaffirming his prior encyclical *Divino Afflante Spiritu* (no. 24), and now referring to an official letter sent to the Archbishop of Paris on January 16, 1948, by the Pontifical Commission on Biblical Studies, he says:

> 38. This Letter, in fact, clearly points out that the first eleven chapters of Genesis, although properly speaking *not* conforming to the historical method used by the best Greek and Latin writers *or by competent authors of our own time*, do nevertheless *pertain* to history in a true sense, *which however must be further studied and determined by exegetes*; the same chapters (the Letter points out), in simple and *metaphorical* language adapted to the mentality of a people but little cultured, both state the principal truths which are fundamental for our salvation, and also give a *popular* description of the origin of the human race and the chosen people. If, however, the ancient sacred writers have taken anything from popular narrations (*and this may be conceded*), it must never be forgotten that they did so with the help of divine inspiration, through

---

of his meaning to extend it to human races, these being as much subject to the struggle for existence and survival of the fittest as plant and animal varieties." Gertrude Himmelfarb, *Darwin and the Darwinian Revolution* (New York: Norton, 1962), 416; emphasis added. But most fundamentalists rejected this interpretation of Gen. 4 (however awkwardly), although it lasted in some pockets as late as the 1970s; see Ronald L. Numbers, *The Creationists: The Evolution of Scientific Creationism* (Berkeley, CA: University of California Press, 1992), 231.

which they were rendered immune from any error *in selecting and evaluating those documents*. (all emphases added)[24]

The papal guidance here might sound vague, since much is still left in the hands of competent exegetes to interpret, and no guidance is given at all in determining what would count as error in selecting and evaluating pre-existing Babylonian documents; but I think the following principles emerge quite clearly from the story of the fall in Genesis 3. First, as Paul Ricoeur (1913–2005) notes, the point of the story is twofold: first "to separate the origin of evil from the origin of the good" (Adam and Eve spent at least *some* time in Eden prior to sinning); and second, the story also

24. Commenting on the Commission's *responsum*, Montague makes this point: "[T]he Commission accepted what was becoming increasingly clear to the scholarly community, that these introductory chapters were concerned to show humanity's need for salvation by portraying the origins of the world and the race in narrative forms familiar to the ancient world. This could mean that the writers were acquainted with the mythologies of the surrounding peoples from which they could borrow motifs to illustrate the monotheistic and salvific faith of Israel." Montague, *Understanding the Bible*, 103. The key passage from the Commission runs as follows: "The question of the first eleven chapters of Genesis is much more obscure and complex [than that of the composition of the Pentateuch in general]. These literary forms do not correspond to any of our classical categories and cannot be judged in the light of Graeco-Latin or modern literary forms. It is thus impossible to deny or to affirm their historicity as a whole without unduly applying to them the rules of a literary form to which they do not belong. If it be agreed that these chapters are not to be looked upon as history in the classic and modern sense, it must also be admitted that the scientific data available to us do not allow of a positive solution to all the problems they present. The prime duty that here devolves upon scientific exegesis consists first of all in the study of all the literary, scientific, historical, cultural and religious problems connected with these chapters. Next it would be necessary to examine closely the literary conventions of the peoples of the ancient Orient, their psychology, their manner of expression and their very concept of historical truth. In a word, it would be necessary to assemble, without prejudice, all the material of the paleontological, historical, epigraphic and literary sciences. It is only thus that one may hope to see more clearly into the true nature of certain accounts of the first chapters of Genesis. To declare *a priori* that their narratives do not contain history in the modern meaning of the word would easily give the impression that they do not contain it in any sense; whereas they relate in simple and figurative language, adapted to the intelligence of a less sophisticated era, the fundamental truths concerning the economy of salvation, while at the same time they give a popular description of the origins of the human race and of the chosen people." Cited in: Henri Rondet, S.J., *Original Sin: The Patristic and Theological Background*, trans. Cajetan Finegan, O.P. (Shannon, Ireland: Ecclesia Press, 1972), 228–29. Clearly, Pius XII's endorsement of this passage in *Humani Generis* shows that he has in no way retreated from what he had said earlier in *Divino Afflante*, as so many have unthinkingly assumed.

stresses the *inherency* of sin, making sin both adventitious (coming from the outside, that is, from the words of the serpent) and ineradicable, setting up what Ricoeur calls a distinction between "a *radical* origin of evil distinct from the more *primordial* origin of the goodness of things."[25] This is crucial, because, as he explains, the story "makes man a *beginning* of evil in the bosom of a creation which has already had its absolute *beginning* in the creative act of God."[26]

Furthermore, the serpent symbolizes the strange reality that malevolence against God's divine counsels somehow *precedes* the creation of Adam and Eve; and therefore the temptation felt by our first parents comes both from within and from without.[27] Finally, the doctrine tells us that it was only our first parents who *originated* sin, which means that henceforward all sin, no matter how malignant or malevolent, *always takes the form of acquiescence.* The only sins that the sons and daughters of Adam and Eve

25. Paul Ricoeur, *Symbolism of Evil*, trans. Emerson Buchanan (New York: Harper & Row, 1967), 233; Ricoeur's italics.

26. Ricoeur, *Symbolism of Evil*, 233; Ricoeur's italics; Ricoeur is seconding here Reinhold Niebuhr's view: "The importance of Biblical satanology lies in the two facts that: (1) the devil is not thought of as having been created evil. Rather his evil arises from his effort to transgress the bounds set for his life, an effort which places him in rebellion against God. (2) The devil fell before man fell, which is to say that man's rebellion against God is not an act of sheer perversity, nor does it follow inevitably from the situation in which he stands. The situation of finiteness and freedom in which man stands becomes a source of temptation only when it is falsely interpreted. This false interpretation is not purely the product of the human imagination. It is suggested to man by a force of evil which precedes his own sin." Reinhold Niebuhr, *The Nature and Destiny of Man*, Volume I: *Human Nature* (New York: Charles Scribner's Sons, 1941/1964), 180–81. The twentieth-century Lutheran martyr to Nazism, Dietrich Bonhoeffer, takes a decidedly Barthian view of the serpent's cleverness: "The serpent asks, 'Did God really say you shall not eat of any tree in the garden?' The serpent does not dispute this word, but it enables . . . [Adam] to be in the position to establish or dispute whether a word is the Word of God or not. . . . The decisive point is that this question suggests to man that he should go behind the Word of God and establish what it is by himself, out of his own understanding of the being of God." Dietrich Bonhoeffer, *Creation and Fall: A Theological Interpretation of Genesis 1–3*, trans. John C. Fletcher (New York: The Macmillan Company, 1959), 66.

27. It was this last point that proved so difficult for Augustine in his polemics against the Pelagians; for if things were *so* perfect in Eden, what would ever prompt our first parents to sin? The serpent, after all, had to tempt them by enticing some motivation already located in their prelapsarian psychology. To which Augustine was forced to reply that, since they were indeed tempted, there must have been at least a smidgen of concupiscence in them before their sin, which was a concession more damaging to his cause than he seems to have realized.

can henceforward commit are ones that go with the flow of the world. In other words, sin now takes the form of *drifting*.

This insight begins to explain the meaning of original sin *on its own terms*, which can indeed stand on its own, with no need to be shorn up by the deliverances of evolutionary biology. Evolution presents no threat to the doctrine of original sin, because it does not touch on its reality. This point can be easily demonstrated by showing what happens when the doctrine is denied. For time and again, the history of theology shows the intolerable conclusions—sometimes bordering on sheer nonsense—that come in the wake of its denial. In an important and influential monograph on this doctrine, N. P. Williams (who happens to be highly critical of certain features of Augustine's version of original sin) says this of Augustine's main critic, the British-born monk Pelagius (*c.* 354–418):

> Pelagius had no patience with moral weaklings or invalids; he could not understand the idea of the "moral struggle." The contention that the frailty of human nature made conformity with the highest ideals a matter of striving and effort seemed to him merely a dishonest excuse, put forward by hypocrites who intended to go on sinning, and a disparagement of the justice and benevolence of God, in that He is thereby accused by implication of having given commandments which are difficult of fulfillment by man.... There are no such things as "sins of weakness": men sin according to Pelagius because they choose to sin, because they have calmly and deliberately faced the question of sin, and decided that sin represents for them the most desirable course of conduct.... So immutable is the freedom of the will that the Pelagians, contradicting the most patent facts of human experience, appeared to deny the existence of any such thing as the tyranny of habit. A man may commit a sin one hundred times, and yet after the hundredth sin he is no more inclined to commit it, his will is no more biased or trammeled than it was before he began the series of sinful acts. It follows that this mechanically flawless free-will is quite sufficient in itself to enable man to live without sin; and in point of fact there were sinless individuals, even before the Incarnation—Abel, Enoch, and many others amongst Biblical characters, and many philosophers amongst the Pagans. Hence, there never can be any sort of excuse for, or palliative of, sin of any kind.[28]

---

28. Norman Powell Williams, *The Ideas of the Fall and of Original Sin: A Historical and Critical Study* (London: Longmans, Green, 1927), 333–34, 341–42. For this reason, Williams

Augustine has often been criticized for his dark and dreary pessimism regarding the salvation of the human race; but, however paradoxical this might sound, Pelagius was worse; for with him there is absolutely no excuse whatever for moral failings of any stripe; no concession is made to habit, to addiction, to one's upbringing, to inherited traits of personality, to dint of circumstance, to economic conditions, to the pressure of joblessness or disease (mental or physical).[29] At all points the individual is fully responsible and free to choose good over evil from an unbiased and lofty aerie.[30] Thus, in a bizarre irony, far more people end up in hell under the Pelagian rubric than under Augustine's, as one shrewd Augustine scholar has noted: "A dreadful rigorism was the result of this exaggeration of the powers of human liberty. Since perfection is possible for man, it is obligatory.... Harnack dared to say that 'according to Pelagius, every man who could have acted better than he did is going to hell.'"[31]

---

rightly concludes: "[Pelagianism's] triumph would have been an unqualified disaster for Christianity. The principal ground for this judgment is the fact that the fundamental assumption of Pelagianism—the assumption of an absolutely undetermined, autonomous sovereign free-will residing in all human beings without exception—is simply untrue. It ignores the agonizing facts of 'incontinence' and the moral struggle.... It forgets that the affections are as capable of being harnessed to bear the will up to heights of heroic endeavor as of dragging it down to depths of moral infamy. It reduces the spiritual life to a dull, mechanical process of conformity with an external code; it is the negation of the profound maxim, of which the truth is daily receiving fresh confirmation from psychological study, 'No virtue is safe which is not enthusiastic'" (ibid., 355–56).

29. "Pelagianism has often been accused of minimizing the 'sense of sin'; but the exact opposite is the truth: by insisting on the unlimited freedom of the will, and by sweeping away the excuses which may be found in natural weakness or the power of habit, it exaggerates the sense of sin (of actual sin, that is) to a degree at which it must become a burden to the sensitive conscience no less intolerable than the opposite error, which bids us mourn for the 'original guilt' of a nature which *ex hypothesi* we cannot help possessing" (Williams, *Ideas*, 357).

30. One cannot help but recall here Mark Twain's mordant and droll observation of the fate of most New Year's resolutions: "Now is the accepted time to make your annual regular good resolutions. Next week you can begin paving hell with them as usual. Yesterday, everybody smoked his last cigar, took his last drink, and swore his last oath. Today, we are a pious and exemplary community. Thirty days from now, we shall have cast our reformation to the winds and gone to cutting our ancient shortcomings considerably shorter than ever.... New Year's is a harmless annual institution, of no particular use to anybody, ... and we wish you to enjoy it with the looseness suited to the greatness of the occasion." Mark Twain, *Territorial Enterprise* (Virginia City, Nevada), January 1, 1863.

31. Eugène Portalié, S.J., *A Guide to the Thought of Saint Augustine*, trans. Ralph J. Bastian, S.J (Chicago: Henry Regnery, 1960), 188, internally quoting Adolf von Harnack's *History of Dogma* V: 196.

More recent deniers of the doctrine also run into their own self-generated contradictions. Perhaps the most significant contribution made by the twentieth-century American Lutheran theologian Reinhold Niebuhr (1892–1971), among his many other merits, was to show the link between ancient Pelagianism and modern liberalism (whether secular or Christian) and then to display that same contradiction in the latter that Williams found in the former:

> The various alternative [liberal] doctrines all may be regarded as variants of what has become known in the history of Christian thought as Pelagianism. The essential characteristic of Pelagianism is its insistence that actual sins cannot be regarded as sinful or as involving guilt if they do not proceed from a will which is essentially free. The bias toward evil, that is, that aspect of sin which is designated as "original" in the classic doctrine is found not in man's will but in the inertia of nature. It is in other words not sin at all. Actual sin is on the other hand regarded as more unqualifiedly a conscious defiance of God's will and an explicit preference of evil, despite the knowledge of the good, than in the classical doctrine. . . . It is not surprising that wherever [these] views of man prevail, as for instance in both secular and Christian modern liberalism, the bias toward evil should be defined as residing not in man's will but in some sloth of nature which man has inherited from his relation to the brute creation. This remains true even when, as in the thought of men like Schleiermacher and in the theology of the social gospel, this sloth is attributed to the institutions and traditions of history rather than purely to sensual passion or to the finiteness of the mind. By thus placing the inherited sloth in history rather than in each man's own sensual nature, some justice is done to the actual historical continuum in which every human action takes place, but the bias toward evil is always outside and never inside a particular will.[32]

---

32. Niebuhr, *Human Nature*, 245–46. This point is no longer Niebuhr's alone but is echoed even by secular commentators, as here: "Liberalism fails to understand evil for just the same reason that it fails to understand love. Its horizon of explanation is framed by reason, on the one hand, and [by] personal well-being on the other. Between reason and interest, it can find no third term. It has no conception of the will that is not absorbed either by the universalism of reason or by the particularism of interest. These always appear to be in a state of actual or threatened tension: reason must rein in interest, which will always seek more than reason allows. This tension remains as long as individuals find themselves living under conditions of moderate scarcity, because even under the best of arrangements, they

Niebuhr fully grants that the doctrine of original sin is, *au fond*, deeply paradoxical; but for him that is the *point* of the doctrine: "The truth is that, absurd as the classical Pauline doctrine of original sin may seem to be at first blush, its prestige as a part of the Christian truth is preserved, and perennially re-established, against the attacks of rationalists and simple moralists by its ability to throw light upon complex factors in human behavior which constantly escape the moralists."[33] No doubt, the doctrine of original sin can seem at first glance intolerably self-contradictory. In one of his works, Augustine quotes Coelestius's withering objection: "We must ask whether sin comes from necessity or from choice. If from necessity then it is not sin; if from choice then it can be avoided."[34] Niebuhr captures this same objection in this passage:

> The Christian doctrine of sin in its classical form offends both rationalists and moralists by maintaining the seemingly absurd position that man sins inevitably and by a fateful necessity but that he is nevertheless to be held responsible for actions which are prompted by an ineluctable fate.... Here is the absurdity in a nutshell. Original sin, which is by definition an inherited corruption, or at least an inevitable one, is nevertheless not to be regarded as belonging to his essential nature and therefore is not outside the realm of his responsibility. Sin is natural for man in the sense that it is universal but not in the sense that it is necessary.[35]

For Niebuhr, the only way to reconcile this apparent contradiction is by showing that in fact this peculiar-seeming doctrine better illuminates the actual workings of the human will better than any alternative (and we have already seen how absurd Pelagius's view of human free will is). For this is now the situation of human will as it currently obtains in our empirically observable world: "Sin is to be regarded as neither a necessity of man's nature nor yet as a pure caprice of his will. It proceeds rather from a *defect* of the will, for which reason it is not completely deliberate; but since

cannot have all that they want. Evil, accordingly, can appear to liberalism only as a failure of reason or as unconstrained desire—two perspectives on the same phenomenon." Paul W. Kahn, *Out of Eden: Adam and Eve and the Problem of Evil* (Princeton: Princeton University Press, 2007), 53.

33. Niebuhr, *Human Nature*, 248–49.

34. Quoted in Augustine, *Anti-Pelagian Works*, Vol. I: *Treatise on Man's Perfection in Righteousness*, 317.

35. Niebuhr, *Human Nature*, 241–42.

it is the *will* in which the defect is found and the will presupposes freedom, the defect cannot be attributed to a taint in man's nature."[36] As Williams puts it more pithily: "We are free to do what we like, but we are not free to like what we ought to like."[37]

Outrageous as that might sound, this conundrum defines the human condition. Perhaps on first encounter with the doctrine, a reader might feel like Oedipus, condemned at birth by a fate he did not choose to carry out a crime that horrified him once he realized what he had done; at which point he then gouges out his eyes in atonement for a crime he never intended to commit! But again, there is a reason Sophocles' *Oedipus Rex* was, by near unanimous acclaim, regarded as the best tragedy the Greeks ever produced (such was Aristotle's verdict, who knew far more of the plays of that time than have survived to us). As the Chorus explains, this is the lot of us all:

> Oh, what a wretched breed
> We mortals are:
> Our lives add up to nothing.
> Does anyone, anyone at all,
> Harvest more of happiness
> Than a vacant image? . . .

> *You are my pattern,*
> *Your fortune is mine.*
> You, Oedipus, your misery teaches me
> To call no mortal blessed. . . .

> Behold, all you who dwell in Thebes: This is Oedipus.
> He knew the riddle's answer, he held great power,

---

36. Niebuhr, *Human Nature*, 242.

37. Williams, *Ideas*, 369. Niebuhr is perhaps less pithy, but no less stark in stressing the paradox: "The whole crux of the doctrine of original sin lies in the seeming absurdity of the conception of free-will which underlies it. The Pauline doctrine, as elaborated by Augustine and the Reformers, insists on the one hand that the will of man is enslaved to sin and is incapable of fulfilling God's law. It may be free, declares Augustine, only it is not free to do good. 'How then do miserable men dare to be proud of free-will before they are liberated or of their own strength after they are liberated?' Yet on the other hand the same Augustine insists upon the reality of free-will whenever he has cause to fear that the concept of original sin might threaten the idea of human responsibility: 'Only let no man dare so to deny the freedom of the will as to desire to excuse sin'" (Niebuhr, *Human Nature*, 243).

And we all looked on his success with envy.
Now a terrible wave of trouble sweeps over him.
Therefore, always look to the last day,
And never call a man happy
Until he's crossed life's threshold free from grief.[38]

By no coincidence whatever, William Shakespeare's most famous play, *Hamlet*, also deals with a man caught in a damned-if-you-do-damned-if-you-don't bind: told by a ghost of whose provenance he cannot be sure to murder his uncle and assume a throne rightfully his, his irresolution over this dilemma leads to catastrophe for all Denmark: "Oh cursèd spite that ever I was born to set it right" (I v, lines 196–87). In fact, as Stephen Greenblatt has pointed out, the play is really about Hamlet's "Reformation dilemma," which is quintessentially an Augustinian one: "The psychological in Shakespeare's tragedy is constructed almost entirely out of the theological, and specifically out of the issue of remembrance that . . . lay at the heart of the crucial early-sixteenth-century debate about Purgatory."[39] And nothing so characterized the Reformation, especially Luther's version, than an acute, entirely Augustinian sense of sin, to which Hamlet confesses here:

I am myself indifferent honest; but yet I could accuse me of such things that it were better my mother had not borne me. I am very proud, re-

38. Sophocles, *Oedipus Rex*, in *Theban Plays*, trans. Peter Meineck and Paul Woodruff (Indianapolis: Hackett, 2003), lines 1186–1196, 1286–1292; emphasis added.

39. Stephen Greenblatt, *Hamlet in Purgatory* (Princeton: Princeton University Press, 2001), 229. Surely Greenblatt is right that only this theological dilemma—whether purgatory exists—can explain Hamlet's indecision: "What has intervened to deflect a direct course of action and to blunt the sharp edge of remembrance? Most obviously, despite attempts at something like the *discretio spirituum*, he is in the grip of continued doubts about the precise nature of the Ghost and hence about the trustworthiness of the Ghost's account of the murder in the garden: 'The spirit that I have seen, / May be the devil' (II ii, lines 575–576). This suspicion—the fear that the devil is manipulating the weakness and melancholy that he recognizes in himself in order to claim his soul—leads Hamlet to seek some further verification, some independent evidence of his uncle's guilt" (ibid., 220). To speak in Greenblatt's favor: The prince was after all studying in Luther's Wittenberg when his father was murdered, and the Ghost clearly tells him he has come from purgatory: "I am thy father's spirit, / Doomed *for a certain term* to walk the night, /And for the day confined to *fast in fires*, / Till the foul crimes done in my days of nature / Are burnt and *purged* away" (I v, lines 9–13; emphases added).

vengeful, ambitious; with more offences at my beck than I have thoughts
to put them in, imagination to give them shape, or time to act them in.
What should such fellows as I do crawling between heaven and earth?
We are arrant knaves, all; believe none of us. (III, i, lines 121–130)

When this cultural wisdom is ignored, as it largely is in secular or
Christian liberalism, naïveté sets in, only to be flummoxed—not to say
led to bitter despair—by the outcome of history, set forth chillingly by
Stephen Duffy:

> In the twentieth century, when human beings have already killed well
> over one hundred million of their kind, disenchantment [with an opti-
> mistic view of human nature] has set in. Two world wars, the Gulags,
> the Holocaust, Korea, Vietnam, the nuclear and ecological threats form
> a somber litany that makes the optimism of the liberals ring hollow
> and naïve. Despite technological progress, evil, far from vanishing, has
> only become more powerful and more fiendish. . . . Artists like Conrad,
> Camus, Beckett, Golding, and Murdoch contend that because of our
> hearts of darkness there may be countless nice men and women but
> few if any genuinely good ones. In all these perspectives evil is held to be
> inherent, somehow structural, ingrained. And its terrible power defies
> explanation and solution. Paradoxically, the silver wings of science and
> technology, on which soared the hopes of the industrialized societies,
> carry the ultimate menace to the human prospect.[40]

One can even plausibly argue that these horrors have in some way
been *caused* by a denial of the fact of original sin. I am reminded in this
context of a shrewd observation by Anatole France to the effect that never
have so many been murdered in the name of a doctrine as in the name of
the principle that human beings are naturally good. When one glances
over the catalogue of evils that have so pockmarked the past century, it is
extraordinary how many have come from doctrines founded on the notion
of the perfectibility of man. As Niebuhr puts it so well:

> The utopian illusions and sentimental aberrations of modern liberal
> culture are really all derived from the basic error of negating the fact of

---

40. Stephen Duffy, "Our Hearts of Darkness: Original Sin Revisited," *Theological Studies*,
Vol. 49, No. 4 (December 1988): 597–622, here 606.

original sin. This error . . . continually betrays modern men to equate the goodness of men with the virtue of their various schemes for social justice and international peace. When these schemes fail of realization or are realized only after tragic conflicts, modern men either turn from utopianism to disillusionment and despair, or they seek to place the onus of their failure upon some particular social group, . . . [which is why] both modern liberalism and modern Marxism are always facing the alternatives of moral futility or moral fanaticism. Liberalism in its pure form [that is, pacifism] usually succumbs to the peril of futility. It will not act against evil until it is able to find a vantage point of guiltlessness from which to operate. This means that it cannot act at all. Sometimes it imagines that this inaction is the guiltlessness for which it has been seeking. A minority of liberals and most of the Marxists solve the problem by assuming that they have found a position of guiltlessness in action. Thereby they are betrayed into the error of fanaticism.[41]

To be sure, these citations do not constitute a positive "proof" in the technical sense but merely point to the consequences of abandoning the doctrine. But such a modest opening gambit at least blocks the way to its outright denial. For it is, after all, mostly because of Augustine's own formulations of a perfect paradise spoiled by a nearly unmotivated sin that make Christians feel stranded in their sense of the doctrine, especially in the light of evolution. On its own terms, however, the doctrine stands as a cipher pointing to what everyone senses in his or her own heart: that sin after Adam always takes the form of acquiescence and not of origination. We are born, that is, into a world where rebellion against God has already taken place, and the drift of it sweeps us along.

Nor, properly understood, is Augustine's rosy scenario of paradise, which John Milton (1608–74) used so effectively in *Paradise Lost*, all that absurd: the *Catechism of the Catholic Church* speaks of the "figurative language" of Genesis 3 (no. 390), and the same must therefore apply, *a fortiori*, to Augustine's portrait of Adam and Evil before the fall.[42] The reason

41. Niebuhr, *Human Nature*, 273–74, footnote 4.

42. As Rondet notes so well, the beginning moment of the "demythologization" of Augustine's literal paradise comes from Thomas Aquinas: "There is no reason to suppose that the material universe in which the first man lived should have been different from ours. Even if Adam had not sinned, the wolf would devour the sheep. It is unreasonable to think otherwise; the nature of the animals was not changed by man's sin [*ST* I, q. 96, a. 1, ad 2]. In order to live, man would have needed to eat and he would have sinned if he did not do so

we are drawn, despite the theory of evolution, to Augustine's and Milton's portrait of paradise before the fall is because of the memory we have of that original justice we once had with God but lost through sin, as Blaise Pascal (1623–62) explains so well:

> The greatness of man is so evident that it can even be deduced from his wretchedness. For what in animals is called nature we call wretchedness in man. From this we realize that, his nature now being like that of the animals, he has fallen from a better nature which once was his. For who can be wretched at not being a king except a deposed king? . . . Who is miserable at having only one mouth? And who would not be miserable at having only one eye? It has probably never occurred to anyone to be distressed at not having three eyes; but those who have none are inconsolable.[43]

So far this argument has proceeded either from the negative consequences that come to society when it establishes itself on a denial of original sin or from obvious empirical facts that testify to its reality. Still to be addressed are the doctrine's more direct affirmations (the positivity of the doctrine, as it were), especially in its most recent articulation, the *Catechism of the Catholic Church (CCC)*. First of all, it teaches the superiority of the doctrine of original sin as the true explanation for evil that fits the data better than any other rival theory, which of course resembles the "negative" arguments of Pascal, Williams, and Niebuhr, but which adds its own positive twist by seeing the doctrine in the light of Christ:

[I, q. 97, a. 3 and ad 3]. The human race would have multiplied by way of generation [I, q. 98, ad 2]. . . . Even if Adam had not sinned, there would have been inequalities among men, masters and servants, and an unequal distribution of material goods [I, q. 98, a. 2 and ad 3]." Rondet, *Original Sin*, 160–61. In this as in so many other issues dealing with original sin, Thomas was more ahead of his time than he is often given credit for. Later his famous commentator Cardinal Cajetan will interpret Eve's creation from Adam's rib purely symbolically (see Rondet, *Original Sin*, 173).

43. Blaise Pascal, *Pensées*, trans. Honor Levi (Oxford: Oxford University Press, 1995), 37; translation amended. The mordant aphorist E. M. Cioran, who once said that he refused to kill himself because it would give his life too much meaning, gets at this same point here: "It would be a torture merely to breathe were it not for the memory or presentiment of Paradise, the supreme object (however unconsciously) of our desires, the unexpressed essence of our memory and expectation." E. M. Cioran, *Historie et utopie* (Paris: Gallimard, 1987), 13; quoted in Henri Blocher, *Original Sin: Illuminating the Riddle* (Downers Grove, IL: InterVarsity Press, 1997), 88.

Only the light of divine Revelation clarifies the reality of sin and particularly of the sin committed at mankind's origins. Without the knowledge Revelation gives of God we cannot recognize sin clearly and are
tempted to explain it as merely a developmental flaw, a psychological
weakness, a mistake, or the necessary consequence of an inadequate
social structure, etc. *Only in the knowledge of God's plan for man* can
we grasp that sin is an abuse of the freedom that God gives to created
persons so that they are capable of loving him and loving one another.
(no. 387; emphasis added)

In other words, the doctrine of original sin is a *retrospective* doctrine
that only becomes clear in the light of Christ's mission to save humanity
by dying on the cross, a point the *Catechism* makes explicitly clear in the
next paragraph:

Although to some extent the People of God in the Old Testament had
tried to understand the pathos of the human condition in the light of the
history of the fall narrated in Genesis, they could not grasp this story's
ultimate meaning, which is revealed *only* in the light of the death and
resurrection of Jesus Christ. *We must know Christ as the source of grace
in order to know Adam as the source of sin.* (no. 388; emphases added)[44]

Of course Adam is not the *sole* source of sin; for, relying on the teaching
of the New Testament (Rev. 12:9), the church identifies the serpent in the
Garden with Satan, who rebelled prior to the creation of the world (nos.
391–95). The *Catechism* also freely grants, as we saw, that the account of the
fall in Genesis 3 "uses figurative language," while adding that it "took place
at the beginning of the history of man" (no. 390). No further explanation is

---

44. As early as the second century Christian writers began to notice the chiasmic parallels between Genesis 3 and the passion narratives, as in this charming account from one
Cosmas the Indicopleustes in his *Christian Topography*: "Just as the two, Adam and Eve,
were at the ninth hour cast out of Paradise, so also at the ninth hour the Lord Christ in the
spirit and the thief entered into Paradise. On the same day, therefore, in which Adam was
made, that is, on the sixth day, there occurred both the Fall and the grief of the angels, the
sentence of death and the expulsion from Paradise; so also at the time of the Passion, on
the same day, there occurred the death of the Savior by the tree of the Cross, the mourning
of creation, and in the afternoon the putting away of this mourning and the entrance into
Paradise." Quoted in Emmanouela Grypeou and Helen Spurling, *The Book of Genesis in Late
Antiquity: Encounters between Jewish and Christian Exegesis* (Leiden: Brill, 2013), 62.

given as to how this phrase "at the beginning of the history of man" is to be interpreted. If it refers to the first emergence of *Homo sapiens* on the stage of history, then presumably this would have taken place in Africa, roughly 200,000 to 300,000 years ago, which seems an unlikely interpretation of the meaning of this passage. Moreover—and however that line is to be interpreted—the *Catechism* goes on to say: "[O]riginal sin is called 'sin' *only in an analogical sense*: it is a sin 'contracted' and not 'committed'—a state and not an act" (no. 404; emphasis added), which means that "original sin *does not have the character of a personal fault in any of Adam's descendants*" (no. 405; emphasis added), both of which teachings are very nearly the opposite positions from those held by Augustine.[45] The idea that original sin is merely "analogical" would have dumbfounded Augustine:

> It follows from this exalted view of man's paradisal condition that the malice of the first sin was infinite in its demerit, precisely because it was the *first*. . . . All subsequent sins . . . have been due to the inordinate power of concupiscence and the corruption of man's nature engendered by the Fall. But the Fall itself was not due to concupiscence, because that *ex hypothesi* barely existed in unfallen man. It was therefore due to pure senseless perversity; it was a sin solely of the will and not of the appetite, and it was committed, not as a result of weakness or frailty, but against a settled habit of virtue. It was not a mere floating with the stream of human tendencies, but a deliberate attempt to swim against the stream. Hence, apart from the question of its consequences, it was a unique and dreadful tragedy, because it was the moral *débâcle* of a saint.[46]

But the contrast between Augustine and the *Catechism* becomes most apparent in their mutually opposite conclusions regarding the fate of the unbaptized, especially of infants who die before baptism. Notoriously, Augustine held that these hapless babies go straight to hell, to suffer for all

---

45. As Williams notes, for Augustine "This 'sin' has become ingrained into human nature and is transmitted by physical heredity. Here for the first time in the history of Christian thought we meet the epoch-making phrase *peccatum originale*, meaning a sinful quality which is born with us and is inherent in our constitution. But this sinful quality, it is clear, is conceived by Augustine to be 'sin' *in the fullest sense of the term*, albeit involuntarily acquired, for *it deserves 'punishment,' and therefore involves guilt*" (Williams, *Ideas*, 327; emphases added; the last internal quote is from Augustine's *Letter to Simplicianus* I, q. 1, 10: "*ex poena originalis peccati*").

46. Williams, *Ideas*, 363–64.

eternity, albeit in a mitigated form. Odious as that conclusion no doubt sounds, it follows directly from his prior insistence that Adam's sin was not only a catastrophic breach of divine law, but entailed a *guilt* that was handed down to all his children via the act of sexual intercourse, on which point Williams catches out the (rather ironically named) *doctor gratiae* in a glaring contradiction:

> It follows, according to Augustine's logic, that all human beings are born subject to the penalty of eternal hell for a sin which they are alleged to have prenatally committed in Adam's loins: and this appalling sentence is duly executed upon all except those whom the inscrutable decree of God's predestination singles out from the "mass of perdition," brings to the absolving waters of baptism, and endows with the grace of final perseverance. The Doctor of Hippo repeatedly and vehemently insists upon the "justice" of this arrangement whereby millions of the human race are condemned to an eternity of torture as the punishment of a crime for which they have *ex hypothesi* no personal responsibility whatever.[47]

The *Catechism*, however, insists that the doctrine, while hardly an "optimistic" one as that term is usually understood, is certainly a *hopeful*

---

47. Williams, *Ideas*, 373. So intensely disagreeable to Williams is this conclusion of Augustine's that he veers into some rather over-the-top *ad hominem* attacks on the bishop's character: "Equally patent is the influence exerted upon his convictions by the less admirable traits of his character. The downright brutality which led him to discard his mistress of fifteen years' standing, the mother of Adeodatus, without, apparently, so much as a thought of making reparation for his fault by marrying her, appears in his theology as the heartlessness which leaves the great bulk of mankind, even helpless infants, in the *massa perditionis*, doomed to everlasting flames for a sin which is not their own. The terrible strength of the sexual passions which devastated his youth and early manhood accounts for the prominence which the idea of 'concupiscence' assumes in his writings; and the apparently instantaneous sublimation of these emotions through his conversion explains the feeling of irresistible grace upon which his theology of predestination and election was founded, as well as the ultra-puritan fanaticism which colored his opinions with regard to wedlock and procreation. . . . It is, perhaps, better not to speculate with regard to the amount of unhappiness which these ideas must have brought to sensitive souls between the time of their first promulgation and that of the final eclipse of Augustinianism by Darwinism in the nineteenth century. . . . The fact that Augustine nevertheless maintained this inhuman theory [of the damnation of unbaptized infants] down to the last days of his life is a melancholy illustration of the way in which the best of men may allow the kindly instincts of human nature to be overridden by the demands of a fanatical logic" (ibid., 330–31, 374, 376–77). Whether Williams is being entirely fair to Augustine here should perhaps best be left to the judgment of the reader.

one. Following Paul here, who said that "as one man's trespass led to the condemnation for all men, so one man's act of righteousness leads to acquittal and life for all men" (Rom. 5:18, cited by the *CCC* at no. 402), the *Catechism* places the event of the fall inside the context of God's wider plan to save:

> But *why did God not prevent the first man from sinning?* St. Leo the Great responds: "Christ's inexpressible grace gave us blessings better than those the demon's envy had taken away." And St. Thomas Aquinas wrote, "There is nothing to prevent human nature's being raised up to something greater, even after sin; God permits evil in order to draw forth some greater good. Thus St. Paul says, 'Where sin increased, grace abounded all the more'; and the Exultet sings, 'O happy fault, . . . which gained for us so great a Redeemer!'" (no. 412)[48]

That the *Catechism* is not trying to sweeten the bitter pill of Augustinianism by introducing a factor of liberal sentimentality is clear from the deeply traditional sources it invokes (all from sources postdating Augustine except for Paul).[49] True, a republication of Augustine's views on the fate of infants who die before baptism would inevitably result in an evangelical disaster, not to mention the fact that such a recrudescence of Augustine's infantile hell would undercut the prolife movement at its

---

48. Italics in the original; the citations are from Leo the Great, *Sermo* 73; Aquinas, *ST* III, q. 1, a. 3, ad 3; Paul, Rom. 5:20).

49. One could of course equally cite any number of parables from Jesus, who makes the same point: that a Christian has no business hoarding salvation like some personal possession, a point that (then Cardinal) Joseph Ratzinger has deftly described here: "We cannot start to set limits on God's behalf; *the very heart of the faith has been lost to anyone who supposes that it is only worthwhile, if it is, so to say, made worthwhile by the damnation of others.* Such a way of thinking, which finds the punishment of other people necessary, springs from not having inwardly accepted the faith; from loving only oneself and not God the Creator, to whom his creatures belong. That way of thinking would be like the attitude of those people who could not bear the workers who came last being paid a denarius like the rest; like the attitude of people who feel properly rewarded only if others have received less. This would be the attitude of the son who stayed at home, who could not bear the reconciling kindness of his father. It would be a hardening of our hearts, in which it would become clear that we were only looking out for ourselves and not looking for God; in which it would be clear that we did not love our faith, but merely bore it like a burden. . . . It is a basic element of the biblical message that the Lord died for all—being jealous of salvation is not Christian." Joseph Cardinal Ratzinger, *God Is Near Us: The Eucharist, the Heart of Life*, trans. Henry Taylor (San Francisco: Ignatius Press, 2003), pp. 35-36; emphasis added.

foundations (no one has ever claimed that the evil of abortion comes from the way it sends fetal souls automatically to hell).[50]

No doubt Paul would have been equally horrified by Augustine's doctrine of an infantile hell of eternal torment and by the use the Doctor of Grace made of Romans, since the whole point of that letter was to explain how grace *trumps* sin:

> But the free gift is not like the trespass. For if many died through one man's trespass, much more have the grace of God and the free gift in the grace of that one man Jesus Christ abounded for many. And *the free gift is not like the effect of that one man's sin*. For the judgment following one trespass brought condemnation, but the free gift following many trespasses brings justification. If, because of one man's trespass, death reigned through that one man, much more will those who receive the abundance of grace and the free gift of righteousness reign in life through the one man Jesus Christ. *Then as one man's trespass led to condemnation for all men, so one man's act of righteousness leads to acquittal and life for all men.* For as by one man's disobedience many were made sinners, so by one man's obedience many will be made righteous. Law came in to increase trespass; *but where sin abounded, grace abounded all the more*, so that, as sin reigned in death, grace also might reign through

50. As the reader already probably suspects, Williams has a much more baroque way of expressing the same point: "No Christian thinker in his senses will maintain that Augustinianism is a heresy. Yet a theological opinion may be profoundly erroneous without being either formally or materially heretical. . . . If Augustine's doctrines of the Fall and of original sin—with their mythological concept of the physical, moral, and mental state of the first man, with their logically incoherent notion of original guilt, their fanatical denial of the possibility of virtue outside the Church, and their horrible corollary of the necessary damnation of unbaptized infants—were really the ecclesiastical doctrine, that is, the doctrine of the Church, as both friends and opponents have, at least in Western Europe, hitherto assumed it to be; if the whole fabric of orthodox dogma were really based upon this one-sided theory of human nature, seamed as it is with so large a vein of mythology and split by a colossal self-contradiction; we should be obliged to conclude that the prospects of defending historical Christianity in the coming generation were of a singularly unpromising kind." Williams, *Ideas*, 382–83. The noted Polish philosopher Leszek Kolakowski agrees: "Proviso being made for the notorious fragility of counterfactuals, one could even imagine that if the Church had (almost *per impossibile*) then adopted the Augustinian-Jansenist theology as the basis of its educational work [during the Jansenist crisis], it would have embarked on the road to self-destruction." Leszek Kolakowski, *God Owes Us Nothing: A Brief Remark on Pascal's Religion and on the Spirit of Jansenism* (Chicago: University of Chicago Press, 1995), 31.

righteousness to eternal life through Jesus Christ our Lord. (Rom. 5:15–20; emphases added)

At this point, however, the party advocating Augustine's theology of sin can point out that Paul's consistent parallelism between the old Adam and the new Adam would seem to require a parallelism of *individuals*, a point Paul makes clear just a few verses earlier:

Therefore as *sin came into the world through one man* and *death through sin,* and so death spread to all men because all men sinned—sin was indeed in the world before the law was given, but sin is not counted where there is no law. Yet death reigned from Adam to Moses, *even over those whose sins were not like the transgression of Adam,* who was a type of the one who was to come. (Rom. 5:12–14; emphases added)

In attempting to get clarity on Paul's meaning here, which seems to imply not only that Adam was a historical figure from a datable time in the past, but also that, had he not sinned, he would have remained immortal, we must also pair this with another passage of equal importance, where Paul also makes the Adam/Christ parallel:

What is sown is perishable; what is raised is imperishable. The body is sown in dishonor, it is raised in glory. It is sown in weakness, it is raised in power. It is sown a physical body, it is raised a spiritual body. If there is a physical body, there is a spiritual body. Thus it is written, "The first man Adam became a living being" [Genesis 2:7], but the last Adam became a life-giving spirit. *But it is not the spiritual which is first but the physical, and then the spiritual.* The first man was from the earth, a man of dust; the second man is from heaven. As was the man of dust, so are those who are of the dust; and as is the man of heaven, so are those who are of heaven. Just as we have borne the image of the man of dust, we shall also bear the image of the man of heaven. I tell you this, brethren: *flesh and blood cannot inherit the kingdom of God, nor does the perishable inherit the imperishable.* (1 Cor. 15:42–50; emphases added)

Without the quite different contrast between the old Adam and the new Adam in Romans 5, and with this passage standing alone, it would be much easier to reconcile Paul's theology of the death of Adam with evolution (and the wider law of entropy); for here death seems to be due to entirely natural processes stemming from Adam's creation out of the dust (Hebrew = *adamah*) of the earth, whereas in Romans Paul says death (first?) entered the world through sin. But this tension can be reconciled, once one takes to heart what the *Catechism* says about the doctrine's retrospective interpretation of Genesis 3 in the light of Christ.[51]

This tension, in fact, is also reflected in human experience. As a biological reality, death comes across as both inevitable (since all cells eventually die) and entirely natural (as seen in the evident aging of all life-forms); but as a spiritual reality *in humans*, it seems a violation of the right order of things, an intrusion of a foreign element, in other words, a "sting" (1 Cor. 15:55). Thomas Aquinas reconciles this tension in this way:

> We may have a suspicion that separation of the soul from the body is not *per accidens* but is in accord with nature. For man's body is made up of contrary elements. Everything of this sort is naturally corruptible. Therefore the human body is naturally corruptible. But when the body corrupts, the soul must survive as a separate entity if the soul is immortal, as in fact it is. Apparently, then, the separation of the soul from the

51. Williams largely misses this point in his polemic against Augustine: "It would seem that the first step [in linking the idea of the Fall with Genesis 3] consisted in the affirmation of a causal connexion between Adam's sin and the fact of human liability to death, that is, in the reading into the story of the hypothesis that man at his creation was endowed with the gift of immortality, but that this was withdrawn from him as part of the punishment for his transgression. In fact, the Scriptural text says nothing of the kind: it implies, on the contrary, that man was created mortal, formed of the dust and destined to return to it, though he might have made himself immortal by eating of the Tree of Life, even after his sin; and that it was precisely in order to keep him mortal that YHWH expelled him from the Garden and posted a cherubic guard to prevent his return. The point of YHWH's warning in Gen. 2:17 as to the fatal consequences which would follow a breach of his command is, not that man would become mortal after being immortal, but that man, mortal by nature and fated sooner or later to return to dust, would suffer death *forthwith* as a punishment for his sin ("*in the day* that thou eatest thereof thou shalt surely die") instead of living out his life to a ripe old age and being re-absorbed into his parent earth through a painless dissolution. It is the ruthless immediacy of the threatened death, not the mere fact of mortality (to which Adam was in any case subject by virtue of his creaturely nature), which constitutes the spear-head of the menace." Williams, *Ideas*, 53. Enns is more balanced when he says: "Paul's reading of Genesis is driven by factors external to Genesis. . . . Paul's view of the depth of universal, inescapable human alienation from God is completely true, but it is also beyond what is articulated on the Old Testament in general or Genesis specifically." Enns, *Evolution of Adam*, 87. The same principle applies to Augustine, and indeed to the whole theological tradition: Genesis 3 must always be read in the light of Christ.

body is in accord with nature. In view of these considerations, we must take up the question of how this separation is according to nature, and how it is opposed to nature. We showed above that the rational soul exceeds the capacity of all corporeal matter in a measure impossible to other forms. This is demonstrated by its intellectual activity, which it exercises without the body. To the end that corporeal matter might be fittingly adapted to the soul, there had to be added to the body some disposition that would make it suitable matter for such a form. And in the same way that this form itself received existence from God alone through creation, that disposition, transcending as it does corporeal nature, was conferred on the human body by God alone for the purpose of preserving the body itself in a state of incorruption so that it might match the soul's perpetual existence. . . . But when man's soul turned from God by sin, the human body deservedly lost that supernatural disposition whereby it was unrebelliously subservient to the soul. Hence man *incurred* the necessity of dying. Accordingly, *if we regard the nature of the body, death is natural.* But if we regard the nature of the soul and the disposition with which the human body was supernaturally endowed in the beginning for the sake of the soul, death is *per accidens* and contrary to nature, inasmuch as union with the body is natural for the [immortal] soul.[52]

Although he was certainly no Thomist, Pascal seconds this view of death's dual visage, although even more than Thomas he stresses death's *irruption* into the complacent life of the "natural man," whom he addresses in these unsparing terms:

You do not need a greatly elevated soul to realize that in this life there is no true and firm satisfaction, that all our pleasures are simply vanity, that our afflictions are infinite, and lastly that death, which threatens us at every moment, must in a few years infallibly present us with the appalling necessity of being either annihilated or wretched for all eternity. Nothing is more real nor more dreadful than that. We may put on as brave a face as we like: that is the end which awaits the finest life on earth. . . . Where can we find the source of such feelings? What reason for joy can we find in expecting nothing but hopeless wretchedness?

52. St. Thomas Aquinas, *Light of Faith: The Compendium of Theology*, trans. Cyril Vollert, S.J. (Manchester, NH: Sophia Institute Press, 1993), 170–71 (no. 152); emphases added.

What reason for pride to see ourselves cloaked in impenetrable darkness? . . . Nothing is so important to man as his condition. Nothing is
so frightening to him as eternity. And so the fact that there are men
indifferent to the loss of their being and to the peril of an eternity of
wretchedness is not natural. They are quite different with regard to
everything else: they fear even the most insignificant things, they fore-
see them, feel them; and the same man who spends so many days and
nights in a rage and despair over the loss of some office or over some
imaginary affront to his honor is the very one who, without anxiety
or emotion, knows he is going to lose everything through death. It is
a monstrous thing to see in the same heart and at the same time both
this sensitivity to the slightest things, and this strange insensitivity to
the greatest.[53]

These attempts to reconcile Romans 5 with 1 Corinthians 15 surely
dovetail with everyone's personal experience as biological beings destined
for death—yet a death that, however biologically inevitable, strangely
looms as a divine judgment to be rendered on a life mired in the acquiescence of sin. But exegetes have also offered their own perspective when
they take up Paul's contrast between the old and new Adam. Given that
Paul says, "Then as one man's trespass led to condemnation for all men, so
one man's act of righteousness leads to acquittal and life for all men" (Rom.
5:18), it can be all too easy to conclude that the old Adam spoken of here
must be an individual human being, since Paul obviously regarded Jesus as
an individual human being in history. While true, that is not *all* that Jesus
meant for Paul, a point that becomes especially clear when one realizes
the manifold ways Paul speaks of *sōma* ("body") in his letters:

One could say without exaggeration that the concept of the body forms
the keystone of Paul's theology. In its closely interconnected meanings,
the word *sōma* knits together all his great themes. It is from the body of
sin and death that we are delivered; it is through the body of Christ on
the Cross that we are saved; it is into His body the Church that we are
incorporated; it is by His body in the Eucharist that this Community is
sustained; it is in our body that its new life has to be manifested; it is
to a resurrection of this body to the likeness of His glorious body that
we are destined. Here, with the exception of the doctrine of God, are

53. Pascal, *Pensées*, 160, 161–62.

represented all the main tenets of the Christian Faith—the doctrines of Man, Sin, the Incarnation and Atonement, the Church, the Sacraments, Sanctification, and Eschatology. To trace the subtle links and interaction between the different senses of this word *sōma* is to grasp the thread that leads through the maze of Pauline thought.[54]

Paul's multivalent usage here obviously far transcends the sterile and jejune categories of "literal" and "symbolic" as those terms are usually bandied about. For one thing, if by "literal" we mean what Paul intended to say, then "literal" here must encompass all the meanings that he sought to get across in all their complexity. Secondly, all these meanings are equally obviously "real" for Paul, just as Catholics insist on the *real* presence of the Body and Blood of Christ in the Eucharist. Something similar is perhaps at work in Paul's invocation of the second Adam. As W. D. Davies points out in his influential study of Paul's debt to rabbinic Judaism, for the rabbis "Adam as created by God was no ordinary man; he was of an enormous size extending from one end of the earth to another, and from heaven to earth."[55] The point is controversial because our sources for first-century rabbinic thought most often come from the Talmud and Mishnah, which only received their final literary forms from the fourth to the eighth centuries of the Common Era, although this particular midrash (embellished commentary) can apparently be traced back to Rabbi Eliezer ben Azariah, who lived around the close of the first century, that is, a generation after Paul's death.[56]

The same must be said for another midrash, somewhat similar to the one given above, and based on the Hebrew pun between *adam* (the generic word for "man") and *adamah* ("ground" or "dust"), according to which God made Adam out of dust gathered from all over the earth, with his head formed from the earth of the Holy Land, the trunk of his body from Babylonian soil, and so forth. While the influence of these specific rabbinic speculations on Paul's thinking must remain merely hypothetical, given

54. J. A. T. Robinson, *The Body: A Study in Pauline Theology* (Philadelphia: The Westminster Press, 1952), 9.

55. W. D. Davies, *Paul and Rabbinic Judaism: Some Rabbinic Elements in Pauline Theology* (London: SPCK, 1962), 45.

56. Philo of Alexandria, who was a contemporary of Paul, reconciled Genesis 1 and 2 by assuming that the first account of creation dealt with the creation of the Heavenly Man, while the earthly man's formation was described in Genesis 2. Two accounts of creation, two different creations of two different men! Details in Davies, *Paul and Rabbinic Judaism,* 47.

the difficulty of dating their provenance, one may at least agree with Enns when he says: "The fact that Paul draws an analogy between Adam and Christ, however, does not mean that we are required to consider them as characters of equal historical standing."[57]

Enns adopts this position, as he makes clear, largely because he holds that evolution renders any other conclusion quite literally incredible. But there is also scriptural and magisterial warrant for refusing a direct equation between Adam and Christ. For, while Adam holds a *temporal* priority over Christ in the history of salvation, Christ is *ontologically* prior, as we learn from all those scriptural passages that speak of creation as being created *through and for* Christ (Col. 1:16b) or of Christ not regarding his equality as something to be grasped but becoming obedient unto death by taking on the form of a human being, indeed of a slave (Phil. 2:5-8).[58] As the papally appointed International Theological Commission (ITC) rightly pointed out, this was the source of Augustine's error, who said, in a telling passage: "Every man is Adam, just as, *in the case of those who believe*, every man is Christ, for they are his members."[59]

As the Commission rightly observes, this inverts the perspective bequeathed to us by revelation: "Many traditional accounts of sin and salvation (and of Limbo) have stressed solidarity with Adam more than solidarity with Christ, or at least such accounts have had a restrictive conception of the ways by which human beings benefit from solidarity with Christ"

57. Enns, *Evolution of Adam*, 125.

58. Notice that the grammatical (nominal) subject of these verses is not the eternal Logos, but Christ: "Put on the mind of Christ Jesus, *who*, though he was in the form of God, did not count equality with God a thing to be grasped, but emptied himself, taking on the form of a slave, born in the likeness of men. And being found in human form he humbled himself and became obedient unto death, even death on a cross."

59. Augustine, *Enarrationes in Psalmos 70*, Book II, chapter 1 (*PL* 36, column 891); emphasis added: "Omnis autem homo Adam; sicut in his qui crediderunt, omnis homo Christus, quia membra sunt Christi." Cited by the ITC Report at note 123. Augustine applies this same restrictive "exegesis" when dealing with Paul's statement that "just as in Adam all die, so also in Christ shall all be made alive" (1 Cor. 15:22), which the African Doctor glosses this way: "[This passage] does not mean that all who die in Adam will be members of Christ, for the great majority of them will be punished with the second death, which is forever. What the Apostle means by using 'all' in both parts of the statement is that no one dies in his animal body except in Adam; and in the same way no one is brought to life in a spiritual body except 'in Christ.'" Augustine, *City of God* (Book XIII, chapter 23), trans. Henry Bettenson (New York: Penguin Books, 1972), 540. The ITC is correct: Augustine consistently interprets Christ inside salvation history and *under* Adam, quite the reverse of the movement of Paul's thought, for whom the "heavenly Christ" perforce comes first.

(no. 91).[60] In other words, this entire debate has been conducted by looking at the issue of limbo, as it were, through the wrong end of the telescope:

> We wish to stress that humanity's solidarity with Christ (or, more properly, Christ's solidarity with all of humanity) must have priority over the solidarity of human beings with Adam, and that the question of the destiny of unbaptized infants who die must be addressed in that light. (no. 91) . . . The traditional view is that it is only through sacramental Baptism that infants have solidarity with Christ and hence access to the vision of God. Otherwise, solidarity with Adam has priority; we may ask, however, how that view might be changed if priority were restored to our solidarity with Christ (i.e., Christ's solidarity with us). (no. 93)

Paradoxically, this stress on solidarity can rescue at least one part of Augustine's doctrine, his notorious and much-criticized interpretation of the received Latin translation *in quo* ("in whom" or "in which") for Paul's original *eph'hō* (ἐφ ᾧ: usually taken to mean "because" or "inasmuch as") in this line: "Therefore, as sin came into the world through one man and death through sin, and so death spread to all men because [ἐφ ᾧ] all men sinned" (Rom. 5:12; RSV). Augustine, however, took the line to mean that sin came into the world through one man (Adam) *in whom* all sinned, which verse he then used to justify his idea that Adam transmitted his sin seminally to all his progeny. That interpretation is now universally rejected; because if that had been Paul's meaning, he would have said *en hō* (ἐν ᾧ). But in an important article Joseph Fitzmyer, after a careful examination of the extant secular and religious literature, shows that the phrase could also be translated as "with the result that" (this is called in the grammar books the "consecutive sense"), which both rescues Augustine from his theory of seminal transmission of original sin while salvaging his main point of human solidarity in sin: "Thus Paul in v. 12 would be ascribing death and human sinfulness to two causes, not unrelated: to Adam and to the conduct of all human beings. . . . For 'no one sins entirely alone and no one sins without adding to the collective burden of mankind.'"[61]

60. International Theological Commission, "The Hope of Salvation for Infants Who Die Without Being Baptized," available on the Vatican website at http://www.vatican.va/roman _curia/congregations/cfaith/cti_documents/rc_con_cfaith_doc_20070419_un-baptised -infants_en.html; quoted here by paragraph number. As Rondet says so well: "Christ cannot have been less powerful to save us than Adam was to ruin us" (Rondet, *Original Sin*, 181).

61. Joseph A. Fitzmyer, S.J., "The Consecutive Meaning of ΕΦ Ω in Romans 5:12," *New*

But this solidarity must work both ways, with the clear priority given to Christ's work of salvation, not Adam's sin. As Pope Benedict XVI solemnly taught in his encyclical *Spe Salvi*:

[W]e should recall that no man is an island, entire of itself. Our lives are involved with one another; through innumerable interactions they are linked together. No one lives alone. No one sins alone. No one is saved alone. The lives of others continually spill over into mine: in what I think, say, do and achieve. And conversely, my life spills over into that of others: for better and for worse. So my prayer for another is not something extraneous to that person, something external, not even after death.... It is never too late to touch the heart of another, nor is it ever in vain. In this way we further clarify an important element of the Christian concept of hope. Our hope is always essentially also hope for others; only thus is it truly hope for me too. As Christians we should never limit ourselves to asking: how can I save myself? We should also ask: what can I do in order that others may be saved and that for them too the star of hope may rise? Then will I have done my utmost for my own personal salvation as well. (no. 48)

This factor of solidarity in salvation as well as sin is largely missing in Augustine, at least when he was tangling with the Pelagians.[62] But that very lack is what transforms baptism into a kind of celestial life-insurance policy, of relevance to the individual alone, which would then lose its monetary value, so to speak, if the non-baptized were to be admitted into heaven. Thus, a kind of binary logic takes over, whereby the believer comes to feel "cheated" if others get in ahead of him, as if St. Peter were standing at the Pearly Gates checking for baptismal certificates like some Manhattan night-club bouncer assigned to weed out the lowly bridge-and-tunnel crowd from New Jersey while the beautiful people are inside with

---

Testament Studies, Vol. 39, No. 3 (July 1993): 321–39; here 339; the internal quotation is from Brendan Byrne, *Reckoning with Romans: A Contemporary Reading of Paul's Gospel*, Good News Studies 18 (Wilmington, DE: Glazier, 1986), 116.

62. As here: "Tell me, then, what sort of justice has recompensed the little ones with a heavy yoke of such great and obvious misery? Tell me, by what justice is one child adopted in baptism, while another dies without such adoption? . . . You do not reply, because, as someone more a Pelagian than a Christian, you do not understand either the grace of God or the justice of God." Augustine, *Answer to the Pelagians, III: Unfinished Work in Answer to Julian*, trans. Roland J. Teske, S.J. (Hyde Park, NY: New City Press, 1999), 68 (I 35).

their Botox souls dancing the night away. But that was Augustine's logic, which George Dyer explains in this unsparing description of his position:

> Augustine had employed his formidable scriptural armament to exclude children from eternal life and from the kingdom of God; . . . and so in language that was largely scriptural he painted a chilling description of the future life of the unbaptized child. He must face the judgment of God, said Augustine; he is a vessel of wrath, a vessel of contumely, and the judgment of God is upon him. Baptism is the only thing that can deliver him from the kingdom of death and the power of the devil. If no one frees him from the grasp of the devil, what wonder is it that he must suffer in flames with Satan? There can be no doubt about the matter, the saint concludes, he must go into eternal fire with the devil.[63]

Augustine's theory of the seminal transmission of original sin through Adam's seed also runs into the contradiction of his theory of the soul. Although he never did finally decide which theory was right, and was at times open to Tertullian's idea that souls were conceived by parents along with bodies (a theory known as "traducianism"), he was, all in all, mostly drawn to the position that God created each soul directly at conception (called "creationism," not to be confused with the creationism that rejects evolution), a position that is now the official doctrine of the Catholic Church, reaffirmed not only in *Humani Generis* but also iterated in Pope John Paul II's "Letter on Evolution" of October, 1996.[64] But once the position that God directly created each soul at conception became settled doctrine, Augustine's theory of the seminal transmission of original sin runs into intolerable antinomies, as even he recognized: for if God directly creates the soul, that soul must be wholly good, since God cannot create evil. But

---

63. George Dyer, *Limbo: Unsettled Question* (New York: Sheed and Ward, 1964), 14–15. In this debate Augustine will recognize only the exclusive and entirely binary categories of right and left: "Judgment will be passed on the living and the dead; some will be on the right, others on the left; I don't know any other destiny. . . . Whoever is not on the right is without a doubt on the left; so whoever is not in the kingdom is without a doubt in the eternal fire." Augustine, *Sermons* III/8 (273–305A), trans. Edmund Hill, O.P. (Hyde Park, NY: New City Press, 1994), sermon 294, 181–82. No doubt!

64. Even at the end of his life, he could not decide: "As regards the origin of the soul, how it comes to be in the body, whether it comes from the first man when he was made living flesh or whether each soul is created for each human being, I did not know at that time, and no more do I know today." Augustine, *Retractions*, I t.3; cited in Rondet, *Original Sin*, 136).

sin is primarily an event of the will, which is a faculty of the soul, with the body receiving its tendency to corruption from the formal properties of the soul.[65]

Thomas Aquinas recognized the problem and in trying to solve it came astonishingly close to the ancient rabbinic idea of a corporate Adam. After rejecting the idea that the rational soul is transmitted by the semen, or that the defects of the body can infect the very substance of the soul (for then there would be no guilt involved), Thomas comes to this solution:

> Therefore, we must explain the matter otherwise, by saying that all men born of Adam may have one common nature, which they receive from their first parents; even as in civil matters all who are members of one community are reputed as one body, and the whole community as one man. Indeed Porphyry says that "by sharing the same species, many men are one man." Accordingly, the multitude of men born of Adam are as to many members of one body. Now the action of one member of the body—of the hand, for instance—is voluntary not by the will of that hand, but by the will of the soul, the first mover of the members. Wherefore, a murder which the hand commits would not be imputed as a sin to the hand, considered by itself as apart from the body, but is imputed to it as something belonging to man and moved by man's first moving principle. In this way, then, the disorder which is in this man born of Adam is voluntary, not by his will, but by the will of his first parent, who, by the movement of generation moves all who originate from him, even as the soul's will moves all the members to their actions. Hence the sin which is thus transmitted by the first parent to his descendants is called *original*, just as the sin which flows from the soul into the bodily members is called *actual*. And just as the actual sin that is committed by a member of the body is not the sin of that member, except inasmuch as that member is a part of the man, for which reason it is called a *human sin*; so original sin is not the sin of this person except inasmuch as this

---

65. "[Augustine's] personal inclination pointed in the direction of 'creationism'; but he found it difficult to explain why God should have created so many millions of souls in a state of innocence, only to be infused into bodies which He knew were bound to pollute them with concupiscence. Moreover, the Pelagians . . . were 'creationists' to a man: hence, when charged by them with holding 'traducianism,' Augustine shows a distinct reluctance to repudiate the accusation." Williams, *Ideas*, 368. For examples of Augustine's wiggling here, see his *On the Soul and Its Origins* I 6, 13; *On Merit and the Remission of Sins* III 5; *Incomplete Work Against Julian* II 178; IV 104; V 17.

person receives his nature from his first parent, for which reason it is called the *sin of nature*, according to the Apostle (Eph. 2:3): "We ... were by nature children of wrath." (*ST* I-II, q. 81, a. 1)

I am not necessarily defending Thomas's position here, especially since the analogy of the murdering hand breaks down when applied to Adam's guilt. For surely he cannot mean that individual souls that command the murdering hand to do the bloody deed are no more guilty as "agents" of Adam than is the hand, the agent of the soul. But the Common Doctor is groping toward a solution, while working under the nearly intolerable antimonies bequeathed by Augustine. But what is fascinating about this passage is that Thomas is groping toward some kind of *corporate solution*. But this "solution" (assuming it works) entails another point, one that will be treated more fully in the next chapter: if Adam and Eve were saved during Christ's descent into the underworld on Holy Saturday (as the entire iconographic and patristic tradition automatically assumed), then how do actual sins count more against the individual than Adam's initial sin, which by definition was the more catastrophic? Why does the "guilt" of unbaptized babies count for more than the supposedly *real* guilt that Adam handed on to all his progeny?

Thomas had at least a provisional solution to that problem when he relied on an increasingly popular medieval doctrine, that of a limbo of unbaptized infants. But Augustine resolutely opposed that idea (to be sure, because it was proposed by the Pelagians, and not very coherently). The trouble is, Augustine *needed* his doctrine of the seminal transition of original sin; otherwise his whole stance on the absolute necessity of baptism would collapse, together with his polemic against the Pelagians on just this point. For as Pier Franco Beatrice notes in his influential monograph on this theme:

> When ... one speaks of hereditary sin, the idea is that Adam transmitted to his descendants not just the punishment for his sin, but the sin itself. In this manner, men are born not only subject to physical death, pain, and the other limitations inherent in their debased nature, deprived as it is of the image of God. In addition, they come into the world in a condition of actual sin, which renders them worthy of eternal damnation.[66]

66. Pier Franco Beatrice, *The Transmission of Sin: Augustine and the Pre-Augustinian Sources*, trans. Adam Kamesar (Oxford: Oxford University Press, 2013), 6. Beatrice claims that

To add to Augustine's difficulties, for him baptism is not all *that* determinative of God's favor, because for him baptism only avails if it is accompanied by God's grace of perseverance, a discussion of which will also be taken up in the next chapter. But at least this can be said in conclusion of this one: Augustine's own highly peculiar interpretation of original sin might well be riddled with internal contradictions, which were indeed noted early on, even by his contemporaries. But time and again in the history of theology, as we have noted, whenever believers or unbelievers in the gospel of Christ deny the doctrine of original sin, and precisely because Augustine's views seem so bizarre, then it is not so much that the dogmatic truth of the doctrine reasserts itself as that the blatant *reality* of what it points to and is meant to illuminate comes roaring back into the foreground of the crisis of civilization. For as Pascal says so well:

> [T]here can be no doubt that nothing shocks our reason more than to say that the sin of the first man made guilty those who, so far from that source, seem incapable of having taken part in it. This contamination seems not only impossible to us, but also quite unjust. . . . Certainly, nothing shocks us more deeply than this doctrine. Nevertheless, without this most incomprehensible of all mysteries, we are incomprehensible to ourselves. Within this gnarled chasm lie the twists and turns of our condition. So, humanity is more inconceivable without this mystery than this mystery is conceivable to humanity.[67]

---

this idea of the seminal transmission of original sin was not Augustine's invention but one that he drew from earlier second-century Jewish-Christian sects in Egypt—the Encratites and the Messalians—who rejected marriage and procreation as inherently evil. At all events, and as already noted above, the *Catechism of the Catholic Church* takes quite the opposite position when it calls "original sin . . . 'sin' only in an analogical sense: it is a sin 'contracted' and not 'committed'—a state and not an act" (no. 404).

67. Pascal, *Pensées*, 42–43.

CHAPTER 4

Free Will and Predestination

> Skepticism always develops when races or classes are crossed suddenly and decisively. In the new generation, which has inherited in its blood diverse standards and values, everything is unrest, disturbance, doubt, attempt. The best forces have an inhibiting effect: the very virtues do not allow each other to grow and become strong. ... But what becomes sickest and degenerates most in such hybrids is the will: they no longer know independence of decisions and the intrepid sense of pleasure in willing—they doubt the "freedom of the will" even in their dreams.
>
> Friedrich Nietzsche, *Beyond Good and Evil*

No issue has proved itself more difficult of resolution, in either philosophy or theology, than the question of free will. If, in philosophy, the presupposition is made that there are no uncaused events in nature—that every event in nature is caused by some preceding natural event—then how can free will exist, especially if free will is defined as that faculty by which the human person makes decisions from his own internal source of *free* choice, decisions that are by definition not compelled by the forces of nature? If, correlatively, theology must presuppose God's sovereignty over human history, then again what happens to human free will? Can man ever really defy God, go against God's will, do what God had never intended in the first place when he created the world? In both systems, the temptation to deny free will seems well-nigh overwhelming.

Philosophers nowadays are nothing if not intimidated by the sciences, especially the hard sciences, which generally brook no opposition to the idea of a self-sufficient nature, even when the random events at the quantum level are taken into account.[1] Nor, as we shall see, has it ever been possible for Christian theologians to defend the idea of free will too much without running into the accusation of having fallen into that dread heresy of Pelagianism, a term that in its generic sense means any heresy that defends the power of human free will to respond to God's offer of salvation quite independent of God's predetermining aid of grace.[2]

The philosophical issue of free will, however, does not "map out" in any exact or isometric way with theology's concerns—although of course there is some overlap. For one thing, at the birth of western philosophy in ancient Greece, the concept of divine agency was much more attenuated (when it was acknowledged at all) than what any Christian theologian could countenance. For the Greeks, no doubt influenced by their prior mythology, impersonal *fate* had a much more determinative role to play in discussions of free will, whereas for monotheists (whether Jewish, Christian, or Muslim) God's own personal *will* was all-determining. This difference in worldview is admirably captured by the Israeli scholar of the Hebrew Bible Yehezkel Kaufmann (1889–1963), who pointed out that in polytheistic belief systems the gods are *born*, which means that they come *from* a prior (and therefore more impersonal) world that existed before they did:

> [Polytheists assumed] that there exists a realm of being prior to the gods and above them, upon which the gods depend, and whose decrees they must obey. Deity belongs to, and is derived from, a primordial realm. . . . They are rooted in this realm, are bound by its nature, are subservient to its laws. To be sure, paganism has personal gods who create and gov-

---

1. Randomness at the quantum level does not really entail an escape from determinism, at least for human behavior. For one thing, such randomness tends to get "washed out" in the probabilistic statistics of subatomic events, after which regularity becomes inevitable. Second, true randomness, strictly defined, means "utterly uncaused," but free will refers to human behavior *caused* by an allegedly free decision made by an agent who is claimed to be free of the determinations of the natural order. As Thomas Pink tartly points out: "Randomness, the operation of mere chance, clearly excludes control. . . . If a process is just random, then it must be taking place outside of our control. Randomness is at least as much a threat to freedom—to our exercising control over how we act—as determinism might be. If our actions are no more than chance occurrences, then how can our action involve an exercise of control on our part?" Thomas Pink, *Free Will: A Very Short Introduction* (Oxford: Oxford University Press, 2004), 16.

2. At least according to Augustine, one of his opponents, Julian of Eclanum, did not hesitate to say that, by his possession of free will, man is "emancipated from God." Augustine, *Incomplete Work against Julian* I, 78. Not the wisest debating ploy on Julian's part against the formidable African *doctor gratiae*.

ern the world of men. But a divine will, sovereign and absolute, which governs all and is the cause of all being—such a concept is unknown. There are heads of pantheons, there are creators and maintainers of the cosmos; but transcending them is the primordial realm, with its pre-existent autonomous forces.[3]

For that same reason, myths often speak of the gods' subservience to fate, as in the famous scene in Homer's *Iliad*, when the father-god Zeus seeks to rescue his mortal son Sarpedon from certain death and is rebuked by his wife Hera in these terms:

> But Queen Hera, her eyes wide, protested strongly:
> "Dread majesty, son of Cronus—what are you saying?
> A man, a mere mortal, *his doom sealed long ago*?
> You'd set him free from all the pains of death? . . .
>
>   . . . No,
> dear as he is to you, and your heart grieves for him,
> leave Sarpedon there to die in the brutal onslaught. . . ."
>
>   . . . So she pressed
> and Zeus the father of men and gods complied at once.[4]

The implied metaphysics of the monotheist worldview is so strikingly different from that of the polytheists that it comes as no surprise to the historian to learn how the two different systems misunderstood each other from the ground up. For, as Kaufmann says:

> The basic idea of Israelite religion is that God is supreme over all. There is no realm above or beside him to limit his absolute sovereignty. He is

---

3. Yehezkel Kaufmann, *The Religion of Israel: From Its Beginnings to the Babylonian Exile*, trans. and abridged by Moshe Greenberg (New York: Schocken Books, 1972), 21–22. Every mythology is carried along by an implicit metaphysics, as can be seen in the theogonies that every mythology describes: "Even the 'primal god' is thought of as no more than 'father' of the gods and the world, engendering these out of his seed or his substance *with no more control over their nature and destiny than a human father has over the nature and destiny of his offspring*. His 'paternity' does not involve universal rule and power. Indeed, it is typical of the ruling gods that they are usually of the second or third generation. The son who dethrones his father, or rescues him from distress, and thus rises above him, is a standing feature of pagan mythologies" (ibid., 22; emphasis added).

4. Homer, *Iliad*, Book 16, ll. 522–24; 535–37; 544 (Fagles's translation); emphasis added.

utterly distinct from, and other than, the world; he is subject to no laws, no compulsions, or powers that transcend him. . . . Israel's God has no pedigree, fathers no generations; he neither inherits nor bequeaths his authority. . . . He has no sexual qualities or desires and shows no need of or dependence upon powers outside of himself.[5]

Given these startlingly different outlooks on the world, in one of which fate operates as the instance of last resort and in the other of which God's will operates as the court of last appeal, the issue of free will was bound to be taken up in different ways in the two systems. Once that point is conceded, however, one does notice in the history of philosophy and theology a certain formal similarity of outcome: efforts to defend free will keep getting outbid by the ultimate "trump card" in each worldview: fate (or, later, scientific determinism) in philosophy, and God's predestining will in theology. Yet, when determinism, whether scientific or divine, begins to win out in the debate, then the idea that human beings are responsible for their actions slowly gets undermined. But *that* conclusion—that humans are not really responsible for any of their actions—itself leads to problems of its own (not least in criminal courts, where human freedom and responsibility must be presupposed), which then provokes an inevitable reopening of the debate.

The problem with determinism is that it keeps running up against basic human *intuitions*, which seem inexpugnable. True, intuition also recognizes a vast range of factors over which we have no control whatever, starting with our births (no one chooses to be born). But along with birth, we have no choice over our sex, our parents, our siblings, our looks, the era of history into which we were born, our mother tongue, even to a large extent our personality and talents,[6] along with desires and feelings that overcome us from time to time (most of the time, actually).[7] Nor may we

5. Kaufmann, *Religion of Israel*, 60–61.

6. "Among the possible determinants of the shape of character, the psychological equipment . . . may have been present from the beginning and independent of instinctual conflict." David Shapiro, *Neurotic Styles* (New York: Basic Books, 1965), 9.

7. Once again, Augustine had the better argument against the Pelagians: "St. Augustine noted this truth of universal experience: that man is not master of his first thoughts. He can influence the course of his reflections, but he himself cannot determine the objects, the images, and consequently the motives which are presented to his mind. 'No one has power over what chances to come into his mind,' he said, 'but to give consent or to withhold it is in the power of one's own will.'" Eugène Portalié, S.J., *A Guide to the Thought of Saint Augus-*

choose the physical laws of the universe, its age, the vulnerability of our planet to earthquakes, our susceptibility to disease, the rate of inflation, the unemployment rate, and a host of other constraints that hem us in.

Yet, there seems to be a whole other range of realities that do seem to be under our control, options that are, both in Aristotle's phrase and in English idiom, "up to us."[8] Such choices that seem to be up to us would include choosing a college major, deciding to read this book now in front of the reader rather than going out to see a movie, voting for one candidate over another in an election, choosing to forgo dessert during Lent, or choosing chocolate over vanilla ice cream when the time for fasting has elapsed. No doubt all of these supposedly free choices are *motivated*; but motivation (such as, say, strong ideological convictions that would make one's vote easily predictable to an outsider) do not obviate the basic intuition, which we all have, that these choices are still *ours*—"up to us," as we say. That intuition has, down through the ages, caused philosophers and theologians to torment themselves in efforts to make that intuition jibe with what is already known about the workings of the physical uni-

---

tine, trans. Ralph J. Bastian, S.J. (Chicago: Henry Regnery, 1960), 199. The internal quotation is from Augustine's *On the Spirit and Letter* 34, 60. This lack of mastery applies most vividly of course to sexual feelings, which arise unbidden and continue to throb away "until the blood is cooled," to borrow Hamlet's famous line; and on no topic has Augustine been most often derided than for his "hatred" of human sexuality. But here too the bishop of Hippo gets the better of his opponents, as Henry Chadwick notes: "His considerable discussions of sexuality are conspicuously free from prudery, so frank that he feared being read by people whose minds were unequal to the seriousness of the subject. Medicine was a department of science on which he made himself informed. His library included clinical textbooks and, while composing his replies to Julian of Eclanum, he studied the best guide to gynecology." Henry Chadwick, Augustine, Past Masters Series (Oxford: Oxford University Press, 1986), 113. Precisely that "clinical" attitude gave him the freedom to point out the obvious: "The physiological changes that make sexual union practicable are uncontrolled by reason and will. Body and reason can often be at loggerheads, the body stirred when the will and reason do not want it, or vice versa" (ibid., 112).

8. Greek: *eph'hēmin*, which exactly corresponds to the English idiom "up to us." Actually, Aristotle never uses the Greek word for "freedom" *(eleutheria)* for this concept of "up-to-us-ness," the former of which had a primarily political meaning in his works (this changed with the Stoics). Rather, Aristotle referred to "voluntary" *(hekousios, hekōn)* and "involuntary" *(akousios, akōn)*, all of which he connects in this way: "Since what is wished for is the end [*telos*], while what we deliberate about and decide on are things that lead to the end [*ta pros to telos*], actions aimed at the latter will be based on choice and are voluntary, which is precisely what the various excellences aim at too, which also depend on us [*eph'hēmin*]." Aristotle, *Nicomachean Ethics* III (5) 1113b3–6.

verse and/or of divine agency; but the intuition just won't go away, as Pink notes:

> The idea of being in control of how we act—the up-to-us-ness of our actions—is an idea we all share. It is a constant and fundamental feature of our thinking, and one that we can all recognize. And the idea is irresistible. However sceptical we may become when doing philosophy, once we fall back into ordinary life we do all continue to think of how we act as being up to us. Thinking of ourselves as being in control of how we act is part of what enables us to see living as something valuable. In so far as we can direct and control how we ourselves act, our lives can be genuinely our own achievement or failure. Our lives can be our own, not merely to be enjoyed or endured, but for ourselves to direct and make.[9]

But our intuitions also testify to other feelings: that we are not as much in control of our lives as it might at first seem. For the intuition of possessing a free will arises most spontaneously when we look toward the future. But when looking back on the past, things often seem more inevitable. When I chose a college major way back in my undergraduate days, for example, how much freedom to choose did I really have? Was I not compelled by anticipated future economic consequences, by such factors as talent, whether I got along with a certain professor, even by scheduling conflicts? Or if I continually "choose" dessert when I am on a diet or am fasting for religious reasons, can I really say I am freely *choosing* dessert? Cardinal Newman once said somewhere that if you want to predict what someone will do tomorrow, look at what is he doing today. If *character* not only gets expressed by our actions but is the very and sole expression *of* our actions, and if character is merely the term for *who* we are, are we really free to act "out of character"? If that were not enough to undermine a sense of freedom, *neurology* and *psychopathology* also work to chip away at the sense of freedom.[10] The

---

9. Pink, *Free Will*, 1–2.

10. In a famous experiment, Benjamin Libet (1916–2007) discovered that electrical charges instructing muscular activity (such as moving one's hand) began more than 300 milliseconds before subjects reported being conscious of the decision to flick their wrists. Many neurologists interpreted the experiment as proving that free will is an illusion, although Libet himself thought his experiments merely showed how and where free will works. See: Benjamin Libet, *Mind Time: The Temporal Factor in Consciousness* (Cambridge, MA: Harvard University Press, 2004), Chapter 4. An even more famous experiment (and one more

conclusion can be dizzying, as Daniel Dennett shows in this scenario we all can recognize:

> Where will it all end? There is no more potent source of anxiety about free will than the image of the physical sciences engulfing our every deed, good or bad, in the acid broth of causal explanation, nibbling away at the soul until there is nothing left to praise or blame, to honor, to respect, or love. Or so it seems to many people. And so they try to erect one barrier or another, some absolutist doctrine designed to keep these corrosive ideas at bay. This is a doomed strategy, a relic from the last millennium.... [For] as we learn more and more about how people make up their minds, the assumptions underlying our institutions of praise and blame, punishment and treatment, education and medication, will have to adjust to honor the facts as we know them, for one thing is clear: Institutions and practices based on obvious falsehoods are too brittle to trust.[11]

But Dennett is far from advocating any wholesale capitulation here. Indeed, the chapter from which this quotation is drawn is called "Holding the Line against Creeping Exculpation," and he holds the line precisely where Pink does: at the human intuition of free will:

> The anxious mantra returns: "But where will it all end?" Aren't we headed to a 100 percent "medicalized" society in which nobody is responsible, and everybody is a victim of one unfortunate feature of their background or another (nature or nurture)? No, we are not, because there are forces—not mysterious metaphysical forces, but readily explainable social and political forces—that oppose this trend, and they

---

easily replicated than Libet's) showed that unconscious patients undergoing brain surgery would spontaneously speak on the operating table, enacting past events as if they were living through them again. See: Wilder Penfield and Phanor Perot, "The Brain's Record of Auditory and Visual Experience: A Final Summary and Discussion," *Brain* 86 (1963): 595–696. Again, while others took these phenomena as proving the physical basis of all mental phenomena, Penfield saw them as evidence of the independence of mind from body: Wilder Penfield, *The Mystery of Mind: A Critical Study of Consciousness and the Human Brain* (Princeton: Princeton University Press, 1975). In cases of psychopathology, the law clearly recognizes that some mental diseases are so severe that the schizophrenic (say) is no longer criminally responsible for his deeds. But what about kleptomania or a warped childhood? The very irresolvability of the question is part of the free will problem: because we cannot answer the latter, we cannot answer the former.

11. Daniel C. Dennett, *Freedom Evolves* (New York: Viking, 2003), 289–90.

are the same sort, really, as the forces that prevent the driving age from rising to, say, thirty. People *want* to be held accountable. The benefits that accrue to one who is a citizen in good standing in a free society are so widely and deeply appreciated that there is always a potent presumption in favor of inclusion. Blame is the price we pay for credit, and we pay it gladly under most circumstances.[12]

Whatever the viability of Dennett's suggestion for a future defense of free will might prove to be, and however the debate on free will in philosophy and the human and biological sciences turns out, all this must be left for philosophers to decide. But the theological discussion of human free will runs into another, and quite different, difficulty: divine causality. In the pithy formulation of Leszek Kolakowski (1923–2009): "Ultimately the whole problem boils down to the perplexing difficulty in reconciling two tenets of Christianity: God is omnipotent and it is impossible to imagine that his will might be foiled by men; men are responsible for their damnation or salvation."[13]

With this additional theological consideration, as the history of Christian thought has shown time and again, theology invariably runs aground when it confronts the issue of divine and human freedom. Every time it tries to steer through these dangerous shoals, it seems either to crash against the rock of divine omnipotence or to run aground on the reef of human freedom, with its (alleged) ability to decide whether to accept the offer of redemption—and so determine its own salvation. The very issue itself seems to carry within it its own contradiction: to deny human freedom seems to lead to fatalism, but to assert it seems to make God's freedom no longer omnipotent. In this dilemma, generally speaking, advocates of divine omnipotence have usually won out, as Jaroslav Pelikan (1923–2006) has noted here: "One horn of the dilemma of Christian anthropology, that of responsibility, seems to be demanded by the polemical situation [when responding to the fatalists]. Yet in the long run the other alternative, that of

12. Dennett, *Freedom Evolves,* 292. He continues: "And so the best strategy for holding the line against creeping exculpation is clear: Protect and enhance the value of the games one gets to play if one is a citizen in good standing. It is erosion of these benefits, not the onward march of the human and biological sciences, that would threaten the social equilibrium. (Recall the cynical slogan that accompanied the decay and ultimate collapse of the Soviet Union: They pretend to pay us, we pretend to work.)" (ibid.).

13. Leszek Kolakowski, *God Owes Us Nothing: A Brief Remark on Pascal's Religion and on the Spirit of Jansenism* (Chicago: University of Chicago Press, 1995), 9.

inevitability, was the one to which the interpretation of Christian doctrine was obliged to give its primary attention."[14]

In that regard, one detects at least a formal similarity between the philosophical and theological debate: defenders of human free will are just that: always on the defensive. The other side—whether that side be called, in different systems of thought, and according to its own lights: fatalism, determinism, inevitability, or predestination—always seems to have a way of getting in the last word. The *onus probandi* is perennially borne by that sorry beast of burden, free will. Perhaps there is something "inevitable" even in that weighting of the debate. For we have already seen that the faculty of free will looks much more plausible when a human person faces the future; but retrospectively, the situation rapidly takes on the coloration of the unavoidable.[15]

For as we saw above, only when looking into the future do we seem masters and pilots of our own ships, who, despite the storms, control the rudders and guide the vessel to its pre-chosen goal. But when looking back on the past, we see how little we knew at the time, how things turned out quite otherwise than our plans had assumed, how the future in fact developed in such a way that our choices, like those of the heroes of Greek tragedy, provoked the very opposite of what they had intended. And who *really* has any control over the economic and political forces of the globe? When the economy tanks, what does one's carefully chosen college major mean now?

So too with predestination: it is largely a *retrospective* doctrine; and, as we will see shortly, it is especially when the doctrine is then projected into the future that knotty problems arise. But the logic of the doctrine is

14. Jaroslav Pelikan, *The Christian Tradition: A History of the Development of Doctrine*, Vol. I: *The Emergence of the Catholic Tradition: 100–600* (Chicago: University of Chicago Press, 1971), 280.

15. One aspect of this debate touches on an issue that is both philosophical and theological: the problem of divine foreknowledge: if God knows "ahead of time" what we are going to do, how can our actions be free rather than inevitable? But that topic pertains more to the area known as philosophical theology and does not really touch on the doctrine of grace *per se*. In fact, in any "hard" doctrine of predestination, whereby God chooses the elect and reprobate antecedent to their actions, the problem of divine foreknowledge cannot even arise, since it gets trumped by God's *decision* to save or damn, as Augustine noted: "sine dubio enim praescivit, si praedestinavit; sed praedestinasse, est hoc praescisse quod fuerat [Deus] ipse facturus." Augustine, *On the Gift of Perseverance* 17, 47. God obviously *knows* what he is going to accomplish if he has already *decided* to do it. For that reason, this chapter will focus solely on predestination and not on divine foreknowledge.

clear when Christians look back at the circumstances of their past and come to see the role that seemingly chance circumstances played in how they first came to accept the faith, so that when they link up these circumstances with a belief in God's providence, the language of predestination spontaneously rises to their lips: "Praise be to God the Father of our Lord Jesus Christ, who has blessed us in the heavenly realms with every spiritual blessing in Christ. For he chose us in him before the creation of the world to be holy and blameless in his sight. . . . And you also were included in Christ, when you heard the word of truth, the gospel of your salvation" (Eph. 1:3–4, 13a).

Predestination, then, is really the resulting realization that comes upon believers when they reflect how graciously they have been received and accepted by God, and how the circumstances that conspired to lead them to believe were not of their own doing, were not, in Aristotle's phrase, "up to them." In other words, the doctrine first arose out of a sense of gratitude for a gift that came "in the fullness of time." In that regard, it represents the convergence of several realizations in a Christian's life: 1) that God is eternal and that his very creation is a gratuitously willed gift that did not have to be; 2) that even though the world is sinful to its Adamic core, God can trump sin and outrun the sinner; 3) that among the mass of human beings on the globe, *I*, for reasons that have nothing to do with my merit (for I did not even choose to be born, let alone where or when), have been given the grace to know of this decision of God to outbid human sin; and 4) that the spontaneous response to this accumulating set of realizations can only be gratitude. This virtue, *gratitude*, is the core of Paul's doctrine, a gratitude that at least in his case is so powerful and overwhelming it spills out in this extraordinary paean:

> What then shall we say to all this? If God is for us, who can be against us? He who did not spare his own Son but gave him up *for us all*, will he not also give us all things with him? Who shall bring any charge against God's elect? It is God who justifies; who then is left to condemn? Is it Christ Jesus, who died, yes, who was raised from the dead, who sits at the right hand of God, who indeed intercedes for us? Who shall separate us from the love of Christ? Shall tribulation, or distress, or peril, or sword? . . . No, in all these things we are more than conquerors through him who loved us. For I am sure that neither death, nor life, nor angels, nor principalities, nor things present, nor things to come, nor powers, nor height, nor depth, not anything else in all creation, will be able to

separate us from the love of God in Christ Jesus our Lord. (Rom. 8:31–35, 37–39; emphasis added)

That is the doctrine of predestination. But three factors, the history of theology shows, can throw off this hope-grounding doctrine and turn it into something very nearly the opposite: 1) the psychology of the supposedly predestined believer; 2) the application of temporal categories of understanding to divine intentionality; and 3) the description of divine causality using human analogies, or at least the wrong ones.

The first factor has generally proved the most pernicious. For once the glance wanders off Paul's response of gratitude to the fate of others who seem to be not so similarly blessed, and once the idle workshop of the self-righteous mind gets to humming, the doctrine of predestination begins to cause problems on which theology has again and again run aground. For if a sense of gratitude is at the root of the Christian doctrine of predestination and if its enunciation is meant to give believers a strong sense of hope that they will persevere to the end (as it clearly is for Paul in the above passage), then the smallest deflection from that gratitude and hope into idle speculation about the fate of non-believers can derail the doctrine completely, so that it ends up leading those who hear of the doctrine, not to gratitude and hope, but rather either to fear and despair, or alternatively, to negligence and presumption, as Dom Farrelly (1927–2011) notes in his influential monograph on this issue:

> Man can by misunderstanding this mystery form for himself a more or less distorted notion of God and his relation to the creature, and therefore commit himself to presumption, despair, negligence, or an unchristian self-confidence. But St. Paul presented this doctrine of predestination to the Christians of Rome as a motive of hope. Hence, a true understanding of it should lead to a strengthening of the motives of true hope and of the vigor of the Christian life, because it will lead to a more adequate understanding of the objective relation between God and the creature in the work of salvation.[16]

16. Dom M. John Farrelly, O.S.B., *Predestination, Grace, and Free Will* (London: Burns & Oates, 1964), 31. Recall from the last chapter that Trent forbade the Catholic faithful from excessive confidence about one's predestined status, a view already defended by Thomas Aquinas, who held that it is not fitting that the outcome of predestination be revealed, "because, if so, those who were not predestined would despair; and security [in knowing one is predestined to salvation] would beget negligence in the predestined" (*ST* I, q. 23, a. 1, ad 4).

The trouble really begins in a too-close identification between the apparent outcomes of salvation history and the eternal decrees of God: since the world is divided between believers and unbelievers, and since one's being a Christian is due to the unmerited grace of God, and since some believers too obviously fall by the wayside and abandon their call before death, it becomes all too easy to read these features of salvation history as being due to the eternal ordinance of God; and so by a weird reversal of intent, the doctrine—originally intended by Paul to forestall pride—ends up making the believer feel set apart and better off than the *massa damnata*, from which pathetic mass he has been plucked by an apparently arbitrary decree of God.[17]

But this same logic can work in reverse, especially among those whose recessive personalities shun the public spotlight and find the notion of bragging and boasting repellent; and when *they* fall, despair can be the only logical conclusion, as we see most luridly portrayed in Nathaniel Hawthorne's novel *The Scarlet Letter* about a Puritan pastor in seventeenth-century Boston, the aptly named the Reverend Arthur Dimmesdale, who collapses at the end of the tale from guilt at having committed adultery. On the day of his death, he preaches his most effective sermon ever on the predestining grace of God, to the great edification of his congregation. But then on leaving church he climbs a different pulpit, the town scaffold. There, attended by the adulterous Hester Prynne and their daughter Pearl, he confesses his sin to the townsfolk while exposing the Scarlet A psychosomatically seared into his chest by his gnawing guilt, and falls dead just after Pearl kisses him.

From the distance of two centuries, Hawthorne made his novel a mordant commentary on Dimmesdale's theology of predestination as the source of his torment. As a "five-point Calvinist," this clergyman subscribed to the five core doctrines of strict Calvinism, usefully captured in the famous acronym, TULIP: Total depravity, Unmerited election, Lim-

---

17. Farrelly deftly describes how this psychology can easily insinuate itself into the thought of a dedicated Christian: "If two men are faced with the same temptation and one overcomes it, his superiority to the other man is due to grace and not to himself in any way that would nourish pride. [Nonetheless] he is *better* than the other because he has received not only sufficient power to perform the good act but the performance of the act itself. In other words, it is God who distinguished him from the other through giving him a prevenient grace which was greater than that given to the other" (Farrelly, *Predestination*, 34; emphasis added). Thus, and by a very rapid logical declension, the "better" Christian finds himself at the front of the synagogue bragging to God that he is not like that penitent publican in the back, beating his breast at his sinful unworthiness.

ited atonement, Irresistible grace, and Perseverance of the saints. Because Dimmesdale had failed to persevere, he recognizes that, despite his zeal for winning Boston souls, he had never been numbered among the elect to begin with, and therefore Christ, *from all eternity*, had never atoned for *his* sins, only for those of the elect. Doom was thus his foreordained end, decided in the eternal counsels of God, even before he had committed any sins, indeed even before creation itself.

In America, the latter conclusion—despair not pride—seems to have been much more common, at least in the colonial period, a problem that became so prevalent that it led to its own moniker, *tentatio praedestinationis*, the temptation to despair at one's future salvation, as we learn in Peter Thuesen's monograph, *Predestination: The American Career of a Contentious Doctrine*.[18] In his account two aspects of the debate on predestination hit Americans with special force: the suicidal torment the doctrine caused to some sensitive souls, and the divisive effect it had on American denominationalism. As to the first, American Puritans took over wholesale the Augustinian and Calvinist position that hell was, so to speak, the default position *from* which one was meant to feel lucky to have been saved.[19] One not terribly helpful strategy would be to say, as one Puritan theologian actually did, that "If among a thousand capital offenders, it were published that one of them should have a pardon, would not everyone hope to be the man?"[20] Obviously that ploy can only offer the hope of desperation. Anyone with the slightest sense of unworthiness, or even a delicate conscience, would easily assume he belonged among the vast number of the reprobate.

So it could hardly have come as much of a surprise when Increase Mather, a well-known Puritan clergyman, announced, in a sermon specifically devoted to his congregation's collective temptation to suicide, that "within the space of but five weeks, there had been five self-murders" in his own congregation.[21] Thus, a doctrine that Calvin had meant to give hope to his persecuted followers in fact became the occasion for their despair.

18. Peter J. Thuesen, *Predestination: The American Career of a Contentious Doctrine* (New York: Oxford University Press, 2009).

19. "The number of the elect is certain and will neither be increased nor decreased." Augustine, *De corruptione et gratia ad Valentinium* 13, 39.

20. Samuel Willard, *Compleat Body of Divinity in Two Hundred and Fifty Expository Lectures on the Assembly's Shorter Catechism* (Boston, 1726), 248–49; cited in Thuesen, *Predestination*, 60.

21. Increase Mather, *A Call to the Tempted: A Sermon on the Horrid Crime of Self-Murder* (Boston, 1724), 1; cited in Thuesen, *Predestination*, 65.

While this kind of despair largely waned under the impact of liberal Protestantism in the nineteenth century, the doctrine of predestination did not in any way disappear from denominational debate—and in nearly every case its impact proved divisive. Generally speaking, the pattern has been this: Usually those denominations that took their identity from their *rejection* of "hard shell" Calvinist predestination, such as John Wesley's Methodism, never felt tempted to return to a strict Calvinist understanding of predestination. Wesley, for example, when he arrived in the American colonies, excised fifteen of the Thirty-Nine Articles of the Church of England in which he had been raised that treated of justification by faith alone and the condemnation of works-righteousness. Obviously, a Methodist stress on the need for good works must equally imply a robust defense of free will, hence Wesley's hostility to Calvinism. As Susanna Wesley wrote to her brother John in 1725: "The doctrine of predestination, as maintained by the rigid Calvinists, is very shocking and ought utterly to be abhorred, because it charges the most holy God with being the author of sin."[22]

But whenever a congregation or denomination *adopted* either five-point Calvinism or its equivalent, such a doctrinal subscription to strict predestinationism invariably served as a catalyst for internal dissent from the doctrine—and a breakup of that denomination into another church formation. The reason why predestination proved so perennially discordant stems, not surprisingly, from the very *tentatio praedestinationis* that so dominated the lives of the devout in Puritan New England, as Thuesen explains here:

> First, [anxiety over one's predestined salvation] entailed something of a Catch-22. If you were not anxious about your eternal election, you were obviously not elect. But continuous (or at least cyclical) anxiety about election denied you the very comfort that predestination was supposed to bring. Comfort, in other words, could be notoriously elusive in this system. Predestinarian anxiety . . . all too easily passed from salutary struggle to genuine distress. The second problem . . . was its sheer intensity. . . . Not everyone was a spiritual marathon runner like Edwards or an accomplished soliloquist like Hamlet. Many Americans, including many Puritan laypeople, were happy simply muddling through. They looked to religion for the sort of automatic and tangible comforts that medieval laypeople once sought in merely watching the Mass. But such

22. Cited in Thuesen, *Predestination,* 73.

a view of the sacrament was the very thing Puritan clerics were bent on dispelling.[23]

Even John Milton, certainly a Puritan of the strict observance (at least up until the time he began defending the legitimacy of Christian divorce when his own marriage broke down), had no patience with the doctrine of predestination, seeing it as a tool forged in Satan's smithy; and in one highly amusing scene in *Paradise Lost* depicts the devils spending their time in hell debating the intricacies of the doctrine!

> Others apart sat on a hill retired
> In thoughts more elevate, and reasoned high
> Of providence, foreknowledge, will and fate,
> Fixed fate, free will, foreknowledge absolute
> And found no end in wand'ring mazes lost.
> Of good and evil much they argued then,
> Of happiness and final misery,
> Passion and apathy, and glory and shame:
> Vain wisdom all and false philosophy! (Book II, lines 557–565)

Even more cheekily (he had a greater sense of humor than he is often given credit for), Milton depicts the Father in Book III denouncing the Augustinian version of predestination to his Son, even though the speech occurs before the creation of Adam and Eve, that is, with the Father's full foreknowledge of the sin that would befall them; and yet in that same foreknowledge he still denounces the idea that his foreknowledge has already trumped the free agency of man:

> They themselves decreed
> Their own revolt, not I. If I foreknew,
> Foreknowledge had no influence on their fault,
> Which had no less proved certain unforeknown. (Book III, lines 116–119)

Puritan sensitivity to this doctrine was of course inevitable, given how foundational it was to their confessional identity and how it bequeathed seemingly mutually exclusive temptations either to despair or to overconfidence. But two other issues have also managed to distort Paul's original

23. Thuesen, *Predestination*, 69.

teaching: the issues of time and the kind of analogies used to describe divine causality. First of all, as to time, one must begin with what is now conceded on all sides—by cosmologists, physicists, philosophers, and theologians—that time is an inherent part of creation. True, in the seventeenth century Isaac Newton had tried to argue that time was an absolute *inside of which* God then decided to create the world; but Gottfried Leibnitz disagreed, and subsequent history would show he got the better of the argument, as one author, Dan Falk, explains:

> Leibniz believed that if time were absolute—continuing even when no change is observed—then time must have been passing even before God created the universe. In that case, God created the universe at some particular time. But why *that* particular time? Why not five minutes earlier or five minutes later? After all, in the Newtonian scheme, every moment is alike. (The best that Newton's ally [Samuel] Clarke could offer in reply was that sometimes God *did* do certain things on a whim. That did not satisfy Leibniz, who said such a notion "is plainly maintaining that God wills something, without any sufficient reason for his will.")[24]

Contemporary physics agrees with Leibnitz here: "What happened before the big bang? . . . The answer is simple: *nothing.* If time itself began with the big bang, there was no 'before' for anything to happen in."[25] And, as it happens, both Leibnitz and contemporary cosmologists agree with Augustine: "There can be no doubt that the world was not created *in* time but *with* time."[26]

One need not be a card-carrying Kantian to realize that all created beings are so deeply entissued in time that its categories always shape our experience, even when speaking of God and his "aboriginal" (another

24. Dan Falk, *In Search of Time: The History, Physics, and Philosophy of Time* (New York: St. Martin's Press, 2008), 132–33.

25. Paul Davies, *About Time: Einstein's Unfinished Revolution* (New York: Simon & Schuster, 1995), 132.

26. St. Augustine, *City of God* IX.6, trans. Henry Bettenson (Harmondsworth: Penguin, 1984), 436; translator's italics. By anticipation, Augustine's argument almost exactly parallels Leibnitz's: "An event in time happens after one time and before another, after the past and before the future. But at the time of creation there could have been no past, because there was nothing created to provide the change and movement which is the condition of time" (ibid.).

temporal word) intentions in creating the world.[27] Even the word *predesti-nation* carries a temporal marker in its prefix. Thus, theologians will often speak of God's will to save all humankind as an expression of his *antecedent* will. But then, when the topic shifts to humans' abuse of freedom, that is, when theologians have to speak of God's will after the fact of sin—whether to punish the ungodly or to save a remnant irrespective of that remnant's merits—that is ascribed to God's *consequent* will, both of which were presumably part of God's eternal counsels "before" he created the world, even though the words themselves come loaded with temporal implications. While the issue is undoubtedly arcane, much depends on the viability of the distinction, as Farrelly lucidly describes:

> For example, if one lives by the conviction that predestination is anterior to any knowledge God has of one's good or evil acts, an injunction to work out one's salvation in fear and trembling seems inappropriate, for it seems that if one has been predestined one's salvation is certain; and if one has not, it is impossible. If one is simply uncertain whether such a divine intention exists or not, it seems that the foundations of hope and thus of a vigorous Christian life are to that extent weakened. If, on the other hand, one accepts the statement that predestination is consequent upon God's foreknowledge of a life lived in fidelity to him and that this grace is rendered efficacious by man's response, then man seems cast back upon himself and his own resources. He seems to have less reason to rely completely on God, for here he is certain that God has not already predestined him. He knows that God waits to see what the outcome of his life will be before predestining him, and what the outcome of his response will be before his grace can be called truly efficacious.[28]

All of these confusions, I maintain, come from an illicit importation of temporal categories into God's eternal counsels, which are by definition beyond time. But a different, third kind of bind traps theologians when they address the *kind* of divine causality that operates to move the human will graciously, a point that can be shown in the famous dispute between the Dominican Dominic (or Domingo) Báñez (1528–1604) and the

---

27. In the rest of the analysis that follows, one must keep in mind the wise words of Henri Rondet: "The priority of grace is a priority of nature, not of time." Henri Rondet, S.J., *The Grace of Christ: A Brief History of the Theology of Grace*, trans. Tad W. Guzie, S.J. (Westminster, MD: Newman Press, 1966), 237.

28. Farrelly, *Predestination*, 31.

Jesuit Louis (or Luis) Molina (1535–1600), a fierce debate that later became known as the *de auxiliis* controversy, drawn from the name of the papal commission appointed to look into this dispute, the *Congregatio de Auxiliis*, appointed by Pope Clement VIII (r. 1592–1605). The scope of this chapter does not permit a full treatment of this controversy, for which we will rely on Farrelly's summary here:

> It was in [the] sixteenth century, when there was a dichotomy in Christendom between a radical supernaturalism and a radical naturalism, that there emerged the two prominent and clearly distinct Catholic interpretations of the mystery of predestination. As was true of the great defenders of the faith in previous ages, each of these schools was an attempt to preserve the doctrine from contemporary errors threatening its purity. Dominic Banez, the principal spokesman for the school since called Thomist or Banezian, in explaining the doctrine of predestination, was particularly careful to defend it against Pelagian interpretations. Louis Molina, on the other hand, the foremost exponent of the doctrine of the opposed school that has since borne his name, stated explicitly that he was harmonizing the doctrine of predestination, grace, God's foreknowledge, providence, and reprobation with the truth of human freedom denied by the Protestants. Thus, though both of these theologians drew on the same heritage of Scripture and tradition and even presented their doctrine in the form of commentaries on the same questions in the *Summa theologiae* of St. Thomas, their interpretations of the doctrine are quite different in detail and in spirit.[29]

For Báñez the starting point was God as first cause and the creature's complete dependence on God in all its actions. God puts into the creature

29. Farrelly, *Predestination*, 4. As far as the Holy See was concerned, the dispute remained at a stalemate and was deliberately kept that way: On March 19, 1598, the *Congregatio* reported back for the first time advising that the circulation of Molina's books be forbidden and that ninety propositions extracted from them be condemned; but the pope declined to ratify the decision. A second attempt to secure his condemnation, when the number of offending propositions had been culled down to twenty, also proved unsuccessful. The next pope, Paul V (r. 1605–21), also proved unsympathetic to the campaign and finally, on September 5, 1607, in an attempt to satisfy both sides, he decreed that the Dominicans could not be justly accused of Calvinism nor the Jesuits of Pelagianism—and that neither side could declare the other side heretical. Thus, at least inside the Roman Church, was prevented what happened in later Protestantism: the fissipiration into ever more sects based on the controversy around predestination.

not only the power of acting, a power the creature then puts into effect precisely by acting; but God also gives *the act itself* to the creature. This principle trumps even the creature called man, as Farrelly explains: "What is true of the creature as such [for Báñez] does not cease to be true when the creature considered is man, for this is a metaphysical truth that depends upon the nature of the creature as creature and God as God. . . . [Thus] if God wants a man to be saved, or if he wants him to perform a good act, it would detract from the divine power to say that he was prevented by man from fulfilling his will. God would not be omnipotent if he could not gain the created will's consent, for there would be something he could not do."[30]

Molina did not exactly disagree with these principles, but still he insisted that human free will, even precisely as a created free will, introduced a new factor, one that could be harmonized with Báñez's axioms. The trouble was that Molina's definition came perilously close to the one espoused by Pelagius: "That agent is said to be free which, once everything necessary for acting is given, is able to act and not to act, or to do one thing in such a way that it could also do the contrary."[31] This definition of course runs into the same difficulty that, as we saw in the last chapter, had afflicted Pelagius: it is not based on any real acquaintance with the facts of human nature. For who has ever made that kind of decision based on such even-steven neutrality?[32] Moreover, it does nothing to explain why, given such neutrality, anyone would ever be so foolish ("ignorant," in Socrates' view) as to choose evil.[33]

30. Farrelly, *Predestination*, 5.

31. Louis Molina, *Liberi arbitrii cum gratiae duobus, divina praescientia, providentia, praedestinatione, et reprobatione Concordia*, ed. Rabeneck (Madrid, 1953), q. 14, a. 13, d. 2, n. 2 (p. 14): "illud agens liberum dicitur quod, positis omnibus requisitis ad agendum, potest agere et non agere, aut ita agere unum ut contrarium etiam agere possit."

32. The eighteenth-century Puritan divine Jonathan Edwards (1703–58) realized that such a view of motiveless volition means no volition at all: "So that in every act, or going forth of the will, there is some preponderation of the mind or inclination, one way rather than another; . . . and that there, where there is absolutely no preferring or choosing, but a perfect continent equilibrium, there is no volition. . . . For the will itself is not an entity that has a will: the power of choosing, itself, has not a power of choosing. That which has the power of volition or choice is the man or the soul, and not the power of volition itself." Jonathan Edwards, *The Freedom of the Will*, in *The Jonathan Edwards Reader*, ed. John E. Smith et al. (New Haven: Yale University Press, 1995), 195, 204. This category mistake infects not only Pelagius and his epigones but also, in my opinion, Molina and his.

33. For what it is worth, Bernard Lonergan, upon starting research for his dissertation on the notion of operative grace in Thomas, came to this conclusion: "Within a month or so it was completely evident to me that Molinism had no contribution to make to an under-

But these obvious objections to Molina's views do not automatically leave the field open to Báñez. True, it was easy for him to reject Molina's doctrine that God was but a *partial* cause of the effect of the human free will (always Molina's Achilles' heel). But his own fateful presupposition was to hold that God's influence on the will was a *physical* influence, as Farrelly notes: "This antecedent movement [by God on the human will] is not simply the moral movement of the object upon the will, . . . but a physical movement, since the effect is itself a physical act of the will."[34] Or in Báñez's own words: "For God applies [*applicat*] a force to our will to [do] a good action and [make] a free consent by a real or physical influence [*applicatione reali seu physica*] . . . and does not just influence as a moral cause by setting before it some object attractive to the appetites."[35]

Clearly something has gone awry here in the presuppositions governing both men. Báñez holds to a physical impulsion of the divine will on the human will, which for Molina leaves no room for human freedom; but, *since he accepted the terms of the debate*, the Jesuit theologian sees no other route out of the dilemma than to resort to a recrudescence of Pelagius's definition of freedom as bland neutrality.[36] Fortunately, recent research into the actual position of the Angelic Doctor has moved the debate beyond these sterile physical categories; and scholarly consensus has opened up new vistas into Thomas's actual teaching in this matter, admirably summed up by Robert Barron's memorable phrase describing Aquinas's teaching on divine causality: *noncompetitive transcendence*, and which he summarizes this way:

---

standing of Aquinas." Bernard J. F. Lonergan, *Method in Theology*, second edition (New York: Herder and Herder, 1972), 163, note 5.

34. Farrelly, *Predestination*, 14. According to Farrelly, Báñez used the term *praedestinatio physica* for the first time in his *Apologia fratrum praedicatorum* of 1599, which was delated to the Holy See by the Jesuits for its implications of fatalism (ibid., 15, note 28).

35. "Deus enim applicat nostram voluntatem ad actionem bonam et consensum liberum applicatione reali seu physica . . . et non solum applicat ut causa moralis proponendo objectum sub ratione appetibilis." Dominic Báñez, *Scholastica commentaria in primum partem Summae theologica s. Thomae Aquinatis* (Madrid, 1934), at *ST* 1–2, 109.1, n.2, page 22. Telling, that Báñez simply assumes without arguing that the terms *real* and *physical* are interchangeable terms!

36. Die-hard defenders of Molina have only one option left, although it was politically impossible for him: they can argue that Molina was wrong to argue the Thomist provenance of his theory but that Thomas got it wrong and Molina was right all along anyway. For something resembling that argument see Thomas P. Flint, *Divine Providence: The Molinist Account* (Ithaca, NY: Cornell University Press, 1998).

Because God is not namable even according to the most generic of categories, he cannot be circumscribed, defined, or grasped. Nor can he be in any sense *a being*, an individual, since this would make him comparable to other individuals. . . . As for Anselm so for Thomas: this strange God, who is not an individual or a specifiable reality, cannot possibly be in competition with the world. Even as he enters most intimately into creation, grounding it and sustaining it, he must allow it to be itself, for to do otherwise would be to compromise his own otherness. . . . If God were a supreme being alongside those other agents, his causality would necessarily compete and interfere with theirs, but because God is somehow else, both immanent and transcendent in the highest degree, he can be, *vis-à-vis* secondary causes, both everything and nothing.[37]

The Dominican Brian Shanley seconds these views by eschewing all unhelpful talk of "physical" causality, drawing rather on the analogy of how two people in love mutually influence each other (this would be real love, of course, not that kind of love that is merely disguised narcissistic self-seeking):

Because we are created to find fulfillment in God, human freedom is inherently relational for Aquinas. In contrast to modern notions of autonomy as the absolute independence and self-creativity of sovereign individuals, Aquinas paradoxically sees human beings as most free when they are most dependent upon and responsive to God. . . . Aquinas does not see God as a rival to human freedom along the lines of the biggest being in the universe throwing his metaphysical weight around by overpowering all other sources of action; God is not a being like any other being, sharing the same metaphysical space as a potential rival. God utterly transcends all creation and stands related to it as creative source. We are free because God creates and sustains us in freedom, not despite God. And though we are compelled to use language drawn from our experience of causation in the physical world, it must be remembered here that we are talking about the action of Creative Spirit upon

37. Robert Barron, *The Priority of Christ: Toward a Postliberal Catholicism* (Grand Rapids, MI: Brazos Press, 2007), 220. The third video presentation of Fr. Barron's popular *Catholicism* DVDs, called "The Doctrine of God," is largely devoted to this theme, thus ensuring that this new scholarly consensus will reach down to the pews.

spirit which finds its consummation in the peculiar kind of causality originating in the love between two persons in grace.[38]

To add to this cloud of witnesses one need only add the formidable authority of Bernard Lonergan (1904–84), who devoted his dissertation to just this doctrinal point in the Common Doctor: "The Thomist higher synthesis was to place God above and beyond the created orders of necessity and contingence: Because God is universal cause, his providence must be certain; but because he is a transcendent cause, there can be no incompatibility between terrestrial contingence and the causal certitude of providence."[39]

38. Brian J. Shanley, O.P., "Beyond Libertarianism and Compatibilism: Thomas Aquinas on Created Freedom," in *Freedom and the Human Person*, ed. Richard Velkley, Studies in Philosophy and the History of Philosophy, Volume 48 (Washington, DC: Catholic University of America Press, 2007), 70–89; here 88–89. If Shanley is right, then Báñez clearly misunderstood Thomas from the ground up: "Aquinas consistently asserts that the divine motion does not determine the will to choose any particular good and he studiously avoids the term *praedeterminatio* precisely to avoid the overtones of divine determinism. He claims instead that God moves the will so that it acts in accord with its own nature as a self-determining power" (ibid., 85–86). Denys Turner makes a similar point when he says: "'Now I call you friends,' says Jesus, and it is from this offer of friendship that the whole doctrine of grace evolves, as also the complexity and precision with which Thomas interlaces the elements of irresistibility on the side of grace and freedom of choice on the side of the human.... Thomas is constrained to speak thus paradoxically, because his central model for the work of grace is that of friendship.... [G]race succeeds without fail but not by force.... It is too easily taken for granted that to speak of God causing my free actions is necessarily a contradiction. For Thomas far from it: worse, to say that my actions are free only insofar as God does not cause them presupposes a plainly idolatrous conception of the divine causality. God is the cause of the free choice that makes the action also mine." Denys Turner, *Thomas Aquinas: A Portrait* (New Haven, CT: Yale University Press, 2013), 151, 152, 154, 157, 160.

39. Bernard Lonergan, *Grace and Freedom: Operative Grace in the Thought of St. Thomas Aquinas* (Toronto: University of Toronto Press, 2000), 81–82. Not to pile it on here, but Reinhard Hütter is the most recent voice in this growing chorus: "God as external cause is in no way extrinsic to the creature's nature or existence but external only to the creature's proximate causality. It is precisely the metaphysics of being that prevents this 'externality' from being understood in the modern sense of a 'first cause,' issued by a 'highest' or 'perfect' being—that is, infinitely superior to all other causes and beings but still on an ontic continuum and hence in a competitive relationship with them because it does not transcend the ontological level of secondary causality. For Thomas, the external causality of grace remains transcendent causality all the way down and hence is not competitive with the internal proximate causality of the will." Reinhard Hütter, *Dust Bound for Heaven: Explorations in the Theology of Thomas Aquinas* (Grand Rapids, MI: Eerdmans, 2012), 274–75. To the best of my knowledge, Henri Rondet was one of the first modern theologians to drive home this

These clarifications of course pertain to strictly metaphysical issues; nor is the mere invocation of "noncompetitive transcendence" meant itself to provide a "solution" to what will always remain deeply mysterious, as Shanley well notes: "The motion by which God moves the will is interior, non-coercive, and non-determining because it is of the nature of the Creator to preserve the modality of what he creates in divine providence. Aquinas is rather spare in his account; he asserts what is metaphysically required without purporting to give a detailed explanation of how God causes freedom."[40] But the very introduction of a whole new perspective on how God moves wills—as a lover wooing and not as some hydraulic motor acting on a pump—not only preserves the mystery at work here, but also provides invaluable service in displacing early attempts to solve the problem of predestination, which had continually run aground on a too-univocal view of God's causality, one that relied too much on how humans conceive of the operation of causes in the world.

But predestination, while often carrying the burden of unacknowledged philosophical presuppositions, still remains fundamentally a theological doctrine; and theology too has resources to help guide theologians in their attempt to understand this deeply puzzling doctrine. The two purely theological considerations that can be brought to bear on this issue are *solidarity* and *Christology*. We have already touched on the issue of solidarity in the last chapter, with a glance at the corporate identity of Adam and the citation of Pope Benedict's encyclical *Spe Salvi*, which pointedly asks if any of us could really feel joy at the damnation of one's neighbor. But it is really *in the identity of Jesus Christ as the ultimate Predestined One* that the solution to this maddening (and basically church-dividing) doctrine can be found, for which the world of Christian believers owes a large debt of gratitude to Karl Barth, who was among the first—and certainly the most influential—theologians to point the way forward.

Perhaps like the famously anti-Communist President Richard Nixon

---

point: "The First Cause is neither necessary nor contingent; it is transcendent. The Thomistic position is impregnable from this metaphysical viewpoint, and it is unfortunate that the twentieth century had to arrive before its real depth was understood. Banezians and Molinists would often be fighting over false problems." Rondet, *The Grace of Christ*, 238–39.

40. Shanley, "Beyond Libertarianism," 86. Another Dominican joins this chorus: "God is not a separate and rival agent within the universe. The creative causal power of God does not operate on me from outside, as an alternative to me; it is the creative causal power of God that makes me *me*." Herbert McCabe, O.P., *God Matters* (London/New York: Continuum, 2003), 13.

going to visit Communist China, it had to be a theologian trained in the Calvinist tradition to solve the problem, and one moreover who firmly rejected liberal sentimentalism, natural theology, works-righteousness, any deviation from the *sola scriptura* principle, or any and all vaguely optimistic doctrines of human progress based on a naïve view of sin. Rather, it was within the resources of his own tradition that he saw where the trouble started, which in fact he spotted as early as his commentary *The Epistle to the Romans*. Commenting on the verse (which for Barth was the lynchpin of Paul's own doctrine): "For those whom he foreknew he also predestined *to be conformed to the image of his Son*, in order that he might be the first-born among many brethren" (Rom. 8:29), Barth gets right to the point:

> Here it is that we encounter the secret of predestination to blessedness, which Augustine and the Reformers represented in mythological form as though it were a scheme of cause and effect, thereby robbing it of its significance. No doubt human love of God, the ordination of men to Sonship, and their calling to be witnesses of the Resurrection, are genuine occurrences, consequent upon God's knowledge of men and taking place in the knowledge of the true and only God. But this must not be taken to mean that His love has brought into being a particular temporal human being . . . [as if it were] the result of a divine causation which took place concretely as the first of a series of temporal occurrences. Predestination means the recognition that love towards God is an occurrence . . . which takes place in no moment of time, which is beyond time, which has its origin at every moment in God Himself, and which must therefore be sought and found only in Him. The man who loves God can never ask "Is it I?" or "Is it Thou?"[41]

But these are only hints of what was to come. For it is in Volume II/2, *The Doctrine of God* (published in 1942) of the *Church Dogmatics* that Barth was now able to devote his formidable mind to resolving the problem of predestination. He begins by focusing on this passage from Paul: "Do I make plans like a man of the world does, ready to say Yes and No in the same breath? As surely as God is faithful, our message to you is not Yes and No. For the Son of God, Jesus Christ, whom we preached among you,

41. Karl Barth, *The Epistle to the Romans*, trans. Edwyn C. Hoskyns (Oxford: Oxford University Press, 1933), 324.

Silvanus, Timothy and I, was not Yes and No; but in him it was always Yes. For no matter how many promises God has made, they are Yes in Christ" (2 Cor. 1:17b–20a). Taking his cue from this passage, Barth bluntly states: "The election of grace is the sum of the Gospel—we must put it as bluntly as that."[42] He can say that because a page earlier he has lanced the Augustinian/Calvinist boil:

> The truth which must now occupy us, the truth of the doctrine of predestination, is first and last and in all circumstances the sum of the Gospel, no matter how it may be understood in detail, no matter what apparently contradictory aspects or moments it may present to us. It is itself evangel: glad tidings, news which uplifts and comforts and sustains. Once and for all, then, it is not a truth which is neutral in face of the antithesis of fear and terror, of need and danger, which the term itself suggests. . . . Its content is instruction and elucidation, but instruction and elucidation which are to us a proclamation of joy. It is not a mixed message of joy and terror, salvation and damnation. Originally and finally it is not dialectical but non-dialectical. It does not proclaim in the same breath both good and evil, both help and destruction, both life and death. It does of course throw a shadow. We cannot overlook or ignore this aspect of the matter. In itself, however, it is light and not darkness. We cannot, therefore, speak of the latter aspect in the same breath. In any case, even under this aspect, the final word is never that of warning, of judgment, of punishment, of a barrier erected, of a grave opened. We cannot speak of it without mentioning all these things. The Yes cannot be heard unless the No is also heard. But the No is said for the sake of the Yes and not for its own sake. In substance, therefore, the first and last word is Yes and not No.[43]

But Barth can say these things precisely because Paul taught him that only in Christ is God always Yes to us; and that is because, in Barth's lapidary line: "In its simplest and most comprehensive form the dogma of predestination consists . . . in the assertion that the *divine predestination is*

---

42. Karl Barth, *Church Dogmatics*, II/2: *The Doctrine of God*, trans. G. W. Bromiley *et al.* (Edinburgh: T. & T. Clark, 1957), 13.

43. Barth, *Church Dogmatics*, II/2, 12–13. A few pages later, Barth makes clear his total break with Calvin on this point: "We cannot regard any doctrine of election as Reformed, or prove it Reformed (let alone Christian), merely in virtue of the fact that it maintains as such the historical characteristics of the Reformed confession and theology" (ibid., 36).

the election of Jesus Christ."[44] Yes, but not just as God's chosen one in whom God is well pleased, but also as the one who bore the curse and wrath of God. Here again Barth relies on Paul: "For our sake, God made him who knew no sin to be sin, so that in him we might become the righteousness of God" (2 Cor. 5:21); and "Christ redeemed us from the curse of the law, having become a curse for us" (Gal. 3:13a). Although the core of Barth's doctrine of Jesus Christ as the predestined one on *both* sides of God's will for sinful creation—both election and reprobation—are clearly adumbrated in II/2, it was when he got to IV/1, *The Doctrine of Reconciliation*, that he was able to set forth in full detail his theology of Jesus Christ as both judge and judged, as here:

> What took place [on the cross] is that the Son of God fulfilled the righteous judgment on us men by Himself taking our place as man and in our place, undergoing the judgment under which we had passed. That is why He came among us. In this way, in this *for us*, He was our Judge against us. That is what happened when the divine accusation was, as it were, embodied in His presence in the flesh. That is what happened when the divine condemnation had, as it were, visibly to fall on this our fellow-man. And that is what happened by reason of our accusation and condemnation: it had to come to the point of our perishing, our destruction, our fall into nothingness, our death. Everything happened to us exactly as it had to happen; but because God willed to execute His judgment on us *in His Son*, it all happened *in His person*, as *His* accusation and condemnation and destruction. He judged, and it was the Judge who was judged, who let Himself be judged.[45]

These conclusions are really but the entailment of Barth's vigorous defense of Chalcedonian Christology, with its acknowledgment of the full divinity and full humanity of Jesus Christ in the hypostatic union, which after all in Greek means God's *substantial* union with humanity in Jesus

---

44. Barth, *Church Dogmatics*, II/2, 103; emphasis added.

45. Karl Barth, *Church Dogmatics*, IV/1: *The Doctrine of Reconciliation*, trans. G. W. Bromiley (Edinburgh: T. & T. Clark, 1956), 222; emphases added. For Barth this convergence of Jesus the judge who is judged in our place—all the while acting justly—teaches us the real meaning of sin: "So great is the ruin of the creature that less than the self-surrender of God would not suffice for its rescue. But so great is God, that it is his will to render up himself. Reconciliation *means* God taking man's place." Karl Barth, *Dogmatics in Outline*, trans. G. T. Thomson (New York: Harper & Row, 1959), 116; emphasis added.

Christ. Especially in his humanity, Jesus is our representative, our stead, the one elect in our place and for us, so that when we see him in his full humanity we see ourselves:

> It is strictly and narrowly only in the humanity of the one Jesus Christ that we can see who and what an elect person is. It is He who is the man distinguished by this special relationship to God. It is His life which is the genuine fulfillment of genuine election. It is to Him that it is truly and essentially said: "I have called thee by thy name; thou art mine." It is He who, in the midst of many others and in the same depths with them, is placed in a special situation and upon a special road. It is He whom God has called His Son and Friend, before and in distinction from all others. It is He who is the elect individual. If there are others who are also elect, it is as a result of and in virtue of the fact that He is originally and properly elect, and *that they are included in his election.*[46]

Probably nothing will strike the reader as untoward here, for no one denies that the baptized Christian is incorporated into the Body of Christ; but then Barth adds a twist, one certainly new to the entire Augustinian/Calvinist tradition: *the same logic of election in Christ applies to the reprobate*:

> But again, it is strictly and narrowly in the portrait of the one Jesus Christ that we may perceive who and what a rejected man is. It is He who—just because of His election—is cast out from the presence of God by His righteous law and judgment, and delivered to eternal death. *In the genuine fulfillment of genuine election* it is His life which is truly the life of the man who must suffer the destructive hostility of God. The peculiarity of the position which He occupies among all others is that He took it upon Himself to be this man. God has made Him who is uniquely His Son and Friend "to be sin." It is He who is the rejected individual. If there are others who are rejected, then it is only . . . in the godlessness which will not accept as a right the right which He has secured for them all. . . . Rejected individuals as such . . . are the evidence of the sin for which He has made Himself responsible, of the punishment which He has borne.[47]

46. Barth, *Church Dogmatics* II/2, 351.
47. Barth, *Church Dogmatics* II/2, 352.

Some of the most remarkable and lyrical passages in the *Church Dogmatics* treat of the famous biblical reprobate/elect "twins" of Cain and Abel, Esau and Jacob, Saul and David, the two thieves on their crosses next to Jesus; and finally there is Barth's great diptych on Judas and Paul. But unlike Augustine and Calvin, Barth refuses to see these pairs on just their own terms as individuals but sees them inside the context of wider salvation history. This *contextualized* doctrine of predestination then opens out into the middle term of election: predestination is not just a matter between Jesus Christ and the individual; rather, the church is the mediating term between Christ and Christian, a point that Hans Urs von Balthasar saw with special acuity:

> Running through all these contrasting "twins" of salvation history is a special interpretation of Mosaic Law and of the relation between Church and Synagogue. And once more, we find a new contrast between Barth's highly biblical doctrine of election and the traditional view in the history of dogma: the place of the Church. Between the election of Jesus Christ and the election of the individual, Barth inserted the election of the People of God, the Church. For it is for the sake of the Church that Christ is the elect of God (and elected to be rejected). And it is only for the sake of the Church that the individual is chosen to become a member of the Church. The moment of community cannot be removed from the biblical doctrine of election without threatening to dislodge the rafters and destroy the whole edifice. Without the moment of solidarity, we cannot describe Christian election in all its depth and uniqueness.... A religion of only provisional, partial, solidarity and of a purely individual fate having no bearing on the fate of the others would in any case not be the Christian religion.[48]

But how far does Jesus' "reprobation" run? How far does he identify with the rejected of God? If he came "in the likeness of sinful flesh" (Rom. 8:3b), if he was "made sin" that we might become the righteousness of God (2 Cor. 5:21), if he endured God's "curse for us" (Gal. 3:13a), how sinful *is* that flesh, how much was he *made* sin, how much *did* he have to endure God's curse for us—*and who is this "us"?* Barth's answer is here; and although a bit long, it must be quoted in full to capture its lyricism:

48. Hans Urs von Balthasar, *The Theology of Karl Barth: Exposition and Interpretation*, trans. Edward T. Oakes, S.J. (San Francisco: Ignatius Press, 1992), 182–83.

What Jesus suffered innocently was undoubtedly the punishment . . . which man brings upon himself and, like Judas, must execute upon himself, in his freedom to continue in evil. Although He Himself was not evil, Jesus had to suffer just what has to be suffered in the freedom to continue in evil: the suffering of Israel given up to idolatry; the suffering of the Gentiles given up to the lusts of their own hearts; the sufferings of Christians given up to Satan. In Gethsemane and on Golgotha Jesus reaches the very place of the [sinner who has taken] this way, and the inescapable distress which he necessarily prepares for himself in consequence. . . . And we must add at once that He alone drinks this cup—not Peter and not Judas, and not those who are delivered up in this way. He alone is delivered up in this way and to this end. How else could it be seriously said or maintained that He was delivered up "for us," in our place? It follows that whatever those who were delivered up have suffered, and whatever all who have deserved the same handing-over may still have to suffer, they do not have to suffer what Jesus Christ suffered, but Jesus Christ has suffered for them what they are spared by His suffering, what God has therefore spared them by not sparing His own Son.[49]

At this point Barth introduces a theme dear also to the theology of Hans Urs von Balthasar: that Christ's identification with sinners went all the way to hell. Not that Barth mitigates what might lie in store for the rebels against God. Yet he also qualifies their fate with this important consideration:

We must certainly take their punishment and suffering in all seriousness. The judgments which fall on them and us are not merely merited but are, in fact, hard and severe. It is a serious matter to be a Pharisee,

49. Barth, *Church Dogmatics*, II/2, 495. This motif that Christ suffered the worst possible of all possible sufferings is of course deeply traditional, as this passage from Aquinas shows: "Christ grieved not only over the loss of his own bodily life, but also over the sins of all others. And this grief in Christ surpassed all grief of every contrite heart, both because it flowed from a greater wisdom and charity, by which the pang of contrition is intensified, and because he grieved at the one time for all sins, according to Isaiah [53:4]: *Surely he hath borne our sorrows.* But such was the dignity of Christ's life in the body, especially on account of the Godhead united with it, that its loss, even for one hour, would be a matter of greater grief than the loss of another man's life for howsoever long a time. . . . And in like fashion Christ laid down his most beloved life for the good of charity, according to Jeremiah [12:7]: *I have given my dear soul into the hands of her enemies.*" Thomas Aquinas, *ST* III, q. 46, a. 6, obj. 4.

a Saul, a Judas, an Alexander or a Hymenacus. It is a serious matter to be threatened by hell, sentenced to hell, worthy of hell, and already on the road to hell. On the other hand, we must not minimize the fact that we actually know of only one certain triumph of hell—the handing-over of Jesus—and that this triumph of hell took place in order that it would never again be able to triumph over anyone. We must not deny that Jesus gave Himself up into the depths of hell not only with many others but on their behalf, in their place, in the place of all who believe in Him.[50]

This chapter is obviously not the place to present an independent treatment of Christ's descent into hell.[51] Crucial here is how Barth uses the line about the descent in the Apostles' Creed to break the Augustinian/Calvinist logic of God's (alleged) *decretum absolutum*, which supposedly determined the number of the saved and damned independent of one's foreseen merits or crimes, indeed even antecedent to the creation of the world. As Barth says so well in his own commentary on the Apostles' Creed:

[I]f, without ceasing to be God, God in Jesus Christ entered into the ordeal, if Jesus Christ descended into hell and thereby actually doubted Himself as to His being God and man in one, what else can we take that to mean than that He did that also for us and so relieved us of it? It is no longer *necessary* that we go to hell. And we shall no longer [have] to go to hell in order to ask ourselves there: why has God forsaken us? If we think we have occasion for this question, we should consider that Jesus

---

50. Barth, *Church Dogmatics*, II/2, 495–96. This motif too is far more traditional than some critics claim, for which this line from Thomas Aquinas's *Exposition of the Apostles' Creed* (written in the last year of his life) will serve for the rest: "There are four reasons why Christ descended in his [human] soul to hell. The first was to take on the *entire* punishment of sin and thereby to atone for *all* of its guilt." "Sunt autem quatuor rationes quare Christus cum anima ad infernum descendit. Prima ut sustineret *totam* poenam peccati, ut sic *totam* culpam expiaret." Thomas Aquinas, *In Symbolum Apostolorum Expositio*, art. 5, 926, in *Opuscula Theologica*, Vol. II, ed. Raimund Spiazzi, O.P. (Turin/Rome: Marietti, 1954), 204; emphases added.

51. For a most fascinating treatment of the similarities and differences between Barth and Balthasar on this theologoumenon, see David Lauber, *Barth on the Descent into Hell: God, Atonement and the Christian Life* (Burlington, VT: Ashgate, 2004). For my own treatment of this theme from the New Testament to Joseph Ratzinger, see Edward T. Oakes, S.J., *Infinity Dwindled to Infancy: A Catholic and Evangelical Christology* (Grand Rapids, MI: Eerdmans, 2011), 382–93.

Christ put it long ago and answered it in our place. How could His way into hell have been other than a victorious way?[52]

A caution should be entered here, at least from my point of view, that Christology (still less a focus on Christ's descent into hell), taken in isolation from other doctrines, does not solve all the problems of predestination, a cavil shared also by Balthasar. He fully concedes that Barth, even and especially within the Calvinist tradition, has broken the back of the logic of predestined perdition. Thus, once Barth's insights are granted, earlier theology no longer remains viable, the kind of theology founded on these principles: 1) that predestination refers to a stable system; 2) that it involves a symmetry between eternal bliss and eternal fire; and 3) that it could be grounded in a prior decree made by God before or outside of Christ. But christocentrism also raises problems of its own for predestination, shown most vividly in this passage from Paul: "For we are the aroma of Christ to God among those who are being saved and among those who are perishing; to one an odor from death to death, to the other a fragrance from life to life" (2 Cor. 2:15–16a). On this basis Balthasar worries that "Barth's doctrine of election does not leave much room open for possibility. There is something inevitable and necessary in his views. What is definitive in Barth's thought is grace and blessing, and all reprobation and judgment are merely provisional."[53]

Recall this verse from the Gospel of John: "They hated me without cause" (John 15:25). If the church is the Body of Christ, and therefore the continuation of his mission on earth, then the same fate must befall his followers. What else but this provocation can explain the persecution suffered by Christians in the first three centuries and which has now broken out in new force in our time? For Balthasar, such persecutions are inevitable precisely because Christ *must* divide the human race if he is to gather it up at the end:

> In setting out to gather all men, Jesus relativizes all religion in the world, Jewish and Gentile. He thereby separates whatever is prepared to respond to his absolute summons from what resists it. So it comes about

52. Karl Barth, *Credo: A Presentation of the Chief Problems of Dogmatics with Reference to the Apostle's* [sic] *Creed*, trans. James Stathearn McNab (London: Hodder & Stoughton, 1936), 93–94; italics in the original.
53. Balthasar, *Barth*, 186.

that the peace-bringing mission ("his is our peace," Eph. 2:14) introduces more division in the world than any other; not through fanaticism but because of an inherent logic: the very One who has come "not to judge but to save" utters that "word" that judges those who reject it (John 3:16–21; 12:47–48).[54]

This insight then leads to Balthasar's doctrine of the *crescendoing No*, whereby all competing ideologies and worldviews gather themselves under the rubric of the slogan "anything but Christianity," the primary manifestation of which is contemporary atheism (especially Nietzsche's). But the "ABC Rule" can also be found in the vain attempts of New Age spiritualities to recover the numinous sense of the divine that had been lost with the advent of Christianity. Resurgent Islam also plays its role: it identifies the new outburst of atheism as a uniquely Western phenomenon and sees the resultant decadence in the West as a ripe target. This passage from Balthasar, though long, neatly captures all the forces at work in the world's *crescendoing No* to the claim of Christ and so must be quoted in full:

> Human reason, in its secularizing role in world history, prevents those who reject Jesus' provocation from returning to a "numinous" worldview in which the divine and worldly commingle, unseparated. . . . This leaves the field clear for what must be called "post-Christian atheism." For when nature is deprived of divinity, the presence of the Creator within it fades. To the observer who sees matters only in terms of the *useful*, God disappears into the background. This is a natural process, and over against it is heard the claim of Jesus to be "*the* way, *the* truth, and *the* life" (John 14:6)—a claim that attracts to itself and concentrates all the religious aspirations of mankind. He goes on to say that "no one comes to the Father except through me." This is not to deny the ultimate salvation of all who do not know him and adhere to other religions; he is saying that the latter religions do not mediate salvation: he alone does. Once this has become sufficiently well known to mankind, the other religions (those that still remain) are bound to acquire a certain anti-Christian slant. They will try to appropriate all the features of the religion of Jesus that seem to commend it to mankind. . . . The only exceptions are those religions that are directly or indirectly dependent on the biblical revelation, first of all Judaism, and then Islam. They constitute a very strange

---

54. Balthasar, *Theo-Drama* IV, 435.

kind of exception, however, for both of them—first of all Judaism, and then Islam—reject the full claim made by Jesus and so will be particularly susceptible to militant atheism (Judaism) or to an emphatically anti-Christian theism (Islam).[55]

Because of the new attention being paid to the theme of universalism among so many theologians across the confessional divide, the worry grows that Christians are becoming susceptible to a facile optimism about the outcome of world history. But hope is not the same thing as expectation. That is, hope (and therefore prayer by the church) for the salvation of all does not in the least entail optimism about the outcome of the plot of theodrama, certainly not in Balthasar anyway, as we see in this sober, even grim, passage:

> We must not be afraid to utter the harsh truth. In making his provocative claim to have reconciled the world in God, Jesus never suggested that he was creating an earthly paradise. The kingdom of God will never be externally demonstrable (Luke 17:21); it grows, invisibly, perpendicular to world history, and the latter's fruits are already in God's barns. Man responds to this provocation by attempting to manufacture the kingdom of God on earth, with increasing means and methods of power; logically this power that resists the powerlessness of the Cross is bound to destroy itself, for it bears the principle of self-annihilation within it by saying No to the claim of Christ. And so we are brought to the following formulation, extravagant though it may seem: *mankind's self-destruction is the only foreseeable end to the world, left to itself, and the only end it deserves,* insofar as it prefers to hoard what is its own (that is, power, Mammon) rather than gather with Christ. It has already decided its own fate.[56]

Even more worrisome is the ease with which *Christians* can be tempted to win favor with the world by trying to make the kingdom of God externally demonstrable, on which efforts Balthasar can be quite scathing (this is the besetting sin of liberal Christianity, especially in the Social Gospel movement): "Further—and this is something that even more clearly unveils the apocalyptic situation—this fascination [with gaining the approval of the world] so weakens the Christian organism that the alien wasp is

55. Balthasar, *Theo-Drama* IV, 438–39.
56. Balthasar, *Theo-Drama* IV, 442; emphasis added.

able to inject its anesthetizing sting and lay its eggs right inside it, with the result that the body, now hollowed out from inside, serves as welcome food for the enemy."[57]

But while Christology cannot be expected to solve all the problems bequeathed to the church by the doctrine of predestination (in fact for Balthasar it shouldn't "solve" them anyway, since that would once again, but from a different perspective, create a closed system, which was the source of the problem to begin with), it can cast a retrospective light on the past history of theology, a light that can show just where so many theologians, at least in the west, went astray. Consider these two notorious verses from Paul: "Jacob I loved, but Esau I hated" (Rom. 9:13, quoting Malachi 1:2–3), and "Has not the potter the right to make out of the same lump of clay some vessels for noble purposes and some for menial use?" (Rom. 9:21). Taken in isolation, of course, these verses not only sound harsh and arbitrary but also have given license down the centuries to the instrumental language so often used when theologians speak of predestination. But christologically considered, one sees that Paul is really making a wider point about salvation history, that is, Paul is speaking this way because he is trying to show that God is "using" Esau (or Israel as a whole) *for wider purposes.*

Many contemporary exegetes echo this point. For example, Joseph Fitzmyer points out in his commentary on Romans that Paul uses the quotation from Malachi about God "hating" Esau "to stress Israel's role in the salvific plan in contrast to Edom's. Jacob and Esau are the representatives of their ethnic groups and are tools in the execution of the divine plan of salvation. God is sovereign and freely chooses Jacob as a tool."[58] But more

57. Balthasar, *Theo-Drama* IV, 441. He knows well the voice that animates this spirit and he mocks them with their own voice here: "Why, if we are serious about God's incarnation in Jesus, should we not salute 'atheism in Christianity'? For the latter's norm now resides in this divine impulse in *man*, not in the alienating spell cast by a *tyrant in heaven*" (ibid.).

58. Joseph A. Fitzmyer, S.J., *Romans: A New Translation with Introduction and Commentary*, The Anchor Bible, Volume 33 (New York: Doubleday, 1993), 563. He also makes the point (as do most commentaries on Romans) that "hated" is a Semitism for "loved less," as can be seen in numerous passages in the Bible: "He loved Rachel more than Leah . . . ; when the Lord saw that Leah was hated" (Gen. 29:30–31). Compare also Luke 14:26 ("If anyone seeks to follow me and does not hate father and mother . . .") with Matt. 10:37 ("Anyone who loves father or mother more than me is not worthy of me"). As Fitzmyer rightly points out: because of this Semitic trope there "is no hint here of predestination to 'grace' or 'glory' of an individual; it is an expression of the choice of corporate Israel over corporate Edom" (ibid.). Elsewhere he says: " 'Jacob' is to be understood as Israel as a whole" (ibid., 625).

crucially, since Paul's readers, especially his Jewish-Christian ones, would have identified not just themselves but also their former co-religionists (the non-Christian Jews) *with Jacob*, the "hate" that God "feels" toward Esau *must* be merely provisional, otherwise the whole point of the entire letter to the Romans would be lost ("first Jews, then Greeks"), a point deftly driven home by John Lodge: "at least up to this point, everything Paul has said *simply reinforces God's irrevocable choice* of the Israelites in Jacob. Paul cannot be making a distinction between historical Israel and some other, theoretical configuration. . . . The implied author is simply stating what everyone would know, that the Jews of his time are descendants of Abraham through Isaac and Jacob, not Ishmael and Esau."[59] But then of course, Paul's *Gentile* readers would identify with *Esau*, and would thus know that God had now reversed his previous "hatred" for Esau by admitting the Gentiles into the Chosen People, albeit only as a branch or shoot engrafted on to the Jewish trunk.

A similar point can be made about the two different vessels formed by the potter out of the same lump of clay. It is not the instrumentalism as such that Paul is stressing, still less the eschatological fate of the more menial vessel, but the different *uses* God makes of different vessels, a point stressed by James Dunn here: "That Paul intended a specific reference with the imagery (individuals and final judgment) is hardly clear; . . . the more natural sense of the metaphor is of vessels put to differing uses *within history*."[60]

One should further add that Paul is drawing on the famous incident in Jeremiah 18, when the prophet came upon a potter trying and failing to shape recalcitrant clay into a useful vessel. As Bernard Anderson rightly notes, Jeremiah took this scene as an instance of Israel's recalcitrance before her Lord. But far from denying human responsibility, Jeremiah was using the potter's failure as a parable to *encourage* responsibility:

> Seeing a potter seated in his pit, his feet spinning the wheel and his hands deftly molding the clay, Jeremiah was reminded that Israel was like clay in the potter's hand. If the vessel was spoiled, owing to some

59. John G. Lodge, *Romans 9–11: A Reader-Response Analysis* (Atlanta, GA: Scholars Press, 1996), 65–66. Most commentaries stress the authors' intentions; but how the biblical books would have been read at their first "publication" must also factor in to any true scientific exegesis, admirably shown in this commentary.

60. James D. G. Dunn, *Romans 9–16*, Word Biblical Commentary, Vol. 38 (Dallas: Word Books, 1988), 557; emphasis added.

imperfection in the material, it could be reworked into another vessel as the potter saw fit. And so it was with Israel. If a nation refuses to be molded by the divine design, and insists on following its own plans, then YHWH will repent of the good he has intended and will visit it with destruction. Notice that the threatened catastrophe is to come as a result of human recalcitrance, not as a result of the arbitrary, capricious wrath of the potter. Again and again the prophet reminded the people that the imminent tragedy would be the consequence of their own actions: "Your ways and your doings have brought this upon you. This is your doom, and it is bitter; it has reached your very heart" (Jer. 4:18). . . . Therefore, in the very passage where Jeremiah proclaims the sovereignty of the potter over the clay, his word is accompanied by an urgent plea that the people amend their ways and doings while there is still time. Divine sovereignty does not erase human responsibility.[61]

Not all commentators agree, of course, with these positions. (For one thing, if exegetes agreed all the time, there would be no need for more than one commentary.) But even those who adopt a Calvinist interpretation of these texts admit that, under that rubric, Paul comes perilously close to contradicting himself. Such, at any rate, is Douglas Moo's conclusion, as we read in this fascinating observation:

I have argued that this passage gives strong exegetical support to a traditional Calvinistic interpretation of God's election. God chooses those who will be saved on the basis of his own will and not on the basis of anything—works or faith, whether foreseen or not—in those human beings so chosen. . . . But if we exclude faith as a basis for God's choice here, what becomes of Paul's strenuous defense of faith as the means of justification? . . . I can only reiterate that the introduction into this text of *any* basis for God's election outside God himself defies both

---

61. Bernard W. Anderson, *Understanding the Old Testament*, third edition (Englewood Cliffs, NJ: Prentice Hall, 1975), 375-76. We know that Jeremiah has not denied human freedom with this analogy of the potter working with recalcitrant clay because in that same chapter he announces this word of the Lord: "If at any time I declare concerning a nation or a kingdom that I will pluck up and break down and destroy it, and if that nation I have addressed turns from its evil, I will repent of the evil I intended to do to it; and if at any time I declare concerning a nation or a kingdom that I will build and plant it, and if it does evil in my sight, not listening to my voice, then I will repent of the good I had intended to do to it" (Jer. 18:7-10). No doctrine of *praedestinatio ante merita praevisa* here!

the language and the logic of what Paul has written. . . . [A]s Augustine stated it: "God does not choose us because we believe, but that we may believe." This way of putting the matter seems generally to be justified by this passage and by the teaching of Scripture elsewhere. But it comes perilously close to trivializing human faith, something that many texts in Romans and in the rest of the NT simply will not allow us to do. We need, perhaps, to be more cautious in our formulations and to insist on the absolute cruciality and meaningfulness of the human decision to believe at the same time as we rightly make God's choosing of us ultimately basic. Such a double emphasis may strain the boundaries of logic (it does not, I trust, break them!) or remain unsatisfyingly complex, but it may have the virtue of reflecting Scripture's own balanced perspective.[62]

But surely part of that "balanced perspective" must include a more full-throated treatment of Romans 11:32 ("God trapped all in disobedience that he may have mercy on all") than Moo provides, who concedes more authority to Calvin than to Paul, whom he cites when he says of this verse: "Considering the corporate perspective that is basic to chapter 11, it seems best to think that 'all' refers to 'all the groups' about which Paul has been speaking, for example Jews and Gentiles. For Paul is not saying that all human beings will be saved."[63] But surely Dunn is following the less strained interpretation by seeing the verse as the culmination of Romans 9–11 (which nearly all exegetes hold to be a single argumentative unit), which therefore casts retrospective light on all the previous instrumental language:

Now at last we can see the whole letter set within the full sweep of salvation-history. . . . The twin aspects of God's purpose of election are reaffirmed in one final breathtaking summary—wrath as well as grace,

---

62. Douglas J. Moo, *The Epistle to the Romans*, The New International Commentary on the New Testament (Grand Rapids, MI: Eerdmans, 1996), 587–88; italics in the original. The internal quotation is from Augustine's *On the Predestination of the Saints* 17.34.

63. Moo, *Epistle to the Romans*, 736. In his commentary for a more popular audience, Moo simply contents himself with this raw assertion: "This verse does not teach universalism, that all people eventually will be saved. In this context, as is often the case in the Bible, 'all' means 'all kinds.' God is working in salvation history to bring all kinds of people to salvation—Jews and Gentiles alike." Douglas J. Moo, *Encountering the Book of Romans: A Theological Survey* (Grand Rapids, MI: Baker Academic, 2002), 172.

severity as well as kindness, hostility as well as love, confined to disobedience as well as subject to mercy.... And the mystery which resolves
the paradox is the revelation that the ultimate purpose is one of mercy:
God hardens some in order to save all: he confines all in disobedience
in order to show mercy to all.... It is the magnificence of this vision of
the final reconciliation of the world to God which makes it possible to
see here the expression of a hope for universal salvation.... But precisely
because it is so summary in its expression and so grandiose in its sweep
it would probably be wiser to assume that Paul is speaking simply in
general terms.[64]

I happen to agree with this last sentence, since, as we have seen, any
closed system of eschatology, whether Origenistic or Augustinian, only
leads to trouble. But I have made this brief survey of some commentaries on Romans not so much to defend an open-ended eschatology as to
show that commentators will always operate, however much they might
be aware of it or not, in a particular ecclesial tradition, which is bound to
affect how they see the text. It was for just this reason, in fact, that Barth
insisted he was being a true Calvinist by rejecting the Calvinist version of
predestination: that by the twentieth century Calvin*ism* had become an
ossified *tradition*, one that needed, ironically, a "reformation" based on the
sola scriptura principle:

Calvinism does not exist as a subject and norm of Christian doctrine....
But we shall be doing Calvin the most fitting honor if we go the way that
he went and start where he started. And according to his most earnest
protestations, he did not start with himself, nor with his system, but
with Holy Scripture as interpreted in his system.... And it is to Scripture
that we must again address ourselves, not refusing to learn from that
system, but never as "Calvinists without reserve." ... Modern Neo-Cal-
vinism involves at once, on its formal side, a mistaken reintroduction

---

64. Dunn, *Romans 9–16*, 696–97. Fitzmyer concludes: "After his firm 'no' to the idea that
God has rejected his people, he now has recourse to God's mercy to all. As human beings
look at Israel's situation, it is its responsibility and tragedy; but as God looks at it, it is the
way to Israel's salvation." Fitzmyer, *Romans*, 629. For his resolute christological interpretation of this difficult passage, see ibid., 620. Lodge holds that the verse is meant to overthrow
the implied self-righteousness in both groups of Christians Paul is addressing, Jewish and
Gentile: "Paul's message disputes the views of these two factions. Neither group is given
comfort in opposition to the claims of another." Lodge, *Romans 9–11*, 204.

of the Catholic principle of tradition [!] repudiated by all the Reformers, and most sharply of all, by Calvin. Out of loyalty to Calvin himself we must never begin by treating the doctrine of predestination as a kind of *palladium* of the older Reformed Church.[65]

The same principle, I argue, applies to Augustine *a fortiori*. To hear some Catholic theologians speak, Augustine holds greater sway and authority than does Calvin in Calvinism. No doubt, nods to his genius are deserved. Who would wish to dispute the assessment of Robert Louis Wilken here? "It is not hyperbolic to say that during his lifetime, he was the most intelligent man in the Mediterranean world. From the time of Plato and Aristotle, the great philosophers of ancient Greece, across more than fifteen centuries until Thomas Aquinas in the High Middle Ages, he has no equal."[66] Quite true, but genius can be mesmerizing, as Wilken also admits: "In reading Augustine it is hard to keep one's distance. His words soar off the page to sink into the soul of the reader, moving the affections as well as stirring the intellect."[67] And geniuses can be wrong. One is reminded in this context of a remark that Etienne Gilson (1884–1978) made about René Descartes (1596–1650):

> No man can fall victim to his own genius unless he has genius; but those who have none are fully justified in refusing to be victimized by the genius of others. Not having made the mathematical discoveries of Descartes and Leibniz, we cannot be tempted to submit all questions to the rules of mathematics; but our very mediocrity should at least help us to avoid such a mistake. There is more than one excuse for being a Descartes, but there is no excuse whatsoever for being a Cartesian.[68]

Yet for nearly a millennium and a half, the western half of Christendom was Augustinian to its core, very much including during the Reformation. For both sides knew their Augustine, quoted him throughout their works, and appealed to his well-nigh unquestioned authority. N. P. Williams is surely not alone when he says:

65. Barth, *Church Dogmatics,* II/2, 36.
66. Robert Louis Wilken, *The First Thousand Years: A Global History of Christianity* (New Haven, CT: Yale University Press, 2012), 183.
67. Wilken, *First Thousand Years,* 185.
68. Etienne Gilson, *The Unity of Philosophical Experience* (San Francisco: Ignatius Press, 1999; originally published New York: Charles Scribner's Sons, 1937), 6.

From Augustine the leaders of the Protestant revolt inherited the overwhelming sense of God's universal causality, of the impotence of human nature and the emptiness of human merit, which in logic makes all sacramental and institutional religion otiose: and in Augustine, too, is to be found that lofty conviction of the divine mission of the institutional, visible Church, which nerved Loyola, Borromeo, and Peter Canisius to roll back the flood of rebellion against the Papacy beyond the Alps and the Rhine. . . . The two main camps into which the Reformation sundered the medieval Western Church continued to take the authority of Augustine for granted, as second only to that of the inspired writers. . . . The doctrines of Grace set forth in the Canons of the Council of Trent, in the Thirty-Nine Articles, in the *Institutio* of Calvin, in the Augsburg Confession, are so many modified and competing versions of Augustinianism.[69]

So the roots of the divisions in the western church really can be found in the many unresolved antinomies in the thought of this African genius, antinomies which have been set out in this and the previous chapter.[70] But

69. Williams, *Ideas*, 322. Williams also makes the perfectly valid point that one can fully admit Augustine's errors without lapsing into the vulgar accusation that he must be a heretic: "No Christian thinker in his senses will maintain that Augustinianism is a heresy. Yet a theological opinion may be profoundly erroneous without being either formally or materially heretical" (ibid., 382). Arnoud Visser has recently shown how both Protestants and Catholics often appealed to the same texts in Augustine: "In similar fashion [to other Catholic polemicists], the Jesuit [Hieronymus] Torrensis urges his readers to turn to Augustine's works, 'the most wholesome sources in these days,' for a comprehensive confession of true faith and religious learning. Adopting a more militant tone, the Reformed preacher Guy de Brès . . . presents his French collection of extracts as a weapon, a 'baton,' to fight the enemy. It is in fact the same weapon, he adds, as the one with which 'they fight against you.' De Brès realizes that some of his readers may not accord any special authority to the church fathers, who, in their view 'are humans, just like they.' Yet, as the minister argues, God sometimes speaks through humans, which one will know from the agreement between their statements and the word of God." Arnoud S. Q. Visser, *Reading Augustine in the Reformation: The Flexibility of Intellectual Authority in Europe, 1500–1620* (Oxford: Oxford University Press, 2011), 83.

70. On the matter of double predestination, readers are directed to the wise words of David Bentley Hart: "Were this so [that God predestined Adam's fall], God would be the author of and so entirely beyond both good and evil, or at once both and neither, or indeed merely evil (which power without justice always is). The curious absurdity of all such doctrines is that, out of a pious anxiety to defend God's transcendence against any scintilla of genuine creaturely freedom, they threaten effectively to collapse that transcendence into absolute identity—with the world, with us, with the devil. For, unless the world is truly set apart

despite these internal tensions and contradictions, Augustine won out in the west, no doubt in part because of the condemnation of Origenism a century later, which (at least in the west) left the field open to Augustine's sole authority, assisted by the collapse of the western half of the Roman Empire and the loss of the knowledge of Greek in the west after the death of Boethius. "Books have their own fate," goes an old Latin proverb; and so in a way do geniuses, on which Paula Fredriksen has this illuminating point to add:

> Their shared focus on Paul and their mutual adherence to the principles of late Platonism notwithstanding, however, these two geniuses of the ancient church also disagreed sharply. According to Origen, Paul's message was that all will be saved; according to Augustine, Paul's message was that all should be damned. According to Origen, all rational beings by definition have free will; according to Augustine, humanity left to its own devices can only sin. According to both Origen and Augustine, God's two great moral attributes are justice and mercy. But Origen's god expresses these attributes universally and simultaneously: God is *both* just *and* merciful. Augustine's god expresses these attributes serially and selectively: he is *either* just *or* merciful. For Origen, even Satan will at last attain redemption; for Augustine, even infants, if unbaptized, go to hell. And their ultimate fates as doctors of the church differed no less sharply than did their signature theological views. Augustine the late Latin bishop and renowned controversialist became a saint, and one of the premier authorities of western Christendom. Origen, lay intellectual and Christian martyr, was ultimately condemned as a heretic, his great literary legacy destroyed.[71]

---

from God and possesses a dependent but real liberty of its own analogous to the freedom of God, everything is merely a fragment of divine volition, and God is simply the totality of all that is and all that happens; there is no creation, but only an oddly pantheistic expression of God's unadulterated power. One wonders, indeed, if a kind of reverse Prometheanism does not lurk somewhere within such a theology, a refusal on the part of the theologian to be a creature, a desire rather to be dissolved into the infinite fiery flood of God's solitary and arbitrary act of will. In any event, such a God, being nothing but will willing itself, would be no more than an infinite tautology—the sovereignty of glory displaying itself in the glory of sovereignty—and so an infinite banality." David Bentley Hart, *The Doors of the Sea: Where Was God in the Tsunami?* (Grand Rapids, MI: Eerdmans, 2005), 90–91.

71. Paula Fredriksen, *Sin: The Early History of an Idea* (Princeton: Princeton University Press, 2012), 99–100.

Yet, in this near total rout, western theologians, very much including during the Reformation, forgot a signal principle that should apply to every theologian, one made all the more forceful by coming from one of Augustine's most sympathetic interpreters, Eugène Portalié: "Every decision of the Church must be preferred to the statements of Augustine. The reason for this is plain, for the Church has the gift of divine assistance; Augustine did not enjoy it."[72] Another sympathetic scholar of Augustine, James Wetzel, seconds this opinion, but also provides an acute analysis of just where Augustine went wrong—his interpretation of the role of Esau in Romans 9:

> There is a dark side to Augustine's reading of Romans 9. It is Esau. Augustine assumes that because Esau is the son not favored, he is forever cast off. Leave aside whether this reading fits Paul (it does not), in subscribing to a doctrine of reprobation, Augustine subscribes to the belief that some who feel abandoned by God are, in fact, abandoned by God. These unhappy souls are the damned, the sons and daughters not favored. The doctrine of reprobation has mixed poison into Augustine's motives for affirming predestination. You do not have to be a Pelagian not to like the taste. His affirmation of reprobation is tragically wrong in two fundamental ways: it assumes that a soul is capable of experiencing the pain of being forsaken by God, and it assumes that God has a motive for inflicting it.[73]

---

72. Portalié, *Guide to Augustine*, 323. The author was prompted to enunciate this axiom by the preceding few pages, where he cites a number of embarrassing encomia to Augustine from both heretics and faithful Catholics. From the former, there is Jansenius himself who said that "Augustine determined the limits of true theological knowledge by his own teaching" (cited at ibid., 322); from the latter, one writer attacked the Molinists on these grounds: "Any teaching of Augustine on grace or predestination must be considered as dogma of the Catholic Church" (cited in ibid., 323).

73. James Wetzel, "Snares of Truth: Augustine on Free Will and Predestination," in *Augustine and His Critics: Essays in Honor of Gerald Bonner*, ed. Robert Dodaro and George Lawless (London: Routledge, 2002), 124–41, here 129. Wetzel fully admits that Augustine had a robust theory of free will down to his last days: "he practically invented the concept," he says (ibid., 127). But for him, the African bishop's interpretation of Esau laid waste to his defense of free will: "At the very least, it must be conceded that Augustine's provocative way of reading Paul disrupts the delicate *pas de deux* of western theism, between ethical self-assertion and religious self-surrender.... In the dance of redemption, it would seem that the human partner arrives empty-handed and lacking in grace; not only does the divine partner supply the grace, God does all the dancing. It is as if sin has drained the human heart of vitality, leaving God to assume (or forsake) a spiritless husk" (ibid., 124–25).

From this conclusion, which Augustine hammered into the theological tradition with uncommon force and rhetorical skill, comes that *tentatio praedestinationis* that regularly afflicts church bodies that take seriously such views. But even among those not tempted to despair—and perhaps especially among them—other dangers lurk, not least the mortal peril of self-righteousness. As Wetzel rightly points out, "After AD 397, that is, soon after he has arrived at his definitive reading of Romans 9, Augustine never tires of citing 1 Cor. 4:7: 'What part of a good do you have that you have not received?'"[74] While Augustine is surely right that this verse leaves no room for boasting or for merit considered as a claim on God, it means more than that; for surely it must also include any sense of hoarding salvation, of feeling resentful if the unbaptized are "allowed in" to heaven, of feeling that one's own salvation is "worth more" if others don't "make it in" to Augustine's exclusive salvation club.

The bishop of Hippo also caused a host of problems inside the technical issues in the theology of grace, especially in the distinction he bequeathed between "sufficient" and "efficacious" grace.[75] To understand the distinction, the reader might be reminded of the fine print in those insurance policies in which the policyholder has dutifully and faithfully paid all premiums only to discover that the costs of repairing his flooded basement are not covered because it was his fault that the pipes leaked, since he owned the pipes. Or to put it less polemically, Karl Rahner (1904–84) and Herbert Vorgrimler (b. 1929) define the difference this way:

> It follows, from the fact of God's universal salvific will on the one hand and human sinfulness on the other, that there is an assistance of grace which is offered but does not take effect, that is, is merely "sufficient" (*gratia sufficiens*). Its character therefore cannot be sought in God's irresistible omnipotence. The difference between merely sufficient and efficacious actual grace, according to the (almost) common teaching (of Banezianism as well as of Molinism), is grounded in God's election prior to man's acceptance or rejection of grace and despite man's freedom either to accept or reject it.[76]

74. Wetzel, "Snares of Truth," 125.

75. Terminology differs among various theologians. What I shall be calling "efficacious" grace throughout is also called by others "effective," "efficient," or "operative" grace, often depending on how the original Latin *gratia efficiens* or *gratia efficax* is translated.

76. Karl Rahner/Herbert Vorgrimler, *Dictionary of Theology*, second edition, trans. Richard Strachen et al. (New York: Crossroad, 1981), 198–99. As we noted earlier, this distinction

This distinction between an allegedly sufficient grace and a truly efficacious grace became increasingly important to Augustine the more he tangled with the Pelagians. After having exaggerated the importance of the rite of baptism of infants to such an extent that one dead baby goes to hell and the other to heaven, based solely on whether that baby had undergone the rite of baptism, Augustine is then forced to admit, like the fine print in an insurance policy, that baptism doesn't really count all that much for adult Christians after all without the grace of perseverance; and of course *that* grace was also predetermined before the creation of the world, and certainly not in view of future "merits" of the adult Christian, as J. Patout Burns explains in his important monograph on Augustine's uses of this distinction:

> In *De corruptione et gratia*, Augustine asserted that within the economy of gratuitous grace final salvation must not be a reward for human merits. He could provide no explanation of the incongruity of God's withholding the efficacious grace of perseverance from those to whom he had already granted faith and charity. He could only assert that those who fail themselves choose the evil for which they are condemned. These were never among the elect and were not true disciples because they did not remain in the justice they possessed. He noted the parallel between the withholding of baptism from dying infants and the withholding of the grace of perseverance from Christian adults. Each is mysterious—*O altitudo* reappears—but undeniable.[77]

---

hardened during the *de auxiliis* controversy, when Báñez used physical motion as his analogue for efficacious grace: "In [Báñez's] view, and in that of nearly all theologians, before man makes a free choice (*in actu primo*) God bestows an actual grace which enables him freely to perform a salutary act. According to Báñez this actual grace is a sufficient grace (*gratia sufficiens*), and the *salutary act is not actually performed until the person is granted an additional efficacious grace* (*gratia efficax*) that is *really different from the first*. More specifically, God himself infallibly causes the human will to pass from a state of potency to a particular free act by a 'physical premotion,' which by its own inner nature produces a free choice" (ibid., 37).

77. J. Patout Burns, *The Development of Augustine's Doctrine of Operative Grace* (Paris: Études Augustiniennes, 1980), 176. This new stress on perseverance as itself both gratuitous and predestined moved *pari passu* with the other shift in the African doctor's thought: "Gradually, however, he moved from the necessity of grace and the inadequacy of human nature to the gratuity of grace and the impotence of human nature" (ibid., 131). Notice as well Augustine's consistent habit of subordinating Christ to Adam because of the latter's chronological priority in the history of salvation: "Augustine defined and contrasted two

The older Augustine got, the more he put hope for salvation of others (he of course never doubted his own predestined status for heaven) in a constricting torque; for now, with his concept of a "sufficient" grace that does not really suffice without a predestined efficacious grace, the passage to heaven becomes ever more fraught, since in the last analysis baptism, faith in Christ, works of charity, count for nothing without the grace of perseverance:

> The significant anomaly in Augustine's division of the two economies is the calling of some to grace but not to glory. Unlike the unrepentant simulators whom he described as weeds among the wheat during the Donatist controversy, these are transferred into the Christic economy. They are converted to faith in Christ and freed from the sin of Adam in baptism. They receive the gift of charity and perform some good works. Yet they do not persevere in good; they fail and are condemned for their personal sins. . . . The non-elect do not persevere; the elect persevere. The grace of God accounts for the perseverance of the saints; the sins of the non-elect account for their condemnation. . . . Augustine insisted that the case of the Christian who is not elected to glory is not more mysterious than that of the infant who is condemned for the sin of Adam alone. . . . He steadfastly refused to lessen God's glory in the saints in order to satisfy human justice in the condemnation of sinners.[78]

A further difficulty with the concept of sufficient grace is that it never seems to suffice unless efficacious grace is at work too, as seen especially in Thomas's image of the cook who uses fire to cook the food: "Thus an artisan who applies the power of a natural thing to some action is said to be the cause of the action; for instance, a cook of the cooking which

---

economies of salvation. The original freedom of Adam was itself the fruit of grace rather than the property of nature. Still, that freedom was a true autonomy which made him fully responsible for his sin and thus justified the condemnation of all his offspring. Those who remain in this economy live out in their individual lives the tragedy in which they all collectively participated in Adam. The Adamic economy manifests the justice of God; his mercy is demonstrated in the economy of Christ. There one finds effective divine operation rather than autonomous human cooperation with God's gifts. Thus one economy leads to life by the mercy of God in Christ; the other leads to death by the sin of Adam and his offspring" (ibid., 179–80).

78. Burns, *Development of Augustine's Doctrine,* 180.

is done by means of fire."[79] But this image can only imply that, as far as getting to heaven is concerned, sufficient grace does not suffice, any more than a fire suffices to cook the food without a cook in the kitchen to set the saucepan on the fire.

So perhaps the Jansenists—who in this and in all matters pertaining to grace may be regarded as Augustinians on steroids—had a point when they asked to be *delivered* from sufficient grace. But that is just the proposition that Pope Alexander VIII condemned in 1690: "Grace sufficient for our state is not so much useful as pernicious, so that we can justly pray: From sufficient grace deliver us, O Lord."[80] That condemnation especially, but also a whole series of papal condemnations pertaining to the Jansenist theory of grace, is what prompted Kolakowski to claim the following:

> Jansenists were on firm ground in saying that they were faithful to the Augustinian teaching, and quite justified in scenting Pelagian errors in the Jesuit theology. The Jesuits were no less right in demonstrating the fundamental conformity of Jansenist tenets with Calvin's theory of predestination. This amounts to saying that Calvin was, on this point, a good Augustinian and that, by condemning Jansenism, the Church was

79. Thomas Aquinas, *Summa contra Gentiles* III, 67.4. William Most glosses this text as follows: "In other words, just as fire in itself really has the ability or power to cook food, yet never will cook food unless the cook *applies* the fire to the food; similarly, through sufficient grace a man really has the *power* or *ability* to perform a good action, yet will not perform it unless God gives also the *application*, that is, efficacious grace." William G. Most, *Grace, Predestination, and the Salvific Will of God: New Answers to Old Questions* (Front Royal, VA: Christendom Press, 1997), 10; all italics in the original. A popular textbook used in theology courses just prior to the Second Vatican Council openly avers: "Sufficient grace is certainly not of itself sufficient for salvation, because it cannot produce any acts by itself." Francis L. B. Cunningham, O.P., *The Christian Life: A Basic Synthesis for the College* (Dubuque, IA: The Priory Press, 1959), 292. For his part, Most works hard to exonerate Thomas from the implications of this image of cook and fire: "St. Thomas does not deserve criticism because he was not able to remove those obscurities, for the impressive weight of the prestige of St. Augustine made St. Thomas think it necessary to accept St. Augustine's interpretation" (Most, ibid., 5). But he also does not hesitate to say: "[I]n the theory of the older Thomists, God actually is the chief author of sin" (ibid., 61), although of course he exempts more recent Thomists who have relearned Thomas's more basic theology of God as pure act who does not compete with human freedom. For those interested in pursuing this issue further, Most's book can be recommended for its thorough—even massive—treatment of predestination.

80. DH 2306.

in effect condemning—without, of course, stating it explicitly—Augustine himself, its own greatest theological authority.[81]

The claim is of course controversial and perhaps best left to historians of theology to adjudicate. But I think we may safely conclude with a warning from Balthasar against seeking to close what must always remain an open question, precisely because revelation has left it open:

> In the long run . . . people cannot rest content with unsolved problems. Faced with man's ambivalence and all the suffering in the world, they try by means of *speculation* to "get behind" the Christian mystery of the God-man who, in pure freedom and love, was crucified for us . . . [and] attempt to trace it back to a source in the Absolute, so rendering it accessible to reason. This suppression of Christian faith by speculation begins as early as the second century in the manner of post-Christian Gnosticism; the dichotomy imported into the Absolute becomes a complete one in Manichaeism. . . . But this speculative rhythm between heaven and hell can also have a retroactive effect on Christian theology: the great shadow that arose from Augustine's later works and, in the form of predestination, darkened the Middle Ages, the Reformation and Jansenism might not have settled [on the west] at all if Augustine had not been a Manichee in his early period.[82]

81. Kolakowski, *God Owes Us Nothing*, 5. Further along he says: "The Jansenists took comfort in the pope's answer to their delegation in Rome; they asked him to confirm that Augustine's teaching on efficient grace had not been affected by the bull, to which the pontiff replied 'O, questo è certo.' This, however, meant little or nothing. No pope, at any time, could ever have admitted aloud that he had made Augustine the author of a heresy, even if, as in this case, this was precisely what he had just done. . . . The Jesuits knew better; the pope did condemn the genuine doctrine of Jansenius and this doctrine was virtually identical with Calvin's. They were as right on this point as were the Jansenists in saying that Jansenius had been a faithful follower of Augustine" (ibid., 26-27).

82. Balthasar, *Theo-Drama* II, 491. The Eastern Orthodox tradition has largely escaped this problem by preferring a different set of images, such as Origen's image of the vessel arriving safely at port after a storm: "To what extent should we say that the [captain's] skill helps in bringing the ship back to the harbor when compared with the force of the winds and . . . the shining of the stars? . . . Why, even sailors themselves, from feelings of reverence, do not often venture to claim they have saved the ship but attribute it all to God; not [implying] they have done nothing, but that the efforts of God's providence are very much greater than the effects of their skill." Origen, *On First Principles* 3.1.19, in *Origen on First Principles*, trans. G. W. Butterworth (Gloucester, MA: Peter Smith, 1973), 199. One author glosses this passage as follows: "Ancient sailors and desert monks modestly ascribed all their

Or in the perhaps more lapidary formulation of Ludwig Wittgenstein: "Within Christianity, it's as though God says to men: Don't act out a tragedy, don't enact heaven and hell on earth. Heaven and hell are *my* affair."[83] Exactly.

---

achievements to God, but their work resulted from a happy synergy between God's grace and their own freely chosen actions." Nonna Verna Harrison, *God's Many-Splendored Image: Theological Anthropology for Christian Formation* (Grand Rapids, MI: Baker Academic, 2010), 27. Origen's image of course is not without its difficulties; but metaphors are our fate, and we are bewitched by language.

83. Wittgenstein, *Culture and Value*, trans. Peter Winch (Chicago: University of Chicago Press, 1980), 14e: "Im Christentum sagt der liebe Gott gleichsam zu den Menschen: Spielt nicht Tragödie, das heißt Himmel und Hölle auf Erden. Himmel und Hölle habe *ich* mir vorbehalten."

CHAPTER 5

Experience and Divinization

But man, proud man,
Dressed in a little brief authority,
Most ignorant of what he's most assured—
His glassy essence—like an angry ape
Plays such fantastic tricks before high heaven
As make the angels weep.

William Shakespeare, *Measure for Measure*

There are in faith two equally constant truths. One is that man in the state of his creation, or in the state of grace, is exalted above the whole of nature, made like unto God and sharing in his divinity. The other is that in the state of corruption and sin he has fallen from that first state and has become like the beasts of the field.

Blaise Pascal, *Pensées*

This chapter will address the following question: what difference does grace make? The discussion will take place under two rubrics: experience and divinization, which can be considered, in a way, as the subjective and objective side of the difference grace makes: the first topic treats the difference grace makes to our outlook on the world and on ourselves; the second the difference grace makes in God's relation to us, as when Paul says "God was in Christ reconciling the world to himself" (2 Cor. 5:19); the first of which will be taken up now.

Experience

If experience is defined (however provisionally) as our only access to the real, then presumably, if grace is real, it must be accessible to experience.[1] For if grace were declared to be *in principle* inaccessible to experience, then it would end up being as hypothetically useless as phlogiston or as embarrassingly vacuous as that now-discredited medium of undulating light, celestial ether. Yet there are problems, as we soon shall see, with asserting outright that grace is directly accessible to experience. For as we saw in the last chapter especially, God is not an item in the world, a being alongside or in competition with other beings and therefore cannot be accessible to experience in the same way those other items are. If, as one venerable tradition in philosophy holds, all knowledge begins in the senses, then by definition God cannot be experienced, at least in any direct, sensory way; and if God cannot be directly experienced, then, *a fortiori*, his grace cannot either, which is, ultimately, the impartation of God's own (invisible) life.[2] But to foreclose the world of grace from the world of experience altogether leads to acute problems of its own, not least pastoral ones, as Hans Urs von Balthasar describes in an acute essay on just this theme:

> In real distress many people nowadays are asking: Can one experience God? For if I do not encounter him in living fashion anywhere in my

1. But experiences can deceive, and that applies *a fortiori* to religious experience. Yet what other access to the real do we have than corrigible experience? The dilemma is deftly described here: "At some very basic level, our 'third person' knowledge always depends upon a 'first person' insight.... Certainly private consciousness can be deceived, confused, diminished, or deranged; if we are wise, we submit our judgments to the judgments of others, offer our testimony expecting to be challenged by those who have very different tales to tell, learn to distinguish opinion from insight and impulse from reflection, rely upon the wisdom of others, cultivate an aptitude for doubt, and so on. Nevertheless, there remains in each of us an unshakable ground of resolute subjective certainty, which forms the necessary basis of all rational belief. The world that appears *in* consciousness is the only world of which we have anything like immediate assurance.... We are not condemned to absolute subjectivity, but our direct experience of reality has to possess an altogether primary authority for us, which may need to be qualified by further experience but which can never be wholly superseded." David Bentley Hart, *The Experience of God: Being, Consciousness, Bliss* (New Haven, CT: Yale University Press, 2013), 315, 316.

2. As Thomas says: "Although by the revelation of grace in this life we cannot know of God 'what he is,' and thus are united to him as to one unknown, still we know him more fully according as many and more excellent of his effects are demonstrated to us" (*ST* I, q. 12, a. 13, ad 1). Also: "Whatever is comprehended by a finite being is itself finite" (*ST* I-II, q. 4, a. 3, ad 1).

existence, how can I believe in him? Let us not be too quick to answer such queries by pointing out the limitless ambiguity of the concept of "experience" in general and of religious experience in particular. Instead, let us consider that the disintegration of a vigorous Christian tradition in family, community and nation, and the isolation of Christians in a faithless society within a practically atheistic, technical civilization make that cry of distress credible and profoundly worthy of consideration over and above every objection.[3]

In his first encyclical, *Lumen Fidei*, Pope Francis echoes this worry and insists that without a palpable sense of God's presence, the whole meaning of the Christian religion will be lost:

Our culture has lost its sense of God's tangible presence and activity in our world. We think that God is to be found in the beyond, on another level of reality, far removed from our everyday relationships. But if this were the case, if God could not act in the world, his love would not be truly powerful, truly real, and thus not even true, a love capable of delivering the bliss it promises. It would make no difference at all whether we believed in him or not. Christians, on the contrary, profess their faith in God's tangible and powerful love which really does act in history and determines its final destiny: a love that can be encountered, a love fully revealed in Christ's passion, death and resurrection. (#17)

The kind of cultural atmosphere Balthasar and Pope Francis are referring to here—one dominated both by an explicit atheism recently become ever noisier by the New Atheism movement and by a *de facto* agnosticism rooted in consumerist materialism—can be seen lucidly typified here in this interview with the famous philosopher of language and mind John

---

3. Hans Urs von Balthasar, "Experience God?" in Hans Urs von Balthasar, *New Elucidations*, trans. Sister Mary Theresilde Skerry (San Francisco: Ignatius Press, 1986), 20–45, here 20. Balthasar is of course not alone in this lament: "The greatest cultural—and ecclesiastical—challenge we have to confront is the loss of a palpable sense that God's life makes all the difference in the world to our social and political decisions. Many things have made this witness more and more difficult in our era, and they touch the wider world as much as they do local American concerns. . . . What we like to call a 'commodified' consumer culture of religion is largely the result of our naïveté that all things can be touched and exchanged without danger or consequence, and this has now come to include religion itself." Ephraim Radner, "Primacy of Witness," *First Things*, no. 235 (August/September 2013): 38–40, here 38.

Searle (b. 1932), of the University of California at Berkeley. At the height of
his fame he was asked by the freethinking magazine *Free Inquiry* whether
he believed in God or the supernatural. Here was his answer:

> *Free Inquiry*: We're a secular humanist magazine, which means that we
> like to think of ourselves as the children of the Enlightenment. So we
> must ask—do you personally believe in God?

> John Searle: I don't. Actually, the best remark about this was by Bertrand
> Russell at a dinner I attended when I was an undergraduate. Russell
> was 85 years old. We were all a bunch of kids, and we thought, he's not
> going to live much longer, and he's a famous atheist, so let's really put it
> to him. So we asked him, What would happen if you were wrong about
> the existence of God? What would you say to *Him*? That is, suppose you
> died and you went to heaven and there you were in front of Him—what
> would you say? Russell didn't hesitate a second. He said, "I would say,
> 'You didn't give us enough evidence.'" And I think that's my attitude. On
> the available evidence we have about how the world works, we have to
> say that we're alone, there is no God, we don't have a cosmic friend, we're
> on our own. I might be wrong about that, but on the available evidence,
> that's the situation we're in. So I guess that makes me a kind of agnostic.

> *FI*: And you have no belief in the supernatural?

> Searle: None. But you see, there's something else that is, in a way, more
> important in this issue of the supernatural. Intellectuals in our culture
> have become so secularized, there's a sense in which the existence of
> the supernatural wouldn't matter in a way that it mattered a hundred
> years ago. Suppose we discovered that we're wrong, that there really is
> this divine force in the universe. Well, then, most intellectuals would say,
> okay, *that's a fact of physics like any other—instead of just four forces in
> the universe we have a fifth force.* In this sense, our attitude about the ex-
> istence of God wouldn't be as important because the world has already
> become demystified for us. Essentially, our world view would remain
> even if we discovered that we had been wrong, that God did exist.[4]

4. John Searle, "God, Mind, and Artificial Intelligence," *Free Inquiry*, Vol. 18, No. 4 (Fall
1998): 39–41, here 39; emphasis added. A variant of this position has been called Argument
from Divine Hiddenness and runs as follows: "If God exists, why doesn't He make His ex-

Searle is obviously operating under a severe category-mistake here, whose only cure would be a crash course in the Thomistic metaphysics of God. For as Balthasar notes so well (and he joins a chorus of other witnesses here, as we saw in the fourth chapter), because God is not an item in the world like other items, the notion of an experience of God or grace must come with a large proviso:

> God is not just one being among others encountered in this world and perceived by human senses and spiritual insight in an experience accumulated in the course of a lifetime. Hence it is to be expected that one cannot experience God as one does a mundane thing or even a fellow human being. God is essentially our origin, from which we are sent forth not by a natural growth, like a branch sprouting from a stem, but in a sovereign freedom that sends us forth in our creaturely independence and freedom, certainly not to expose us on a desert island, but rather so that we may set out on a free search back to our origin and "in feeling for him, come to find him. Yet he is not far from any of us" (Acts 17:27). If we view God and man only as the opposites Creator and creature, this "feeling" is comparable to the groping of a blind person who, beyond this space crammed with finite objects, fumbles around in infinity trying to find something to touch with his spiritual hand.[5]

Complicating this issue of experiencing God even further, the role of experience as such in both philosophy and theology has been quite transformed by René Descartes (1596–1650) and Immanuel Kant (1724–1804) in philosophy and by Friedrich Schleiermacher (1768–1834) in theology. Notorious nowadays among postmoderns for his so-called "foundationalism," Descartes sought to establish all truth on the one feature of reality he could not doubt: his own subjective experience as a thinking being. On that basis he believed he could prove the existence of God without taking into account the external world (which at the moment he was still "doubting," if only for methodological purposes); but God's inherent goodness would

---

istence more obvious, such that it could not be rationally doubted? . . . God supposedly loves us, and so desires our ultimate well-being. . . . So if God really existed and loved us, He would make sure that all of us believed in Him. Yet the world is full of rational persons who blamelessly fail to believe in God." Travis Dumsday, "A Thomistic Response to the Problem of Divine Hiddenness," *American Catholic Philosophical Quarterly*, Vol. 87, No. 3 (Summer 2013): 365–77, here 365.

5. Balthasar, "Experience God?", 21.

itself, Descartes thought, guarantee the reality of the external world; for otherwise the massive testimony of the senses to the overpowering reality of the external world would be a lie, which God would never permit.

It is not the place here to critique the obvious flaws in this overloading of all the burdens of epistemology onto the lonely subjective ego, but only to note how much weight subjective experience now has to carry in the Cartesian schema.[6] For now subjective experience becomes the all-judging *bar* against which all other truth claims must be adjudicated, a point Kant later made explicit when he insisted, as the title of one of his books had it, that religion must be confined "within the limits of reason alone."

True, that overweighting of all of reality onto the subjective ego has now largely collapsed. Led by Friedrich Nietzsche (1844–1900) in the nineteenth century and carried to fruition by Martin Heidegger (1889–1976) in the twentieth, that view of experience has now been almost universally abandoned, especially by continental philosophers.[7] In *Being and Time* (1927), Heidegger demonstrated, through powerful phenomenological analyses, that the Cartesian ego could not bear the foundational weight Descartes claimed for it; for when we come to *be* (*sein*), we find that we are already *there* (*da-sein*). So, we can never get behind ourselves to see ourselves coming into being, nor can we jump out of our skins to see ourselves from above: we are, in Heidegger's useful term, *thrown* into existence.[8] This "thrownness" means that we emerge into history with a pre-given perspective, an "angle" on the world, one that distorts, to be sure, but one that is also our only access to reality.

---

6. One obvious flaw no doubt has already struck the reader: if God's omni-beneficence "guarantees" the veracity of the senses when they testify to the reality of the external world, why are the senses then allowed to deceive us in particular matters, such as the oar that looks bent when placed in the water?

7. Analytic philosophers in the Anglo-American tradition also scorn Descartes, but more because of his mind/body dualism than for his excessive valorization of subjective experience as the foundation for a reliable epistemology.

8. "Thrownness" (*Geworfenheit*) was Heidegger's neologism for that reality we noticed in the last chapter: that no one chooses to be born, still less does anyone choose his or her sex, nationality, parents, race, mother tongue, and so forth. The sense of thrownness comes upon us especially in those moments when we ask: "What am I *doing* here?" Even Adam was in that sense "thrown," as shown most vividly (and again, not without his wonted humor) by John Milton: After Adam has been expelled from Paradise and is understandably feeling "put out," he hurls an objection against God rather reminiscent of a teenager saying to his father "I didn't ask to be born" after having been told to mow the lawn: "Did I request thee, Maker, from my clay/ To mould me Man; did I solicit thee/ From darkness to promote me" (*Paradise Lost* X, ll. 743–45).

Ludwig Wittgenstein (1889–1951) performed a similar inversion of the Cartesian ego by pointing out that there is no such thing as a private language, so that famous Cartesian words like "I," "doubt," "consciousness," and "clear and distinct" are all loaded down by history (in Descartes' case, by the history of medieval scholasticism). This means, in the words of John Caputo: "There is no such thing as a pure, private, pre-linguistic sphere— and, once again, it is a misunderstanding of language even to seek one."[9]

Many Christian theologians obviously find these developments to be a godsend, so to speak. Caputo is a bit less sanguine, for he recognizes the deeply anti-religious, Nietzschean strain in many postmodern thinkers, who can be positively phobic toward religion (or at least toward Christianity). As he tartly notes: "When philosophers really have an axe to grind about theology, that axe trumps the distinction between modern and postmodern. When it comes to theology, some philosophers take no prisoners."[10] Despite that almost instinctual post-Christian allergy against the Christian religion, theologians would be rash to dismiss these potential allies, not least for the way they can reopen the case for a proper appreciation of the Christian experience of grace. Let us begin with what Caputo regards as the central legacy of the Enlightenment's definition of reason:

> Reason does not take what is out there on face value and then adjust to it. On the contrary, by reason we mean the authority to determine what is out there in the first place and to set the standards to which things have to measure up. That is what the "Age of Reason," the "Enlightenment," means. It all has to do with who has the "authority" and the power—faith or reason. . . . God, the subject matter of theology par excellence, has come under the principles of reason, which are the jurisdiction of philosophy, rather than reason coming under God, the subject matter of theology. God has to stand in line like everyone else; what's fair is fair.[11]

That this exaltation of reason is not the view of the Bible can go without saying; but, in a manner of speaking, it is also not the view of Nietzsche, Heidegger, or Wittgenstein either, for all their internal differences. Accord-

9. John D. Caputo, *Philosophy and Theology* (Nashville: Abingdon Press, 2006), 46.
10. Caputo, *Philosophy and Theology*, 52.
11. Caputo, *Philosophy and Theology*, 26, 27–28.

ingly, I maintain, Christian theologians should be grateful for the opening or "clearing" (*Lichtung:* another key word in Heidegger's lexicon) that they provide for a proper understanding of experience. For just as these three worthies showed that "Enlightened" reason was looking at reality from the wrong end of the telescope from the outset, the same can be said for its view of the God of the Bible: the modern outlook completely upends the message of revelation because for Caputo it gets the Bible wrong from the start, by the very nature of its methodology:

> To say that God "obeys" these principles [of reason] is to put it all perversely, wrong-headedly, even impiously, like saying that a father resembles his son instead of the other way around. For, on the contrary, as reflections of God's being, necessity, and truth, the principles obey God. As St. Augustine said, when we human beings think something true, that is in our own imperfect way to think something about God, who *is* truth. God is not "true" but Truth. God is the original; the principles are the reflections in the water.[12]

Schleiermacher, too, contributed to the transformation of the meaning of experience by adding the element of *feeling* to the debate. This redefinition of experience now made the turn to experience conducive (or so he thought) to respond to Christianity's Enlightened despisers rather than just capitulating to them. But again, he did this in ways that still imported the overvalorization of subjective experience inherited from Descartes and

---

12. Caputo, *Philosophy and Theology,* 28–29. As an aside, Caputo notes another category mistake, one perhaps that lurks as the source of Searle's confusion about God being a possible "fifth force" in the universe yet to be discovered: "Descartes established what would become standard practice among the moderns, to refer to God as the 'cause of itself' (*causa sui*) whereas for Aquinas, God is the 'first cause uncaused,' the cause of everything else but himself without a cause. If something else were the cause of God, then God's cause would be greater than God. Then why not say that God is the cause of himself? Because that makes no sense. It would mean that a thing gives itself what it does not have—like lifting yourself up by your own bootstraps, or bringing yourself into being where you previously did not exist. To be your own cause is to be before your time, to be there ahead of your own coming into being, which you then bring about; it is to be there already when you are not there yet. Like being your own father or mother. And that makes no sense. But while such things are impossible for us, surely they are possible with God, for whom all things are possible? Not so fast, answered Aquinas. It makes no sense to say that God can do things that make no sense, not when God is the very height of sense and meaning and truth. It pays God no real compliment" (ibid., 23).

Kant. The stress on feelings did, however, add a new twist, helped not least by the fact that Schleiermacher was writing in the heyday of German Romanticism, with its stress on sentiment. Like Kant, he maintained that religion was an anthropological constant; but he saw the universality of religion as based on a more fundamental reality than the dreary Kantian stress on the morality of mere duty. For he held that, from the time of his conception, man is utterly dependent on others, indeed on his whole environment, for his existence. But since everyone, however dimly, recognizes that even the universe as a whole cannot account for its own existence, man's consistent feeling of dependence—on the womb, on his parents, on air, water, food, society, and so forth—implicitly recognizes an *absolute* dependence, whence arises the feeling of the need for God.

Polytheism refracts that feeling through the prism of humanity's *multifaceted* dependence (on air, rain, favorable weather for farming, and so forth) by positing many gods, each differently responsible for the outcome of certain natural phenomena on which human society depends. But the great virtue of monotheism, for Schleiermacher, is that this feeling of absolute dependence comes to its purest expression in the recognition that, whereas the gods are born from the universe and thus in some sense dependent on it as well, monotheism recognizes the dependence of the universe as a whole on the absolutely independent God. Hence, Schleiermacher thought he could "prove" the superiority of monotheism using the combined Enlightened/Romantic view of subjectivity.

Doctrine, therefore, for Schleiermacher is but the second-order reflection on prior experience. Hence a theologian cannot claim for dogmatics a foundation in deductive proofs based on revelation. On the contrary, theology can only be pursued "by each man willing to have the *experience* [of being a Christian] for himself. . . . [It] can only be apprehended by the love that *wills* to perceive."[13] Even more explicitly, he tells us that Christian doctrines are but "accounts of the religious Christian *affections* set forth in speech."[14] Applied to Christology, the doctrine of Christ will now have to be based on the subjective *experience* of redemption in Christ.[15]

---

13. Friedrich Daniel Ernst Schleiermacher, *The Christian Faith*, trans. H. R. Macintosh and James Stuart Stewart (Edinburgh: T. & T. Clark, 1928/1999), §13.2; emphases added. Because of the variety of editions and translations, citations will not give the page numbers, but section numbers, which all German and English editions share.

14. Schleiermacher, *Christian Faith*, §15.

15. As George Montague rightly points out: "The pertinent point for hermeneutics is this: for Schleiermacher language expresses the subject's *experience* but not *what* is expe-

But this same principle also operates not just in the heart of each individual Christian but also in Jesus Christ too, who, precisely as fully human, must also share fully in this feeling of absolute dependence, only now to a degree unmatched by any other human, as shown by, among other events of his life, the Our Father, which he taught his disciples. On the basis of Christ's singular feeling of absolute dependence, Christians are permitted to take Jesus as their Lord and Savior. No doubt Schleiermacher's Christology is the weakest part of his system; for, as Karl Barth noted, not without a certain fillip of sarcasm: if that is all Jesus represents in salvation history, then his coming is about as remarkable in mankind's religious history as "the formation of a new nebula" would be for the cosmologist.[16]

A loss, no doubt. But for Schleiermacher the price was worth it, considering what he gained: a *publicly accessible and therefore academically respectable* theology. Even if he did not share the presupposition of the roughly contemporaneous British utilitarians like Jeremy Bentham (1748–1832) and John Stuart Mill (1806–73) that feelings could be measured along a pain/pleasure calculus ("the greatest happiness for the greatest number"), he did hold that all human beings had some inkling of the feeling of absolute dependence. Indeed, this for him was the anthropological basis for explaining the universality of religion in human societies. Furthermore, he believed he could show that, on strictly descriptive, phenomenological grounds, monotheism represents a more pristine expression of that feeling of absolute dependence and that, among the monotheistic religions, Christianity represents the most pristine expression of monotheism because Jesus was himself the one human being who most lived out—and showed us how to live out—that feeling.[17]

---

rienced. . . . Since words are only labels for the individual's experience of God, the question immediately arises: Whose experience is authoritative? Evidently none. One person's experience of God is just as authoritative as another's. The consequences for building a universal community based on an authoritative revelation are dire. And as for scriptural interpretation, the text becomes only a triggering device to put the reader's experience in contact with the experience (the 'consciousness') of Christ." George T. Montague, *Understanding the Bible: A Basic Introduction to Biblical Interpretation* (New York: Paulist Press, 1997), 109; italics in the original.

16. Karl Barth, *The Theology of Schleiermacher: Lectures at Göttingen, Winter Semester 1923/24*, ed. Dietrich Ritschl, trans. Geoffrey W. Bromiley (Grand Rapids, MI: Eerdmans, 1982), 205.

17. In a book written twenty-five years after his Göttingen lectures, Barth gives a more neutral description of what Schleiermacher is trying to do here (which of course he will also go on to criticize): "Schleiermacher's presentation of the faith . . . rests on the basis of a

At first glance, this move seems to solve two problems at once: the problem of the public accessibility to academic study of the faith-claims of theology, and the question of religious pluralism. But as subsequent history would show, the results did not live up to the promise. First, how can something as evanescent as feelings be measured and against which standard? Second, according to Nietzsche, feelings are fundamentally biological reactions arising out of the struggle for life and thus are at root expressions of the "will to power," and so do not lend themselves to the adjudication of a more rational schema. Seen from that point of view, Schleiermacher's assertion of the superiority of Jesus Christ is unveiled as the inner expression of Christianity's hegemonic drive to obliterate other cultures and religious worldviews.

The Nietzschean rejoinder obviously comes from the non-Christian side, but it does reveal that the more the academy became influenced by post-Nietzschean relativism, the less Schleiermacher's version of theology could gain a hearing from the Christian religion's "cultured despisers." But there is another, and a more telling, objection that came from within: that what Schleiermacher has in effect done is to subsume Jesus Christ into a more overarching framework (founder of a world religion on the analogue with other founders; prime exemplar of the feeling of absolute dependence which all other human beings share, albeit to a lesser degree, etc.), whereas the Christian kerygma proclaims Jesus Christ as the sole and definitive incarnation of God the Son "in whom the fullness of the deity was pleased to dwell" (Col. 1:19).[18]

But even when one grants the ultimate failure of both Descartes and Schleiermacher to carry through on their projects, their influence still lives on, often in out-of-the-way and habitually unnoticed corners of the culture. I am thinking especially of an odd linguistic tic that indicates their (no doubt unacknowledged) influence: the habit people seem to have more

---

highest knowledge of human feeling or immediate self-awareness in its correlation to God, upon the basis of a highest knowledge of the nature and value of faith and the diversity of ways of believing altogether. It is not the Christian religion but the type to which this phenomenon belongs, religion as a necessary manifestation of human intellectual life, which is for Schleiermacher an object of speculative knowledge of an *a priori* kind." Karl Barth, *Protestant Theology in the Nineteenth Century: Its Background and History*, trans. Brian Cozens and John Bowden (Grand Rapids, MI: Eerdmans, 1947/2001), 435.

18. The preceding paragraphs borrow somewhat from what I had to say on Schleiermacher in my textbook on Christology, *Infinity Dwindled to Infancy: A Catholic and Evangelical Christology* (Grand Rapids, MI: Eerdmans, 2011).

and more of speaking not of someone *converting* but of having a conversion *experience*. Thus, in this new patois, Paul did not convert to the Christian religion on the road to Damascus but had a "conversion experience." Augustine did not convert to Christianity when he randomly found a passage from Paul's letter to the Romans in a garden in Milan but had a "conversion experience," and so forth. Now, no doubt Paul did experience *something*, and that "experience" is vividly described in Acts:

> As he neared Damascus on his journey, suddenly a light from heaven flashed around him. He fell to the ground and heard a voice say to him, "Saul, Saul, why do you persecute me?" "Who are you, Lord?" Saul asked. "I am Jesus, whom you are persecuting," he replied. "Now get up and go into the city, and you will be told what you must do." The men traveling with Saul stood there speechless; they heard the sound but did not see anyone. (Acts 9:3–7)

But the crucial point of the story is not the experience as such (after all, his companions shared in at least part of the "experience," which left them understandably baffled) but its effects in history: "At once he began to preach in the synagogues that Jesus is the Son of God" (9:20). Surely, even scoffers, atheists, or non-Christians of any stripe can admit that, historically speaking, Paul did after all *convert*, one of the most uncontested facts of early Christian history. Yet we continue to speak coyly of conversion "experiences," whereas the New Testament simply describes the event of conversion.

In fact, the very notion of experience is unknown to the New Testament. The ordinary Greek word for "experience" is *peira*, which occurs only twice in the New Testament, both in the Letter to the Hebrews, where it is coupled with the Greek word *lambanō*, forming an idiom that means "to attempt" (Heb. 11:29) or "to undergo" (Heb. 11:36). But like English, the Greek word for "experience" is etymologically related to its word for "experiment," as in a test; and that is the key to the New Testament meaning of what we moderns call "experience." But the difference between experience and experiment is crucial, as Balthasar notes:

> It is not man who is to experience God; rather, God wants to experience and to ascertain (*peirazesthai*) experimentally by means of *testing* whether the commissioned person is walking the path indicated by God. Whereas the Bible nowhere speaks of an experience (*peira*) of God on

man's part, the theme of God's experience of man by means of testing (*peirasmos*) appears throughout the whole of salvation history.[19]

This divine testing will be something that every Christian experiences who chooses to respond to God's call; but it is not the experience that counts, only the testing.[20] St. Ignatius Loyola (1491–1556) says in his *Spiri-*

19. Balthasar, "Experience God?", 23–24 italics in the original. This is of course the Old Testament view as well, as shown not only in the command to Abraham to sacrifice his son Isaac, but in numerous other divine callings as well, which are neatly summarized in the Book of Judith: "Remember what he did with Abraham, and how he tested Isaac and what happened to Jacob in Mesopotamia in Syria, while he was keeping the sheep of Laban, his mother's brother. For he has not tried us with fire, as he did them, to search their hearts, nor has he taken revenge upon us; but the Lord scourges them who draw near to him, in order to admonish them" (Jud. 8:26–27). One could easily cite other passages from the Bible that show the distance between its authors and ourselves in this matter, as Balthasar does here: "Withstanding God's testing leads to man's being *approved*. Therefore Paul says he 'can boast about our sufferings, knowing that suffering brings patience, and patience brings approval [*dokimē*, which Luther translated as 'experience'], and approval brings hope, and this hope is not deceptive' (Rom. 5:3–5). This hope is like the light reflected onto man from God's joy over his successful testing, so that James can even say: 'My brothers, count it sheer joy when you meet various trials (*peirasmoi*), knowing that the testing (*dokimion*) of your faith makes you patient; but patience too is to have its full effect so that you will become perfect, complete, with nothing missing' (Jam. 1:2–3)" ("Experience God?", 24–25).

20. This testing has its own teleology, one determined by the essentially prophetic dimension in every vocation, which requires of every experience of God that it be set against the norms of the world, as all the Hebrew prophets attest. For example, God sends Ezekiel to preach "lamentation and woe" (Ez. 2:10) to "a nation of rebels, who have rebelled against me to this very day" (Ez. 2:3), for "hard of face and stubborn of heart are they to whom I send you" (Ez. 2:4), so that God must make the prophet's "face hard against their faces, and your forehead hard against their foreheads; like stone harder than flint have I made your forehead" (Ez. 3:8–9). The ultimate example of the priority of testing over experience comes of course from Jeremiah, who famously accused God of having "duped" him: "O Lord, Thou hast deceived me, and I was deceived; Thou art stronger than I, and Thou hast prevailed" (Jer. 20:7), a passage that Abraham Heschel makes bold to translate as: "O Lord, Thou hast seduced me, and I let myself be seduced; Thou hast raped me, and I am overcome," which he glosses as follows: "The call to be a prophet is more than an invitation. It is first of all a feeling of being enticed, of acquiescence or willing surrender. But this winsome feeling is only one aspect of the experience. The other aspect is a sense of being ravished or carried away by violence, of yielding to overpowering force against one's will. The prophet feels both the attraction and the coercion of God, the appeal and the pressure, the charm and the distress. He is conscious of both voluntary identification and of forced capitulation." Abraham J. Heschel, *The Prophets* (New York: HarperCollins, 1962), I: 114. This bind can put the soul of the prophet in danger: "Avenge me on my persecutors" (Jer. 15:15), the prophet prayed, to which Heschel appends this observation: "Adversaries endangered the preaching of God's

tual Exercises that "everyone must keep in mind that, in all that concerns the spiritual life, his progress will be in proportion to his surrender of self-love and of his own will and interests."[21] That is the key to the experience of grace: any "felt" sense of God's presence in grace that is not grounded in the fertile soil of self-denial will not be grace but mere self-deception.[22]

It must of course be conceded that the entirety of these Ignatian Exercises is founded on getting the exercitant to "experience" various movements of spirits; and when no movement seemed to be occurring, Ignatius knew something was amiss: "When the one who is giving the Exercises perceives that the exercitant is not affected by any spiritual experiences, such as consolations or desolations, and that he is not troubled by different spirits, he ought to ply him with questions about the exercises. He should ask him whether he makes them at the appointed times, and how he makes them."[23] But the key is not to cultivate experiences for their own sake, but to discern a calling that comes directly from God from within that inevitable turbulence; and the director of the Exercises must avoid the temptation to play God:

> The director of the Exercises ought not to urge the exercitant more to poverty or any promise than to the contrary, nor to one state of life or way of living more than to another. Outside of the Exercises, it is true, we may lawfully and meritoriously urge all who probably have the required fitness to choose continence, virginity, the religious life, and every form of religious perfection. But while one is engaged in the Spiritual Exer-

---

word; the prophet lost patience. He exhorted God to depart from merciful longsuffering. Thus it developed that the prophet's indignation was stronger than God's anger, that the prophet's sympathy for the divine pathos went beyond the divine pathos. Divine forbearance and human indignation conflicted, and the prophet had to be told that God was concerned about the disciplining, not the destruction, of His adversaries" (ibid., 126).

21. *The Spiritual Exercises of St. Ignatius*, trans. Louis J. Puhl, S.J. (Chicago: Loyola University Press, 1951), 78 (#189).

22. As one author points out, Christology is the key here: "[T]he experience created by grace cannot be separated from the form of God's revelation as it appears in the surrender of the whole person to God—intellectually, volitionally, and emotionally—in the act of faith.... The formal object which creates the experience of faith is the Logos itself.... As the form of all perceptible and intelligible expression, the Logos condescends to finite forms of expression, which includes but is not limited to the grammatically ruled utterances of human speech." Peter Casarella, "Experience as a Theological Category," *Communio: International Catholic Review*, Vol. 20 (Spring, 1993): 118–28, here 119–20.

23. *The Spiritual Exercises of St. Ignatius*, 3 (#6).

cises, it is more suitable and much better that the Creator and Lord in person communicate Himself to the devout soul in quest of the divine will, that He inflame it with His love and praise, and dispose it for the way in which it could better serve God in the future. Therefore, the director of the Exercises, [like] a balance at equilibrium, without leaning to one side or the other, should permit the Creator to deal directly with the creature and the creature directly with his Creator and Lord.[24]

But the whole point of generating all these "feelings" and "experiences" of the divine is not to take them at face value but to *discern* the movement of these turbulent spirits, which requires extraordinary skill and subtlety, for the devil is himself a master at the subtle arts:

It is a mark of the evil spirit to assume the appearance of an angel of the light. He begins by suggesting thoughts that are suited to a devout soul, and ends by suggesting his own. For example, he will suggest holy and pious thoughts that are wholly in conformity with the sanctity of the soul. Afterwards, he will endeavor little by little to end by drawing the soul into his hidden snares and evil designs.... When the enemy of our human nature has been detected and recognized by the trail of evil marking his course and by the wicked end to which he leads us, it will be profitable for one who has been so tempted to review immediately the whole course of the temptation.... The purpose of this review is that

24. *The Spiritual Exercises of St. Ignatius*, 6 (#15). In an important short essay on St. Ignatius in a book that was the last of his to be published, Balthasar explains this enigmatic passage this way: "By their relentless practicality the Exercises shove the searcher into the center of the gospel and leave him alone there with Christ, with the triune God who speaks to him. In this way the book sweeps away the hundreds of pious 'manuals for perfection' that abounded during the high and late Middle Ages. I used the word *shove* deliberately, for, in order to be sure to arrive at the center, one must first be stripped of his illusions about himself, his fantasies and sins, so that 'naked he can follow the naked Christ,' so that God's Word—Christ—can confront him personally, nose to nose. This happens not somewhere at the edges but in the center of his existence, so that the call becomes a turning point in his life. 'Being called' constitutes the sole center, meaning and purpose of the whole book and is surrounded with much prudent advice ('pertaining to a proper carrying out of one's call'). The rest of the Exercises merely have to do with sharing Christ's path: Incarnation, birth, hidden and public life and work, Passion, Resurrection, and the founding of the Church." Hans Urs von Balthasar, *You Have the Words of Eternal Life: Scripture Meditations*, trans. Dennis Martin (San Francisco: Ignatius Press, 1991), 82–83. Balthasar had finished proofreading about one third of the galleys of this book when he died on June 26, 1988.

once such an experience has been understood and carefully observed, we may guard ourselves for the future against the customary deceits of the enemy.[25]

But how can this be done if subjective experience is all the exercitant has to go on, especially when the director of the retreat is told in no uncertain terms to keep the retreatant focused solely on the movements of spirits perceived in the hours of prayer? Here Ignatius offers some double-sided advice: "In souls that are progressing to greater perfection, the action of the good angel is delicate, gentle, delightful. It may be compared to a drop of water penetrating a sponge. The action of the evil spirit upon such souls is violent, noisy and disturbing."[26] But the mere fact of turbulence is not in and of itself an indicator of the devil's malign influence. For the situation of the individual soul is crucial, for which only self-knowledge can provide the key: "In souls going from bad to worse, the action of the spirits mentioned above is just the reverse. The reason for this is to be sought in the opposition or similarity of these souls to the different kinds of spirits. When the disposition is contrary to that of the spirits, they enter with noise and commotion that are easily perceived. When the disposition is similar to that of the spirits, they enter silently, as one coming into his own house when the doors are open."[27]

From these considerations drawn from one of the church's great masters at *discretio spirituum* (discernment of spirits), we now can understand the great gulf that separates the Bible's understanding of how God communicates his divine call from how we moderns typically understand experience. As Balthasar puts it with his usual lapidary flair: "We have said that the Bible has no word for religious experience, because it is not concerned primarily with man's religious sensibility, but with his docility to the divine self-revelation and to the mission it entails."[28]

---

25. *The Spiritual Exercises of St. Ignatius*, 148–49 (#332, 334). Not that the complexities end there of course (ibid., 149, #335).

26. *The Spiritual Exercises of St. Ignatius*, 149 (#335).

27. *The Spiritual Exercises of St. Ignatius*, 149 (#335).

28. Balthasar, "Experience God?", 35. This teaching falls especially hard on those whose acquaintance with the Christian religion has been attenuated by the popularity of New Age spiritualities, on which Balthasar issues this wise warning: "The law of renunciation can become very difficult for the individual in times when genuine ecclesial life finds feeble expression and numerous sects offer the enticement of immediate 'experiences.' But no one who experiences this difficulty should think that the mystic, with his apparently immediate

Moreover, God can paradoxically often be most active in a soul that feels only darkness and desolation, a point stressed particularly in the Carmelite tradition but which also came to full public consciousness when the private journals and other unpublished writings of Blessed Mother Teresa of Calcutta were published under the title *Come Be My Light*, wherein it was revealed how desperately poor in religious experience she was.[29] Her notes from a retreat she made from March 29 to April 12, 1959, make for especially painful reading, where she says things like "I don't believe I have a soul. . . . There was a burning zeal in my soul for souls from childhood until I said Yes to God, and then all is gone. Now I don't believe."[30]

What had happened was that for the first sixth months after she felt called to leave the Sisters of Loreto in India and to establish her own order, the Missionaries of Charity, she felt the consoling presence of Jesus. Then that feeling disappeared and was never to return for the rest of her life. At first her (many) spiritual directors understood her torment as part of the usual Carmelite template: first comes purgation, then illumination, then union. But that never happened, only the torment of never feeling God's presence or his grace. But then, on April 1, 1981, a breakthrough of sorts happened, when she realized that in fact she was participating in the same suffering that Jesus had undergone on the cross. As she said on that day to her Sisters in the Missionaries of Charity:

> At the Incarnation Jesus became like us in all things except sin; but at the time of the Passion, He became sin. He took on our sins and that was why He was rejected by the Father. I think that this was the greatest of all the sufferings that He had to endure and the thing He dreaded most in the agony in the Garden. Those words of His on the Cross were the expression of the depth of His loneliness and Passion—that even His

experiences of divine things, has an easier life. For every true mysticism, however rich it may be in visions and other experiences of God, is subject at least as strictly to the law of the Cross—that is, of non-experience—as is the existence of someone apparently forgotten in the desert of secular daily life. Perhaps the mystic has to pass through dry periods that are even more severe. Where this is not the case, where we are offered acquirable techniques to attain a mysticism without bitterness and the humiliations of the Cross, we can be certain that it is not authentically Christian and has no Christian significance" (ibid., 44–45).

29. Mother Teresa of Calcutta, *Come Be My Light: The Private Writings of the "Saint of Calcutta,"* edited and with commentary by Brian Kolodiejchuk, M.C. (New York: Doubleday, 2007). The book prompted a lengthy cover story in *Time* and an editorial in the *New York Times* on September 5, 2007.

30. Mother Teresa of Calcutta, *Come Be My Light*, 349.

own Father didn't claim Him as His Son. That, despite all His suffering and anguish, His Father did not claim Him as His beloved Son, as He did at the Baptism by St. John the Baptist and at the Transfiguration. You ask "Why?" Because God cannot accept sin and Jesus had taken on sin—He had become sin. Do you connect your vows with this Passion of Jesus? *Do you realize that when you accept the vows you accept the same fate of Jesus?*[31]

This is exactly the same point that Balthasar makes when he says that faith is not so much a matter of having a certain kind of feeling or experience but of actually following Jesus and sharing *his* fate, who himself knew desolation and rejection: "Active faith means following Jesus, but Jesus' mission leads him on a course from heaven deeper and deeper into the world of sinners, until finally on the cross he assumes, in their stead, their experience of distance from God, even of abandonment by God, and thus of the very loss of that lucid security promised to the 'proven' faithful."[32]

Of course, "the Spirit bloweth where it listeth," and God is free to distribute graces in such a way, as Paul says, "death is at work in us, but life in you" (2 Cor. 4:12). Or as Balthasar puts it: "God is always free to withdraw special graces from an individual (especially one who is completely surrendered!) in order to give them to other members of the mystical body of Christ."[33] In fact, such "feelings" of presence and absence can be intermingled in one person, as the saints often attest:

A person can experience extreme affliction outwardly and at the same time be inwardly "comforted," that is, know that he is living fully within God's will; many martyrs knew this. It can also happen that a person experiences darkness in the depths of his being—is submerged in God's "testing," . . . and in his darkness radiates light to others, though he himself does not feel or realize it at all. This is surely the case with many seriously ill people who can no longer see any meaning in their hopeless suffering, any more than he who was crucified for us all could see any meaning in his godforsakenness.[34]

31. Mother Teresa of Calcutta, *Come Be My Light,* 250–51; emphasis added.
32. Balthasar, "Experience God?", 37.
33. Balthasar, "Experience God?", 39.
34. Balthasar, "Experience God?", 38–39. I am reminded here of the wise words of Cardinal Bernardin when he was undergoing treatment for pancreatic cancer: "I wanted to pray, but the physical discomfort was overwhelming. I remember saying to the friends who visited

So it is not experience that should be the focus, only God's will; not a conversion "experience" but a true conversion; not a "feeling" of being loved and forgiven, but a turn toward God in true indifference that finally comes to understand how and why God loves us. As Balthasar says in another work: "It can be arrogance not to accept God's rewards and promises for the afterlife, that is, not to want to integrate them into one's motives for acting. But it can equally be selfish to want to serve God on account of this reward, to want to become rich 'off him.' We escape the dilemma if we consider that our reward is God, that God is Love, and that Love does not look to itself, much less to a reward."[35]

It would of course be absurd to say that the notion of experience has no role to play in faith, in a sense of vocation, in detecting the movements of grace, and in reading the signs of the times. Cultivation of a sense of the divine certainly forms an essential element in any dedicated Christian's life. But still, all that is secondary to "the one thing necessary," which is God's will: "Through prayer we should come to perceive and savor God within us (the *interne sentire et gustare* of Ignatius)," Balthasar concedes. "And yet," he continues, "in prayer, we should not be seeking any enjoyment but rather the pure service of God. In order for us to learn how to unite both things, God takes us into his school, which consists in a continual alternation of consolations and abandonments, until we have learned how one can even enjoy in a wholly selfless manner and how to experience enjoyment itself as service."[36]

There can be no doubt that a deeper analysis of the notion of an experience of grace leads to real paradoxes; but these paradoxes have been bequeathed to us by Scripture. Paul tells us that God "dwells in inapproachable light" (1 Tim. 6:16); yet elsewhere he tells us that we are to draw near to the inaccessible one "in boldness and confidence through our faith in Jesus Christ" (Eph. 3:12). The Gospel of John explicitly says that "no one has ever seen God," yet in that same verse John says that "the One who is at the Father's side has made him known" (John 1:18); and for this author

---

me, 'Pray while you're well, because if you wait until you're sick you might not be able to do it.' They looked at me, astonished. I said, 'I'm in so much discomfort that I can't focus on prayer. My faith is still present. There is nothing wrong with my faith, but in terms of prayer, I'm just too preoccupied with the pain. I'm going to remember that I must pray when I am well!' Since then prayer has been more important to me than ever before." Joseph Cardinal Bernadin, *The Gift of Peace* (New York: Doubleday/Image Books, 1997), 67–68.

35. Hans Urs von Balthasar, *The Grain of Wheat: Aphorisms*, trans. Erasmo Leiva-Merikakis (San Francisco: Ignatius Press, 1995), 9.

36. Balthasar, *Grain of Wheat*, 11.

Jesus could not be more concrete and accessible to the senses: "That which was from the beginning, which we have heard, which we have seen with our eyes, which we have looked at and our hands have touched—this we proclaim concerning the Word of life. This life appeared; we have seen it and testify to it, and we proclaim to you the eternal life which was with the Father and has appeared to us. We proclaim what we have seen and heard, so that you also may have fellowship with us" (1 John 1:1–3a). How can these statements be reconciled? Here at least is Balthasar's answer:

> Christians today must be capable of withstanding the tension which is contained within these statements. On the one hand, they must abandon every attempt to penetrate into the hidden and free being of God with unbaptized reason, and on the other, they may reject no path which God himself offers men into the mystery of his eternal love. They may neither, on the one hand, push God away into a realm of inaccessible transcendence which then ultimately becomes a matter of indifference for men nor, on the other hand, so draw him into the historicity of the world that he forfeits his freedom over the world and falls victim to human *gnosis*.[37]

This program of Christian *askesis* is of course easier said than done; but the task is also ineluctable, for it is intimately linked with the paradoxical way God is present to the world: both utterly transcendent and totally other than what he has created; and yet more intimate to us than we are to ourselves. This double present-yet-absent ubiquity of God to the world he created allows us to see why religious experience can be so fleeting, so evanescent. But the nature of God demands no less, even if that means we are left only groping for God in the dark; yet in that darkness he is also there. In other words, the problem of religious experience is rooted in the Christian doctrine of God:

> For human thought, and still more for human feeling and experience, God's presence and absence in the world are an unsearchable mystery. It would seem that we can think and speak of it solely in dialectical, mutu-

---

37. Balthasar, *Grain of Wheat*, 45. In a way, God's transcendence only becomes a living doctrine inside a life following the concrete demands of Christ: "When God draws near to us in Jesus Christ, even desiring to dwell in us, it does not mean that he forfeits any of his grandeur and incomprehensibility. Indeed, these attributes, which until then were hardly more than abstractions to us, suddenly acquire a splendor that makes them concrete for us at the moment when we realize that we are called and are children of the divine Father." "Experience God?", 45.

ally invalidating statements. This is because when the concept "God" is outlined as to its content, God is "everything" (*to pan estin autos*: Sirach 43:27), since nothing can exist outside God and nothing can be added to him; and he is at the same time "above all his works" (*para panta ta erga auton*: Sirach 43:28), for none of these works is God; each is distinct from him by virtue of the infinite distance and contrast between the absolute and relative. The more God has to be in all things so that they may exist at all, the more he is in them as the one who is completely other than them: the more immanent he is, the more he is transcendent. In itself, this dialectic is correct, but it sounds hollow and is difficult to translate into religious experience.[38]

Indeed it does.[39] But I wonder if the problem has not been exacerbated by an excessive dwelling on these theological paradoxes. For paradoxes,

38. Hans Urs von Balthasar, "The Absences of Jesus," in Hans Urs von Balthasar, *New Elucidations*, trans. Sister Mary Theresilde Skerry (San Francisco: Ignatius Press, 1986), 46–60, here 46. In an acute and sensitive novel on the life of Jeremiah, the Austrian novelist Franz Werfel (who later became famous for his *Song of Bernadette*) captures just this kind of dilemma that plagued Jeremiah soon after he received his first call: "During those days when he was beseeching God ardently, Jeremiah for the first time in his waking existence experienced the complete absence of God. It was as if in the first hour between the night of Passover and the coming of dawn [when he first heard the prophetic call] too much had been expended both by Him who gave and by him who received. . . . If the patriarch Abraham, the exemplar of faith and trusting confidence, had even for an instant been able to conceive the thought that the voice which commanded him might not be serious, might be fickle and false or even a complete illusion, he would in that same instant have fallen dead from horror at the power of doubt. Jeremiah, however, was no mighty man of antiquity. He was the child of a new and faint-hearted, distrustful generation. He doubted. He doubted even as he prayed and struggled with temptation. Yet the clear and gentle voice of Adonai had revealed mysteries to him that could not have sprung from his own mind: 'Before I formed thee in the belly I knew thee; and before thou camest forth out of the womb I sanctified thee.'" Franz Werfel, *Hearken Unto the Voice*, trans. Moray Firth (New York: Viking Press, 1938), 120–21. A bit later, as he grows more skilled in the discernment of spirits, Jeremiah comes to this "Ignatian" insight: "The God who demanded from men a festive joy at their sacrificial rites, and who required eternal rejoicing from His angels, was it possible that this same God filled those whom He had 'touched with His hand' with the spirit of sadness?" (ibid., 130).

39. As Thomas Aquinas says: "Although uncreated truth exceeds all created truth, yet there is nothing to prevent created truth from being better known to us. Things that are less known in themselves are known better to us." *De veritate* X, 12, ad 6; cited from *The Human Wisdom of St. Thomas: A Breviary of Philosophy from the Works of St. Thomas Aquinas*, arranged by Josef Pieper, trans. Drostan Maclaren, O.P. (San Francisco: Ignatius Press, 2002), 98 (#507).

strictly defined, are sentences whose surface meaning apparently contradicts what those sentences are obviously trying to say (like "too swift
arrives as tardy as too slow"). But that is a grammatical issue. *Christian*
paradoxes, however, are meant to open the believer to venture into what
the New Testament prefers to call *mysteries*, as Balthasar explains: "It is
very easy to ask Christians perplexing questions, because from the outside
Christ's mysteries appear to be mere paradoxes, and it is very difficult to
solve them at this level. (The attempt often leads to a false apologetics.)
The chief concern here, rather, should be to awaken in the questioner an
elementary sense for mystery and awe."[40] *Mystery* explains why Balthasar
can bluntly say on one occasion: "The supernatural can in no case be immediately experienced."[41] Yet in another context he can urge a cultivation
of a sense of the divine: "We cease to perceive water that continually flows.
We hear our innermost wellspring, which flows from God, only when we
make a conscious effort. That is why the saying of the Pythagoreans that
the wise man perceives the music of the spheres is truly a religious saying.
We should always be hearing, as with bodily ears, the gurgling wellspring
of our origin in God."[42] In this same work, he reconciles these two different
statements with this programmatic axiom: "Perfect (intuitive) self-awareness would be an awareness of one's own origin from God. . . . This is said
ontologically speaking, without prejudice to a practical education in the
love of God, which naturally cannot be attained through introversion, but
only through the 'leap out of oneself.' "[43]

Nor are we as bereft as the preceding analysis might suggest, shuttle-
cocking between unreliable subjective experiences yet having no other
access to God since reality can only come to us via experience. True, all
experience of God and his grace will be an oblique one, as it were, one that
must be left behind as soon as experienced so that we can advance to the
ever-greater God, who transcends not just all our experiences but also all
our concepts.[44] But there is one foothold, and it is given to us as an axiom

40. Balthasar, *Grain of Wheat*, 31.
41. Balthasar, "Experience God?", 45.
42. Balthasar, *Grain of Wheat*, 1.
43. Balthasar, *Grain of Wheat*, 6.
44. In the wise words of Pope Benedict XVI: "Believing is nothing other than, in the
darkness of the world, touching the hand of God and thus, in silence, listening to the Word,
seeing Love." Benedict XVI, "Pope Concludes Lenten Retreat," Vatican City, February 23, 2013,
Vatican Information Service, full text at: http://www.news.va/en/news/pope-concludes
-lenten-retreat; accessed August 5, 2013.

by Jesus himself: "By their fruits shall ye know them" (Matt. 7:16). Do you want to experience grace? Follow that rule, as Paul does here:

> The whole law is fulfilled in one command: "You shall love your neighbor as yourself." . . . I say, walk by the Spirit, and do not gratify the desires of the flesh. For the desires of the flesh are against the Spirit, and the desires of the Spirit are against the flesh. . . . Now the works of the flesh are plain: fornication, impurity, licentiousness, idolatry, sorcery, enmity, strife, jealousy, anger, selfishness, dissention, party spirit, envy, drunkenness, carousing, and the like. . . . But the fruit of the Spirit is love, joy, peace, patience, kindness, goodness, faithfulness, gentleness, self-control; against such there is no law. And *those who belong to Christ Jesus have crucified the flesh with its passions and desires.* (Gal. 5:14–24; emphasis added)[45]

According to Origen (182–254), wherever there is division there is sin; and wherever there is sin there is division. Conversely, wherever there is grace, there is unity, harmony, peace, and goodwill, which of course requires that Christians in community "do nothing from selfishness or conceit but in humility count others better than [themselves]" (Phil. 2:3). For grace, as we noted early in the first chapter, is simply love under a different name, and "love does not insist on its own way, nor is it resentful or irritable; love does not rejoice at wrong but rejoices in the right. Love bears all things, hopes all things, endures all things" (1 Cor. 13:5b–7).

All of the above considerations have been admirably synthesized in this concise summary of church teaching on the matter in her most recent catechism:

> Since it belongs to the supernatural order, grace *escapes our experience* and cannot be known except by faith. We cannot therefore rely on our feelings or our works to conclude that we are justified and saved. However, according to the Lord's words—"Thus you will know them by their fruits" (Matt. 7:20)—reflection on God's blessings in our life and in the lives of the saints offers us a guarantee that grace is at work in us and

---

45. Notice that few of the sins of the "flesh" herein enumerated deal explicitly with sins of sex or sensuality but arise out of an attitude that the world is, ultimately, really all there is, which inevitably leads to idolatry and its attendant sins. The fundamental sin of the "flesh," then, *vis-à-vis* God is lack of trust, just as Jeremiah says: "Cursed is the man who trusts in man and makes flesh his arm and whose heart departs from the Lord" (Jer. 17:5).

spurs us on to an ever greater faith and an attitude of trustful poverty. A pleasing illustration of this attitude is found in the reply of St. Joan of Arc to a question posed as a trap by her ecclesiastical judges: "Asked if she knew that she was in God's grace, she replied: 'If I am not, may it please God to put me in it; if I am, may it please God to keep me there.' "[46]

Divinization

At first glance the doctrine of divinization or deification—that the goal of grace is to make us "gods"—would seem preposterous. The idea that this forked mammal we deign to call *Homo sapiens* (the "wise" human) could ever approach the ontological status of the Creator God—immutable and all-holy—is both biologically and religiously garish. Just considering the twentieth century, the human race has displayed such a record of unmitigated folly and destruction—from cultured Germany's romance with that ridiculous runt of a bigot Adolf Hitler to the infatuation of vast swaths of the human race with Communism and its attendant Gulags and mass starvation—that the idea that grace intends to make us "divine" seems absurd on its face. The very aspiration seems to rely on a complete lack of self-knowledge. As Blaise Pascal says so well, *that* kind of self-knowledge comes only to the humble, not the proud: "Two sorts of people have such knowledge: those who have a humble heart and who embrace lowliness, whatever their degree of mental power; or those who have sufficient understanding to see the truth, whatever resistance they might have."[47]

Not only that, but it would seem that Scripture itself strictly forbids any human aspiration toward deification; for the serpent first tempted Adam and Eve *with* that very temptation to become like God:

> Now the serpent was more subtle than any other wild creature that the Lord God had made. He said to the woman, "Did God say, 'You shall not eat of any tree of the garden'?" And the woman said to the serpent, "We may eat of the fruit of the trees of the garden; but God said, "You shall not eat of the fruit of the tree which is in the midst of the garden, neither shall you touch it, lest you die." But the serpent said to the woman, "You

46. *CCC* #2005; italics in the original.
47. Blaise Pascal, *Pensées*, trans. Honor Levi (Oxford: Oxford University Press, 1995), 7 (#13).

will not die. For God knows that when you eat of it your eyes will be opened, and you will be like God, knowing good and evil." (Gen. 3:1–5)[48]

If those two considerations were not enough to count against the doctrine, the Roman world at the birth of Christianity was awash in the twaddle of divinizing anyone who struck the populace as in any way out of the ordinary, as we learn from this amusing scene depicted in Acts of the Apostles:

Now at Lystra there was a man sitting who could not use his feet, for he was crippled from birth and had never walked. He listened to Paul speaking; and Paul, looking intently at him and seeing that he had faith to be made well, said in a loud voice: "Stand upright on your feet." And he sprang up and walked. And when the crowds saw what Paul had done, they lifted up their voices, saying in Lycaonian: "The gods have come down to us in the likeness of men!" Barnabas they called Zeus, and Paul, because he was the chief speaker, they called Hermes. And the priest of Zeus, whose temple was in front of the city, brought oxen and garlands to the gates and wanted to offer sacrifice with the people. But when the apostles Barnabas and Paul heard of it, they tore their garments and rushed out among the multitude, crying: "Men, why are you doing this? We are also men, of like nature with you, and bring you good news, that you should turn from these vain things to a living God who made heaven and earth and the sea and all that is in them. In past generations he allowed all the nations to walk in their own ways; yet he did not leave himself without witness, for he did good and gave you from heaven rains and fruitful seasons, satisfying your hearts with food and gladness." With these words they scarcely restrained the people from offering sacrifice to them. (Acts 14:8–18)

Even the more "enlightened" pagans seemed to have been on to the game, especially when it came to the ever-more-frequent practice of the imperial Senate declaring a recently deceased emperor to be now suddenly

48. Although he does not explicitly rely on Genesis 3 here, the Psalmist depicts a thoroughly realistic view of the pretensions of man: "You have given me a short span of days; my life is nothing in your sight. A mere breath, the one who stood so firm; a mere shadow, the passer-by. Mortal man is no more than a breath. . . . In your house I am a passing guest, a pilgrim, like all my fathers. Look away that I may breathe again before I depart to be no more" (Psalm 39:5–6, 12–13).

"divine." The ancient historian Suetonius reports the amusing story that on his deathbed the emperor Vespasian let out this droll exhalation: *Vae, puto deus fio* ("Oh dear, I think I'm about to become a god.")[49] And of course, at least in the eastern portions of the empire, living emperors had to be acknowledged as in some way divine.[50]

Christians, too, were on to this game; only they weren't playing. The whole *reason* they were persecuted (however sporadically and locally) was because they refused to give what they regarded as the quintessential divine title *Lord* to the emperor. However seriously and literally the Romans did or did not take their ritual of acknowledging the divine status of their own living emperor, the ritual itself was part of their *religio*, that set of customs and norms that itself was a binding agent holding society together. But precisely because the ritual entailed an explicit acknowledgment of the emperor's divinization, Christians could not participate, and did not. Given the episode in Acts recounted above, we know that pagans might hand out divine honors to all and sundry, and thus would have thought little of adding a powerful emperor to this increasingly overpopulated pantheon. But for Christians, the issue was make-or-break: in obedience to the first of the Ten Commandments, no human being gets to be divinized.[51]

---

49. Although the remark is well attested in the ancient sources, Norman Russell cautions against the idea that Vespasian was a Voltaire born before his time, precisely because divinization by then was so taken for granted: "Vespasian's remark was probably an expression of modesty or may just have been a nervous joke." Norman Russell, *The Doctrine of Deification in the Greek Patristic Tradition*, Oxford Early Christian Studies (Oxford: Oxford University Press, 2004), 23. Perhaps, but one must still salute the emperor's sense of humor and insouciance before death.

50. Metaphysically speaking, the step cannot have been that much of a stretch, for as Pindar said: "Men and gods are of the same race; and both from the selfsame mother we draw our breath. . . . In some measure we come near at least to the Immortals, either in respect of mind or in our outward form." Pindar, *Nemean Odes* VI, 1-2, 6-8; quoted in Abraham J. Heschel, *The Prophets*, I: 46.

51. One might also mention that this pagan fascination with the divine has been secularized in western civilization by the notion that the human race is making progress, a legacy from the so-called Enlightenment that still lives on, despite the horrors of the twentieth century: "The Victorian celebration of technology-driven advance has looked a bit fishy to most people since two world wars, the Holocaust and Hiroshima showed the kinds of uses to which allegedly ameliorative science can easily be put: so easily indeed, and so frequently, that we might well ask whether such uses are not in some way inherent in the scientific method that enables them. That is the truly heretical question of our time. . . . It is relatively easy to admit that what we have seen as scientific advance and economic enrichment are meaningless. It is much more difficult to conceive them as actively evil

Nor, apparently, can anything resembling a teaching on divinization be located in the teachings of Jesus in the Synoptic Gospels, who taught this parable:

> "Will anyone of you who has a servant plowing or keeping sheep, say to him when he has come in from the field, 'Come at once and sit down at table'? Will he not rather say to him, 'Prepare supper for me, and gird yourself and serve me until I eat and drink'? Does he thank the servant because he did what was commanded? So you also, when you have done all that is commanded of you, say, 'We are unprofitable servants; we have only done what was our duty.'" (Luke 17:7–10)

Yet, despite this contemporary pagan "divinization sprawl," despite this handing out of divine honors even to those who explicitly eschewed that "honor," despite the persecution Christians faced over just this issue, nonetheless the doctrine of the divinization of man through divine grace goes back deep into the tradition, and indeed to Scripture itself (2 Pet. 1:4), and has been made part of the official teaching of the Catholic Church:

> The Word became flesh to make us "partakers of the divine nature" (2 Pet. 1:4). "For this is why the Word became man, and the Son of God became the Son of man: so that man, by entering into communion with the Word, and thus receiving divine sonship, might become a son of God." "For the Son of God became man so that we might become God." "The only-begotten Son of God, wanting to make us sharers in his divinity, assumed our nature, so that he, made man, might make men gods."[52]

The impression has somehow arisen that the doctrine of divinization is peculiar to the Eastern Orthodox tradition; and indeed the teaching did fall into a certain desuetude in the wake of Baroque scholasticism (which tended to speak of sanctifying grace instead of divinization). But even a

---

and destructive, to imagine Enlightenment as the Fall. But we may soon have to do just that. The question of whether history is progress will not be answered in theory but in practice." David Hawkes, "Backwards into the Future," *Times Literary Supplement*, No. 5761 (August 30, 2013): 7.

52. *CCC* #460, internally quoting Irenäeus, Athanasius, and Thomas Aquinas.

quick glance at theologians in the west disproves any explicit rejection of the doctrine; in fact, most explicitly affirm it, very much including Protestants, where at least in the classical Reformers the doctrine has been ably defended, especially by John Calvin, as here:

> This is the wonderful exchange which, out of his measureless benevolence, he [Christ] has made with us: that, by his descent to earth, he has prepared an ascent to heaven for us; that, by taking on our mortality, he has conferred his immortality upon us; that, accepting our weakness, he has strengthened us by his power; that, receiving our poverty unto himself, he has transferred his wealth to us; that, taking the weight of our iniquity oppressing us upon himself, he has clothed us with his righteousness.[53]

Admittedly, after the sixteenth century the theme of divinization rather loses its traction among western theologians, both Protestant and Catholic. On the Protestant side, Schleiermacher had no interest in the doctrine; and in the nineteenth century the great historian of dogma Adolf von Harnack (1851–1930) accused the notion of deification of being another import from Hellenism that spoiled the Semitic simplicity of the Gospels.[54] Catholics also neglected this important theme, perhaps because their energies were so taken up by the *de auxiliis* controversy, which put the stress more on grace as an aid to help one avoid sin and "get into heaven." But it never quite died out. For example, John Henry Newman says this about deification in his *Lectures on Justification*:

> [Christ's] ascent bodily [on Ascension Thursday] is his descent spiritually; his taking our nature up to God is the descent of God into us. . . . Thus, when St. Paul says that our life is hid with Christ in God, we may suppose him to intimate that our principle of existence is no longer a mortal, earthly principle, such as Adam's after his fall, but that we are baptized and hidden anew in God's glory, . . . that we are newly-created, transformed, spiritualized, glorified in the Divine Nature—that through the participation of Christ we receive, as through a channel, the true

53. John Calvin, *Institutes of the Christian Religion* 4.17.2.

54. This last charge has recently been disproved by Russell's massively learned and lucidly written monograph: "Briefly, the Christian usage of deification terms expressing the soul's ascent to God precedes the pagan usage, rather than the other way around, as is often assumed." Russell, *Doctrine of Deification*, 8.

presence of God within and without us, imbuing us with sanctity and immortality.[55]

Since Newman's day, there has been a remarkable renaissance of interest in this theme, largely due to the influx of Orthodox theologians to the west after the Bolshevik revolution of 1917 and then again later, after the inroads into other lands of Orthodoxy by the Soviet Union after World War II. Western theologians also had a minor role to play (for example, Maximus the Confessor was almost entirely unknown in the west until Balthasar published his monograph on him, *Cosmic Liturgy*, in 1961). Thus we may conclude that E. L. Mascall is entirely correct when he says:

> Christian theologians, from the Fathers to the present day, . . . have been equally convinced that no term less than "deification" is adequate to describe the condition of the human being who has been taken by grace into the supernatural realm; and, let us note, not simply the condition of the mystic united to God in the spiritual marriage or of the saint enjoying the beatific vision in heaven, but also that of the newly baptized infant at the font or of the newly absolved sinner in the confessional.[56]

No theologian nowadays demurs from this judgment. On the contrary, ever new appreciation has been voiced for the importance of this theme, not just as an arcane moment in historical theology, but pastorally as well. Daniel Keating has assembled a useful catena of citations from the "great tradition" in his own seminary textbook on this issue.[57] Because this book is not itself a work in historical theology, I will content myself merely with this citation from Irenaeus, who may be considered (outside of Scripture) to have begun the tradition of speaking of divinization, even if he too never used the word as such:

> Unless it had been God who had freely given salvation, we could never have possessed it securely; and unless man had been joined to God, he could never have become a partaker of incorruptibility. For it was in-

55. John Henry Newman, *Lectures on Justification* (London: Longmans, Green, and Co., 1872), 218–19. Note, however, that while the doctrine of divinization is there, Newman never uses the term itself or its cognates.

56. Eric Mascall, *The Importance of Being Human: Some Aspects of the Christian Doctrine of Man* (Oxford: Oxford University Press, 1959), 64.

57. Daniel A. Keating, *Deification and Grace* (Naples, FL: Sapientia Press, 2007).

cumbent upon the Mediator between God and men, by his relationship
to both, to bring both to friendship and concord, and present man to
God, while he revealed God to man.[58]

While such citations could be multiplied at will, their consistent presence throughout the tradition, both east and west, does raise a problem:
given what was said above about the Christian doctrine of the radical distinction between God the infinite Creator and his finite creation, given the
wild abandon with which pagans bestowed divine titles on the powerful in
their midst, why did Christians come to a doctrine of divinization so early,
and above all what did they mean by it?

Surely, Keating is right when he says that the key to this enigmatic
doctrine must be found in *Christology*, where one human being alone, Jesus
Christ, was himself substantially united to the godhead. But the real key
to what Christians down through the ages have meant by divinization lies
not just in Christology strictly defined as a separate doctrine of the hypostatic union; rather, soteriology—the doctrine of what Christ actually did
for our salvation—is the key. As Keating rightly notes: "There is no better
place to begin a study of deification than with what is commonly termed
the 'formula of exchange' (often designated in the Christian tradition as the
admirabile commercium). In essence, this formula states that the eternal
Son of God became what we are so that we could become what he is."[59]
In that regard, we may consider Paul, and not Peter, as the real instigator
of the doctrine: "For you know the grace of our Lord Jesus Christ, that for
your sake he became poor, though being rich, so that by his poverty you
may become rich" (2 Cor. 8:9).

To be sure, when treated incautiously, the doctrine can veer into gnos-
ticism in the wrong hands, as if we have been made gods *by nature*, or were
so from the beginning. But orthodox authors never veer in that direction,
and often warn against taking the doctrine too "literally." Augustine strikes
just the right note when he says:

> It is evident, then, that he [Christ] has called men gods, who are dei-
> fied of his grace, not born of his substance. For he justifies, who is just

58. Irenaeus, *Against the Heresies* 3.18.7, trans. Alexander Roberts and James Donald-
son, *Ante-Nicene Fathers* (Edinburgh: T. & T. Clark; Grand Rapids, MI: William B. Eerdmans,
reprint 1996) 1: 448.

59. Keating, *Deification and Grace*, 11.

through his own self, and not [through] another. But he that justifies does himself deify, in that by justifying he makes sons of God. "For he has given them power to become sons of God" (John 1:12). If we have been made sons of God, we have also been made gods; but this is *the effect of grace adopting, not of nature generating*.[60]

As we saw in the first chapter, no one has worked out more carefully the subtle relationship between nature and grace than Thomas Aquinas; and so we are not surprised to learn that his formulation has not only stood the test of time but perhaps best summarizes what is and is not entailed in this teaching: "For he did not love them to the point of their being gods by nature, nor to the point that they could be united to God so as to form one person with him. But he did love them up to a similar point: he loved them to the extent that they would be gods by their participation in grace—'I say you are gods' (Ps. 82:6), 'He has granted to us a precious and very great promise, that through these you may become partakers of the divine nature' (2 Pet. 1:4)."[61]

60. Augustine, *Commentary on the Psalms*, at Ps. 49:2 NPNF, first series, VIII: 178; emphasis added. Again, note the Pauline provenance of the doctrine: "For you know the grace of our Lord Jesus Christ, that for your sake he became poor, though being rich, so that by his poverty you may become rich" (2 Cor. 8:9).

61. Thomas Aquinas, *Commentary on the Gospel of St. John*, trans. J. A. Weisheipl and F. R. Larcher (Petersham, MA: St. Bede's, 1999), II: 397. Nonetheless, to avoid any implication of Gnostic theopanism, Thomas also insists that grace is an accident of the soul; for if it were part of the soul's substance, it would be part of God's own substance, an impossibility. Thomas's teaching here is controversial, because it makes grace seem but a superficial supplement to the soul's nature. But the Common Doctor makes clear that is not his meaning: "Every substance is either the nature of the thing whereof it is the substance, or it is a part of the nature, even as matter and form are called substance. And because grace is above human nature, it cannot be a substance or a substantial form but is an accidental form of the soul. Now what is substantially in God becomes accidental in the soul participating in the divine goodness, as is clear in the case of knowledge. And thus because the soul participates in the divine goodness imperfectly, the participation of the divine goodness, which is grace, has its being in the soul in a less perfect way than the soul subsists in itself. Nevertheless, inasmuch as it is the expression or participation of the divine goodness, it is nobler than the nature of the soul, though not in its mode of being." *ST* I-II, q. 110, a. 2, ad 2. As Thomas says immediately before: "Grace, as a quality, is said to act upon the soul, not after the manner of an efficient cause, but after the manner of a formal cause, as whiteness makes a thing white, and justice, just"(ibid., ad 1). In other words, some accidental changes are more accidental than others, as it were. A moustache on a man does not affect his substance from what he had been when he had been clean-shaven; but a moustache painted on the original of the Mona Lisa would utterly change the painting. Thomas is here implying that grace makes us,

So while there is considerable unanimity among theologians of all schools that the nature/grace distinction must be preserved even in moments of highest union with the divine nature, one can detect different emphases in these different schools, a difference in stress particularly noticeable in the first seven centuries of reflection on this theme, one that Russell has usefully summarized:

> In summary, until the end of the fourth century the metaphor of deification develops along two distinct lines: on the one hand, the transformation of humanity in principle as a consequence of the Incarnation; on the other, the ascent of the soul through the practice of virtue. The former, broadly characteristic of Justin, Irenaeus, Origen, and Athanasius, is based on St. Paul's teaching on incorporation into Christ through baptism and implies a realistic approach to deification. The latter, typical of Clement and the Cappadocians, is fundamentally Platonic and implies a philosophical or ethical approach. By the end of the fourth century the realistic and philosophical strands begin to converge. In Cyril the realistic approach becomes more spiritualized through the use he makes of 2 Peter 1:4; in Maximus the philosophical approach comes to be focused more on ontological concerns under the influence of his post-Chalcedonian christology.[62]

The reason that nearly all forms of the defense of divinization ultimately rest on Christology can be seen in the way the Alexandrians (with their heavy stress on the hypostatic union creating a complete union of divine and human nature in the divine person of Jesus) and the Antiochenes (with their insistence that the two natures must always remain distinct, even while granting a "moral" union between the two natures) interpret the meaning of divinization, where any reconciliation between the two views completely breaks down (as it did with their respective Christologies). Again, Russell captures the difference quite succinctly here:

> The Antiochene fathers are different. They speak of men as gods only by title or analogy. When the Antiochenes are compared with the Alexandrians, the correlation between deification and christology becomes

---

as it were, God's work of art: "Light implies something in what is enlightened. But grace is a light of the soul. . . . Therefore grace implies something in the soul" (ibid., a. 1, *sed contra*).

62. Russell, *Doctrine of Deification*, 14.

clear, the contrast between the metaphysical union of the Alexandrians and the moral union of the Antiochenes in their christology being reflected in their respective attitudes toward deification. For the Alexandrians the transformation of the flesh by the Word is mirrored in the transformation of the believer by Christ. For the Antiochenes the deliberate and willed nature of the union of the human and divine in Christ finds its counterpart in the moral struggle that human beings need to experience before they can attain perfection. Just as without Platonism there is no philosophical approach to deification, so without a substantialist background of thought in christology there is no basis for a realistic approach.[63]

In other words, without a vigorously orthodox and Chalcedonian Christology, which stresses the substantial union of divine and human natures in Christ, there is no doctrine of deification; correlatively, an affirmation of Chalcedon's teaching on the hypostatic union itself directly entails by logical necessity the direct implication that grace is bestowed on the human race in order to make it a partaker in the divine nature.

Although he died several years before the convocation of the Council of Chalcedon in AD 451, Cyril of Alexandria (376–444) has been universally recognized as one of its chief architects; and so we are not surprised to learn how vigorously he defended his Christology precisely for the sake of man's ultimate goal of being deified, although he too can be sparing in his use of the actual term.[64] Ever since Edward Gibbon (1737–94) accused Cyril of being a patriarchal thug in his epochal *Decline and Fall of the Roman Empire*, commentators on Cyril's thought have often expressed puzzlement at the tenacity with which he held to his views; but at least as what touches his Christology and its inherent links with man's divinization, the tenacity is understandable, precisely because of what is at stake for Cyril: our ultimate goal to share in God's own nature. As Keating rightly observes: "More

---

63. Russell, *Doctrine of Deification*, 14–15.

64. "Cyril of Alexandria has often been identified as the theologian *par excellence* of what is variously termed 'divinization,' 'deification,' or *theōsis*. . . . These claims, however, must be reconciled with the surprising fact that Cyril only rarely employs the technical terminology of divinization, which was so well established in the Alexandrian theological tradition and was widely employed by Athanasius before him." Daniel A. Keating, "Divinization in Cyril: The Appropriation of Divine Life," in *The Theology of St. Cyril of Alexandria: A Critical Appreciation*, ed. Thomas G. Weinandy, OFM, Cap., and Daniel A. Keating (London: T. & T. Clark, 2005): 149–85, here 149–50.

frequently than any other Christian writer before him, Cyril of Alexandria either cites or makes allusion to the phrase from 2 Peter 1:4, 'that you may become partakers of the divine nature.'"[65]

But besides having to live under the burden of Gibbon's accusation of thuggery, Cyril has often been accused of stressing divinization so much that he ends up slighting not just the humanity of humans but also that of Jesus, an accusation that has almost become a commonplace: "Perhaps the most frequent criticism of Cyrilline Christology, and of the Alexandrian school in general, concerns the specifically human element in Christ, and correspondingly, the human reception of salvation and the divine life."[66] But this charge misunderstands Cyril from nearly the ground up. Speaking specifically in his commentary on John 16:33: "But be of good cheer, I have overcome the world," Cyril states that Christ has overcome the world, not "as God" but "as man," and the adverbial phrase is crucial: "For Christ overcame it [fear] for us as man (ὡς ἄνθρωπος), being also in this a beginning and a gate and a way for human nature. For we who were fallen and vanquished of old have conquered and have overcome on account of the one who overcame as one of us and for our sake. For if he conquered as God (ὡς Θεός), it profits us nothing; but if as man (ὡς ἄνθρωπος), we have conquered in him."[67]

Cyril also frankly avows that Christ experienced all the emotions attendant upon being a fully human being, for he "experienced every human characteristic except sin alone. Now fear and timidity, being natural emotions in us, are not to be classified among the sins. . . . Just as he experienced hunger and weariness as a man, so too he accepts the disturbances that come from the emotions as a human characteristic."[68] According to Thomas Weinandy, this frank avowal means something quite radical, and goes far to resolving the dilemmas thrown up by the doctrine of divinization: "The Son did not merely appear to be man, nor was his life a mere fiction, but being truly born of a woman. . . . This means then that even the Son's humanity needed to be saved and sanctified."[69]

65. Keating, "Divinization in Cyril," 176.

66. Keating, "Divinization in Cyril," 173.

67. Cyril of Alexandria, *Commentary on John*, at 16:33; trans. by Keating at ibid., to whom I owe this reference.

68. Cyril of Alexandria, *Commentary on the Gospel According to John*, trans. T. Randell (London: Walter Smith, 1885), II: 120, at John 12:27.

69. Thomas G. Weinandy, OFM, Cap., "Cyril and the Mystery of the Incarnation," in *The Theology of St. Cyril of Alexandria*, ed. Weinandy and Keating, 23–54, here 26–27.

With Cyril, perhaps more than any other theologian, the conjoining of Christology, soteriology, divinization, and the "wondrous exchange" that happened at the incarnation comes to its most perfect expression: "For this cause, though he is Life by nature, he became as one dead, that, having destroyed the power of death in us, he might mold us anew into his life; and being himself the righteousness of God the Father, he became sin for us."[70]

Thus we arrive at a peculiar paradox: often those spiritualities in the west that stressed the humanity of Christ, his suffering along the Via Dolorosa, the agonies he suffered on the cross, and so forth (as in the popularity of the Stations of the Cross, which began in the late middle ages), are, however unbeknownst to themselves, expressions of the doctrine of divinization. For provided one holds fast to the doctrine of the substantial union of divine and human natures in Christ, then any stress on Christ's humanity is itself a portal to God's revelation in Christ, an aperture opening to the divine, and a sure access to our true path to real divinization, and not the merely titular kind promoted by the Romans in the earlier years of their empire.

Nonetheless, tensions with the doctrine still remain. The doctrine of divinization can never be used to obliterate the radical distinction between Creator and creature, a point that Balthasar stressed time and again, as here:

> "Divinization" (in Christ and through a participation in him) can never express the whole relationship between divine and created being. Even the fact that we are "born of God" (John 1:13) and thus (especially according to Eckhart) are drawn into the Son's "coming forth" from the Father, cannot alter the truth that we are creatures and not the eternal Logos. All the same, notwithstanding the incommensurability involved, there is an analogy between the Son's being begotten and the creatures' being freely and sovereignly created by God. This analogy can form a bridge

---

70. Cyril of Alexandria, *Commentary on the Gospel According to John*, trans. T. Randell, II: 316, at John 14:20; cited in Weinandy, "Cyril and the Mystery of the Incarnation," 25. Cyril repeats the point later in the same commentary, although with a more tangled syntax: "He that is God by nature became, and is in truth, a man from heaven; not inspired merely, as some of those who do not rightly understand the depth of the mystery imagine, but being at the same time God and man, in order that, uniting as it were in himself things widely opposed by nature, and averse to fusion with each other, he might enable man to share and partake of the nature of God" (ibid., II: 359, at John 17:19).

both to the Son's "becoming a creature" and to our being "reborn" (John 3:3, 7). After all, the incommensurable distance does not mean that the created world is alienated from its origin; the gradations in the created world's "imaging" of God (*vestigium-imago-similitudo*) show that this is not so. The trinitarian analogy enables the Son too, without abolishing the *analogia entis*, simultaneously to do two things: he represents God to the world—but in the mode of the Son who regards the Father as "greater" and to whom he eternally owes all that he is—and he represents the world to God, by being, as man (or rather, as the God-man), "humble, lowly, modest, docile of heart" (Matt 11:29). It is on the basis of these two aspects, united in an abiding analogy, that the Son can take up his *one*, unitary mission.[71]

Perhaps the central controversy surrounding divinization centers on the question of uncreated or created grace, or in other words the difference between Thomas Aquinas and Gregory Palamas, his near contemporary (Aquinas: 1225–74; Palamas: *c.* 1296–1359), who both lived just before the time of the final schism between East and West. For Thomas the (actually rather odd) term "uncreated grace" can only refer to the divine processions, the inner life of God "in himself." All other graces, starting of course with the grace of creation, inside of which all other graces are bestowed, are by definition created graces, very much including the graces in the human soul of Christ. But for the great Palamas, this distinction renders the very notion of deification otiose, which is why he distinguished the divine essence (always inaccessible to human participation, even in heaven) from the divine energies, which are God's effects in salvation history, but which are still truly part of the divine nature.

It is the opinion of some that this difference of opinion between Thomas and Palamas is more central to the schism between East and West than the *filioque* or the exercise of papal authority outside the Latin Church, a view shared by both Catholic and Orthodox theologians. For example, Vladimir Lossky says this:

> In the West, there was no longer any place for the conception of the energies of the Trinity; nothing was admitted to exist, outside the divine essence, except created effects, acts of will analogous to the acts of creation. Western theologians must profess belief in the created character

71. Hans Urs von Balthasar, *Theo-Drama* III: 229.

of the Glory of God and of sanctifying Grace and renounce the conception of deification or theosis; in this way they are consistent with their [trinitarian] premises.[72]

Other authorities, however, are not so pessimistic; and in fact A. N. Williams insists that both men are in fundamental agreement about the gratuity of divinization, which obviates any danger of pantheism in Palamas or of empty moralism in Thomas, so that the two merely disagree about where to place the emphasis:

> Aquinas and Palamas undoubtedly differ, then, in their appropriation of the patristic tradition, inasmuch as they emphasize different elements of it. When we measure . . . in what manner and to what extent they differ, we find the surprising result that it is Aquinas who generally lies closer to it. Nevertheless, although they sometimes represent a healthy development of the tradition (as with, for example, the vigorous insistence on grace), none of these differences represents an abandonment of the Fathers' model of deification. Rather, both theologians take patristic conceptualities and through an extended meditation on them, not so much extend, as deepen them.[73]

This startling claim can be backed up by a passage from Thomas we have already seen in the first chapter but which now takes on a new meaning in the context of man's deification:

> Now man's happiness is twofold. . . . One is proportionate to human nature, a happiness, to wit, which man can obtain by means of his natural principles. The other is a happiness surpassing man's nature, and which man can obtain by the power of God alone, by a kind of participation of the Godhead, about which it is written that by Christ we are made "partakers of the divine nature" (2 Pet. 1:4); and because such happiness surpasses the capacity of human nature, man's natural principles which

---

72. Vladimir Lossky, "The Procession of the Holy Spirit in the Orthodox Triadology," *Eastern Churches Quarterly*, Vol. 7 (1947–48): 31–53, here 52. The great twentieth-century Dominican Yves Congar agreed that this distinction between uncreated and created graces was the *punctum saliens* between East and West and will probably remain unresolved until the eschaton. See A. N. Williams, *The Ground of Union: Deification in Aquinas and Palamas* (Oxford: Oxford University Press, 1999), 7, for details and citations.

73. Williams, *Ground of Union*, 165.

enable him to act well according to his capacity do not suffice to direct him to this same [latter] happiness. (*ST* I-II, 62, a. 1)[74]

Only the future can tell if the differences between Thomas and Palamas are more apparent than real. But perhaps both sides can find solace and support by focusing on what Paul meant by faith. For I believe we can come to a proper understanding of the doctrine of both experience and divinization focusing on a neglected aspect of Paul's theology of faith. Leaving aside its connection with justification, treated already in the second chapter, one must note how for Paul faith means placing our trust (and ultimately our experience) in heaven:

If then you have been raised with Christ, seek the things that are above, where Christ is, seated at the right hand of God. Set your minds on things that are above, not on things that are on earth. For you have died, and your life is hid with Christ in God. When Christ who is our life appears, then you also will appear with him in glory. . . . Put on then, as God's chosen ones, holy and beloved, compassion, kindness, lowliness, meekness and patience, forbearing one another and, if one has a complaint against another, forgiving each other; as the Lord has forgiven you, you must also forgive. And above all these put on love, which binds everything together in perfect harmony. And let the peace of Christ rule in your hearts, to which indeed you were called in the one body. And

74. Further: "It is impossible that any creature should cause grace. For it is as necessary that God alone should deify, bestowing a partaking of the divine nature by a participated likeness, as it is impossible that anything except fire should enkindle" (*ST* I-II, q. 112, a. 3). Even Thomas's alleged "moralism" takes on a different coloration when seen inside his doctrine of deification, as Williams notes: "The prime form in which Thomas sees grace as resulting in deiformity is not through some unspecified gift of grace but grace bestowed in the form of the theological virtues. He terms faith, hope and charity the theological virtues not because they derive from the New Testament rather than from Aristotle but because these are the virtues that direct us to God. In his very definition of why a virtue might be called theological, then, Thomas intimates his doctrine of deification. The highest of the virtues are not those which enable the right ordering of human relations but those which order humanity to God. Sanctity is therefore defined not in human, but divine terms. This close relation between the doctrine of sanctification and the doctrine of God is one of the characteristics of the patristic formulation of theosis" (Williams, *Ground of Union*, 35). As Thomas himself says in a lovely passage: "He will have a fuller participating in the light of glory who has more charity; because where there is greater charity, there is more desire; and desire in a certain degree makes the one desiring apt and prepared to receive the object desired" (*ST* I, q. 12, a. 6).

be thankful. . . . And whatever you do, in word or deed, do everything in the name of the Lord Jesus, giving thanks to God the Father through him. (Col. 3:1–4, 12–15, 17)

"Your life lies hid with Christ in God." In that line, the tensions and dilemmas in the doctrine of divinization can be resolved. As Pascal put it so well: "God wanted to be hidden. If there were only one religion, God would be clearly manifest. If there were martyrs in only one religion, the same. God being therefore hidden, any religion which does not say God is hidden is not true. And any religion which does not give the reason why does not enlighten. Ours does all this: *Vere, tu es Deus absconditus*: "Truly, thou art a hidden God" (Isa. 45:15).[75]

---

75. Pascal, *Pensées*, 81 (#275). See also: "It is the glory of God to conceal things" (Prov. 25:2).

CHAPTER 6

Mary, Mediatrix of Graces

This air, which, by life's law,
My lung must draw and draw
Now but to breathe its praise,
Minds me in many ways
Of her who not only
Gave God's infinity
Dwindled to infancy
Welcome in womb and breast,
Birth, milk, and all the rest
But mothers each new grace
That does now reach our race.

Gerard Manley Hopkins, S.J.,
"The Blessed Virgin compared to the Air we Breathe"

Of all the topics covered in this book, perhaps none is more controversial than the idea that in some way Mary the Mother of Jesus can and does mediate the grace of redemption to her children. No Protestant affirms the notion, since it would violate so obviously the core Protestant doctrine of *solus Christus*, that Christ alone mediates salvation. But Catholics, too, shy away from the idea, partly for ecumenical reasons, claiming that a formal definition by the church of Mary as Mediatrix of Graces would be a disaster for ecumenical relations with Protestants; but they also have their own objections, not least scriptural: "For there is one God, and there is one mediator between God and men, the man Jesus Christ, who gave himself as a ransom for all" (1 Tim. 2:5–6a).

In what follows, I shall be suggesting that Mary can be properly understood as in some way a Mediatrix of Graces precisely by taking these (largely Protestant, but also Catholic) concerns into account.[1] Specifically, I will maintain that the doctrine of Mary's Immaculate Conception—that she was conceived from the first moment of her existence without the "taint" of original sin—holds the key to resolving the issue. Admittedly, the task is formidable, for Catholic Marian doctrine is widely regarded— by both Catholics and Protestants—as a stumbling block to ecumenism, especially in its most recent developments in the nineteenth and twentieth centuries, when (according to Protestant accusation) things *really* got out of hand.[2] For one thing, the Catholic-specific doctrines of Mary's Immaculate Conception and her bodily Assumption into heaven at the

1. Most of what follows has been reprinted from my article "Predestination and Mary's Immaculate Conception: An Evangelically Catholic Reading," *Pro Ecclesia*, Vol. XXI, No. 3 (Summer 2012): 281–98, with the kind permission of its editor.

2. To keep this chapter within suitable bounds, I will be concentrating here solely on Protestant objections—and the way those objections might be answered using specifically Protestant axioms. Of course, there are ecumenical issues with the Orthodox tradition here as well; but they map out differently, not least because (ironically enough) Roman mariological doctrine owes so much to Orthodox Marian devotion, as Brian Daley notes: "My point here (which needs no long argument for those familiar with the world of Byzantine liturgy and theology) is that what many—including Karl Barth—think of as characteristically Western, Catholic ways of conceiving and approaching Mary are as much Orthodox as Catholic, as much Eastern as Western." Brian Daley, S.J., *Woman of Many Names: Mary in Orthodox and Catholic Theology*, The Theotokos Lecture in Theology, 2008 (Milwaukee: Marquette University Press, 2008), 20. Of course that does not mean that the Roman-defined dogma of Mary's Immaculate Conception is problem-free for the Orthodox. Along with the issue of papal authority, whose rejection is shared by Protestants (see the next note), the Orthodox often demur at the Augustinian presuppositions shared by both Roman Catholics and Protestants, as again Daley notes: "Always nervous about what they understand to be Augustine's influence, Orthodox theologians of the [twentieth] century have pointed out that the main difference between East and West on the doctrine of Mary's predestined holiness is that the East has never understood the effects of the fall in terms of shared guilt for an 'original sin,' as Western theology has done since Augustine, so that the work of divine grace in her is seen less in terms of a radical reconditioning of human nature than it is in the West" (ibid., 21). Nonetheless, the *substance* of the Roman doctrine largely overlaps with the Orthodox position, at least if we may take Sergei Bulgakov as representative: "It goes without saying that, even if we do not accept the Catholic dogma of the 'immaculate' conception, we must confess that the Mother of God is entirely full of grace." Sergius Bulgakov, *The Bride of the Lamb*, trans. Boris Jakim (Grand Rapids, MI: Eerdmans, 2002), 411, note 23. See also Sergius Bulgakov, *The Burning Bush: On the Orthodox Veneration of the Mother of God*, trans. Thomas Allen Smith (Grand Rapids, MI: Eerdmans, 2009). For a more pessimistic, or at least minimizing, view, see: John Meyendorff, *Byzantine Theology: Historical Trends and Doctrinal Themes* (The Bronx, NY: Fordham University Press, 1974), 165.

end of her earthly life are intimately bound up with the exercise of papal magisterial authority—another neuralgic point for Protestants (and not a few Catholics too).[3]

Second, these two doctrines cannot be found in Scripture, or so goes the claim, which if true would violate one of the central axioms of the Reformation: the *sola scriptura* principle. The case of the Immaculate Conception is even more dire, for here the Bible is not just silent on the issue but seems directly to contradict the doctrine. For according to Paul, "all have sinned and fallen short of the glory of God" (Romans 3:23). If Paul does not mean *all* here—everyone without exception—when he *uses* the word "all," then why have a Bible at all?

Third, Catholic Marian doctrines are accused of drawing their sustenance from the surrounding pagan culture—just what we would expect to happen, given their unscriptural provenance. As Joseph Ratzinger said back in his days as a professor of dogmatics in Regensburg, "many find no embarrassment in identifying the non-Christian origin of Marian belief

---

3. But can there be a concept of revelation without an infallible magisterium? Not for the future Cardinal Newman, who—while still an Anglican—insisted that the concept of revelation *directly* entails an infallible magisterium, or else there is no revelation to speak of. Since Catholic Marian doctrine is intimately bound up with claims to magisterial infallibility, we must note, at least in passing, his defense of a teaching office endowed with the grace of infallibility: "The most obvious answer, then, to the question, why we yield to the authority of the Church in the questions and developments of faith, is, that some authority there must be if there is a revelation given, and other authority there is none but she. A revelation is not given if there be no authority to decide what it is that is given. . . . If Christianity is both social and dogmatic, and intended for all ages, it must humanly speaking have an infallible expounder. Else you will secure unity of form at the loss of unity of doctrine, or unity of doctrine at the loss of unity of form; you will have to choose between a comprehension of opinions and a resolution into parties, between latitudinarian and sectarian error. You may be tolerant or intolerant of contrarieties of thought, but contrarieties you will have. By the Church of England a hollow uniformity is preferred to an infallible chair; and by the sects of England an interminable division. Germany and Geneva began with persecution and have ended in scepticism. The doctrine of infallibility is a less violent hypothesis than this sacrifice either of faith or of charity. It secures the object, while it gives definiteness and force to the matter, of the Revelation." John Henry Newman, *An Essay on the Development of Christian Doctrine*, in *Conscience, Consensus, and the Development of Doctrine*, ed. James Gaffney (New York: Doubleday, 1992/1845), 111–12. Not surprisingly, while these words were being typeset at the printery, Newman was received into the Roman Church. Protestants who reject the dogma of the Immaculate Conception will of course have to reject simultaneously papal claims to infallibility. Newman's point is simply that such a rejection is not consequence-free. For a balanced Protestant engagement with this issue, see Mark E. Powell, *Papal Infallibility: A Protestant Evaluation of an Ecumenical Issue* (Grand Rapids, MI: Eerdmans, 2009).

and devotion: from Egyptian myths, from the cult of the Great Mother, from Diana of Ephesus who [surreptitiously] became 'Mother of God' (*Theotokos*) at the council convened in Ephesus.'"[4]

Fourth—and once again keeping strictly to the Immaculate Conception—the issue was hotly debated in the Middle Ages, with no less an authority than Thomas Aquinas holding against it, which hardly speaks to the unanimity of tradition.[5] If this dogma is supposed to be located in some putative unbroken oral Tradition (with a capital T), handed down by the apostles intact as a "second source" of revelation operating independently of the Bible, and whispered in the sacristy by each ordaining bishop to his successor at the conclusion of the rite, then how did Thomas never come to hear of it? Thus we may conclude: a doctrine less palatable to the prospects of ecumenical *rapprochement* would be hard to imagine.

In what follows, I shall be discussing only the Immaculate Conception and will leave out any treatment of Mary's bodily Assumption into heaven; for that is a topic that deserves separate treatment and raises issues specific to itself.[6] But I wish to focus here on the Immaculate Conception not

4. Joseph Cardinal Ratzinger, *Daughter Zion: Meditations on the Church's Marian Belief*, trans. John M. McDermott, S.J. (San Francisco: Ignatius Press, 1983 [German original 1977]), 9–10.

5. Traditional Dominican opposition to the doctrine led to a noticeable eclipse of the order in the Rome of Pius IX: "In the eighteenth century the Dominicans had 25,000 members in the whole Order. The Napoleonic Revolution left them with almost none. For a time they remained under a cloud at Rome because of their opposition, which was traditional, to the doctrine of the Immaculate Conception of the Virgin. In 1876 they were still only 3,341." Owen Chadwick, *A History of the Popes: 1830–1914* (Oxford: Clarendon Press, 1998), 516.

6. I can note here in passing, however, that ecumenical discussion of Mary's Assumption might best begin with an investigation of the wide range of meanings given to the word *body* that can be found in the New Testament, especially in Paul, on which the Anglican bishop and noted New Testament scholar John Robinson had fascinating things to say: "One could say without exaggeration that the concept of the body forms the keystone of Paul's theology. In its closely interconnected meanings, the word *soma* [body] knits together all his great themes. It is from the body of sin and death that we are delivered; it is through the body of Christ on the Cross that we are saved; it is into His body the Church that we are incorporated; it is by His body in the Eucharist that this Community is sustained; it is in our body that its new life has to be manifested; it is to a resurrection of this body to the likeness of His glorious body that we are destined. Here, with the exception of the doctrine of God, are represented all the main tenets of the Christian Faith—the doctrines of Man, Sin, the Incarnation and Atonement, the Church, the Sacraments, Sanctification, and Eschatology. To trace the subtle links and interaction between the different senses of this word *soma* is to grasp the thread that leads through the maze of Pauline thought." J. A. T. Robinson, *The Body: A Study in Pauline Theology* (Philadelphia: The Westminster Press, 1952), 9. To what

just for reasons of limited time and space but also, paradoxically enough, *for its ecumenical potential*. For, when looked at more closely, the doctrine actually dovetails quite neatly with important Reformation concerns, especially the *topoi* of unmerited grace and predestination. One can, after all, hardly "merit" grace until one first exists; but Mary was given a singular grace *at* the first moment of her conception, which also means that she must in some sense have been predestined for her role as Mother of God from all eternity and quite independent of any later "merit" on her part (what is known as *ante merita praevisa*, in the traditional terminology).

Not only have the ecumenical implications of this dogma gone relatively unappreciated, we must also take into account the doctrine's extraordinary fruitfulness, which for Cardinal Newman was itself a sign of authentic development—the authenticity of which can be detected from what he calls a doctrine's "power of assimilation" and its "chronic vigor." I am reminded here of Jaroslav Pelikan's observation that the manifestation of Our Lady of the Immaculate Conception in 1858 to Bernadette Soubirous at Lourdes proved to be Catholicism's greatest evangelizing and revitalizing force in the nineteenth century, far exceeding any other:

> There is good reason to believe that neither the intellectual defense of Christian revelation by the apologetic enterprise in nineteenth-century Roman Catholic theology, including the revival of Thomistic philosophical apologetics, nor the political defense of the institutional church and its prerogatives against the anticlericalism of that time was as effective a campaign, particularly among the common people, as the one that the Virgin Mary waged. For it has been well said that "Rome is the head of the Church but Lourdes is its heart."[7]

In what follows I will be focusing on a central paradox embedded in *all* Marian doctrines across the board (of which the dogma of the Immac-

---

extent does the doctrine of Mary's bodily Assumption jibe with one or more of these multivalent meanings, if any? In addition, the interchangeability—indeed total and complete equivalence—of matter and energy in Einsteinian physics would presumably have to play a role as well in any discussion of bodily resurrection/assumption, obviously a topic too broad and complicated to be taken up here.

7. Jaroslav Pelikan, *Mary Through the Centuries: Her Place in the History of Culture* (New Haven: Yale University Press, 1996), 184, internally quoting Andrea Dahlberg, "The Body as a Principle of Holism: Three Pilgrimages to Lourdes," in *Contesting the Sacred: The Anthropology of Christian Pilgrimage*, ed. John Eade and Michael J. Sallnow (New York: Routledge, 1991), 35.

ulate Conception is but one example), one that first came to light during the controversy set in motion by Patriarch Nestorius (386–450) when he had objected to Mary's traditional title as Theotokos or Mother of God. His logic, at first glance, seemed impeccable: the pagan god Apollo, after all, had a mother (Hera), but the Christian God—by definition the Ungenerated and Unbegotten—could not possibly be said to have a mother. To say otherwise would be to lapse back into pagan polytheism.[8]

While Nestorius no doubt found his reasoning airtight (who doesn't think that of his own convictions?), his vehement critic Cyril of Alexandria pointed out—with his usual unsparing vigor—that a denial of this title to Mary came at the price of bifurcating the person of Christ. For if Mary gave birth only to the *human being* Jesus, then Christ could only be divine either by the legal fiction of adoption or by awkward juxtaposition, with the divinity conjoined to the humanity like two oxen yoked to a plow. But that would mean that Christ died only in his human nature. *God* doesn't die, after all, who is the immutable source of all life—only biological beings do; and since no human being on his own can save, Christ's death by crucifixion in the Nestorian schema would be no more saving than was the death by crucifixion of the slave Spartacus.

Cyril was of course perfectly aware that calling Mary the Mother of the Ungenerated and Unbegotten—who by definition sprang from no other being—was paradoxical; but for him that was the whole *point*: "The one incapable of suffering did suffer" (*ho Apathos epathen*), goes his most fa-

---

8. As described by Yehezkel Kaufmann: "We designate as pagan all the religions of mankind from the beginnings of recorded history to the present, excepting Israelite religion and its derivatives, Christianity and Islam. . . . In myth the gods appear not only as actors, but as acted upon. . . . Corresponding to the birth of the gods through natural processes is their subjection to sexual conditions. All pagan religions have male and female deities who desire and mate with each other. . . . The basic idea of Israelite religion, [however], is that God is supreme over all. There is no realm above or beside him to limit his absolute sovereignty. He is utterly distinct from, and other than, the world; he is subject to no laws, no compulsions, or powers that transcend him. He is, in short, non-mythological. This is the essence of Israelite religion, and that which sets it apart from all forms of paganism. . . . *Israel's God has no pedigree*, fathers no generations; he neither inherits nor bequeaths his authority. He does not die and is not resurrected. He has no sexual qualities or desires and shows no need of or dependence upon powers outside himself." Yehezkel Kaufmann, *The Religion of Israel: From Its Beginnings to the Babylonian Exile*, trans. Moshe Greenberg (Chicago: University of Chicago Press, 1960), 21, 22, 23, 60–61; emphasis added. To Nestorius, calling Mary the Mother of God had the disastrous consequence of undercutting this absolutely crucial distinction between pagan polytheism and Christian monotheism.

mous formulation: a logic-defying, oxymoronic "impassible suffering" that took place in God's providence so that, as Cyril says, "we might see side by side the wound together with the remedy, the patient with the physician, what sank towards death together with him who raised it up to life, ... that which has been mastered by death with him who conquered death, what was bereft of life together with him who was the provider of life."[9]

Now there can be no doubt that Cyril defended Mary's title as Mother of God entirely for christological reasons, which is why the Reformers in the sixteenth century—at least the christologically orthodox Lutherans and Calvinists—defended the teaching of the Council of Ephesus of AD 431, which affirmed Mary's title of Theotokos and solemnly declared its denial to be heretical. But ideas as fruitful and paradoxical as this one never sit still; and it was inevitable that the constant iteration of calling Mary Mother of God in liturgical worship and private piety would lead to further reflection on Mary's role in salvation, as Newman saw:

> In order to do honor to Christ, in order to defend the true doctrine of the Incarnation, in order to secure a right faith in the manhood of the Eternal Son, the Council of Ephesus determined the Blessed Virgin to be the Mother of God. Thus all the heresies of that day, though opposite to each other, tended in a most wonderful [albeit for the heretics obviously unintentional] way to her exaltation; and the School of Antioch, the fountain of primitive rationalism, led the Church to determine first the conceivable greatness of a creature, and then the incommunicable dignity of the Blessed Virgin.[10]

But this dignity was itself the outcome (as we saw above) of pure, unmerited grace—one that, moreover, was meant both to typify and embody the reality of the church. In what follows, I shall be relying on the interpretation of Hans Urs von Balthasar, who helpfully contextualized this doctrine in terms of salvation history. Traditionally, the doctrine of the Immaculate Conception spoke of Mary being free from any "taint" of sin (*macula* being the Latin word for blot or stain), which links the doctrine, at least by implication, with Old Testament purity laws. But Balthasar sees

9. Cyril of Alexandria, *Commentary on John*, at John 1:14a, in *Cyril of Alexandria*, trans. Norman Russell (London: Routledge, 2000), 105–6.

10. John Henry Newman, *An Essay on the Development of Christian Doctrine* (Notre Dame, IN: University of Notre Dame Press, 1989 [1845]), 135.

the doctrine more in terms of prevenient grace, that is, of God's radical inbreaking into salvation history via a totally *human* Yes to his prior *divine* Yes:

> Now, suddenly, we see the meaning of this [doctrine]. The God who pulls down the barriers erected by men does not want to keep his own total lack of barriers to himself: he wants to bring this absolute positivity into the world and communicate it to the earthly realm as well, like rain and dew falling on the soil. Somewhere on earth there must ring out, in response to this word, not a half answer but a whole one, not a vague answer but an exact one. . . . By the power of heaven, the earth must accept the arrival of grace so that it can really come to earth and carry out its work of liberation . . . [via] a word of consent [that] can only be given to earth from heaven's treasure house of love.[11]

Although this doctrine is highly controversial because of its Protestant rejection, it is Balthasar's reading that first taught me how this doctrine actually resonates quite remarkably with the Reformation stress on *sola gratia*. As pointed out above, one can hardly "merit" grace until one first exists; but Mary received this special grace, by definition, *at* her conception. Furthermore, far from denying Christ's unique and irreplaceable role in effecting salvation, this doctrine, properly interpreted, *relies* on it:

> In the course of unfolding these implications, two difficulties were encountered that have occupied theology right up to medieval and modern times. The first arose from the realization that God's action in reconciling the world to himself in the cross of Christ is exclusively his initiative: there is no original "collaboration" between God and the creature. But . . . the creature's "femininity" possesses an original, God-

---

11. Hans Urs von Balthasar, "Abolishing the Boundaries," a radio sermon delivered on the Feast of the Immaculate Conception, in *You Crown the Year with Your Goodness: Sermons through the Liturgical Year*, trans. Graham Harrison (San Francisco: Ignatius Press, 1989 [German 1982]), 267. Further: "This quality of Mary's Yes is wholly a function of the requirements of Christology. . . . [T]hat she 'was conceived immaculate' says nothing but what is indispensable for the boundlessness of her Yes. For anyone affected in some way by original sin would be incapable of such a guileless openness to every disposition of God." Hans Urs von Balthasar, "Mary in the Church's Doctrine and Devotion," in Hans Urs von Balthasar and Joseph Cardinal Ratzinger, *Mary: The Church at the Source*, trans. Adrian Walker (San Francisco: Ignatius Press, 2005 [German original, 1997]), 99–124, here 105.

given, active fruitfulness; it was essential, therefore, if God's Word willed to become incarnate in the womb of a woman, to elicit agreement and obedient consent. . . . But where did the grace that made this possible come from—a consent that is adequate and therefore genuinely un-limited—if not from the work of reconciliation itself, that is, from the cross? (And of course the cross is rendered possible only through Mary's consent.) Here we have a circle—in which the effect is the cause of the cause—that has taken centuries to appreciate and formulate, resulting in the dogma of the Immaculate Conception and the exact reasoning behind it.[12]

In other words, what Balthasar seems to be saying here is that the *denial* of the doctrine leaves the way open to a kind of Pelagian Mariology. For if Mary had been tainted by original sin, there would have to be in her an element of struggle against its legacy, what Augustine called the *fomes peccati* (tinderbox or powder-keg of sin), which would imply either a blemish of works-righteousness in her assent, or at least a struggle to obey God, a distracting effort that would obviously inhibit the total Yes that God was expecting of his creature in response to his own total Yes in Christ (2 Cor. 1:20). Not of course that the singular grace she received made her less free; for it has been the consistent doctrine of the churches (especially those most heavily influenced by St. Augustine) that the freedom to sin is no freedom at all. Mary's Yes to God in her *fiat* is entirely free precisely because it is entirely a graced assent.[13]

For that same reason, Mary can also be called "Mother of the church," for the church's own true identity must also include being the "spotless and

12. Hans Urs von Balthasar, *Theo-Drama: Theological Dramatic Theory*, Volume III: *Dramatis Personae: Persons in Christ*, trans. Graham Harrison (San Francisco: Ignatius Press, 1992 [German, 1972]), 296–97.

13. Recall here that for Augustine concupiscence in children is sinful: *Contra Julianum* 2: 5, 12; *Opus incompletum contra Julianum* 4: 41; 5: 20, a view that would later be condemned by Trent when Martin Luther made it an operative principle of his *sola fide* axiom. Aquinas began to move away from this extreme pessimism, but not enough to lead him to the con-clusion of Mary's Immaculate Conception: "ita peccatum originale non est peccatum hujus naturae, nisi inquantum haec persona recipit naturam a primo partente. Unde et vocatur peccatum naturae; secundum illud Eph. II, 'eramus filii irae.'" *ST* I-II, q. 81, a. 1, *in fine* c. On the differences between Augustine and Thomas here see Mark Johnson, "Augustine and Aquinas on Original Sin: Doctrine, Authority, and Pedagogy," in *Aquinas the Augustinian*, ed. Michael Dauphinais, Barry David, and Matthew Levering (Washington, DC: The Catholic University of America Press, 2007), 145–58.

pure bride" spoken of by St. Paul, a church "without stain, wrinkle or any other blemish, but holy and blameless" (Eph. 5:27). Such sinlessness does not currently obtain, of course, in the church that Augustine called a *corpus mixtum*; but that is surely the church Christ *intends* and was accordingly instantiated at the first moment of his mother's earthly existence, who thereby becomes the church's truest identity.

Speaking very generally, Protestant ecclesiology would reject such an implication, based on Luther's forensic theory of justification, which in most Lutheran views effects no genuine transformation in the soul of the believer: for Luther, the Christian is always *simul justus et peccator*, with the *peccator* describing the believer's earthly status and the *justus* referring to his *predestined* status as one of the elect of heaven irrespective of any "works" done on earth. The irony in this position, however, is that it was this same theme of predestination that played so important a function in eventually convincing the Catholic Church of the doctrine of the Immaculate Conception.

The role of Blessed John Duns Scotus (*c.* 1266–1308) in arguing for Mary's Immaculate Conception has long been recognized; but crucial in his argument is the part predestination plays. Besides famously disagreeing with Thomas on the Immaculate Conception, Scotus also insisted against Thomas that Christ would have become man quite independent of the sin of Adam and Eve, a doctrine technically known as "the priority of Christ." This term, when used in its technical sense, does not refer to Christ's priority as savior of the human race over against other founders of world religions (which of course no medieval theologian would have disputed in any event). Rather, the term refers to the priority of Christ in God's aboriginal decision to create the world, which God did, according to Scotus, and relying on Paul here, through and *for* Christ (Col. 1:16b), that is, regardless of whether our first parents would have sinned or not.

Thomas is generally taken to hold that the incarnation would not have taken place had not our first parents sinned, but actually his position is far more nuanced, at least earlier in his career, when he is writing his commentary on Peter Lombard's *Sentences*. In that early text, he admits that the majority position opts for contingency, but then he concedes that Christ's predestination to become man independent of sin cannot be disproved:

> The truth of this question is known only to God. We can know what depends solely on the divine will only insofar as we can glean some knowledge from the writings of the saints to whom God has revealed his purpose. The canon of Scripture and the quotations from the Fathers

mentioned above [chiefly Augustine, Gregory] assign one cause only to the incarnation: man's redemption from the slavery of sin. . . . Other theologians, however, hold that the purpose of the incarnation of the Son of God was not only freedom from sin, but also the exaltation of human nature and the consummation of the whole universe. It follows that even had there been no sin, the incarnation would have taken place for these other reasons. This opinion is equally probable.[14]

Writing about twenty years later, however, he seems to give the argument, on balance, to the defenders of contingency: "In Scripture the cause of the incarnation is always given as the sin of the first man. It is therefore more conveniently said that the incarnation is a work ordained by God as a remedy for sin. Wherefore: no sin, no incarnation. However, God's power is not limited to this, and even without sin he could have become man."[15]

What is fascinating about this increased diffidence toward the absolute priority of Christ is that Thomas also grows, *pari passu*, more diffident toward the idea of affirming Mary's Immaculate Conception. In his *Commentary on the Sentences* he inclines to the view that Mary was immaculately conceived.[16] But once again, roughly twenty years later, he retreats from entertaining this affirmation in his second *Summa* and rejects the idea outright:

If the soul of the Blessed Virgin had never incurred the stain of original sin, this would be derogatory to the dignity of Christ, by reason of his being the universal Savior of all. . . . For Christ did not contract original sin in any way whatever, but was holy in his very conception. . . . But the Blessed Virgin did indeed contract original sin, but was cleansed therefrom before her birth from the womb.[17]

14. Thomas Aquinas, *III Sent.* d. 1, q. 1, a. 3.

15. *ST* III, q. 1, a. 3. In other words, God *could* have but *didn't*. Whether the different Christologies of Thomas and Scotus are affected as well by their different definitions of what it means to be a *person* is addressed by James B. Reichmann, S.J., "Aquinas, Scotus, and the Christological Mystery: Why Christ is not a Human Person," *The Thomist* 71 (2007): 451–74.

16. Thomas Aquinas, *In I Sent.* d. 44, q. q, a. 3, ad 3: "Item, videtur quod nec Beata Virgine, quia secundum Anselmum, decuit ut virgo quam Deus Unigenito Filio suo praeparavit in matrem, ea puritate niteret, quo major sub Deo nequit intelligi. Sed nihil potest Deus facere quod sibi in bonitate vel puritate aequetur. Ergo videtur nihil melius Beata Virgine facere possit."

17. *ST* III, q. 27, a. 2, ad 2. So categorical was this statement that it seems to have blocked the bishops assembled at the Council of Trent from declaring as defined dogma Mary's Im-

John Duns Scotus, however, was entirely unequivocal in his defense of the absolute priority of Christ, who (according to the Subtle Doctor) would have become man even if our first parents had not sinned. This dispute between Thomists and Scotists might seem arcane and often provokes impatience in modern readers, very much including theologians, but more rides on this issue than might be evident at first glance, especially regarding our topic and perhaps can even explain why Thomas went astray on Mary's Immaculate Conception.[18] The conjoined importance of predestination, the priority of Christ, and Mary's Immaculate Conception can be seen in the *locus classicus* of the Scot's argument:

Quaero: I ask, was Christ predestined to be the Son of God?

Respondeo: I reply that predestination consists in foreordaining someone, first of all to glory and then to all other things which are ordained to that glory. . . . At this point, however, two doubts arise: *First*, does this predestination depend necessarily upon the fall of human nature? Many authorities seem to say as much when they declare the Son of God would never have become incarnate had man not fallen. Without passing [invidious] judgment [on these authorities], it can be said that so far as priority of the objects intended by God is concerned, *the pre-*

---

maculate Conception: "We know that the vast majority of the Council Fathers [at Trent] were of the opinion that they might there and then define the Immaculate Conception as a Catholic truth already sufficiently accepted by the Church; they refrained from doing so, however, out of respect for the small number of the members of this venerable assembly [presumably Dominicans] who still professed the opposite opinion." Dom Prosper Guéranger, *On the Immaculate Conception*, trans. by a Nun of St. Cecelia's Abbey, Ryde (Farnborough, Hampshire: Saint Michael's Abbey Press, 2006 [French original 1850]), 25. Trent did, however, explicitly exempt Mary from its decree on original sin, which held that all the children of Adam have fallen under its curse: "Declarat tamen haec ipsa sancta Synodus non esse suae intentionis comprehendere in hoc decreto, ubi de peccato originali agitur, Beatam et Immaculatam Virginem Mariam, Dei Genitricem." *Session V decretum de peccato originali*.

18. Thus I disagree with E. M. Mascall, who claims "The controversy is largely an academic one." E. M. Mascall, *The Importance of Being Human* (Oxford: Oxford University Press, 1959), 92–93. For a brief account of the medieval debate between Thomas and Scotus on the Immaculate Conception, see Paul Haffner, *The Mystery of Mary* (Chicago: Hillenbrand Books, 2004), 81–89; a fuller account can be found in the monograph of Hugolinus Storff, O.F.M., *The Immaculate Conception: The Teaching of St. Thomas, St. Bonaventure and Bl. J. Duns Scotus on the Immaculate Conception of the Blessed Virgin Mary* (San Francisco: St. Francis Press, 1925). That Fr. Storff was already able to call Scotus "Blessed" in 1925, when in fact he would not be beatified by Pope John Paul II until 1992, must be due to the author's clairvoyance.

destination of anyone to glory is prior by nature to the prevision of sin or damnation of anyone. . . . . So much the more is this true of the predestination of that soul [Christ's] which was destined beforehand to possess the very highest glory possible.[19]

For the Subtle Doctor it inexorably followed that the manner of Christ's birth had to be aboriginally predestined too, making his mother thereby the premier example of the elect of the human race. Furthermore, among the important implications of the Scotist doctrine of the priority of Christ is that *sin was never part of the original predestining intention of God when he created the world,* a point that would come to be increasingly appreciated by Catholic theologians in the twentieth century, as we can see by the example of the Franciscan theologian Jean-François Bonnefoy (1887–1958):

> The place of Mary in the divine plan appears more and more clearly in proportion as the eminence of her grace is grasped by the Christian sense. Here again, the Scotistic school has shown itself to be consistent. If by the fullness of her grace and her divine maternity, the blessed Virgin is situated immediately after Christ in the ontological order, then she must be accorded the same place in the order of predestinations [*sic*]. *Her destiny was decided even before,* according to our human but quite valid way of thinking, *there was any question of Adam or of the foresight and permission of sin.* There was, then, no real reason to subject her to the law of original sin, and her Immaculate Conception flows logically from the priority of her predestination as it is conceived and propounded by the Scotistic school.[20]

This passage deftly captures the reasoning behind the official definition of the doctrine by Pope Pius IX in his 1854 Apostolic Letter *Ineffabilis Deus* infallibly decreeing the truth of Mary's Immaculate Conception. The definition is of course well known, but less well known is the pope's Scotist reasoning. Admittedly, its most famous passage speaks of Christ's exclusive

19. John Duns Scotus, *Ordinatio* III, d. 7, q. 3. The full Latin text with facing English translation can be found in Allan Wolter, "John Duns Scotus on the Primacy and Personality of Christ," in *Franciscan Christology,* ed. Damian McElrath (St. Bonaventure, NY: Franciscan Institute Publications, 1980), 139–82; here 147, 149; italics added.

20. Jean-François Bonnefoy, O.F.M., *The Immaculate Conception in the Divine Plan,* trans. Michael D. Meilach, O.F.M. (Paterson, NJ: St. Anthony Guild Press, 1967), 13; emphasis added.

role as redeemer (thereby foreclosing any implication that Mary might have some salvific role independent of her Son):

> We declare, pronounce, and define that the Most Blessed Virgin Mary, at the first instant of her Conception, was preserved immaculate from all stain of original sin, by the singular grace and privilege of the Omnipotent God *in virtue of the merits of Jesus Christ, the Savior of mankind.*[21]

But earlier in the encyclical, in his exposition of the traditional provenance of the doctrine, the pope notes how the church's liturgy has regularly used passages from the Wisdom writings of the Old Testament on feasts of the Virgin. Tellingly, the Scotists also often used passages that speak of Uncreated Wisdom to justify their position that Christ was always intended to assume his role as first-born of creation from all eternity, irrespective of the contingency of sin. For the pope, too, the use of the same Wisdom passages in liturgies celebrating the Virgin means the same logic of predestination applies to her as well, from which fact Pius draws this conclusion:

> For this reason, the very words by which the Sacred Scriptures speak of Uncreated Wisdom, and by which they represent his eternal origin, the Church has been accustomed to use not only in the ecclesiastical Office [that is, the Liturgy of the Hours or Breviary] but also in the Sacred Liturgy itself [the Mass], applying them to this Virgin's origin. *For her origin was preordained by one and the same decree with the Incarnation of Divine Wisdom.*[22]

In other words, Mary's Immaculate Conception both illuminates the doctrines of predestination, election, and *sola gratia* and also depends on them for its justification. Moreover, using this same Scotus reasoning, predestination is now seen as logically prior to the contingency of sin. This priority, in turn, entails the final conclusion that *God's predestination of Christ and Mary precedes God's predestination of the elect and reprobate at the end of time, indeed precedes God's permissive will allowing the sin of our first parents and their progeny.*

---

21. Pius IX, *Ineffabilis Deus*, paragraph 39, text in *Mary Immaculate: The Bull Ineffabilis Dei [sic] of Pope Pius IX*, trans. Dominic J. Unger (Paterson, NJ: St. Anthony Guild Press, 1946), 21; emphasis added.

22. *Ineffabilis Deus*, paragraph 6, in Unger, *Mary Immaculate*, 3; emphasis added.

Those familiar with Karl Barth's Christology will spot this early papal adumbration of his own theology of predestination, although Barth would of course apply that papal insight solely to Christ's predestination. His own way of overturning the teaching of Augustine and Calvin on double predestination is through Christ's atonement on the cross, as we already saw in the fourth chapter. For Barth, the predestination of Christ to be simultaneously priest and victim means that Christ is simultaneously both elect and reprobate (2 Cor. 5:21; Gal. 3:13). Nonetheless, the convergence between the new Catholic understanding of predestination catalyzed by the doctrine of the Immaculate Conception and Barth's revolutionary Protestant interpretation is real, for both now see that the doctrine of *predestination subserves Christology* and does not operate as a separate motivation in God's eternal counsels before the creation of the world and independent of Christ. Barth's Scotist logic is especially evident here:

By virtue of this primal decision [of predestining Christ], God is in every way a gracious God. The doctrine of election tells us that we may be certain that God's self-determination is identical with his decision to turn to us. And this turn toward us is the best thing that could ever happen, for *Jesus Christ himself is the reality and the revelation of this turn,* which means that it is both eternal and yet encompasses our temporal lives. . . . And this holds true for all God's ways and works without exception. There is no created nature that does not have its being, essence and continued existence from grace or that can be known in any other way but through grace.

Sin and death, the devil and hell, God's permissive will and knowledge, his power to negate, do not form exceptions to this doctrine. For God's will and knowledge are gracious even where he works his will by negating and denying (or permitting). God's foes are also his servants— and thus the servants of his grace. . . . God remains gracious even in his denial of grace [*Ungnade*]. . . . The doctrine of election testifies that God's grace is the origin of all his works and ways. It is therefore the "common denominator" that cannot be ignored throughout the rest of the arithmetical operation, for it is the numeral that makes the rest of the addition add up.[23]

23. Karl Barth, *Church Dogmatics*, Volume II/2: *The Doctrine of God*, ed. G. W. Bromiley and T. F. Torrance, various translators (Edinburgh: T. & T. Clark, 1957), 91–93; my translation; emphasis added.

Catholics of course would insist that without a correlative confession of Mary's Immaculate Conception, the "arithmetic" of God's logic also does not add up. How, then, can Paul's line that "all have sinned and fallen short of the glory of God" (Romans 3:23) be interpreted? First, one would have to insist that, unless Paul was specifically thinking of the mother of Jesus in this context, the verse is not probative. To take an example from a much different and rather offbeat topic: it has often been asserted that if extra-terrestrial intelligence should ever be discovered, this would prove to be a body-blow to Christocentrism; for how could Christ be the savior of the *universe* if he could never be known by other *worlds*?[24]

To maintain Christocentrism in this scenario of a discovered exo-intelligence, one could always cite Scripture to answer the question: "[Christ] is the atoning sacrifice for our sins; and not only for our sins but the sins of the whole world [*holou tou kosmou*]" (1 John 2:2). But what does *kosmos* mean here in this context: *our* world or the world of extraterrestrial intelligent life? Since the question never arose in the first century, the verse, taken alone, cannot be probative. But clearly the Scotist doctrine of Christ's predestined priority does answer that question, since all of creation was aboriginally meant *for* Christ (Col. 1:16b: "All things were created through him and for him"), which gives a retrospective plausibility to the interpretation that holds that Christ's atoning sacrifice applies to all conceivable worlds.[25]

Similarly, since Paul was clearly not thinking of the Immaculate Conception (one way or the other) at Romans 3:23, other considerations have

24. This dilemma would become even more exigent if some future human astronauts were to discover an exo-civilization on another planet that had long died out.

25. Thomas, as we saw, was at the very least diffident toward the priority of the incarnation independent of the contingency of sin, and grew increasingly so; thus this Scotist answer is blocked for him. Oddly, though, he does address the question of other worlds and is (to the best of my knowledge) the first to do so, although he addresses the question not so much from Christology as from his Pneumatology, and does so in one of the most charming things he ever said, as Matthew Lamb explains: "In commenting on John 3:34 'For he gives the Spirit without measure,' Aquinas makes the startling affirmation that the grace of Christ is not only more than sufficient to save the entire world, but that it is more than sufficient to save 'even many worlds, if they were to exist' (*In Joan.* 3, lect. 6, n. 544)." Matthew Lamb, "Eternity and Time in St. Thomas Aquinas's Lectures on St. John's Gospel," in *Reading John with St. Thomas Aquinas: Theological Exegesis and Speculative Theology*, ed. Michael Dauphinais and Matthew Levering (Washington, DC: The Catholic University of America Press, 2005), 127–39; here 127. (There is a typo in the text: Lamb gives the passage as John 3:24, but it is in fact located at John 3:34.)

to be brought to bear, especially his line that Christ wants to present his church to himself "as a radiant church, without stain or wrinkle or any other blemish, but holy and blameless" (Eph. 5:27). As we already noted above, such ecclesial purity does not currently obtain, of course; but that is surely the church Christ *intends* and was accordingly instantiated at the first moment of his mother's earthly existence, who thereby becomes the church's truest identity.

This Catholic use of Ephesians to illuminate (if not exactly justify) the dogma of Mary's Immaculate Conception highlights the two issues that most divide Catholics and Protestants on this specific doctrine: the place of Scripture in theological argumentation and ecclesiology. As to the first issue, the real dividing line, at least as pertains to Mariology, is not just the Protestant *sola scriptura* principle over against the Catholic countenancing of tradition, but also the "ditch" that separates ancient vs. modern methods of interpreting the Bible.[26] Pelikan rightly observes that just as the Church Fathers and medieval theologians universally interpreted the Old Testament christologically, so too they also applied the same method to Mariology:

> For with their belief in the unity of the Bible, where "the New Testament is hidden in the Old and the Old becomes visible in the New [*Novum in Vetere patet, Vetus in Novo latet*], and with the consequent ability to toggle effortlessly from one Testament to the other and from fulfillment to prophecy and back again, biblical interpreters throughout most of Christian history have had available to them a vast body of supplementary material to make up for the embarrassing circumstance that, as quoted earlier, "the reader of the gospels is at first surprised to find so little about Mary."[27]

We have already seen an example of this type of holistic interpretation in Pius IX's 1854 encyclical *Ineffabilis Deus*, which relies so heavily on the Wisdom books of the Old Testament; but traditional use of typology ranged much farther than just the Wisdom literature:

26. For a riveting account of how this "ditch" came to be dug, see Michael C. Legaspi, *The Death of Scripture and the Rise of Biblical Studies* (New York: Oxford University Press, 2010).

27. Pelikan, *Mary Through the Centuries*, 23. The internal quote is from Raymond E. Brown, Karl P. Donfried, Joseph A. Fitzmyer, and John Reumann, eds., *Mary in the New Testament: A Collaborative Assessment by Protestant and Roman Catholic Scholars* (Philadelphia and New York: Fortress Press and Paulist Press, 1978), 29.

If "son of David" was in the language of the Gospels a way of affirming the continuity of Jesus Christ with Israel and the continuity of his kinship with that of his celebrated forefather, then his descent from David had to be through his only human parent, Mary, who must then also have been "of the house and lineage of David." That reasoning has provided the justification for the practice of going far beyond and behind the New Testament, by searching through the ancient Scriptures of Israel for prophecies and parallels, topics and typologies, that would enrich and amplify the tiny sheaf of data from the Gospels: Miriam, sister of Moses, of course, because of her name, but also Mother Eve; and then all the female personifications, above all in the writings carrying the name of King Solomon, particularly the figure of Wisdom in the eighth chapter of the Book of Proverbs . . . and the Bride in the Song of Songs, which was the longest and the most lavish portrait of a woman anywhere in the Bible.[28]

In other words, whenever the principle of *sola scriptura* is invoked, the question immediately arises: not so much *which* Scripture (since most of the Old Testament passages used in traditional Mariology are recognized by both Catholics and Protestants, the Wisdom of Solomon being the chief exception), but rather *how* the Old relates to the New Testament, which is a point that the mere invocation of *sola scriptura* cannot settle—as the dispute between Lutherans and Calvinists on just that point proves. By a similar logic, nothing in the principle of *sola scriptura* forbids us, as a principle, from noticing the typological parallels and reversals between, say, Eve and Mary; any more than it forbids us from recognizing the similarities and differences between Moses and Jesus.

At all events, there can be no question that the biblical justification for the dogma of the Immaculate Conception stands or falls with the admission of the typological interpretation of the Old Testament, as again Pelikan rightly notes:

The process of appropriating this material for the purposes of Marian devotion and doctrine, which may be described as a methodology of amplification, was, on one hand, part of the much larger process of allegorical and figurative interpretations of the Bible, to which we owe some of the most imaginative and beautiful commentaries, in words

28. Pelikan, *Mary Through the Centuries*, 24–25.

and in pictures, in all of Medieval and Byzantine culture. It was, on the other hand, and almost against the intentions of those who practiced it, a powerful affirmation that because Mary was . . . "of the house and lineage of David," she represented the unbreakable link between Jewish and Christian history, between the First Covenant *within* which she was born and the Second Covenant *to* which she gave birth, so that even the most virulent of Christian anti-Semites could not deny that she, the most blessed among women, was a Jew.[29]

Mary thus stands athwart any and all Marcionite tendencies in theology: for she establishes in her own person—as daughter of Zion and simultaneously as Mother of the church—the crucial hinge, who both links Old and New Covenants and marks their transition, from the former to the latter. If the history of Israel serves as God's preparation to make the world ready for his Son (as for the New Testament it clearly does), then Mary's role as the New Eve *embodies* that transition in her own person, first in her life as a pious Jew and, above all, in her predestined role of giving birth to our Savior.

Furthermore (and this point is crucial), medieval theologians explicitly invoked predestination to justify their application of key passages from the Old Testament to Mary, and did so well before Scotus, indeed centuries before Thomas was born, especially when they came to interpret this verse: "The Lord possessed me in the beginning of his ways, before he made anything from the beginning" (Prov. 8:22), a point lucidly described by an art historian:

> The idea of the predestination of Mary was one of the earliest ideas forwarded in the West by Immaculist writers to explain Mary's exemption from Original Sin. The idea of an Original Grace, counteracting the curse brought on mankind by the Original Sin of Adam and Eve, *is already forwarded in the fifth century* by St. Maxim of Turin. And the passages from Psalms, Proverbs and Ecclesiasticus quoted above found their way into the liturgy of the feast of the Immaculate Conception from early times.[30]

29. Pelikan, *Mary Through the Centuries*, 25.

30. Mirella Levi D'Ancona, *The Iconography of the Immaculate Conception in the Middle Ages and Early Renaissance* (New York: The College Art Association of America, 1957), 51; emphasis added. She goes on to note that "Proverbs 8:22–23 was part of the Office of the Nativity of the Virgin in the twelfth century, when Godefridus, Abbot of Admont in Syria, asks himself why this text, which refers to Divine Wisdom, is used in reference to the Virgin

In other words, without a robust Scotist interpretation of Mary's predestination, the justification for the typological application of Old Testament Wisdom language to Mary collapses; but with that concept it gains new plausibility.

Finally, there is the ecclesiological issue. Catholics, as we saw above, tend to look askance at any ecclesiology that sees the spotless and pure church located only in the predestined heavenly Jerusalem without any material instantiation in the church below, composed though it truly is of saints and sinners (a dolorous reality that recent headlines confirm, if nothing else does). Despite that ongoing sinfulness of the empirical church, though, the Catholic sensibility resists a bifurcated ecclesiology and is resolutely incarnational, all the way from the Catholic understanding of Jesus as the enfleshed Son of God to the church as the very Body of that same enfleshed Christ. The church is, accordingly, the continuation of his enfleshment.[31]

I do not propose to resolve that ecclesiological issue here, for it goes back to the central issue of the Reformation: the dispute over the kind of change effected by justification (real or forensic), the role of merit in the life of a Christian (necessary or otiose), how much Christians are expected

---

Mary as well. His answer is that Mary was foreseen from eternity and that she existed in the mind of God as an idea, in the exact way in which she was to appear as a living being in the world after her birth" (ibid.).

31. One example of this sensibility will suffice, taken from some recent remarks penned by the Catholic historian Eamon Duffy: "Christianity is a material religion. Its central tenet is that in the man Jesus the eternal God united himself to human nature and human flesh, and thereby opened both humanity and matter itself to the possibility of divinization. So Christians place their eschatological hope not in the survival of a disembodied soul, but in the resurrection of the body, the transformation into another order of being of the whole person, flesh and spirit. In heaven Christ himself retains his body, glorified and transcendent, but bearing still the physical traces of his human suffering. 'With what rapture,' says Charles Wesley's great hymn, 'gaze we on those glorious scars.' Perhaps the most unabashedly materialist form of Christianity is Catholicism, centered around the sacraments, and making material things—bread, wine, water, olive oil, the touch of human hands—vehicles of divine power. In the Mass, Catholics believe, Christ himself is made present in the elements of bread and wine, to nourish and transform those who eat and drink them. Catholics venerate the relics of the holy dead, they bless material *stuff*—water, salt, oil, wax, medals, holy pictures, palm branches—and the formulas traditionally used in such blessings more often than not implied that those objects, called sacramentals, thereby became *objectively* holy, changed in themselves, and capable of effecting change at the material as well as the spiritual level." Eamon Duffy, "Sacred Bones & Blood," a review of Caroline Walker Bynum, *Christian Materiality: An Essay on Religion in Late Medieval Europe*, in *The New York Review of Books*, Vol. LVIII, No. 13 (August 18, 2011): 66–68, here 68, Duffy's italics.

to reflect a life of holiness in their lives in order to make their religion plausible to their non-Christian neighbors (the classical debate on the tension between justification and sanctification), all topics too large to be addressed in this chapter. But here again I refer back to my initial thesis: that the grace given to Mary at her conception is the quintessential example of unmerited grace.

In that light, one cannot help but detect a new appreciation for how unmerited *all* grace really is. Often because of an overreaction to the Reformation, Catholics have, in their stress on merit, tended to lose sight of Augustine's oft-repeated maxim: *tua merita sunt dona Dei.* But if Mary is the "Mother of Graces" (in the language of the Jesuit poet Gerard Manley Hopkins, who says that Mary "but mothers each new grace / That does now reach our race"), then that must mean that she mothers *unmerited* grace. For what is grace but that which we do not, and cannot, merit?

> Like the rest of mankind, we were sons of wrath. But God, who is rich in mercy, out of the great love with which he loved us, even when we were dead in our transgressions, made us alive together with Christ. . . . For it is by grace that you have been saved, through faith; and this not from yourselves, it is God's gift—not by works, so that no one can boast. For we are God's workmanship, created in Christ Jesus to do good works, which God prepared in advance for us to do. (Eph. 2:3c–5, 8–10)

It is that last verse of this passage from Ephesians that legitimates occasional Catholic talk of Mary's "merit" in being given the grace to bear the incarnate Son of God, as in the famous hymn *Regina caeli*, which asks the Queen of Heaven to rejoice, "for he whom thou didst merit to bear, alleluia, is risen as he said, alleluia."[32] This language, far from countenancing any "works-righteousness," points to the fact that under grace, decisions are not coerced but remain entirely free, precisely *because* they are graced decisions.[33] Thus, while good works are expected of the Christian, as Paul

---

32. *Regina caeli, laetare, alleluia: Quia quem meruisti portare, alleluia, resurrexit, sicut dixit, alleluia.*

33. This point was effaced by the Jansenists, who evaded Augustine's correlative stress on true freedom and who thus came to their grim doctrine of double predestination and limited atonement: "Grace [for Augustine] never fails of the effect which God intends it to cause, because God is omniscient; but that effect is a free act of man. . . . It is not characteristic of a free man to choose slavery: 'freedom to sin' is a contradiction in terms." Nigel Abercrombie, *The Origins of Jansenism* (Oxford: At the Clarendon Press, 1936), 39.

insists, they do not entail any claim on God, the same point already made in Mary's Magnificat: "[The Lord] has looked on the lowliness of his servant. Henceforth all generations will call me blessed, *because* the Almighty has done great things for me" (Luke 1:48–49).

Thérèse de Lisieux, the most popular Catholic saint of the twentieth century and named by Pope John Paul II in 1997 Doctor of the church, exemplified this Marian stance to an extraordinary degree. In her remarkable autobiography, *The Story of a Soul*, she recounts her prayer four months before her difficult death:

> I am very happy that I am going to heaven; but when I think of this word of the Lord, "I shall come soon, and bring with me my recompense to give each one according to his works," I tell myself that this will be very embarrassing for me *because I have no works.* . . . Very well, he will render to me according to *his* works for his own sake.[34]

The Little Flower's is precisely the attitude that suffuses the Magnificat, whose whole thrust may be summarized as: gratitude for unmerited grace.

In conclusion, perhaps enough has been outlined here to give encouragement. While much continues to divide Catholics and Protestants, very much including the doctrine of Mary's Immaculate Conception, nonetheless there are enough resources in that doctrine and in the reasoning that led to its solemn declaration to make us see why the Protestant poet William Wordsworth could call Mary "our tainted nature's solitary boast."

---

34. Cited in Hans Küng, *Justification: The Doctrine of Karl Barth and a Catholic Reflection*, trans. Thomas Collins et al. (New York: Thomas Nelson & Sons, 1964), 274; emphases added. Her whole family had a deep devotion to Our Lady of Lourdes; and although she never went to Lourdes herself, her mother and three of her sisters did. For details on the trip, and on the general Carmelite eschewal of any talk of "merit," see Thomas R. Nevin, *Thérèse of Lisieux: God's Gentle Warrior* (Oxford/New York: Oxford University Press, 2006), 108–11; 113–18.

Glossary of Terms

There can be no doubt that the large number of distinctions thrown up in the course of the history of the theology of grace can try the patience of many readers. But equally there can be no doubt that it is hard to master that history without understanding why these distinctions were first drawn and what role they play in the controversies displayed in this book. This glossary of course makes no claim regarding the legitimacy of any particular distinction listed here, a question perhaps best left to the decision of the reader. Nor should these distinctions necessarily be understood as referring to different kinds or species of grace, as if habitual grace, say, were a different item from sanctifying grace. In most authors these distinctions were drawn for the sake of conceptual clarity and not to provide a taxonomy of grace.

Unlike most glossaries, this one is not alphabetized but arranged according to the conceptual structure within which the distinctions first arose, which will perhaps lend them a more convincing arrangement.[1] The structure of the arrangement will make the reasons for the distinctions, if not more convincing to the skeptic, at least more sensible to the sympathetic reader.

I. Uncreated grace *(gratia increata):* a perhaps peculiar term referring to God's inner life, the circuminsession of the divine processions of the Trinity.

II. Created grace *(gratia creata):* all other graces without exception.

1. Drawn from Georg Kraus's article on Grace in *Handbook of Catholic Theology,* ed. Wolfgang Beinert and Francis Schüssler Fiorenza (New York: Crossroad, 1995), 302–10; slightly altered and amplified.

a. Grace of creation *(gratia creationis):* a direct outcome of what is known as God's aseity, the fullness of life within himself. Therefore God did not create the world out of necessity (Plotinus) or need (Hegel), but "gratuitously." Creation is, strictly speaking, a grace also because it was created through the Logos (John 1:1–3) or Christ (Col. 1:16b). Against Baius the church teaches that Adam and Eve were also created in a state of supernatural grace elevating them to union with God (*gratia elevans*). This elevating grace is more usually referred to, especially in the Orthodox tradition, as divinization or deification.

b. Grace of redemption (*gratia redemptionis* or *gratia redemptoris*): all graces given to the human race subsequent to the fall of our first parents, making this grace both elevating and healing *(gratia elevans* and *sanans).*

   1. External graces of redemption *(gratia externa):* these include all graces that come from outside the soul: the church, her sacraments, the Bible (which is the Word of God by virtue of the grace of inspiration: *gratia inspirationis*), or any other outside occasion which God uses in his providence to move the soul, from a homily to a chance bar of music. External graces are ordered to internal graces as to their goal.

   2. Internal graces of redemption *(gratia interna):* all graces that move the soul to God and which are entirely gratuitous, that is, not based on merit, whether foreseen or predestined *(gratia gratis data).* From Augustine these are usually understood by what they do *(gratia faciens).*